I0445928

PEACE AND CONFLICT SERIES

Ron Milam, General Editor

ALSO IN THIS SERIES:
Crooked Bamboo: A Memoir from Inside the Diem Regime, by Nguyen Thai; edited by Justin Simundson

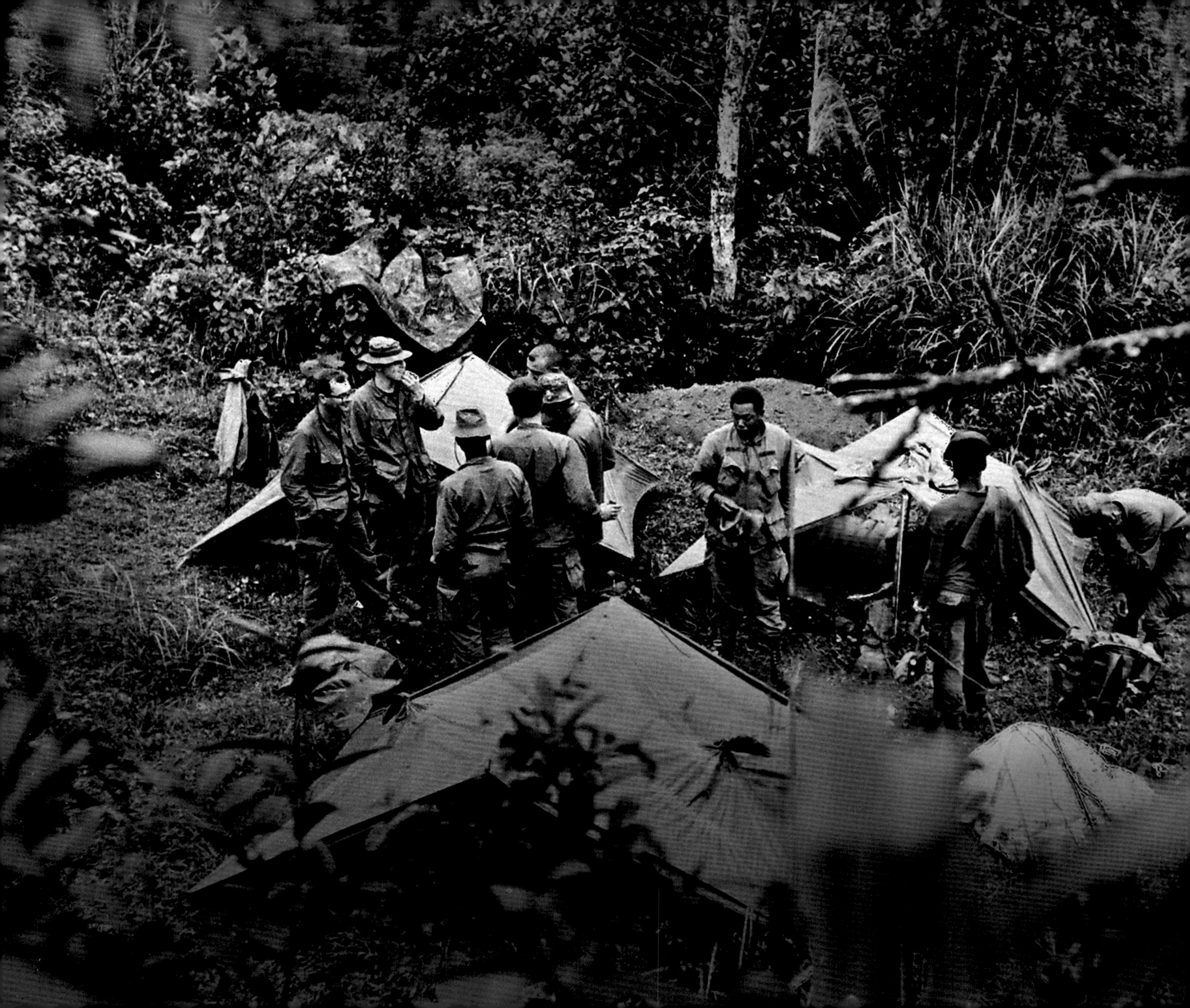

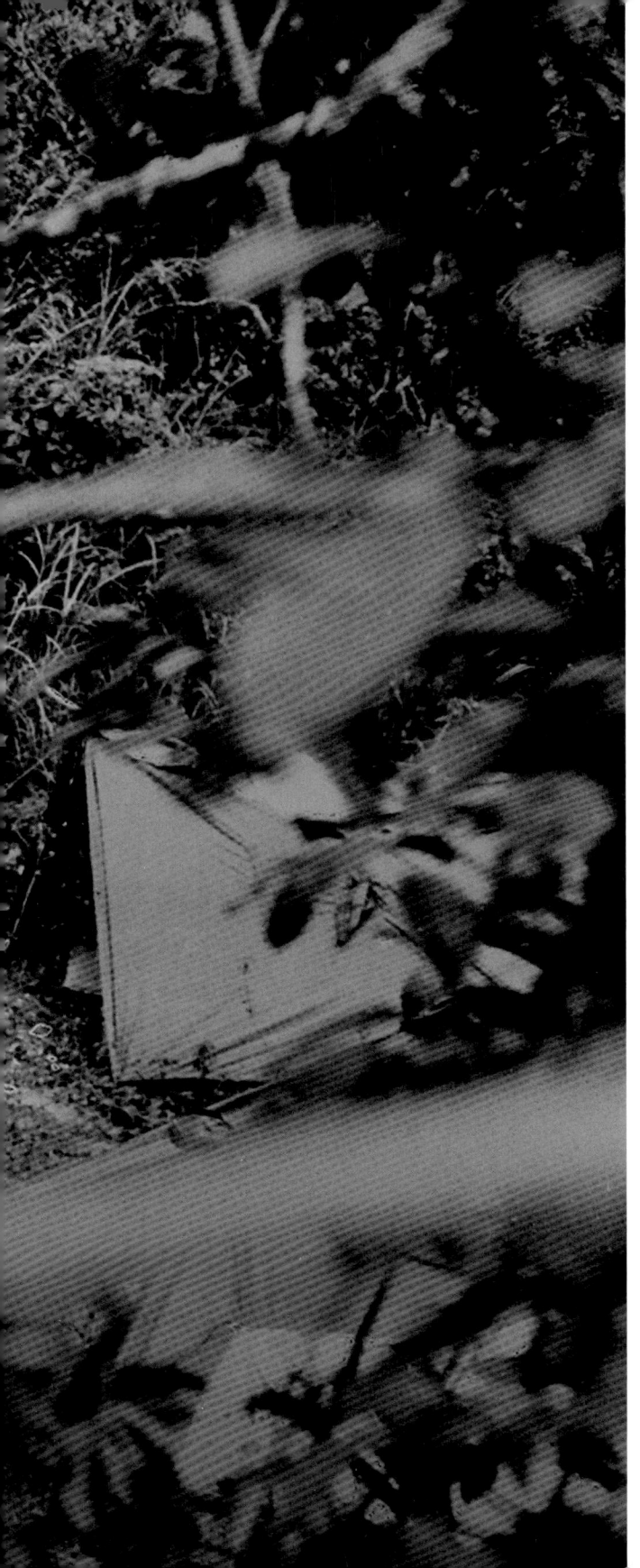

Rain in Our Hearts

Alpha Company in the Vietnam War

James Allen Logue and Gary D. Ford

TEXAS TECH UNIVERSITY PRESS

Copyright © 2020 by James Allen Logue and Gary D. Ford
All rights reserved. No portion of this book may be reproduced in
any form or by any means, including electronic storage and retrieval
systems, except by explicit prior written permission of the pub-
lisher. Brief passages excerpted for review and critical purposes are
excepted.

This book is typeset in Sabon LT Std. The paper used in this book
meets the minimum requirements of ANSI/NISO Z39.48-1992
(R1997). ∞

Designed by Hannah Gaskamp
Cover photograph by James Allen Logue

Names: Logue, James Allen, 1947– photographer. | Ford, Gary D.
(Gary Dean), 1948– author.
Title: Rain in Our Hearts: Alpha Company in the Vietnam War /
James Allen Logue and Gary D. Ford.
Description: Lubbock, Texas: Texas Tech University Press, [2020] |
Series: Peace and Conflict series | Includes bibliographical references
and index.
Identifiers: LCCN 2020010308 | ISBN 9781682830673 (cloth)
Subjects: LCSH: United States. Army. Infantry, 31st. Battalion, 4th.
Company A—History. | Vietnam War, 1961–1975—Regimental
histories—United States. | Vietnam War, 1961–1975—Personal
narratives, American.
Classification: LCC DS558.4. L64 2020 | DDC 959.704/34092 [B]
—dc23

Printed in Canada
22 23 24 25 26 27 28 / 9 8 7 6 5 4 3 2

Texas Tech University Press
Box 41037
Lubbock, Texas 79409-1037 USA
800.832.4042
ttup@ttu.edu
www.ttupress.org

I dedicate this book to the men of Alpha Company, 4/31, 1969–1970, and especially to those among them who gave all:

SERGEANT KEITH ALAN LOCHNER, FAIRMOUNT, INDIANA
KIA 22 APRIL 1970

SERGEANT DUANE ARVID PETERSON, ISANTI, MINNESOTA
KIA 5 MAY 1970

SERGEANT DONALD GARY KUZILLA, RADFORD, MICHIGAN
KIA 14 MAY 1970

SERGEANT WILLIAM DAVID MENSCER, STATESVILLE, NORTH CAROLINA
KIA 16 MAY 1970

SERGEANT FIRST CLASS EVERETTE BRENT CALDWELL, TULSA, OKLAHOMA
KIA 6 JUNE 1970

SPECIALIST 4 DENNIS NORMAN HOGENBOOM, CLYMER, NEW YORK
KIA 6 JUNE 1970

CORPORAL MARK EDWARD KLEVER, MILWAUKEE, WISCONSIN
KIA 6 JUNE 1970

SPECIALIST 4 LARRY WAYNE RASEY, TAFT, CALIFORNIA
KIA 26 JULY 1970

MEDIC THOMAS JOHN ROBERTS, CEDAR PARK, WISCONSIN
KIA 22 AUGUST 1970

Especially I dedicate this book to the memory of Sergeant Benjamin Ellis Perry of Worchester, Massachusetts, my forever friend who first recognized in these images and the story of Alpha Company the confluence of art, history, and the triumph of the human spirit.

JAMES ALLEN LOGUE

We must remember that one man is much the same as another,
and that he is best who is trained in the severest school.
THUCYDIDES (C. 460 BC–C. 400 BC)

History of the Peloponnesian War

Monotonously the lorries sway, monotonously come the calls, monotonously falls
the rain. It falls on our heads and on the heads of the dead up in the line, on the
body of the little recruit with the wound that is so much too big for his hip;
it falls on Kemmerich's grave; it falls in our hearts.
ERICH MARIA REMARQUE (1898–1970)

All Quiet on the Western Front

Contents

Illustrations

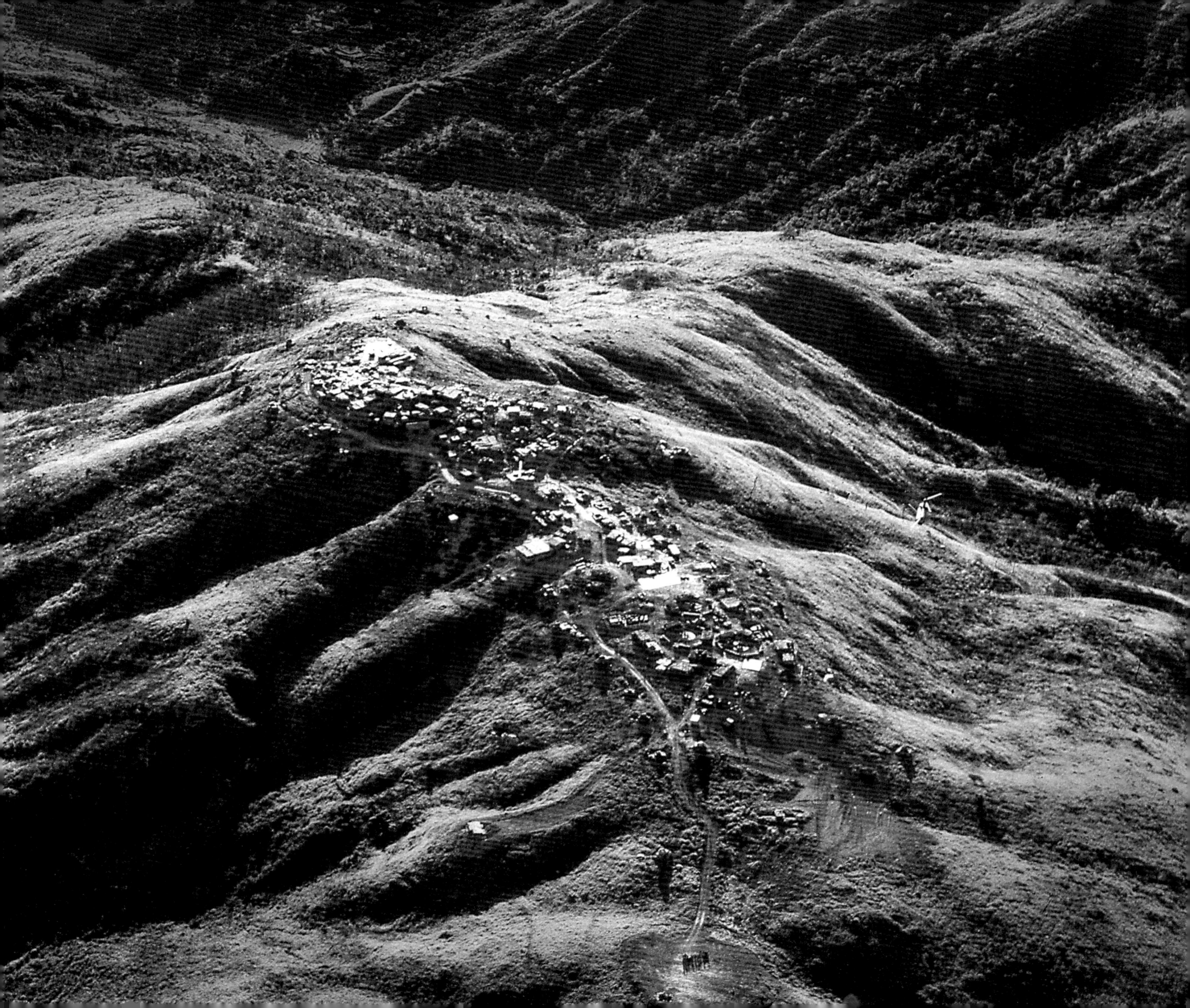

Preface

IT WAS A WAR AGAINST TIME.

Those who fought the Vietnam War flew out alone, served one year, and came home alone. They survived. In that single way, they won.

Then they locked away memories, resumed lives, and learned never to speak the word "Vietnam."

"No one listened. No one cared," recalls one Illinois veteran.

Time fades memory of the conflict, even about the date the war "began":

- As the number of US military advisers in the Republic of Vietnam grew to 23,000 through the Eisenhower, Kennedy, and Johnson administrations.

- 2 August 1964, when North Vietnamese "fired" upon US Navy vessels in the "Gulf of Tonkin Incident."

- 8 March 1965, when US combat troops stepped ashore at China Beach. Soon forces spread through four military zones, from IV Corps in the Delta, north to I Corps (pronounced "Eye" Corps) in the vaulting uplands of South Vietnam.

- 30 January 1968, the year US troop strength reached its zenith at 536,100: North Vietnamese Army (NVA) and Viet Cong forces attacked throughout South Vietnam, including Saigon, in the weeks-long Tet Offensive. The enemy gained no permanent ground and sustained heavy losses—in any other conflict, a major military victory for American and Army of the Republic of Vietnam (ARVN) forces.

Not in this war.

Venerable CBS news anchor Walter Cronkite, with his grandfatherly brush of a mustache, broadcast a rare editorial

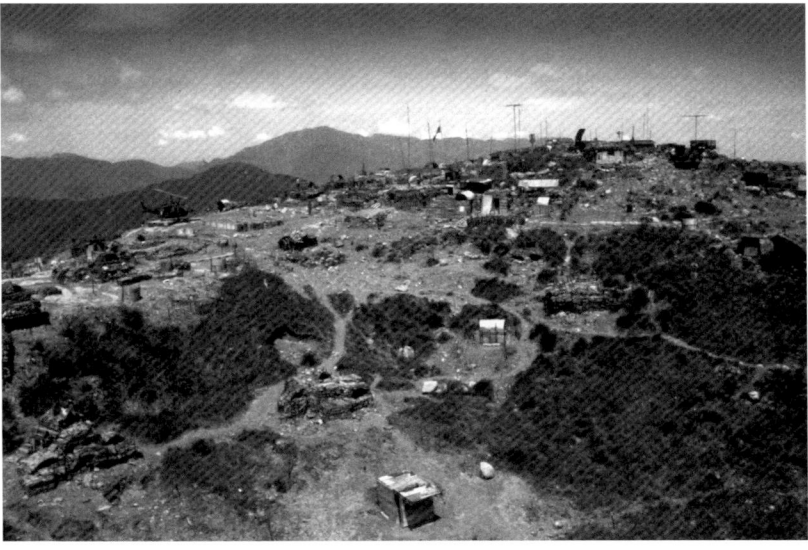

During monsoon, mud cakes boots, fouls equipment, and dampens morale. On LZ West, wooden walkways led to artillery positions. Elsewhere men slosh through mud.

Left: In Quang Tin Province, LZ West crowned *Núi Liêt Kiêm* (mountain of leeches), where the defoliant, Agent Orange, opened "fields of fire." James Logue photographed his "home away from home" in October 1969.

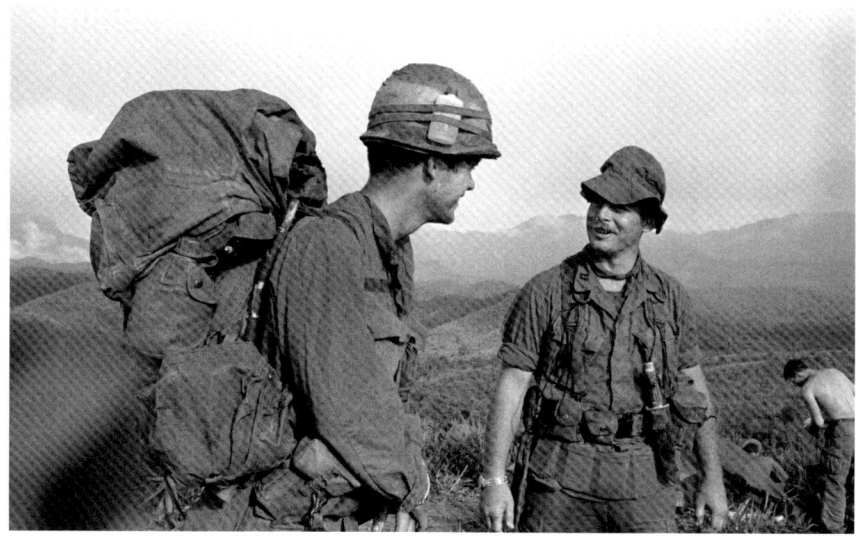

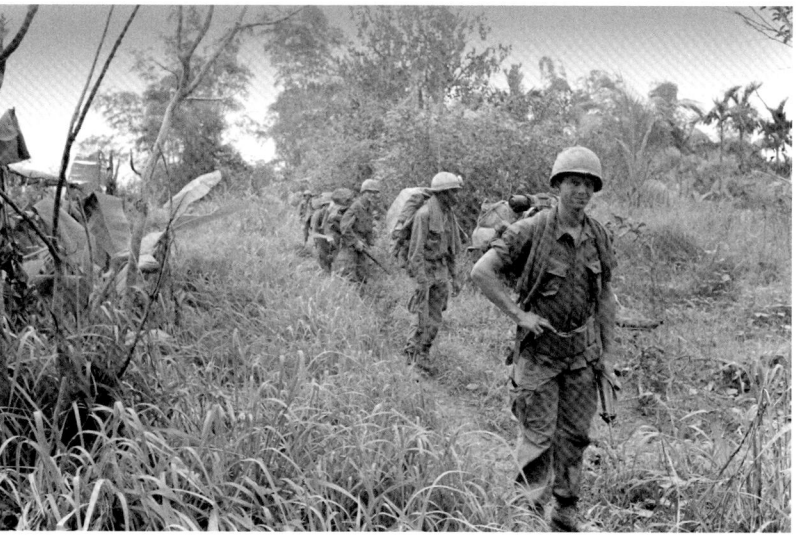

Medic Dennis Mack humps his rucksack and medical supplies, a 75-pound load. Captain John Wilson shoulders two heavy burdens: rucksack and heart in striving to lead his men and see them home safely.

When Logue photographed John Ansley, the Georgian had only nineteen days left in Vietnam, so "short" he did not have to go to the field. He went anyway.

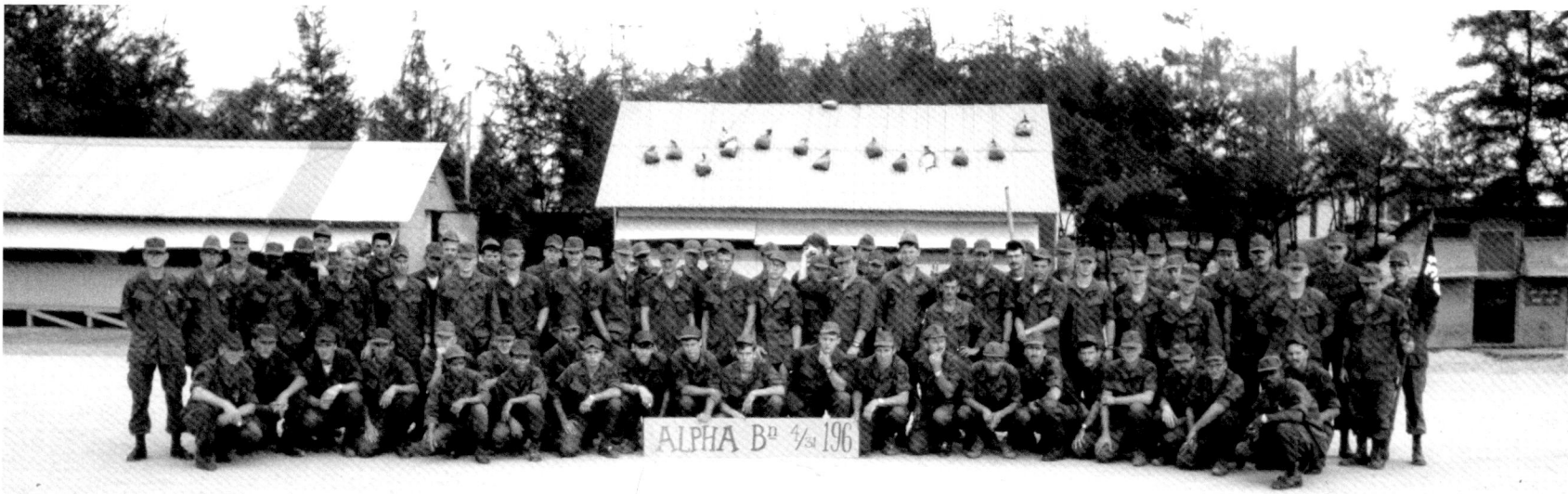

Logue portrays Alpha at full strength of more than 125 in February 1970. By early June, deaths, wounds, and illness had sliced Alpha's strength to less than forty, the size of a single platoon.

comment on 27 February 1968, declaring American forces in Vietnam to be "mired in a stalemate." President Lyndon Johnson reportedly turned off the television and said, "If I've lost Cronkite, I've lost Middle America." Soon after President Richard M. Nixon was inaugurated in 1969, Washington began seeking "Vietnamization," an effort to hand the fighting to the South Vietnamese and wriggle out of the war through a "peace with honor." In 1969–1970, the number of US troops declined from 475,200 to 334,600. Knowing American forces would never plant the Stars and Stripes in Hanoi, both enlistees and draftees arrived in-country with a single goal: "Just stay alive."

Among this group was James Allen Logue, a professional photographer and draftee from Clayton, New Jersey. In the autumn of 1969, just as monsoon season began, he was placed as a rifleman in Alpha Company, 4 Battalion 31st Infantry, 196th Light Infantry Brigade, Americal Division.

The 4/31 infantry battalion occupied LZ (landing zone) or FSB (fire support base) West, atop a high mountain in Quang Tin Province in I Corps. LZ West, which opened in 1967, soared above the southeast end of Hiêp Dúc Valley, and overlooked Song Chang River. While West served as battalion headquarters, it was also the full-time base for a battery of the 3/82nd Artillery's 155mm howitzers. A, B, C, and D (Alpha, Bravo, Charlie, and Delta) companies of 4/31 rotated onto "the hill," so that one company for two weeks guarded the high ground. The main mission for 4/31 was securing the resettlement villages within the Hiêp Dúc Controlled Fire Zone from encroachment of NVA and Viet Cong (VC) forces: a job that kept them in the valley and always in danger.

While the men slept in bunkers atop the mountain, LZ West was never "home" for Logue, Alpha, and the other companies of 4/31.

"Home" they bore on their backs: rucksacks of nylon stretched between aluminum frames, with compartments holding what they needed and what they wanted. Quickly, "fucking new guys" (FNGs) learned they wanted less with each step.

FNGs bent forward like crooked old men from rucks stuffed with ammunition for M16s and M60 machine guns, grenades, claymore mines, canteens, cans of C-rations, a book or a few magazines for spare-time reading, a Bible, goodies from homes—all weighing seventy-five pounds and often more.

As they learned they needed less, they stood taller. Lighter rucks rode higher on backs. Always they bore weapons and ammunition. Other things they needed just as much weighed less: purifying tablets and Kool-Aid for safety and taste of water; malaria pills; a poncho for the rain by day and a tent for night. And socks. They remain as necessary to infantry as weapons. Without them, soles of feet soon resemble hamburger and render infantry immobile.

All turned sodden in monsoon, October to June, when 55 to 94 inches of rain fell. It fell day and night, in the field or on LZ West; the crest of solid red clay after applications of Agent Orange denied enemy close cover.

Of all they bore, their heaviest burdens encircled wrists: watches with hands that crept minute to minute while they walked, fought, and watched friends die or disappear in a twinkling aboard a medevac. On they walked, burdened even more knowing that living was just waiting to die—or, by some miracle, surviving a year and releasing them to life denied to so many.

Two of those in Alpha 4/31 granted life were James Allen Logue of Osteen, Florida, and his best friend from the Vietnam year, Benjamin Ellis Perry of Worcester, Massachusetts. When I met them at a 31st Infantry reunion in Columbus, Georgia, in 2011, Jim had archived his war photography and self-published *Vietnam Hiêp Dúc, LZ West: Images of Alpha Company, 4/31, 196th Lib., Americal Division*, a volume long on photographs and maps but brief in text.

Who and where are these men? If they live, will they speak of the war? What may they say to lend voice to those who are mute?

In 2012, Jim and I called Alpha Company of 1969–1970 into its last formation.

We traveled more than 54,000 land and air miles in a four-year odyssey across America, interviewing whom we could find, those who agreed to talk. In all, we interviewed sixty-nine people.

Why not more? We found no complete roster of Jim's time in Vietnam. Also, soldiers went by nicknames, last names, or first names. Additionally, a soldier knew most in his squad (8 to 10); a few in his platoon (30 to 40); and fewer still in other platoons. As Perry Stemen of Whitehall, Michigan, recalled, "I can still see all the faces; most of the names I've forgotten."

We interviewed most in their homes, often with spouses who never had heard their husbands speak of Vietnam. We recorded not only "war stories" but also life stories: family history, boyhood, Vietnam, and later life. We cried some, laughed more.

Jim looked over veterans' own photographs. He scanned military documents. He photographed artifacts—from P-38 can openers to entire uniforms. Several brought forth correspondence, written to and from, in this last major American conflict featuring handwritten letters.

The interviews constitute a random sampling of one infantry company, as we visited those we could find. Alpha in 1969–1970 dispels stereotypes about "typical" Vietnam veterans as poor, urban, high school dropouts. Of those interviewed, only one enlisted at age 17. Most, from privates to captains, ranged in age from 20 to 28.

Among their numbers, six were high school dropouts. Of the fifteen who attended college, nine held bachelor's degrees, and three, postgraduate degrees. Most were single when they went to war. Before he left, one had time just enough to hold his newborn daughter. Another had yet to see his infant son.

Post-bellum narratives tend to sound similar. Many of the men furthered their educations. Most married; all built careers and worked *hard*, not only to provide for families but also to silence the murmur of Vietnam memory.

Alpha veterans often glanced nervously at the red eye of my recorder but soldiered on, recounting rain, hunger, exhaustion, rain, jungle rot, rain, malaria, rain. They described firefights and watching friends die, their own wounds, and begging God for mercy. Some wept at the guilt of life granted them but denied to friends.

They remain bitter at the overarching order denying them of any chance of victory: Take no territory; just kill the enemy. To do so, comments Robert Scott of Virginia Beach, Virginia, the men were basically bait, "dangled like worms on a hook," to draw out and kill the enemy.

Because forces were not advancing on the enemy's capital, President Lyndon Johnson needed some measurement to indicate progress. This pressure led to the routine dissemination of the most brutal statistic of the conflict, created in a meeting with President Johnson and Secretary of Defense Robert McNamara on 17 April 1965: body count. Soon thereafter, afternoon television news programs broadcast weekly body counts of "us versus them" as if they were sports scores.

In initial interviews, many said, "This is the first time I've talked about Vietnam." All were proud of serving. They humbled me when they would "strip their sleeves and show their scars," representing the great divide between those who went and those who did not.

"Only this matters," one said, tapping his finger thrice on the table: "You . . . were . . . there!"

I was not . . .

Before each interview, I informed each veteran of my (low) two-digit number in the first draft lottery. When I graduated from college in August 1971, I was Vietnam-bound, and I did not want to go.

A coincidence kept me in America. Many who filled reserves and National Guard units in 1965 fulfilled their six-year obligation in 1971. I joined my hometown Texas National Guard unit and completed basic training and advanced individual training in infantry at Fort Ord, California, in 1972. My having fired the weapons, humping a rucksack, practicing squad- and platoon-level fire and maneuver tactics, and learning Vietnam-era slang and acronyms helped greatly in interviewing.

Regarding my absence in Vietnam, all, except one, said I was fortunate. Still, as Shakespeare wrote, I "hold my manhood cheap" that I do not qualify in the three taps of that veteran's finger.

A canyon yawns between those who went to the war and those who did not. In Cove, Oregon, Gerald Parmele pointed to one of Jim's black-and-white photographs and said to me, "When I look at this, I see the war in color. You see it only in black and white."

Our last interview took us to Thomson, Georgia, where John Ansley recalled arriving in Vietnam. The green newcomers in their crisp uniforms stepped outside and gaped at veterans waiting to fly home. Faded fatigues hung like shrouds on skeletal frames. Weathered skin was cracked like old leather. The vets stared into the distance, seeing nothing. John recalls, "We looked like new growth on a tree. They looked like old, dried-up leaves."

Now has come the withering time for those who fought the war, when their autumns gnaw at the edges of recollection. Time, however, leavens memory with the wisdom longer lives grant. These recorded brushstrokes of breath paint masterpieces of memory and preserve voices beyond life.

Jim and I are profoundly grateful to all for their kind hospitality. To mothers, widows, and siblings of loved ones lost in the war, we bow humbly for their courage in opening again the eternal wound of memory.

Jim and I are humbled that this book joins the ranks of good works in the Peace and Conflict Series of Texas Tech University Press. Many, many thanks go to Director Brian L. Ott and Managing Director Joanna Conrad, who quickly saw both art and history in Jim Logue's photography. In the words, they "heard" the courage of breath itself—not only of veterans, but also of families of the fallen. All gave voice to memories still so hard on their hearts. Many, many thanks, too, go to Acquisitions Editor Travis Snyder, who selected from Jim's 2,500 Vietnam images those depicting best the misery, fear,

and bravery of boys that war shape into men. Senior Designer Hannah Gaskamp gracefully wove words and images into a unified story. Editor Christie Perlmutter pointed out my many errors and with soft smile but sharp pencil (metaphorically speaking) straightened my slumping shoulders of prose. To Marketing and Sales Manager John Brock, thank you for delivering this work around the nation. And finally, to all who fought the Vietnam War, both men and women—medevac pilots, doctors, nurses, and yes, Donut Dollies: From lifting morale to saving lives, they returned home veterans whose voices enrich the public discourse of America.

To our wives, Jim's Jeanne and my Cynthia, we bow in deep love and gratitude. Thank you both for your patience, your prayers, and your abiding love while we crossed America and flew fifty years into Vietnam's past.

I thank most of all James Allen Logue. He counseled me with the wisdom of an older brother and quickened miles with laughter. As a research partner, from the National Archives to local libraries, he flooded my files with his findings, then read, reread, and corrected errors in these stories. Any mistakes in the writing are mine. Jim, you are my hero.

I leave the last words to Cleveland Crist of Grand Junction, Colorado. At his kitchen table he peered at each photograph, this one eliciting laughter, another tears. Then he squinted out at the morning sun, his voice a whisper.

"We were so young," he said. "We were so very, very young."

GARY D. FORD

Rain in Our Hearts

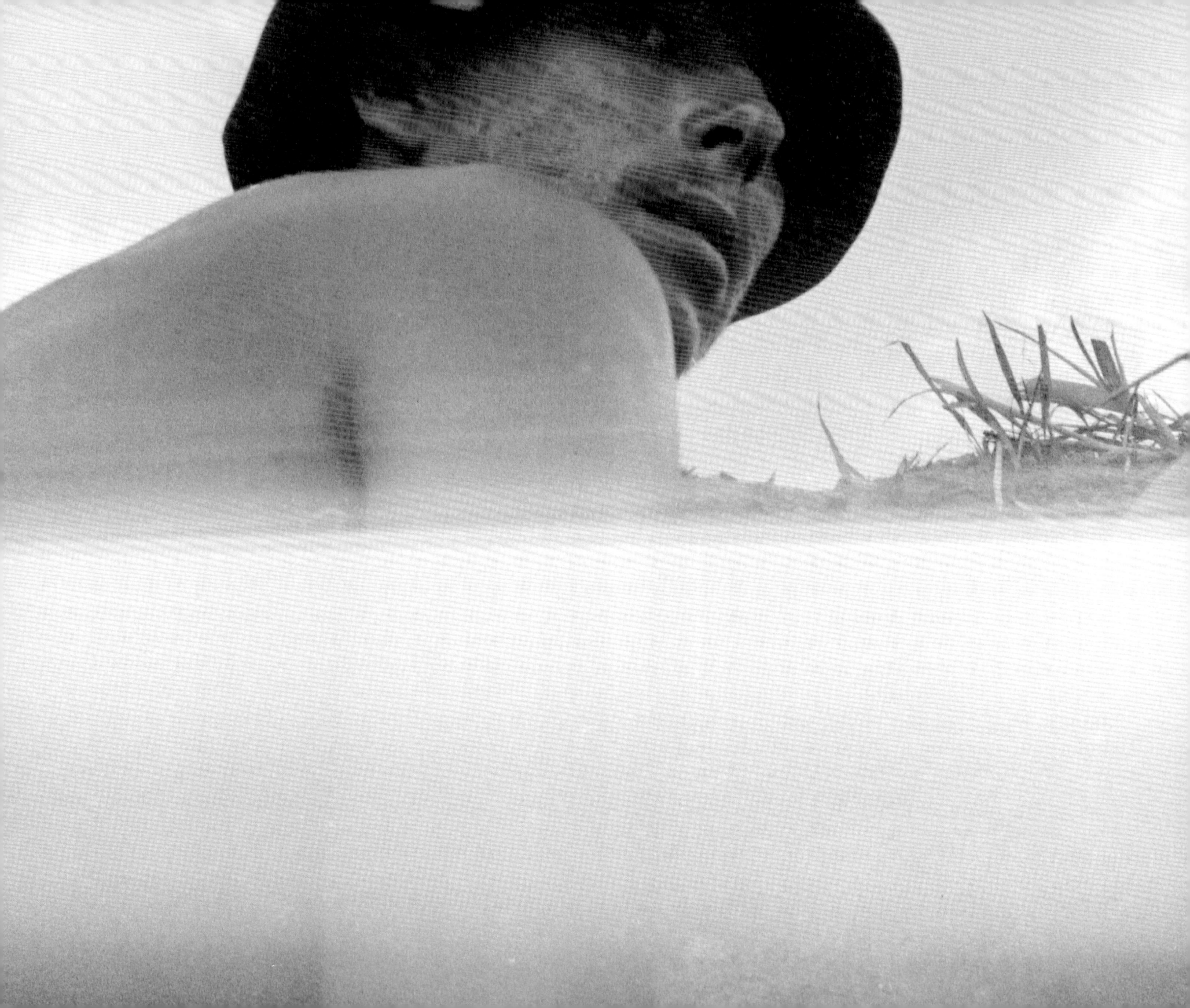

Chapter 1

To Take My Mind off the War, I Took Pictures

Specialist 4 James Allen Logue

FROM THE THROAT OF THE JUNGLE BELOW CAME A SMALL "cough."

All on the hill heard.

All knew they had twenty-one seconds left to live.

"INCOMING!" they screamed and burrowed into foxholes, some as deep as graves. Down rained enemy 82mm mortar rounds. Up sailed curses, screams of agony, and shouted prayers. Out went grenades and gunfire of M16s and M60 machine guns, blazing away at the enemy below. It was 10 May 1970, and James Allen Logue thought surely he would die this day, Mother's Day, on a hill with no name.

With each cough of enemy mortar tubes, another round arched high, then hurtled to earth, scattering thousands of razor-sharp shards across the hilltop; each cycle took twenty-one seconds.

Earlier, upon reaching this night laager (defensive position), Logue and James Lemmon of Robinson, Illinois, dropped their "heavies" and slammed at the hard, red earth to dig a foxhole, six feet deep, eight feet long, two feet wide. Why dig so deep? From the stench of NVA dead below, they knew their foe had been denied this hill at least once and coveted it still.

The enemy seemed everywhere. After monsoon season, 2nd NVA Division arose from its highland lairs on 29 April and struck across rice-rich Quang Tin Province in the Republic of South Vietnam. They smashed into Hiêp Dúc and other villages, burning and wrecking buildings and murdering citizens. They fought American and ARVN forces in the field and attacked mountaintop firebases. Into summer, Alpha and all of Americal Division threw land and air power against the NVA, whose accuracy with mortars seemed mystical.

"Seven rounds I counted in the air at one time. Four of them hit so near that I could touch them from inside my foxhole," Logue recalls.

Between bursts, Lemmon peered above the foxhole to spot puffs of smoke from mortar tubes. That's when Logue, his neck bloody from a shard of steel, grabbed his Nikonos 35mm camera. He forced shaking hands still and snapped a black-and-white photograph of Lemmon daring death.

Nearby, Captain John Wilson knew this rain of steel would kill them all. There was no recourse but to run before the enemy cut off their retreat.

Left: As enemy mortars fall, James Lemmon peers from a foxhole. Logue's hands were shaking when he grabbed this shot of Lemmon, both aware the next round might kill them both.

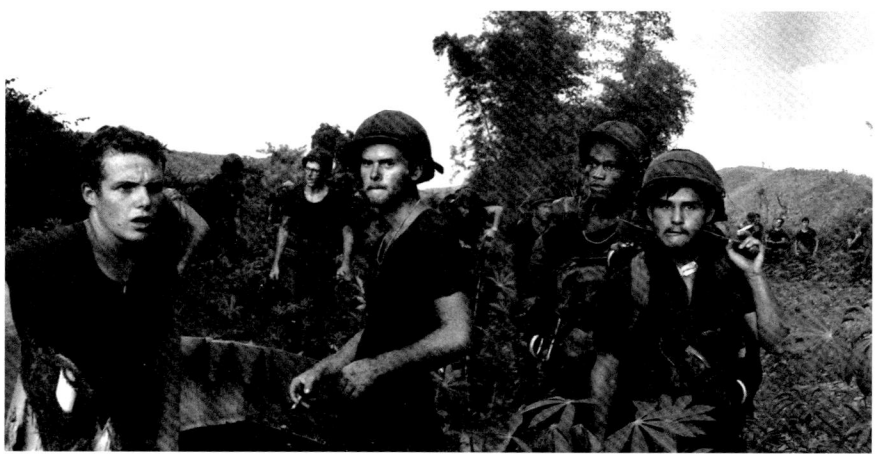

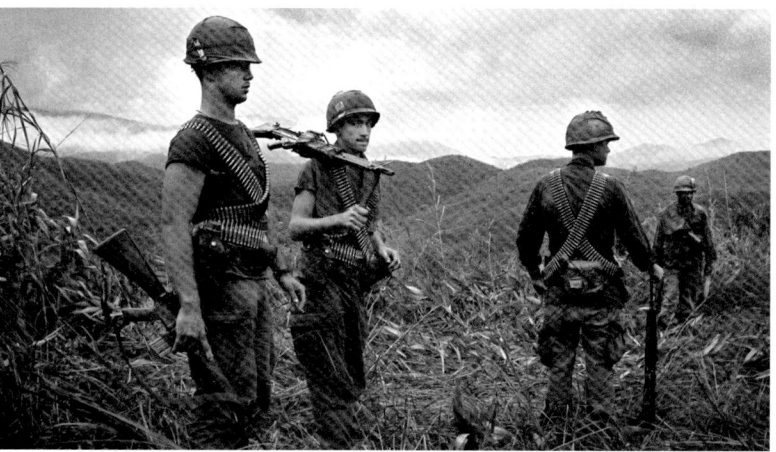

These men survived a vicious NVA attack on 10 May 1970. Left to right are David Gould, John Oiestad, Ron Hicks, and Mark Klever.

The M60 ("the pig") provided most firepower for each squad. The soldier at left with bandoliers of M60 ammunition is likely the assistant gunner. Note his "church key" (bottle opener) in helmet headband.

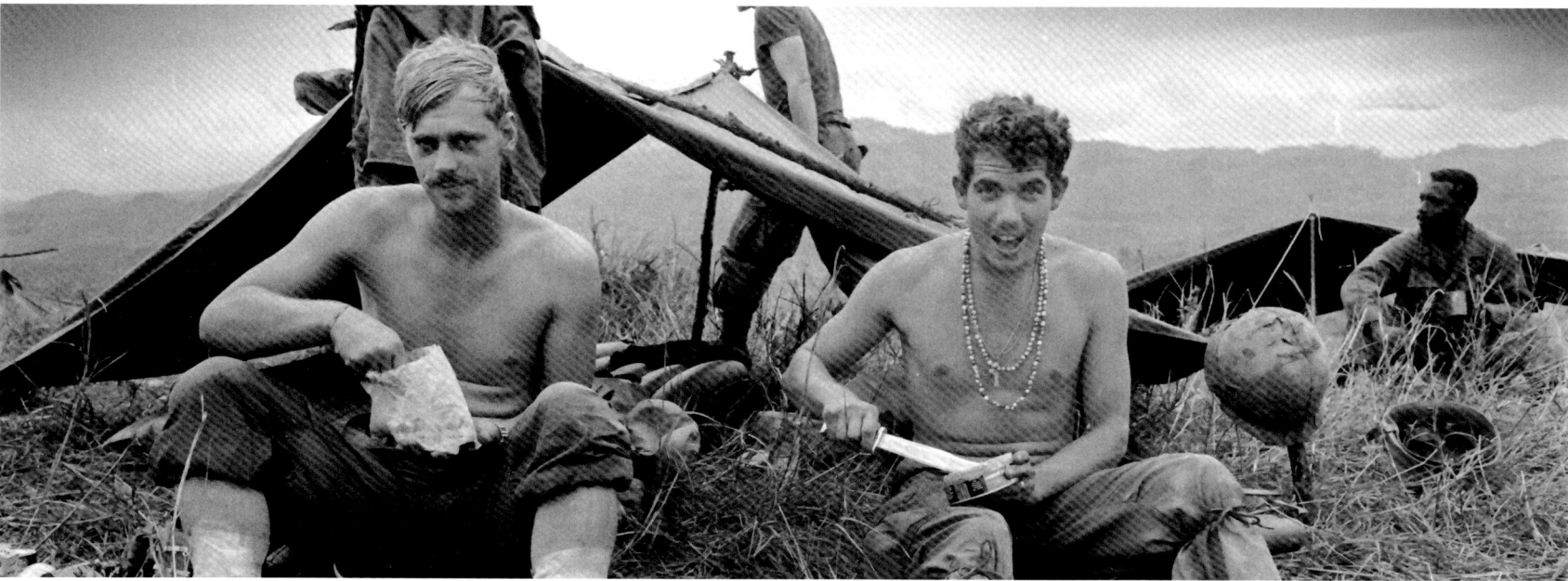

Shelter halves form a night laager hooch for Richard Knowlton (left) and Tim Cruthers. They wear "Ho Chi Minh" sandals while boots and socks dry. Soldiers stored letters in their helmets.

"LET'S GO!" he shouted.

Burdened with wounded, Alpha crashed down the opposite side of the hill and cleared a wooded area for a medevac. Soon, #614, pilot number of 236th Medical Detachment, inserted his bird into the clearing and soared away with the worst of eleven wounded, including Lemmon, who had lost his hearing.

Jim anxiously looked around and breathed easier when he spotted his best friend, Ben Perry, an artist from Worcester, Massachusetts, uninjured. Then he aimed his camera at four soldiers in waist-high brush. Filth, fear, and exhaustion etch their faces. In the foreground, from left to right, stand Dave Gould of Pennsylvania; John Oiestad, a Montana cowboy; Ronald Hicks, an African American soldier from Clearwater, Florida, eyes lost in the mental distance of a "thousand-yard stare"; and Mark Klever of Milwaukee, gazing at the camera, his thin wisp of a mustache revealing a teenage attempt to look older than his nineteen years.

Logue clicked the shutter and froze in time and place four men surviving one more day of war. One was wounded but walking. Another had twenty-seven days left to live.

Why did Logue photograph those four?

"To take my mind off the war, I took pictures," he says, five decades later.

IN HIS NATIVE CLAYTON, NEW JERSEY, "JIMMY" LOGUE BEGAN looking through a viewfinder in the fifth grade when he bought a camera from a classmate for two dollars. Jimmy struggled with undiagnosed dyslexia and ADHD, but with photography he discovered creativity, self-confidence, and eventually a life of art and business.

Soon, with a Mamiya C330 twin-lens reflex, he was photographing high school football games, parades, even an autopsy of a murder victim while the coroner explained the wreckage of a round fired into flesh.

"It was a wonderful lesson. I'd never have gotten that out of my biology class," he says of a dyslexic's different way of learning.

"Boy tycoon," schoolteachers called this only child of Jacqueline Joyce Logue and James P. Logue, a coal salesman, World War II Navy veteran, and mayor of Clayton. Meanwhile, no mentor assisted Jim in improving his camera skills.

"Everything I learned, I learned hands on," he says.

"Lesson One" was to husband film, a trait that would be essential years later in Vietnam.

After graduating from Brooks Institute of Photography in Santa Barbara, California, Jim was back home, working at Pitman Camera Shop, running his own studio, and attending Glassboro State College when his draft board reclassified him 1A. Inducted 19 May 1969, he completed basic training at Fort Dix, New Jersey, and Advanced Individual Training (AIT) in infantry at Fort Lewis, Washington. Jim was confident, however, that he'd carry a camera in the Army rather than a rifle. He shakes his head when recalling this exchange: "They said, 'We don't need photographers. *You're* going to be in the infantry.'"

Aboard the Flying Tiger Airlines "with a bunch of smelly guys," he arrived in Vietnam, which was drenched in monsoon, on 6 October 1969. Flown to Alpha in the field, the chopper hovered just long enough for Jim to jump from the skids. There he stood, soaked, like a foundling on a jungle doorstep.

"Somebody grabbed me and introduced me to Captain [James] Mantell and then to 'Top' [Sergeant James] Price. He took me over to Dick Oswald, a Nebraskan, and said, 'Dick will be your squad leader,'" he recalls.

Assigned to 1st Squad, 1st Platoon, Jim crouched in a foxhole in the rain and began the yearlong, two-hour ordeal of nightly guard duty.

"That became the hardest part about Vietnam. It was difficult to stay awake. You couldn't listen to a radio, read a book, or smoke. You just sat and looked into black for two hours and listened," he says.

It rained his first six days. He wrote his father: "The country is beautiful; the weather is awful." It would rain steadily from then on through April and many days the rest of the year until the next monsoon.

The base for Alpha Company, 4/31, part of 196th Light Infantry Brigade, Americal Division spread atop a mountain called *Núi Liêt Kiém*, or "Mountain of Leeches." Up there no vegetation grew; sprayed Agent Orange (a defoliant / herbicidal chemical) had scoured its crest and slopes of greenery. West was only an occasional "retreat," with bunkers, one indoor latrine, and hot food enough for a week or so.

Alpha stepped down from its crest onto the floor of Hiêp Dúc Valley in Quang Tin Province, part of I Corps area of operations. There the valley rose and fell in the sough of small hills, jungles thick with wait-a-minute vines and fields with razor-sharp elephant grass, until it reached the Song Thu Bon River, flowing beneath vaulting green mountains.

Alpha was plodding single file across an open field on a soggy November day when two farmers grabbed rifles and fired. For the first time, Jim heard the "crack-pop" of an AK-47 round zip past him.

"I learned this: There is a difference between a round being fired and a round being fired at *you*," he says of the day he earned his Combat Infantry Badge (CIB).

He also was learning how to pack his rucksack for maximum need but minimum weight; how to climb mountain slopes of red clay as slippery as ice; how to add iodine tablets and Kool-Aid to render water from streams safe and sweet.

He learned to avoid sharp elephant grass and escape clutches of wait-a-minute vines; to bind trousers with blousing rubbers from boots to knees against intrusion of leeches; and to live in filth.

Cleanliness is always an early casualty of war. On his first stand-down in Chu Lai, Jim bought a bologna-and-cheese sandwich at a vendor's booth, then noticed bugs baked into the bread.

"So I threw it away. On the second stand-down, I bought that sandwich again and pulled out the bugs and ate the sandwich.

By the end of my tour, I just ate the sandwich, bugs and all," he recalls.

Yet, he marveled at Vietnam's natural beauty and listened to its whispered secrets: to peel cinnamon bark as a flavoring for tea; to savor the sweet, star-shaped fruit, *Averrhoa carambola*; and to pluck a plant that served as a small candle. For night movements, men inserted *lân rêu* into helmet-cover bands. The plant's phosphorescent glow provided enough light with which to follow the man ahead.

He had ordered a Nikonos underwater camera. Its body armor of brass, he believed, would withstand Vietnam's climate and the rigors of infantry life. Jim's need to shoot pictures was twofold—foremost to "get out of the field." As soon as he reached Vietnam, he began lobbying for a secondary MOS (Military Occupational Specialty) of 84B20 as still photographer.

"I've been pushing my 'photo-ability' and things sound good. I might have to hump it in the field for a while but hopefully not too long," he wrote his father on 22 October 1969.

Jim yearned for a camera for a greater reason. Like writers and artists driven to pen and paints, photographers *must* photograph. To capture life with the click of a shutter is breath itself.

The Nikonos arrived in early December while Alpha enjoyed a three-day stand-down. Some of Jim's first photos were of entertainers.

"Tonight we have two live stage shows, strippers and all. Wow. Then I think they have some skin flicks. They shouldn't ought to do that to a guy who has been out in the field for two months," he wrote his dad.

While on stand-down, he photographed life on base, friends, and Alpha's new commander, Captain John Wilson.

Soon, friends in Alpha asked him to take their pictures to send home. So Jim devised a trans-oceanic, field-expedient photography business model. He mailed exposed film to his dad, who developed black-and-white negatives and sent color slide film to professional labs. Mr. Logue printed three 8 x 10 proof sheets of each roll, kept one, and sent two to Jim. From proof sheets men ordered photos, Jim sent his dad the negative numbers, when and where (in grid coordinates) he took the shots, and to whom to mail the prints, usually a mother or wife. He charged the princely sums of fifty cents for a 5 x 7, one dollar for an 8 x 10.

"I was fighting communism and practicing capitalism," he quips of his side-business that lasted him about one month and earned him $152. He sank that sum into more film.

In documenting his images, Jim mailed his dad a topographical map of the battalion's Area of Operations, as well as descriptions of movements and actions, with "Fire Zones," "No Fire Zones," and "Controlled Fire Zones" drawn in red pencil. He also mailed home after-action reports he acquired in that time-honored G.I. tradition, the "moonlight requisition." With a topographical map for illustration and reports for narrative, Mr. Logue followed his son's faraway footsteps.

Most days, Jim was walking. Through each month, Alpha spent about two weeks on LZ West, then two weeks in the field. Then one platoon after another guarded the small artillery base, LZ Siberia, for four to five days. Every two months came two days of stand-down.

After six months in the field, Jim earned R&R. In Japan, he toured a Nikon factory, then with dread he flew back to his war's next chapter.

"You went through three phases in Vietnam," he says. "Your first three months was the dangerous time. Then, guys in the middle of their time didn't give a damn about anything. The slogan became, 'It don't mean nuthin'.' You knew people were going to shoot at you. You didn't care. The last three months, you were 'short'! You could see the light! You didn't want to miss going home, and a lot of guys did. And when you saw them die, that's when it really hurt. Most of the guys who got killed were [either] 'new meats' or 'short-timers.'"

Photography quickened time's snail pace. Jim snapped shots atop LZ West and LZ Siberia. He photographed civilians, French colonial ruins, and a land of wending rivers, rolling valleys, and green mountains—a vacation paradise were it not a death-haunted battlefield.

Jim strove to keep film on hand, his supply at the mercies of quirky mail service. He also worked without civilian photographic safety nets: no meter to measure light; no strobes to fill in shadows; no tripod to steady a camera; no lens filters to polarize the sky to a cerulean blue. All he had was camera, film, and an artist's instinct for a good photograph.

As skies cleared in spring, Jim was handed a PRC-25 "prick" radio and designated RTO (radiotelephone operator) for Captain John Wilson. Although the "prick" added twenty-five pounds to his rucksack, Jim walked with the CP (command post), giving him a "heads up" on impending action.

Meanwhile, Jim was *not* capturing award-winning scenes of combat. He did not click a frame of dead or badly injured civilians or soldiers, friendly or enemy. Those were subjects of news photographers such as Larry Burrows (1926–1971), who earned reputations by racing from one battle to another. Jim, instead, was building an archive as someone rare: a combat soldier *and* professional photographer who both fought and documented this last major American conflict shot in black-and-white and color film.

Jim's sense of the importance of the ordinary preserves visual provender for future historians. At one night laager, he documented the small rituals of two soldiers settling in for the night. Richard Knowlton and Tim Cruthers snap together shelter halves for their hooch. Fatigue blouses dry atop its "roof." Cruthers wears a necklace of love beads and a cross—popular fashion statements of peace and piety. They slip on rubber sandals called "Ho Chi Minhs" so boots and socks may dry.

On Knowlton's legs, bandages cover lesions of *cutaneous leishmaniasis*—tropical ulcers or "jungle rot." Cruthers has crisscrossed blousing rubbers from ankle to knees to prevent leeches from burrowing under trousers. Still, bloodsuckers managed to slither beneath fabric.

One also sniffs a C-ration supper. Knowlton heats his canteen cup of chocolate atop a slice of C-4 explosive. Cruthers

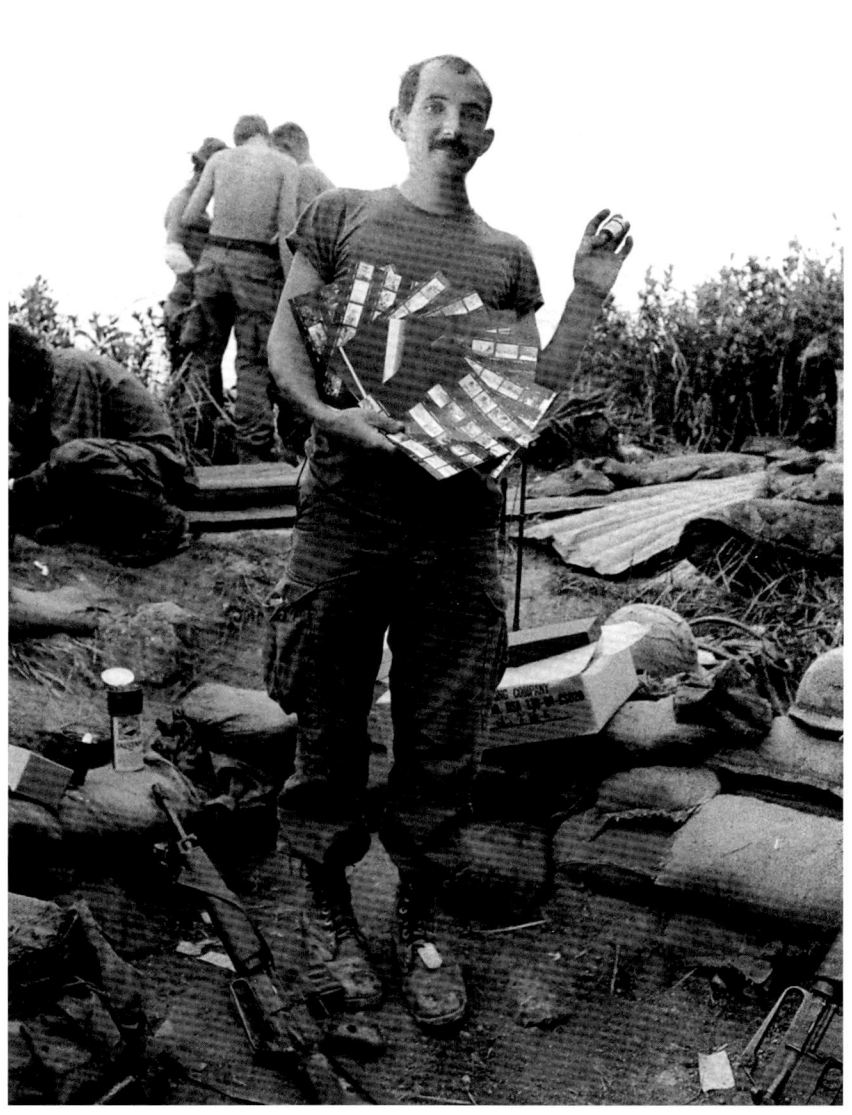

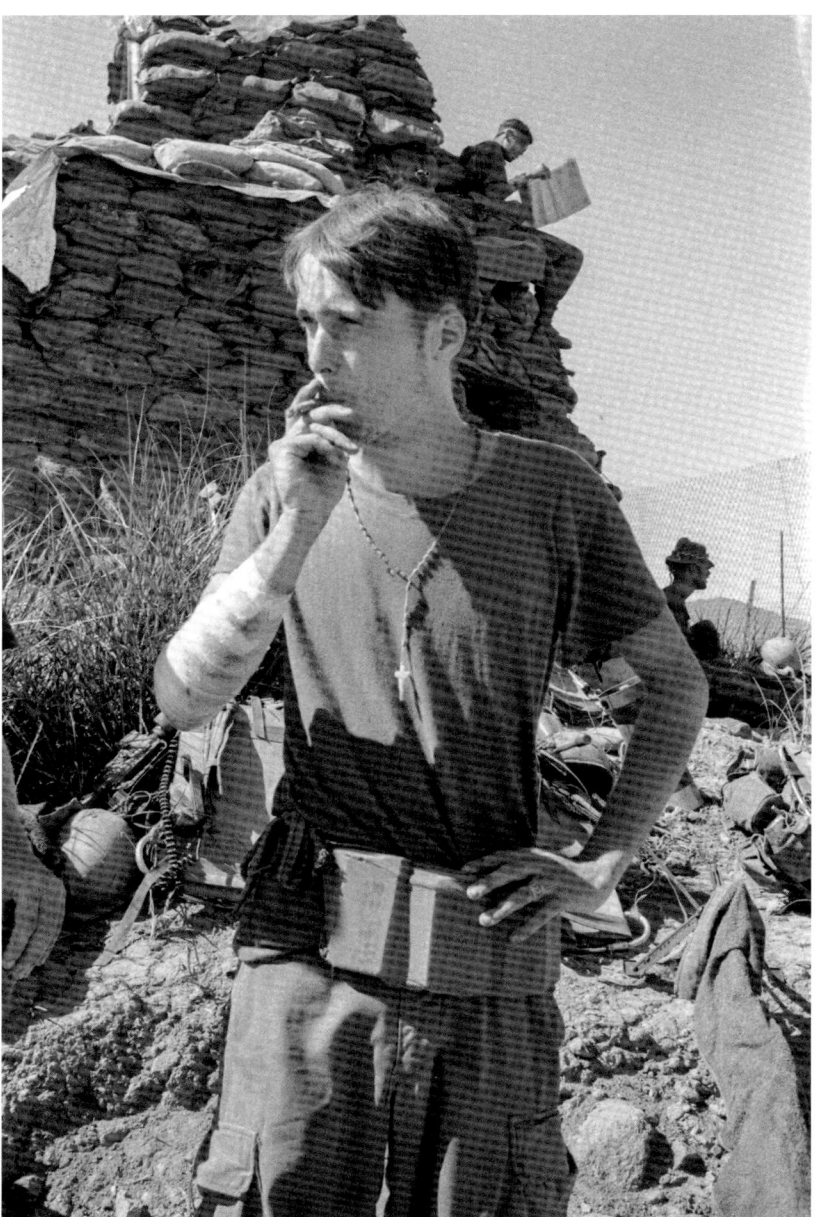

Logue displays a fan of contact sheets of exposed 35mm film. At the PX, he purchased Kodak Tri-X if it were in stock, a "fast" film best for capturing motion and shooting in low light.

With art as a common passion, Ben Perry quickly struck up a lifelong friendship with Logue.

opens a can with a Case XX fixed blade knife, popular among soldiers who found Army-issue bayonets of little use.

In the webbing of Knowlton's helmet liner, a plastic-wrapped packet protects correspondence from home—a grunt's field-expedient filing system. Such photographs illuminate nuggets of daily life in the Vietnam War.

With each click, Logue mined more: Andy Rowell of Monroeville, Alabama, tosses cases of C-rations from a resupply chopper; Dan Simmons, now of Prescott, Arizona, smiles wanly while surrounded by youngsters.

A photo of Ben Perry reveals the physique of Vietnam grunts: more like that of long-distance runners than the iron-pumped build of today's infantrymen. Other images display a wide range of the demographics of an infantry company, from a boy who joined at seventeen to a grizzled veteran the age of a grandfather; from high school dropouts to a doctoral candidate.

At least three enlisted men held master's degrees: Dennis Hogenboom, Peter Hummeland (slated to begin doctoral studies), and Charles Mann, a schoolteacher. Among officers with degrees are First Lieutenant Marvin Kay, now a tenured professor of anthropology at the University of Arkansas–Fayetteville, and First Lieutenant Ross Joplin, a graduate of Texas Tech University.

Meanwhile, he also trained his Nikonos on civilians, especially children, some of whom were the enemy, too. Not until he enlarged a particular negative forty years later did he notice that one small boy was grasping an American hand grenade.

Logue also shot in action the "Zippo Squad," a detail of men named for the popular cigarette lighters. While all citizens were supposed to reside in protected villages, Alpha often found hooches in jungle clearings, tended by a few women and small children, as a way station for passing enemy soldiers. Quick searches often uncovered arms, ammo, medical supplies, and rice.

So Alpha burned the supplies and instructed residents to return to American- and ARVN-protected towns such as Hiêp Dúc. Jim winces in recalling young and elderly nationals trudging away with backs bent from hauled belongings, as the Zippo Squad touched lighters to thatched roofs.

Spirits soared when 28 April brought a stand-down. That night, a Filipino band performed on a makeshift stage, concluding with the finale all soldiers demanded. When the band struck up The Animals' "We Gotta Get out of This Place," Alpha stood as one and roared out the unofficial anthem of the Vietnam War.

Hours later, Alpha was shouted awake. The 2nd NVA Division, as it had in previous summers, was attacking both military targets and civilian villages, wrecking buildings and murdering noncombatants.

Jim fought in every engagement of "Task Force West," or what Alpha veterans call "the May–June Battle." Neither side amassed large numbers on battlefields. There was no Gettysburg, no Saint-Mihiel, no Battle of the Bulge, but men died, and by June, the company fielded about forty effectives (those fit for active service), the average size of one platoon in a company numbering around 120.

In late June, after nine months in the field, Jim was released for duty on LZ West. He revived the defunct battalion

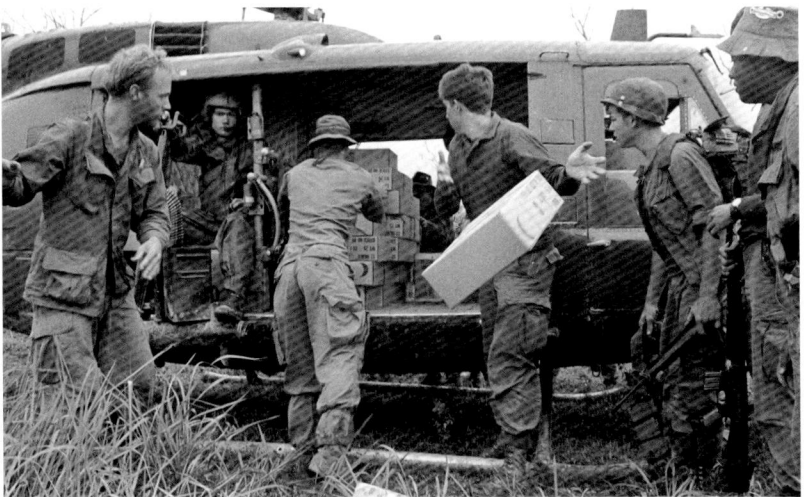

Choppers were vulnerable on the ground. Several men help unload so the bird can lift up and away within seconds. Andy Rowell tosses a box to the ground.

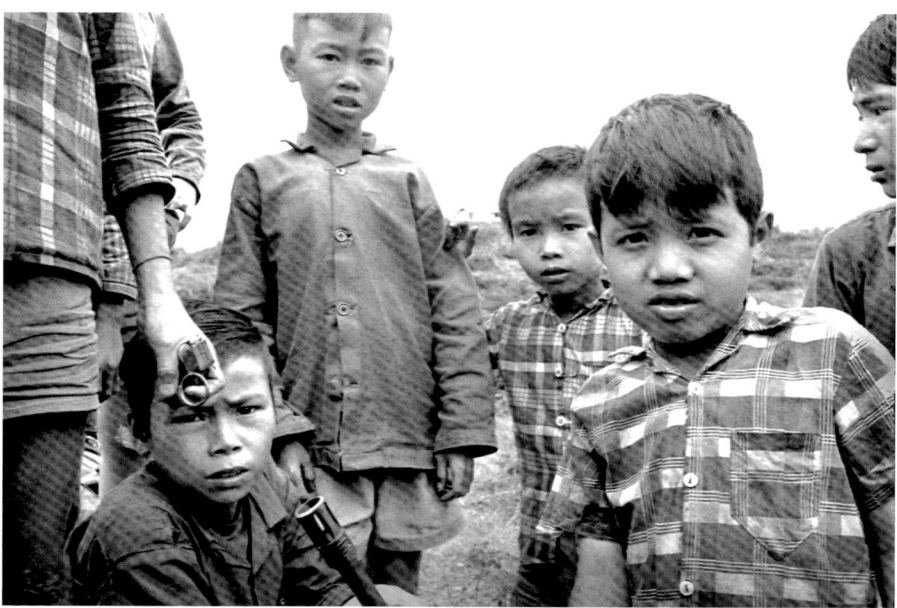

Only decades later, when Logue enlarged this image, did he notice this youngster was clutching a grenade. Viet Cong wired such American munitions into booby traps.

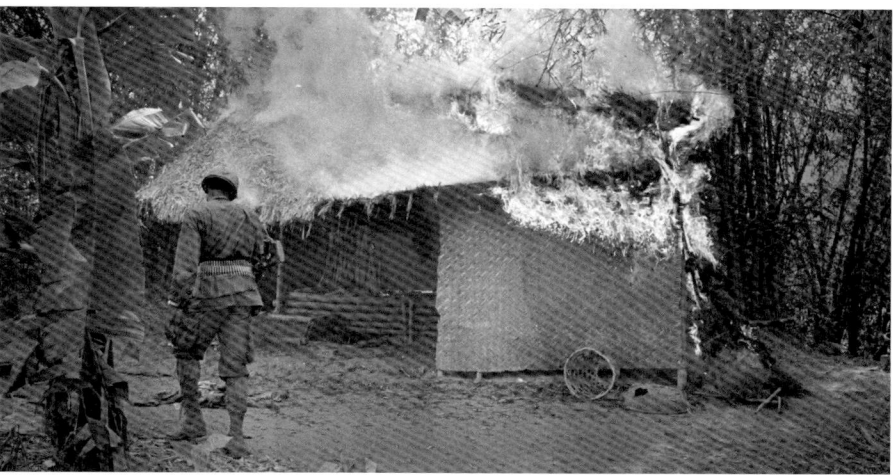

The enemy fired at Alpha from this hooch, where soldiers advanced and discovered munitions. The so-called "Zippo Squad" set it afire with one click of a Zippo, a popular brand of cigarette lighter.

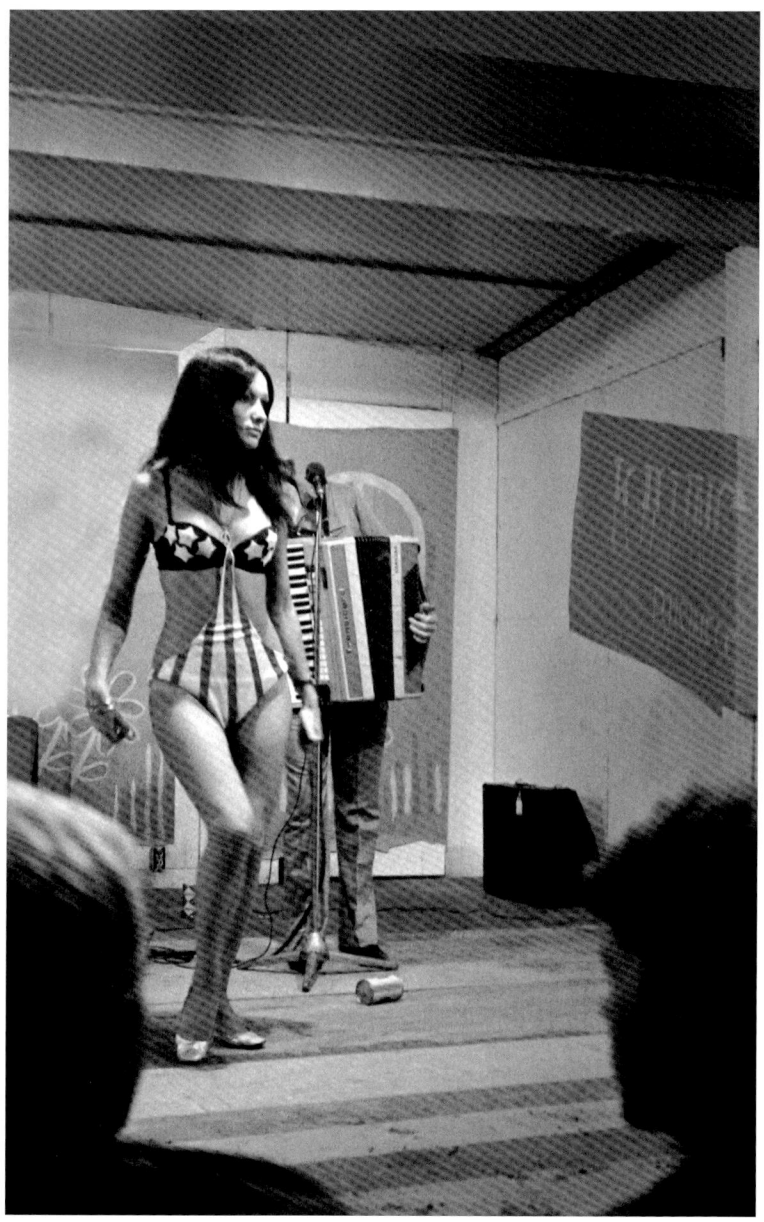

Stand-down promised beer, steaks, and outdoor shows with bands and scantily clad singers / dancers. Performance ended with the unofficial Vietnam War anthem, "We Gotta Get Out of This Place" by The Animals.

newspaper but did not cling to the safety of a desk. To gather material for stories, he often "rucked up" and accompanied Alpha's airborne combat assaults, including one on 22 August, a day that still sears his memory.

ON 6 OCTOBER 1970, JIM SAID GOODBYE TO BEN AND OTHER friends and "skyed up." One day he was at war; the next, home and guest of honor at a welcome-home party.

"It was just family and friends. That was the end of my war," Jim says.

He completed service at Aberdeen Proving Ground in Maryland, unaware that his "second" Vietnam War had begun. For years, he went about the business of living as though he had "won."

"Never thought about it," he said of the war and of the men of Alpha. "I didn't write anybody. I didn't call anybody. When you left Vietnam, you *left* Vietnam. You were *done*. You didn't want to *think* about it. You didn't want to *talk* about it. You were *done*."

In Pitman, he reopened his photography business, The Studio, and married Deanna Baum, with whom he had a son and daughter. The couple later divorced.

For Hallmark Color Labs in Millers Falls, Massachusetts, then for Segal Majestic, Inc. in Baltimore, he built college and high school yearbook photography divisions.

In 1981, Jim married Jeanne Delaney. They would have two daughters. That decade, Segal Majestic created Elegant Images, for whom Jim helped popularize the genre of "glamour photography." He built studios in twenty-three shopping complexes in eight states. He also pioneered digital photography with Sony Corporation. "Boy Tycoon" truly earned his nickname.

The Logues moved to Florida, where Jim joined another photography business, but the owner soon sold out. For the first time since the fifth grade, Jim wasn't looking at life through a viewfinder. The bad times began.

Within three years, his father died. His stepmother died. His grandson died. His son died.

"It was my 'job period,' when you just take it and keep going," he recalls.

Then, it seemed, all life stopped. Jim retreated to his home office, to his desk, artifacts, and photographs. Outside, a swamp swallows a far side of his front yard. Gray moss weeps from cypress trees. Saw palmetto open fans of sharp, green sabers. Alligators and water moccasins glide through black, tannic-stained water. Jim closed curtains, strung a hammock, and for months spent days in what had been his office. Now, it was his bunker.

He developed a stutter. He wept easily. He bolted upright from sleep, screaming from nightmares. Jeanne calmed him, but he lay awake, as if again staring into black Vietnam nights. The war had found him in the green, tangled Florida countryside, slithering like a sapper through Jim's mental claymores and the tangles of concertina wire he raised against the assault of memory.

Finally, Jim met with a psychologist, Dr. Jeanine Kubiak, at a nearby Veterans Administration facility. To battle his PTSD, she urged him to face again his old photographs to see them as they are—just pictures, no larger than 24 x 36 millimeters.

So he pulled out slides and sleeves of negatives untouched for four decades. From scanner to computer emerged faces that his camera, like a sculptor, had chiseled into the stone of eternal youth. He was not *done* with Vietnam, after all.

Steadily, Jim broke from the cell that incarcerates so many veterans: their own silence. He and Ben resumed their friendship. At Ben's urging, Jim began posting his images on military websites. Many from Alpha saw them and began corresponding.

Those photographs brought us together and began our four-year odyssey across America to interview as many in Alpha whom we could find and who agreed to interview. We also conducted research: from local newspapers, morgues, libraries, county courthouses, the National Archives in College Park, Maryland, and the National Historical Center in Carlisle, Pennsylvania. From 2012 to 2017, we gathered material.

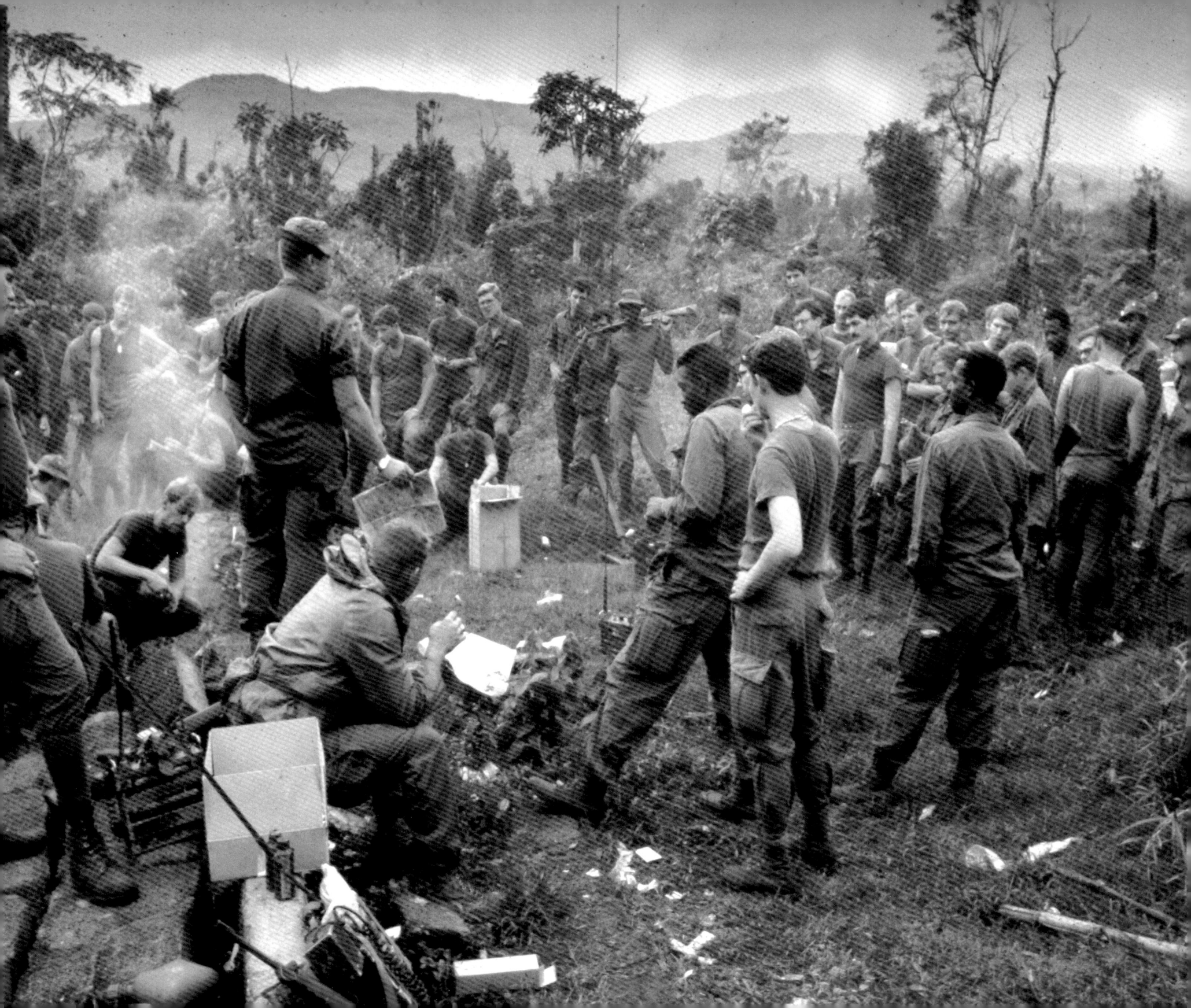

Chapter 2

My Goal Was to Get Everybody Home

Captain John A. W. Wilson

THE BATTLE WAS YET TO BE JOINED, AND ALREADY A SOLDIER lay dead among many more wounded. Captain John Wilson was sickened, heartbroken. And furious.

All had seemed so promising that morning. Alpha waited, hidden in brush, facing the NVA across an open field. Captain Wilson was confident that soon fire from 155mm howitzers from LZ West, directed by the new forward observer (FO), would soar above and beyond Alpha and explode among the enemy.

Instead, rounds fell short among 2nd Platoon, an incident known as "friendly fire" that ranks high among military oxymorons.

As soon as a medevac had lifted away the casualties, Captain Wilson sent word for the new FO to report to him.

Four decades later, Wilson remembers the rookie red leg (artilleryman) as "such a green seed he didn't have any reason to be in the field." Instead of apologizing for the botched fire mission, the FO screamed at Wilson, protesting his innocence.

Today, Wilson's voice is low and measured in speaking of his response.

"I expressed my disdain for his poor performance. I recall pulling my .45. And then I invited him to get out," he says.

The red leg boarded the next chopper, leaving Wilson heartsick as he recalled the promise he made to Alpha when he took command in December 1969.

JIM LOGUE'S PHOTOGRAPH OF THAT DECEMBER DAY DEPICTS Wilson in a clearing, addressing the company clustered around him "at ease." They are a blended group: survivors of summer's slugfest with 2nd NVA Division, men now "short" and soon to "sky up" and new meats—replacements like Logue who had trickled in through late summer and monsoon downpours.

Seasoned veterans included Robert "Prune" Jeans of Kenilworth, New Jersey. He was walking point for 1st Platoon when an NVA ambush roared to life on 22 August 1969. Prune dived beneath a small rise of thick bush, quickly realizing NVA were concealed just above him. He would have died in a dash to his lines, but the enemy could not move from Alpha's withering fire. Fiercest of the fire came from an M72 LAW (Light Anti-tank Weapon), with its rocket-propelled grenades, with which an M60 machine gunner nicknamed "Weird" kept the enemy hugging the earth.

Weird wasn't weird at all.

Left: Logue calls this his "all-time favorite picture," portraying men with whom he formed a lasting bond. In this jungle clearing, Captain John Wilson (center left) addresses Alpha.

"There was a man named Harold in the company earlier. Everybody called him 'Weird.' Then I came in. My name is Harold. So, 'Weird Harold,'" he explains in his Kentucky home, four decades later.

Barry Parsons, a Pennsylvanian, also kept firing at the enemy, with a collapsible tube that held a single round. All day, helicopters supplied him with ammo for the LAW, the Vietnam-era version of the World War II bazooka.

Under cover of night and Weird's fire, Prune crawled back to Alpha's lines. Prune served his year, went home to Kenilworth, New Jersey, and spent his life in (and retiring as chief of) the police department.

Also sizing up Wilson was Sergeant Richard "Dick" Oswald, a Nebraskan and leader of 1st Squad, 1st Platoon. Among enlisted men who'd never held command, Dick had "it"—that innate quality of leadership that made new guys, such as Specialist 4 Alvin Merryman, follow him like a disciple.

No one in Alpha, perhaps, knew the heartbreak of "goodbye" better than Al, who had grown up in rural Prince George County, Virginia, on the family farm, where he plowed with a mule and cut wood to warm the home. For the Merrymans, the 1960s blended past and present technology.

While Al, 19, served in Vietnam, his bride, Margie, 17, tended her vegetable garden, cooked over a wood-burning stove, and watched war news on television. Four times during service, Al had to say goodbye to Margie: leaving for basic training; leaving for Vietnam; coming home on leave for his father's funeral and returning to war; after a week of R&R in Hawaii. Inseparable since then, they live in a prim Victorian cottage, also headquarters of Merryman Painting.

Such good men Wilson would command and Logue would photograph. Encircling Wilson stood enlisted and drafted soldiers from across America. Two held master's degrees and taught school. There was a cooper, a baker, a candy maker. There were mechanics, an engineer, farmers, a rodeo cowboy, an artist, Logue the photographer, and, after the war, at least two attorneys and an anthropologist.

All hoped Wilson wouldn't "play John Wayne" with their lives while "punching his ticket." Junior officers in the combat arms required six months in the field to be "bloodied," to lead men into battle, to earn a Combat Infantry Badge, perhaps a Purple Heart, a Bronze Star or Silver Star. In leading men in combat, they boarded the express to higher ranks in an Army career. Wilson wanted to be on that train.

At least Alpha knew he wasn't a "cherry," having served as 4th Battalion S2 (intelligence) and earning his CIB. Still, he knew he had to earn the men's respect.

Ending his stump speech, Wilson announced he was renaming the company "Alpha Battalion," because of all they had accomplished. What he said next made all breathe easier. He lifted an index finger and raised his voice:

"I have one job: To get all of you, and me, back home safely," he said.

In Logue's photograph, Wilson wears his boonie (short-brim hat) with the back turned up and the front turned down. It resembled the snap-brim fedoras men wore in Grove Hill, Alabama, where he was the son of a widowed mother. All World War II or Korean War veterans, they served as mentors, while his mother nurtured in him a servant's heart.

Oh, he was no angel, Alpha learned. He drank. He cursed. He chewed tobacco. When we told Alpha veterans of Wilson's later life, many exclaimed, "You gotta be kiddin' me!"

Jim and I found the captain and his wife, June, in their comfortable home beside Lake Martin, on an impoundment of the Tallapoosa River in Alabama. Rods and reels leaned beside the front door, available for guests to "wet a hook" from the Wilsons' pier.

In the South, it is proper for new acquaintances to ask two questions: "Where are you from?" and "Who are your people?" In football-mad Alabama, a third query is likely: "Who are you 'for': Auburn or Alabama?"

John Wilson grins when asked the latter.

"Auburn! And I'll tell you why. Shug Jordan's father was a depot agent in Whatley, Alabama." Ralph "Shug" Jordan was head football coach at Auburn University from 1951 to 1975.

John continues, "Shug was a schoolmate of my mother. People kidded her about him being her boyfriend. I aspired to play football at Auburn but wasn't quite big enough."

His mother, Nell Wilson Creighton, grew up on "a little dirt farm," earned her college degree, and taught school until losing her job in the Depression. She married, but John's father soon died, leaving widow and child in near penury. Town citizens, including members of the family's Methodist church, stepped up to help.

"They took the scriptural reference of taking care of widows and children to heart. I had plenty of mentors helping me with part-time jobs," John says.

At Huntingdon College in Montgomery, he planned to enter seminary but was drafted and found another family, the US Army. After Officer Candidate School at Fort Benning, Georgia, and service in West Germany, he flew to Vietnam, along the way chatting with Lieutenant Colonel Colin Powell, who was en route to his second tour in the country. Both saw the beginning of American denouement in the war.

"We were tired. The country was tired. The leadership was tired. There was an attitude: 'Let's get the heck out. We don't have any business here,'" he recalls.

Still, he had men to lead. Beneath LZ West, fields, jungle, and mountains spread out like a game board where geography and population demanded different rules of engagement. As per orders from MACV (Military Assistance Command, Vietnam), various swaths of land were designated "Free Fire Zones" and "Controlled Fire Zones." In contrast, in "No Fire Zones"—which included areas with "pacified" villages such as Hiêp Dúc—Alpha, once fired upon, had to obtain permission from higher command to return fire. All forces complied, except the enemy.

Alpha fought the enemy with one hand and with the other upgraded civilian lives. In pacified Hiêp Dúc, 4th Battalion S5 (civilian affairs) units constructed schools and public buildings, while Military Assistant Teams (MAT) trained local Popular Forces. US medical teams (MEDCAPS) provided health services, including transporting and treating ill and injured civilians and handling births.

The American military mission was *not* to destroy the enemy, capture its territory, and force surrender. Rather, it aimed to pacify and protect citizens while blunting the NVA appetite for conquest.

"That was the tactical mission. People like General [William] Westmoreland had backgrounds of World War II land warfare where you moved and took territory. That wasn't *ever* the case in Vietnam. You didn't take territory. You became a part of it," John says.

Two phrases particularly Wilson detested. The first was initially spoken in the White House on 17 April 1965, when President Lyndon Johnson called for a "body count" of enemy and friendly forces—a gory way of measuring the success of a war without a front. Such quantitative analysis appealed to Secretary of Defense Robert McNamara, with his business background. To report "progress," network television news plastered on screens body counts as if they were sports scores.

By 1969, many new meats understood this was a war without end and were utterly weary of anti-war activists labeling them "baby killers." Soon enough, they scratched on helmet camouflage covers the nihilistic message Wilson despised: "It Don't Mean Nuthin'."

"I'd go crazy when somebody had that written on his helmet. I tried to help people understand that it meant something to somebody," he recalls.

In monsoon, he led rain-soaked Alpha in hunting a phantom, 2nd NVA Division, that seemingly disappeared. Mid-April 1970 opened "Task Force West," a battalion-size search of Hiêp Dúc Valley and its vaulting uplands for the NVA. Wilson, and

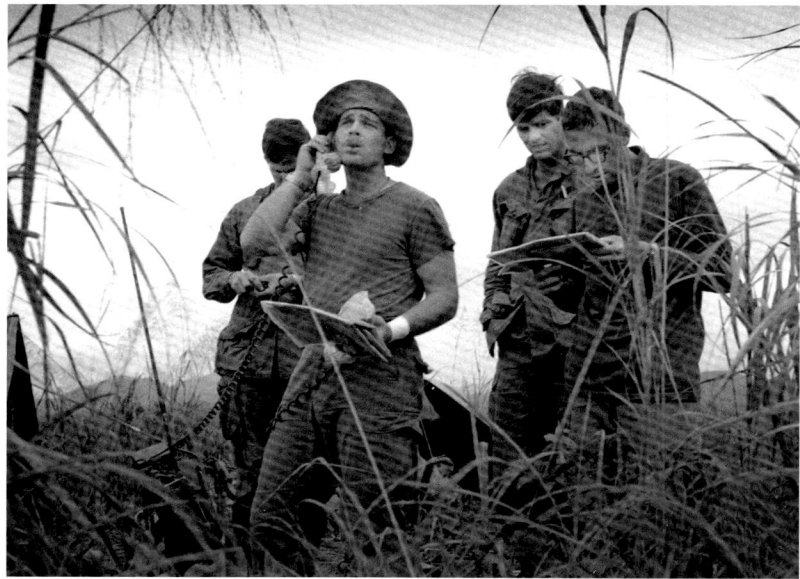

On a rainy January day, Captain Wilson orders artillery strikes on a Viet Cong position. The men admired Wilson for always "softening" the enemy before the company attacked.

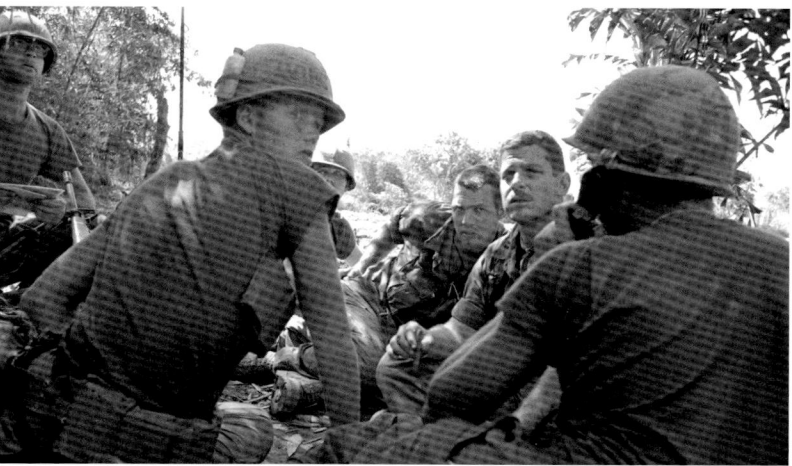

Captain John Wilson (center), First Lieutenant Donald Pettit (behind Wilson), and Specialist 4 Alvin Merryman (left) listen to the direction of enemy fire. An RTO is calling in artillery on the enemy in February 1970.

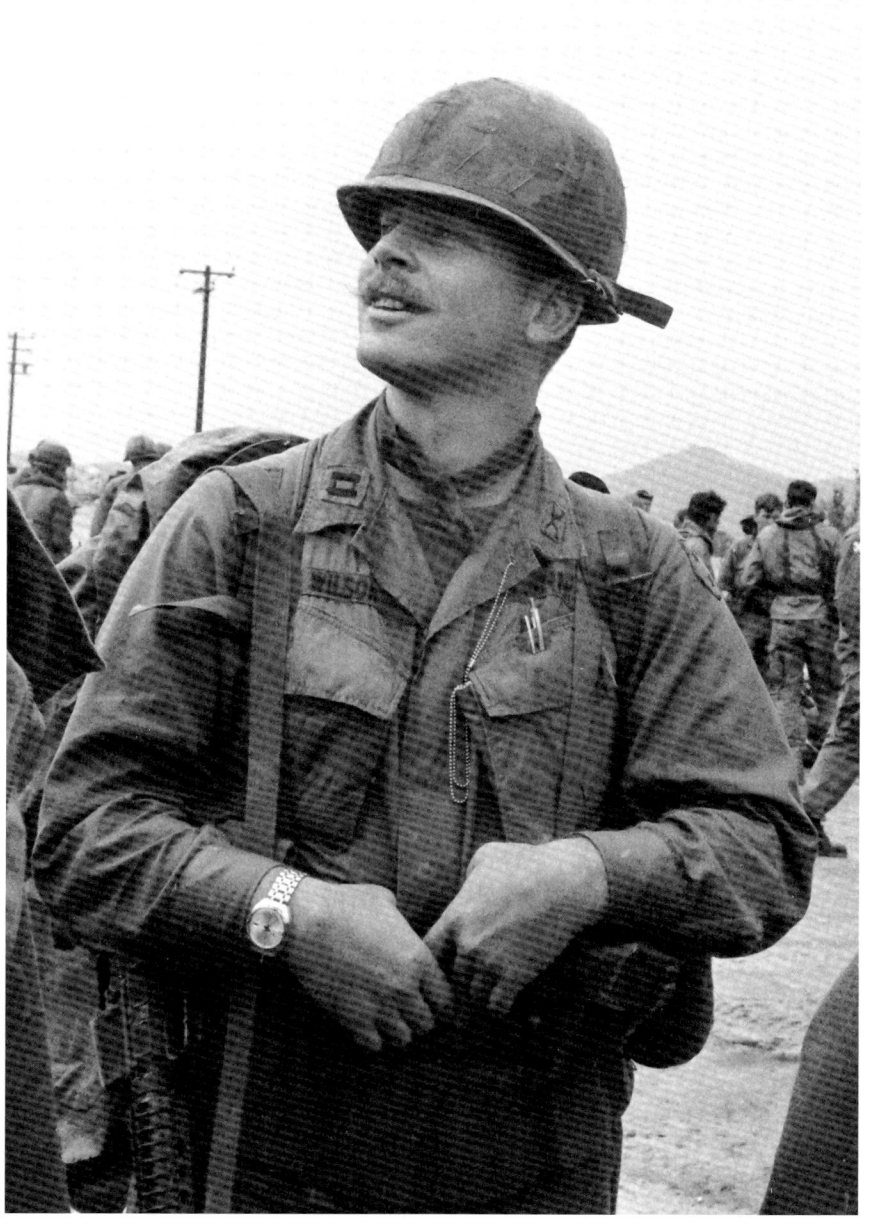

Captain John Wilson later served as a school principal, National Guard company commander, and ordained Methodist minister.

those in Alpha who grew up in the outdoors, sensed enemy presence like unseen game in a forest.

"They were sitting there the whole time, watching every move we made. You could almost *see* eyes. You could *feel* eyes. I was scared to death," he remarks.

On 28–29 April in dim moonlight, 2nd NVA Division attacked throughout Quang Tin province, wrecking villages, confiscating food, murdering civilian leaders, and striking American firebases. On 3 May, with Wilson in his sixth month in the field, Alpha began a two-month-long running fight. The company attacked here, served as a blocking force there, and walked and walked and walked.

Men died, fell wounded, and went hungry for days when fog often grounded resupply choppers. The company marched on empty bellies and dry canteens. The sick and lame leaned on friends' shoulders. Men slept on their feet, fell to the ground on minutes-long rest stops, then plodded on again when someone prodded them awake. Readiness suffered from weariness.

The enemy killed with their own weapons as well as with rucksack contents GIs tossed aside to lighten loads: hand grenades, extra ammo, claymore mines, and C-ration cans—all flotsam the VC fashioned into booby traps. Malaria, jungle rot, heat exhaustion, and trench foot sidelined many. One soldier stepped into a punji pit of razor-sharp iron spikes smeared with feces. Still, Alpha fought on. They fought the enemy, fought their own fear, fought the land itself.

Then, back at LZ West in late May, the men of Alpha looked around. Wilson was gone. After six months with Alpha, the captain had punched his ticket in the field. Command of Alpha temporarily devolved to First Lieutenant Erwin Esterling, the well-respected 1st Platoon leader.

Wilson loved his men and felt confident he had done all he could to keep them alive, often calling forth overpowering resources to save lives. He leans forward and taps the table.

"If I had the opportunity to put a jillion tons of ordnance on enemy areas before we set foot on it, that's what I'd do. If there was one sniper and I had five hundred-pound bombs at my disposal, I was going to give it to him before I put a soldier's boots on the ground," he says.

After his R&R, Wilson served the rest of his tour on LZ West as adjutant for 4/31 Headquarters Company, then as Headquarters Company Commander (HCC) at Americal Division in Chu Lai.

Homebound servicemen and women were advised to wear civilian clothes to avoid anti-war confrontations. John refused to do so. In a San Francisco airport restroom, a protestor spat out at him "baby killer." John, wearing his dress greens, slammed the door on the man's face.

He grins sheepishly.

"The MPs came. That was my 'welcome home,'" he says.

Months later, while Wilson was serving at Fort Carson, Colorado, Vietnam laid him low with malaria. Then, the Army swung another body blow. Wilson's military career ended with an acronym: Reduction in Force (RIF) claimed the careers of some 4,200 young officers after Vietnam. He was devastated.

"I was twenty-eight years old and having to start life again. That was a dark time for me," John says.

Meanwhile, he and his wife had adopted an infant girl through Catholic Social Concerns in Colorado Springs. Back in Alabama, John completed his bachelor's degree at Huntingdon College and earned MS and M.Ed. degrees from Auburn University. For his next career of service, he stepped into Montgomery's Carver Junior High School, a predominantly African American institution. It was 1973, when Southern schools were still desegregating. John was one of the school's "three or four" Caucasian teachers that first year.

He eventually rose to the role of principal, while also serving as a soldier, if part time, as commander of an Alabama National Guard transportation company.

"I had a ball," he said of both academic and National Guard service.

His third career began after his retirement from public education. Long a lay speaker in the United Methodist Church,

John completed seminary and served two decades as pastor of rural and small-town churches. He now fills in for area Methodist ministers, while enjoying the serenity of his lakeside home. There, at water's edge, he stalks bass and bream, if only to release his catch. As sunset fires the water, he sees again those young faces gathered around him on that December day in 1969, a moment Logue preserved on film. Wilson looks at Logue's photograph for a long time. His voice is barely a whisper.

"I think of them every day," he says.

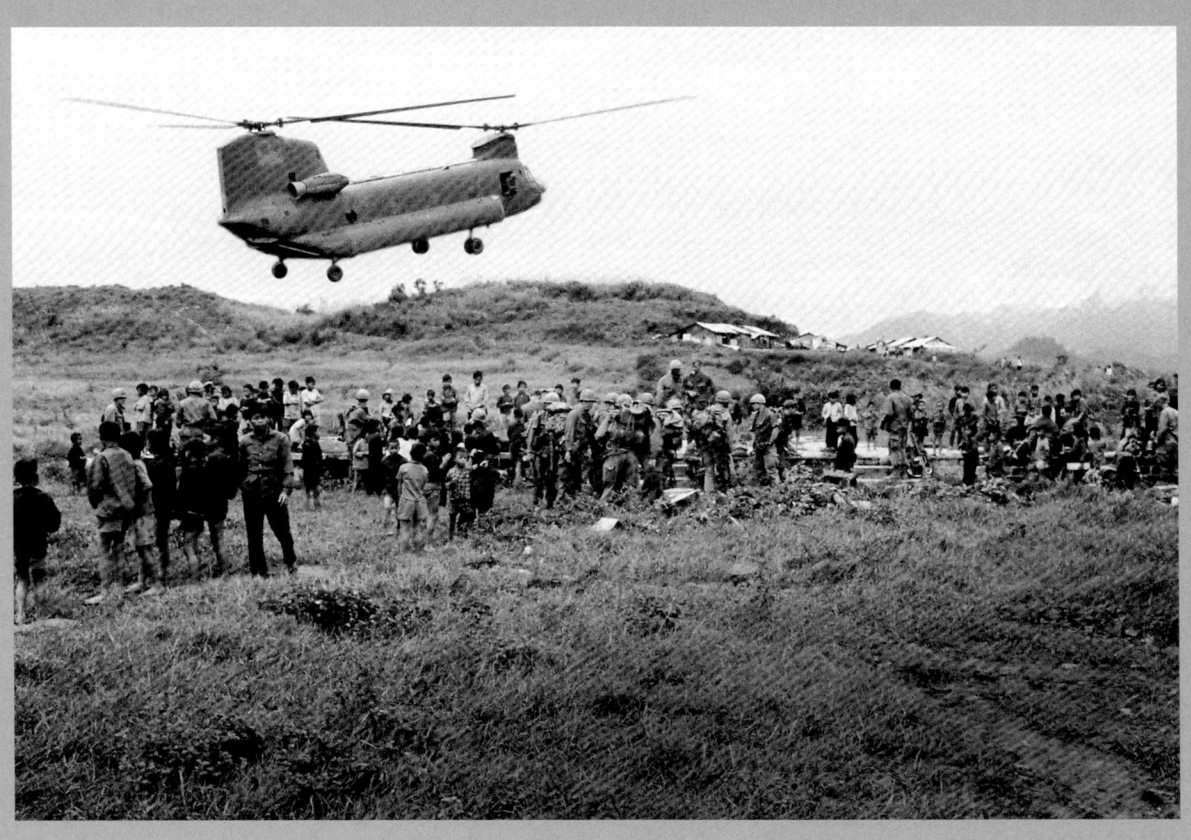

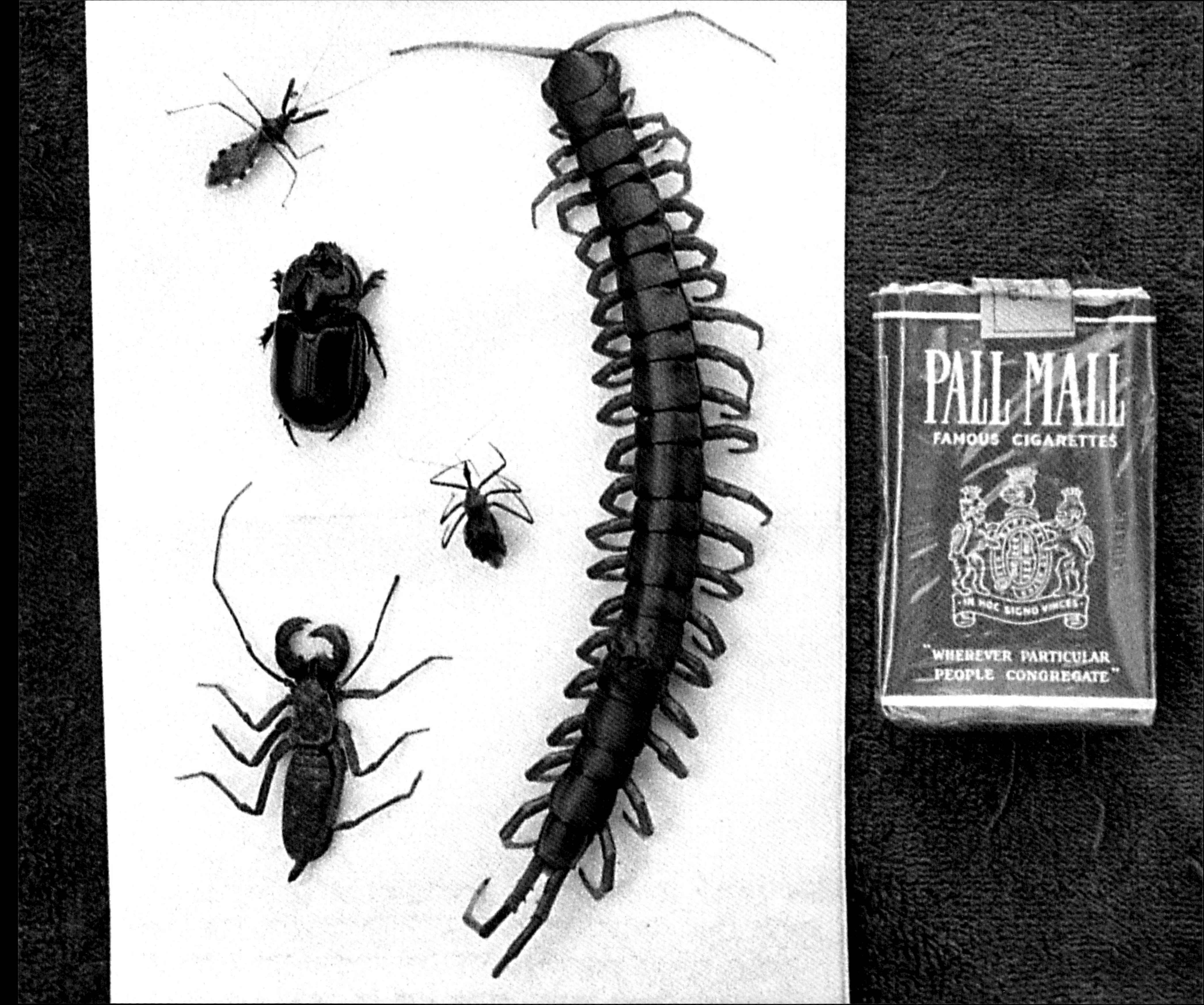

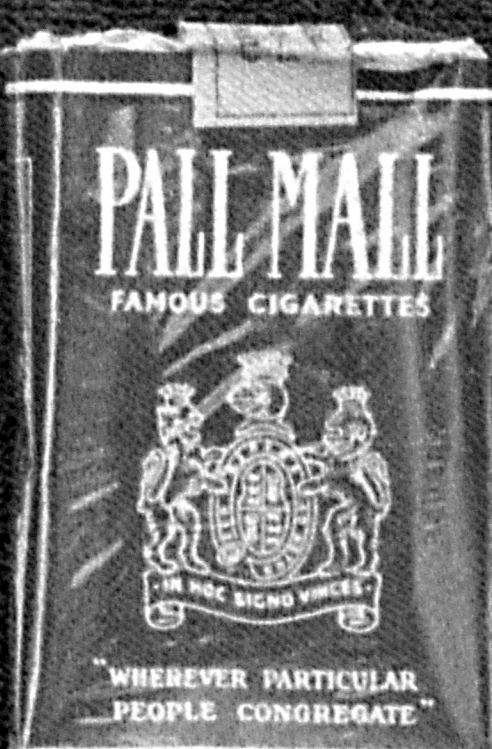

Chapter 3

I Had No Fear, None at All

Sergeant John Sigve Oiestad

AS HE FLEW WEST TO WAR, JOHN SIGVE OIESTAD WRESTLED WITH all the "what ifs" of Vietnam: Would he exhibit cowardice? Would he sustain wounds? And would he ever see his beloved Montana again? On that long sky ride, this cowboy could not know that a single "voice" would grant him peace of mind, even in combat.

That voice spoke months later when the lanky Montanan, dreading the vicious Vietnam heat, arrived on 23 June 1969. He peered across the tarmac from inside the plane.

"I thought, well, it's kind of cloudy today. It ain't gonna be too bad. I stepped out of that plane. It about knocked me right back in. It was *hot*!"

It is not hot on this August morning in 2013 in Bozeman. Breezes carry a cool whisper of approaching autumn when John and Shari Matheson Oiestad meet Jim Logue and me. John is tall, his face ruddy from a life spent outdoors. He never removes his western hat. Like all plainsmen, for whom hat is required work attire, not fashion statement, he knows its safest place is on his head.

He was born to the sun and snow and soar of mountains, to farms and ranches and highland forests, to crops and cattle and horses. An expert in range management, he knows his homeland from the grass up.

John began life in Norway but drew first breath in Big Timber, Montana, as the son of immigrant parents: his loving mother, Kari Ronneberg Oiestad, and stern, taskmaster father, Sverre.

In Norway in World War II, Sverre fought as a partisan against German occupation. Eventually captured, he nearly starved in a concentration camp where prisoners were fed only boiled peelings of rotten potatoes.

Kari suffered horribly, too. She was going into labor with the couple's first child when German SS soldiers made her scrub floors on her hands and knees almost to the moment she delivered. As soon as the child was born, they forced her back on hands and knees to finish her chore.

Kari was pregnant with her second son when the Oiestads sailed for America. John, one of six siblings, was born in 1949 in south-central Montana among Norwegian neighbors.

The Oiestads ate well with Kari's old-country cooking, including *kumle*, or potato dumplings, that provided calories

Left: A pack of Pall Mall cigarettes indicates the size of these insects, like the centipede at right. Such "critters" tormented the men, especially leeches that wriggled beneath clothing and sucked blood.

for daylight-to-dusk chores. John recalls a boyhood that was happy and harsh and filled with work.

"We had a lot of discipline when we were growing up. My dad never gave us anything. You couldn't hardly even get a candy bar out of him," he says.

By age 6, John was milking cows. Soon he was cutting and stacking bales of hay, a chore that brought him a lifelong satisfaction in measuring accomplishment.

"At the end of the day I could always look up at the haystack and see exactly what I'd done that day and be proud of it. My dad always taught us to be proud of what we did," he remarks.

Like most rural Montanans, he was born to the saddle.

"I had a horse you could trot almost all day. He was a cayuse. He'd never wear out, but a cayuse would just as soon bite you as look at you," he remarks of these feral-born ponies.

As a teenager, John welcomed work on larger ranches far from Big Timber. In this manner he escaped Sverre's iron will

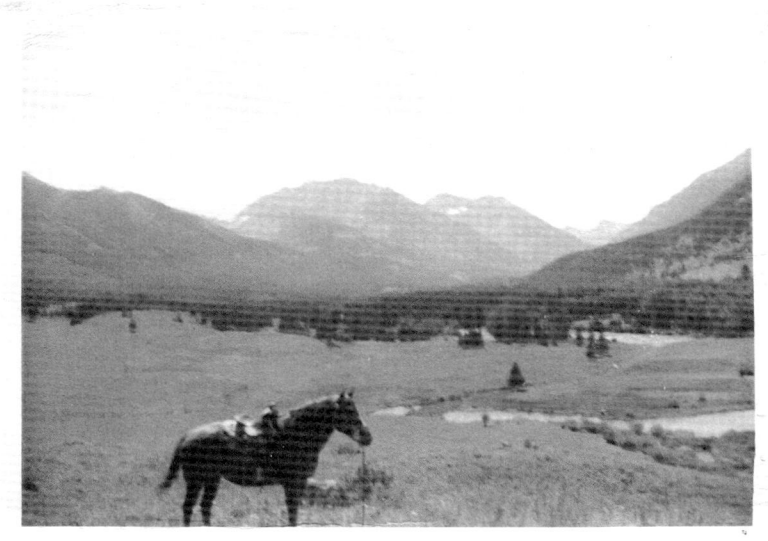

With no sweetheart back home, John Oiestad carried this image of horse, valley, and soaring mountains of his beloved Montana.

and lessened the burden on Kari. The children also spent stints with an aunt and uncle while Kari was bedridden with what John believes was diabetes-related symptoms. He smiles wanly.

"Mom was an angel. In Norway, back then, the women were submissive. That's the way it was with my dad and mom," he recalls.

Restless in classrooms, John would often let his eyes drift from textbooks to window-framed canvases of grasslands and distant mountains. After high school, he completed his freshman year at Montana State College (now Montana State University) in Bozeman. Earnings from a summer job with the US Forest Service fell short of fall semester tuition for his sophomore year. Drafted, he entered service on 23 January 1969.

This muscular farmer-rancher breezed through basic training and infantry Advanced Individual Training (AIT) at Fort Lewis, Washington. By late June 1969, he was baking in the sweatbox of Hiêp Dúc Valley. He was placed in Alpha, 4/31, 1st Platoon, 1st Squad, with Richard "Dick" or "Dickie" Oswald, a Nebraskan, as squad leader.

Soon nicknamed "John-John," Oiestad quickly proved a tough and trustworthy soldier. Oswald assigned him to walk point, a job that required nerves of steel, near fearlessness, and the abiding trust of those who followed. With Oswald behind him as "slack," John walked point "about eight out of twelve months."

Slowly his body adjusted to Vietnam's hellish heat in long "humps" across fields, hacking through jungles, and climbing mountains. He kept walking, well or ill.

"One time I had about a hundred-and-four, maybe a hundred-and-five-degree temperature. They didn't take you out of the field. If you weren't going into convulsions or something, they wouldn't take you out," he recalls.

Neither could anyone avoid night movements that Alpha Company commander, James Mantell, ordered. In the darkness awaited the enemy, venomous reptiles, booby traps, and a medieval torture chamber called a punji pit with upright bamboo or iron stakes sharpened and feces slathered on that lacerated and infected feet.

Getting lost could prove fatal.

"You had to feel with your feet where the trail was. We all put [on their helmets] this stick with moss or lichen on it, about four or six inches, and that stuff would illuminate, so you could actually see the guy in front of you," he remembers of the plant *lân rêu*.

By day, Vietnam's natural world disgusted him, he says, in expressing a plainsman's view that any place south of Amarillo is a miasmal swamp.

"I've always said that the Lord put everything that was nasty in Vietnam," he remarks wryly. "You had the wait-a-minute vine. You had all kinds of insects. You had leeches. They'd almost jump over on you."

Even grass hurt. Elephant grass grew in expansive fields, its edges razor sharp.

"You'd get cuts. You get that jungle rot. I don't know how many penicillin pills we took over there. I have no desire to go back to Vietnam. That's a nasty damn country," he says.

While June and July proved relatively uneventful, August turned to agony. On 11 August 1969, the 2nd NVA Division attacked throughout Quang Tin Province. For nearly a month, 196th Light Infantry Brigade threw everything into the fray.

"I was walking point, and there were people dying behind me and getting wounded. There was so much chaos. And it was really affecting me. Bad," John recalls.

The 196th held. The NVA melted back into mountain lairs to wait out monsoon and reinforce. That summer campaign, however, changed John-John. He grew silent and sat alone in night laagers. Friends understood. All dealt with their demons differently. This was just John-John's way.

"For at least two weeks I wouldn't talk to a soul," he recalls.

He communicated only in letters home. Without a girlfriend, he carried no photograph of a local beauty. Instead, he wrapped in plastic and inserted inside in his helmet liner a Montanan's image of home: a photograph of a horse grazing, mountains rising in the distance. He still has the photograph.

He wrote family and friends, including this excerpt from an undated letter to his sisters: "I got something like 275 days left here, and it seems like I got a lifetime." At least his body had adjusted to high heat, enough that "I don't feel like I'm going to faint any minute." He then composed a short treatise on leeches and how their anti-coagulant in human hosts caused continued bleeding. In closing he asked for a "Care Package of Copenhagen snuff, sunflower seeds, and corn nuts."

Summer fighting had greatly depleted Alpha's ranks. By September, the company assembled no more than thirty-five men. Until more new meat arrived, all had to hump extra ammo and firepower. John-John hefted the 60mm machine gun and strapped on 700 rounds of its ammunition.

John, who by then weighed 140 pounds, was humping at least eighty more. To bear such loads, all learned anew how to stand. First, you find a tree. "You had to roll over, get on your hands and knees, and crawl up on it, just to stand up," John remarks.

Alpha's replacements often arrived in the bush from resupply choppers. As green as their new fatigues, they marveled at such grizzled veterans as John-John, by then deeply tanned and with blond hair sun-bleached. He soon grew weary of one new guy who was assigned to his squad in October. John grins and points at Jim. Both laugh.

"We hated him for a while because he was always clicking those damn pictures," John remarks.

In December, choppers airlifted Alpha to a three-day stand-down at the Spartan facilities of "Charger Hotel" at American Division headquarters in Chu Lai. One day, John slipped away and splashed into the shallows of the South China Sea. There he sat and gazed across the water, pondering one question: "Why wasn't I getting killed, when all these people around me were dying?"

For a moment John cannot speak. He pauses, staring at his boots. When he looks up, his eyes blaze in conviction, but he speaks softly: "And I saw Christ walk off the ocean, a vision of Him or whatever. And He was saying to me, 'Don't worry. I'll take care of you the rest of the time over here.'"

When John finds his voice again, it's clear and adamant.

"And that changed everything. I had no fear. None. None at all, even in the battles we had later. He was protecting me. I truly believe that."

"You heard a voice?" I ask.

He nods.

"Heard the voice. Absolutely. It was real. Guilt, fear—all that stuff was gone. Completely gone. I wasn't one to kill people. I was there to come out alive."

At Christmas, his mother wrote, his youngest brother, Steven, now a noted western artist, sang "Let There Be Peace on Earth" in Norwegian and English in the family's Lutheran church, as a tribute to his brother in Vietnam. That touched him, John says.

He mentioned neither to the men nor in letters to family what he saw in the South China Sea, but Dick Oswald sensed that John-John, by then brandishing a 12-gauge shotgun with double-ought buckshot, had "some kind of a spiritual thing going on. He wouldn't let anybody else walk point," Oswald recalls.

He did have something "going on." He kept hearing the voice that spoke from the sea. He said he would "feel" his mother's prayers.

While he drew inner strength from the voice, he remained neither foolhardy nor fearful, nor was he a saint. In January, he flew to the R&R destination thousands of single GIs favored: the fleshpots of Bangkok, Thailand.

Upon returning, John landed at Cam Ranh Bay. Dreading months more at war, he went AWOL, drank heavily, and lost his wallet, which was returned to his family. Not until he wrote them did they learn he remained alive.

"I finally made it back and went out in the field. They told me they'd keep me out there longer, but not how much longer," he explains of his punishment. He grew very careful with five months remaining.

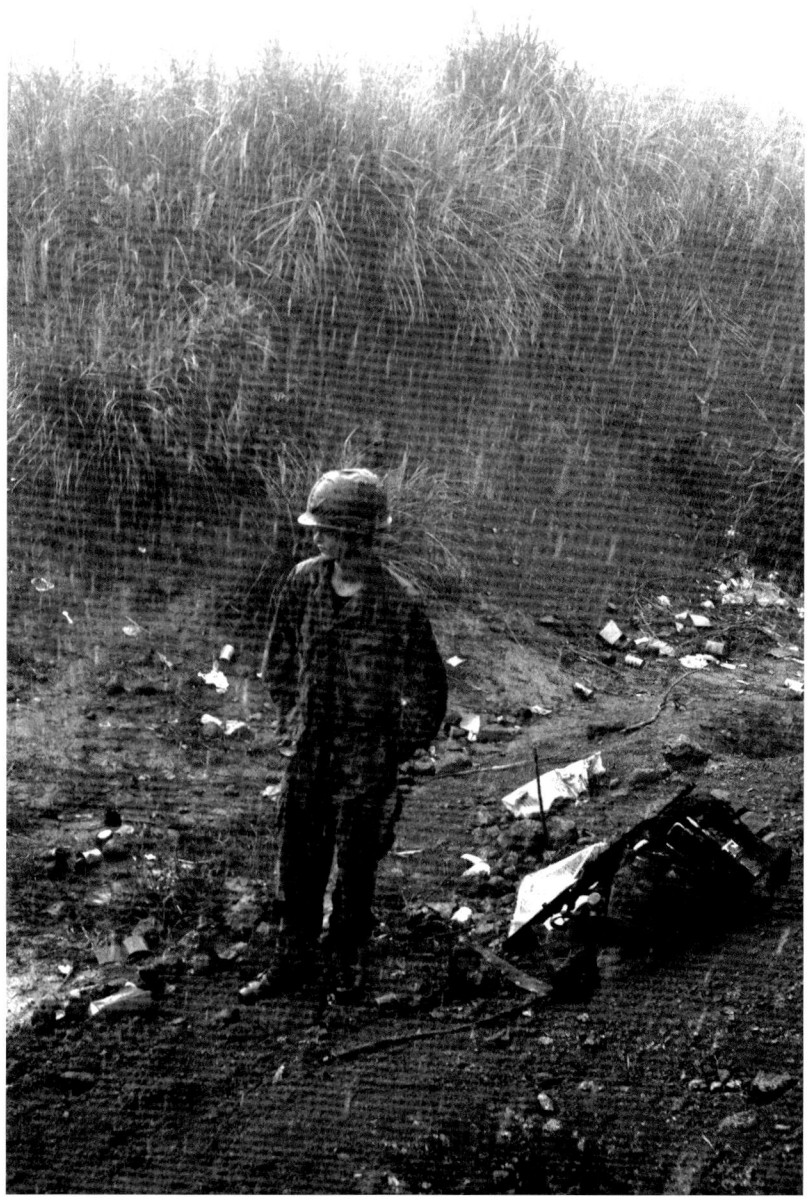

On a rain-soaked afternoon, John Oiestad stands in a bomb crater that will serve Alpha as a night laager. Later, three men would die nearby in an NVA ambush.

"I started digging foxholes like the NVA did. I'd dig them down, and then back under," he explains, demonstrating an L-shaped excavation.

John's year at war ended much as it began: fighting another campaign against the old nemesis, 2nd NVA Division. Between 10 and 14 May, he recalls, fog grounded resupply choppers and medevacs. Rations ran out. Medics had little with which to treat sick and wounded, some who needed to be in hospitals. Still, all of them—fit and ill, short-timers and new guys—plodded on.

"I think some days we'd go ten miles with those damn packs on our backs. I think one time we stayed up three days straight without any sleep," he remarks.

Among his worst times were helping "bag and tag" American dead.

"That was terrible duty. They'd be lying out there for three or four days, all puffed up. Rotted humans are way worse than animals. Way, way worse," he recalls.

By late May, casualties had whittled Alpha's strength to the size of a platoon. Short-timers, terrified of dying in their last few days in Vietnam, begged for safer duty. With ranks depleted, few, if any, such requests were granted.

John, on his 362nd day, was still "paying" for his AWOL spree.

With two days left in country, he boarded a chopper to begin the first leg of his journey home. He fulfilled the final months of his military obligation with other Vietnam veterans at Fort Carson in Colorado, playing war games in the snow.

Back home, John found two weapons to exorcise the demons of Vietnam: He drank. And he fought.

Bars in downtown Bozeman, he recalls, catered to two kinds of clientele. Vietnam veterans and cowboys patronized beer joints on one side of a street; "hippies" with their long hair and hatred for anything or anyone "military" encompassed the other. Fights often broke out between the two sides. John eagerly jumped into these Wild West barroom brawls.

Love uncurled his fists.

"When I met him, he had two black eyes," Shari recalls.

John, smitten, left the bars and married Shari Matheson on 23 August 1975. Living in married housing at Montana State University, he buckled down and a year later earned a degree in range management.

Employed by the US Forest Service, John was in the field again, this time alone. Projects often sent him high into the mountains on horseback, riding Ole Slim, and trailing a pack mule of supplies. He cooked his dinner over a campfire and slept under the stars.

"I was out there for ten days at a time. Alone. No radio. Nothing. Bears all over the place. I would come back and somebody would say, 'How can you stay up there alone with those bears?' And I would say, 'Hell, this is nothing. Nobody's shooting at me! Just don't bother the bear; he ain't gonna bother you,'" he recalls.

For John, up there in the high country, grass, forest, stars, and sky soothed his soul. Up there, Vietnam vanished in the crackle of his campfire. Up there, he made his separate peace.

"Until Jim called, I hadn't thought about Vietnam for years," he remarks.

He and Shari, a schoolteacher and genealogist, have two children and two granddaughters. John has been sober for twenty-three years.

After our interview, the Oiestads took us on a windshield tour of the nearby countryside, where three streams—Jefferson, Madison, and Gallatin—converge to form the Missouri River. Perhaps Lewis and Clark stood here, too, when they named the rivers on their cross-country journey.

Months later, the Montanan was rewarded for his lifelong efforts of service to the land he loved. John and Shari flew to Washington, DC, where he was one of twelve Americans from among more than 200 nominees to accept the Unsung Hero Award for his work with the Natural Resources Conservation Service.

John has thrived in a long career as a hunting guide and in range management, helping ranchers and farmers maintain Montana's fields, forests, and soaring highlands. He treasures one memory of Vietnam that never vanished in the smoke of his mountain campfires: that December day he sat in the sea, transfixed by an image and a voice he adamantly claims was that of Jesus Christ.

He calls himself a "lukewarm Lutheran" who attends services only on special occasions, such as Christmas and Easter.

"I listen to some preachers, and they teach you the fear of God. That's not my take on it. You don't have to be afraid of Him. He's my friend," he says of the image from the sea that told this Montana cowboy to fear not.

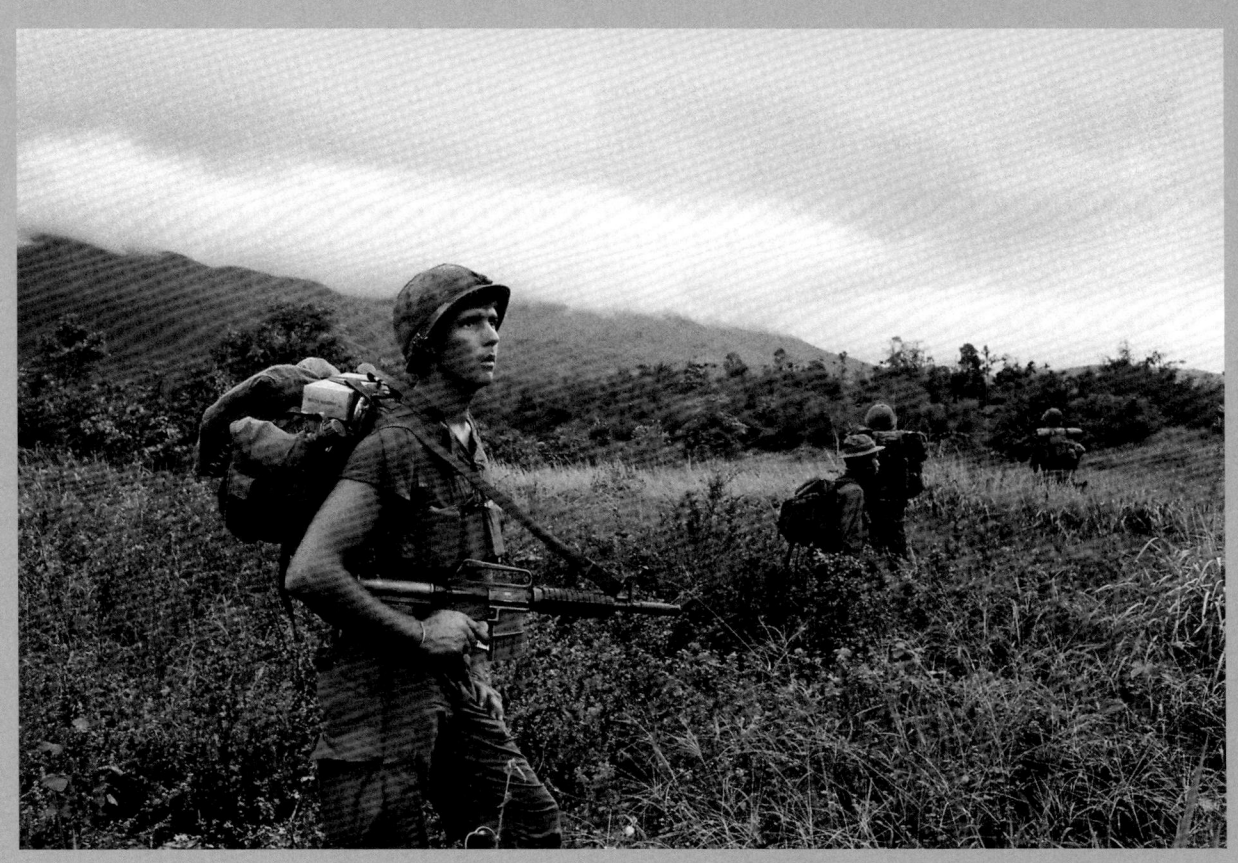

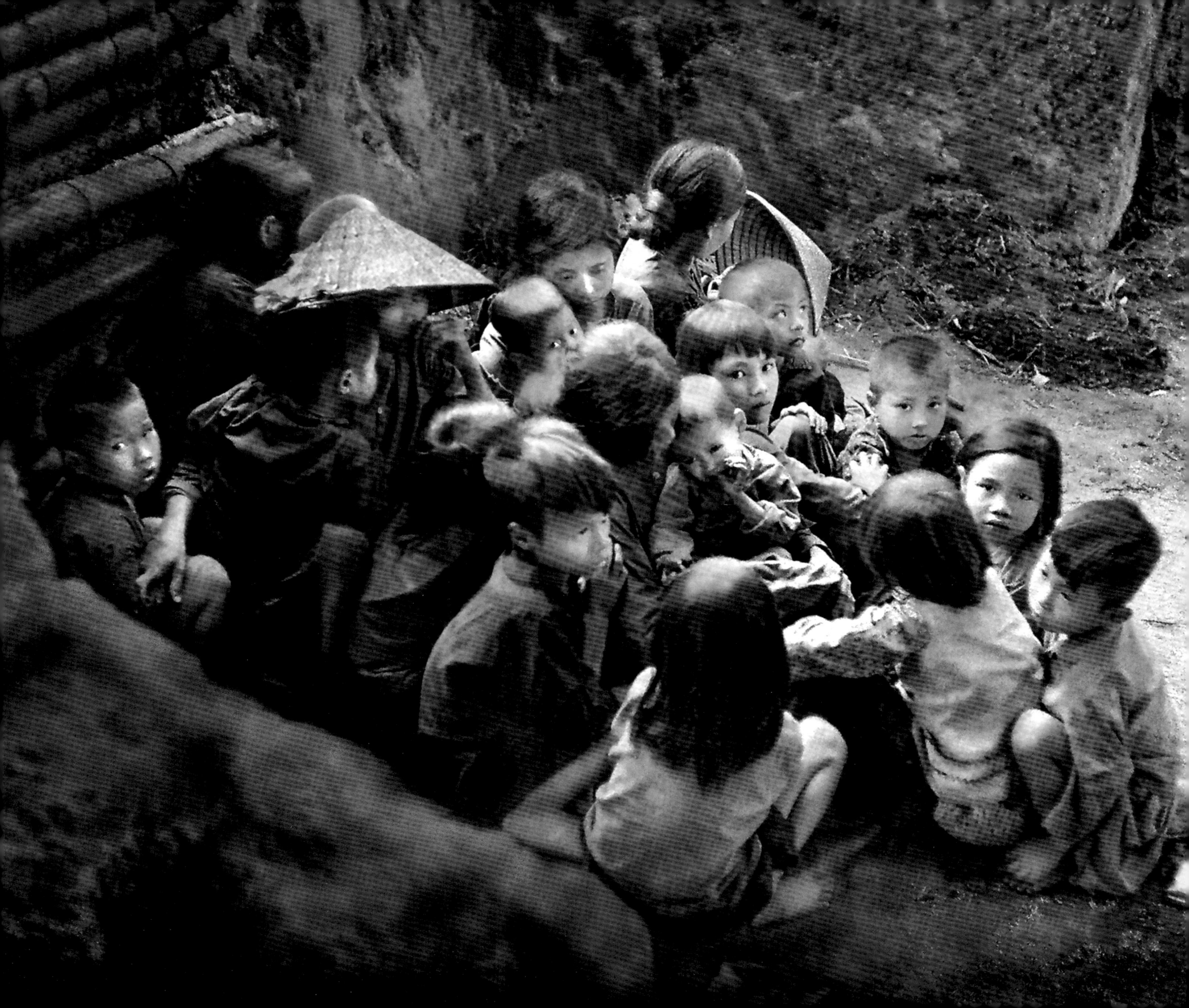

Chapter 4

The Hard Part Is Living With It the Rest of Your Life

Sergeant Philip Morgan Pruett

AS A BOY, HE WOULD FACE ANY FEAR AND FIND A WAY TO BEAT IT.

He was afraid of heights.

"I'd climb a water tower and overcome that."

He was afraid of small confined places.

"I had my brother lock me in a footlocker. I didn't like the feeling of something bothering me."

Jim and I did not know, on this summer day in the clearing of a Florida forest, that Philip was afraid of his own voice.

It didn't seem so, when we arrived at the home of Philip and Rebecca Pruett near Crawfordville. Six feet, three inches tall and sculpted from regular workouts, Phil, smiling broadly, grabbed Jim in a bear hug—two soldiers meeting again after nearly half a century.

Inside, he spoke of early fall 1969 and his fear in flying to Vietnam. He was convinced he wasn't coming home alive.

"I was never afraid of death," Phil says. "I didn't think I was going to live, that I was going to do something stupid and get myself killed."

This athlete and hunter *wanted* to go to Vietnam. He *wanted* to serve at the point of the spear. He *wanted* to fight the enemy. He would do all that, and as a medic save lives. All in Alpha loved their medics, including this big football player voted "Most Happy-Go-Lucky" in high school.

Phil began life wrapped in swaddling clothes of Air Force blue as a son of Sergeant Paul Russell Pruett Jr. and Frances Lydia Henry Pruett. From Scott AFB, Illinois, Sergeant Pruett's next assignment sent the family to Alaska. With four fidgeting brothers in the backseat, the Pruetts drove the 1,700-mile ALCAN (Alaska–Canada) Highway, then a dirt road, to Elmendorf Air Force Base.

Alaska's exotica fascinated young Phil: Eskimo graveyards, the blanket toss, dog sledding. His dad often hosted hunting trips for VIPs. Young Phil tagged along.

"Guns were everywhere," he says of Alaska. "I probably learned how to shoot before I learned how to go to school."

The Air Force soon transferred the family to Eglin Air Force Base near Niceville, Florida. There, Phil continued hunting with his dad, who insisted on either killing game with headshots or not firing at all.

"It was something just kind of ingrained into me," he remarks.

Left: Children are clustered among women in this jungle hooch. Such hooches in jungles were supposed to look like innocent family dwellings; actually, they were VC and NVA resupply stations.

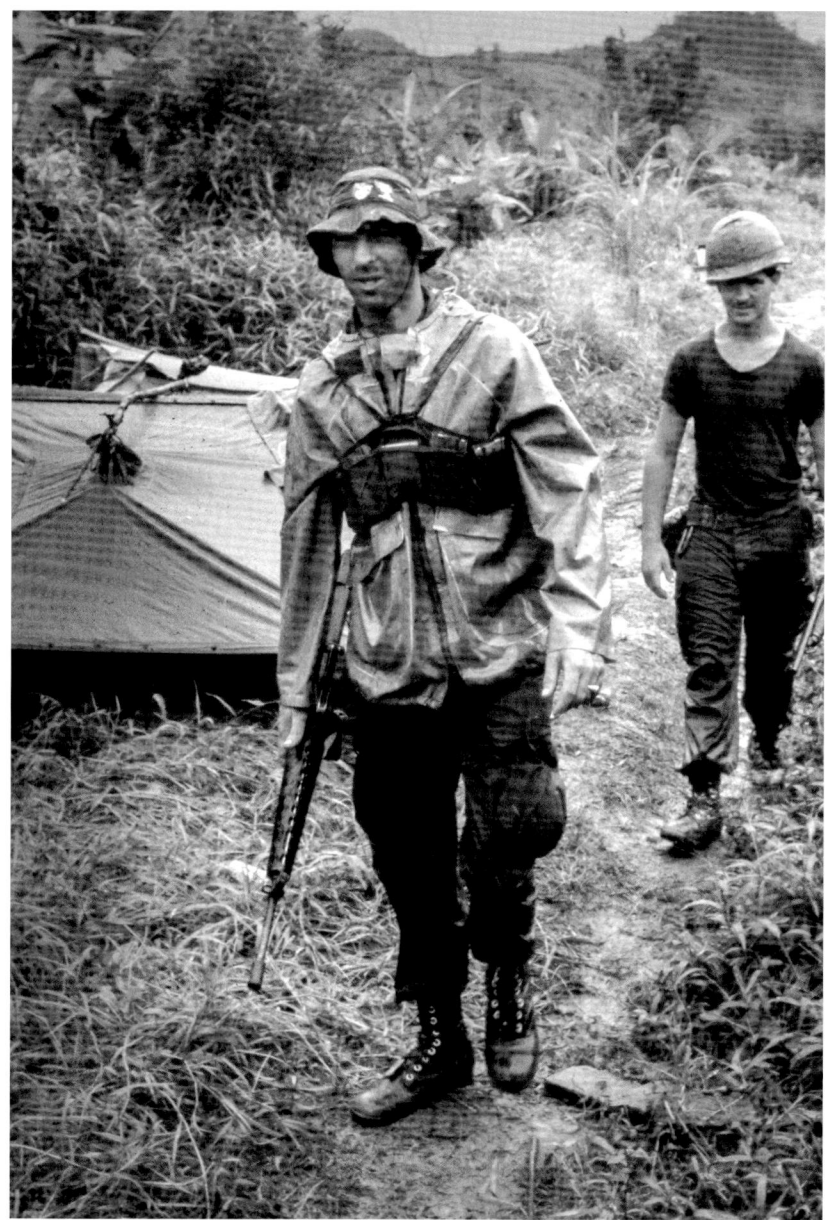

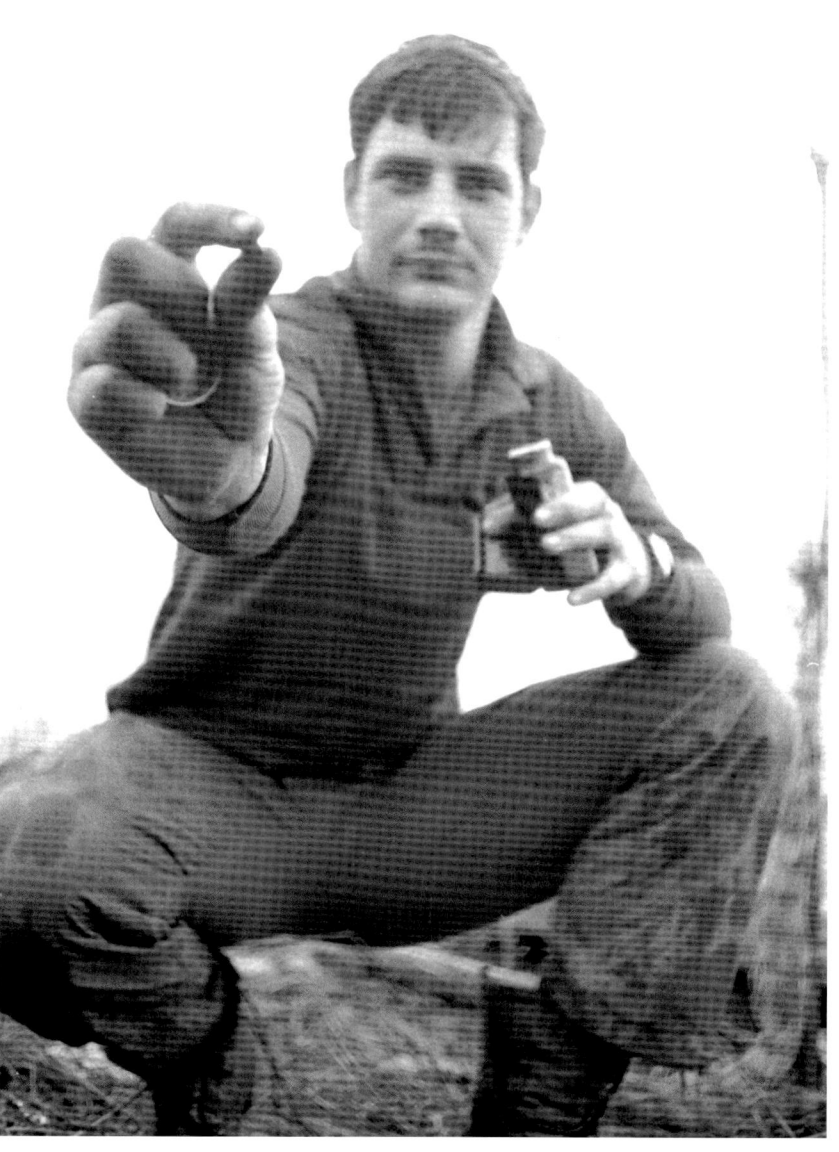

Sergeant Aldo Bastinancic, nicknamed "Mondo" (Italian for "large"), served 2nd Platoon as point man until he stepped on a booby trap. Hospitalized, he never returned to the Company. Alpha veterans recall him as a great operatic singer.

Medic Philip ("Doc") Pruett distributes daily malaria pills and watches each man swallow them. Some in Alpha tried not to swallow, preferring to fight malaria in a hospital than enemy in the field.

Meanwhile, he worked odd jobs to help stretch a sergeant's pay. He also grew taller, stronger, faster, excelling in school sports that consumed his life.

"I'd go to school. I'd go to practice. I'd know what season it was by what sport I was playing," he says.

College recruiters soon came calling. The 220-pound linebacker accepted an athletic scholarship from the University of Iowa but first was sent to Taft Junior College in Taft, California, to improve his grades. Instead, injuries slowed him. Brushes with the law ended his academic and athletic life. A judge told him he could go to jail or leave the state.

"I chose to leave the state. How many people get thrown out of a state?" he says, chuckling.

He joined his mother (his father died when Phil was 16) in Kansas City; Phil had a job pouring concrete there when his draft notice arrived. At Fort Leonard Wood, Missouri, he found basic training a breeze.

"I had football practices that were harder than basic," he notes.

At Fort Sam Houston in San Antonio, he finished at the top of his class in medic training, then completed jump school at Fort Benning, Georgia. At Fort Bragg, North Carolina, he found brutal Special Forces training strangely familiar.

"They tie you up. They punch you. No big deal. Just like home," he remarks.

Reaching Vietnam on 14 October 1969, he was placed not in Special Forces but in Alpha Company 4/31 and attached temporarily to Medical Civilian Assistance Program (MEDCAP). In rendering aid to civilians, he quickly learned his benevolent efforts weren't welcome.

"I've been working on the Med-Cap team where we go down into the village . . . . Working with the kids is . . . a lot of fun. Right now it has been called off because we have had several incidents where people in the village have pulled guns on us, pulled pins out of grenades and shot over our heads," he wrote his mother on 15 November.

In December, he requested and was granted reassignment to Alpha's Reconnaissance Platoon. Walking point one day, Phil rounded a sharp turn in a trail and startled three armed civilians.

"They took off running. If they run, you shoot," he recalls of standard procedure.

As they sprinted away, their *nón lá* straw hats served as excellent targets. Phil shot twice. Two went down. A third leapt into brush, Phil still firing.

"I first felt a rush of excitement. It was my first encounter. I had done well. I wasn't hurt, and I had three kills," he states.

He falls silent for a moment.

"I went up and checked them. It was two women," he says painfully. Then he found the third body, a girl, perhaps ten years old.

"You know what was strange? It didn't bother me. It was like a deer hunt. It was funny how easy it was to kill somebody. The hard part is living with it the rest of your life," he remarks.

Recon often involved privations. Once, with empty canteens, the team survived for twelve days on water from bamboo, which carried the parasite *Entamoeba histolytica*. Racked with amebiasis, Phil spent a week in a hospital.

Back with Recon in December, Phil felt his spirits sink from constant movement and monsoon. He wrote his mother:

> If this isn't a waste of a year of a man's life I don't know what is. You go months without changing clothes or taking a bath! You get eaten up by bugs 24 hrs a day and everyone has diarrhea so bad that they go in their pants including myself . . . . You have to sleep in your clothes and I haven't had dry clothes since I've been out in the field.

By Christmas, Phil was reassigned to Alpha as a medic for 2nd Platoon. For the field, he packed his M-5 Medical Bag, containing IV bottles, a jar of morphine syrettes, sulfa powder, ointments for jungle rot, small splints and bandages, the streamlined M-3 Medical Bag, and a Field Surgical Kit with scissors, clamps, scalpels, tweezers, sutures, and four canteens.

He also carried his M16 and wore three bandoliers of M60 and M16 ammunition. In all, he humped at least seventy pounds. With little to no action, however, the walking and the weight seemed extraneous.

"We couldn't find anybody," he says of the enemy. "The first five or six months we were in country, nothing was going on. You got cocky. You were almost looking for a fight. You figured everybody knows you're in town and they don't want to mess with you."

You would be wrong, he soon learned.

As if hibernating, the NVA spent monsoon in mountains north of Hiệp Dúc. Local VC counterparts, however, scattered deadly calling cards. On 18 April 1970, an explosion erupted from the front of the column. Phil sprinted forward to find at least four wounded, the worst of whom being Specialist 4 Aldo Bastinancic, nicknamed "Mondo," a point man.

The booby trap exploded at groin level. Phil puzzled over the wound.

"How do you attach the bandage? What do you do with the parts?" he exclaims in exasperation. He improvised a "diaper-like" bandage to cover wounds and transport severed organs.

Each day, medics strove to keep all healthy, while thwarting soldiers who courted illness. Preferring a hospital to the field, soldiers sidled up to sick men hoping for infection or tossed away malaria pills, preferring to fight the illness rather than the enemy. Medics made daily rounds to watch each man swallow the antidote.

Feet problems felled men, too. "Trench foot," as it was called in the world wars, punched another free ticket out of the field. Nightly, Phil ordered all in 2nd platoon to strip off boots and socks to dry.

"I *still* have the smell in my head of rotting feet," he says.

A brief respite came on 28 April with stand-down: three days of beer, steaks, showers, and sweet sleep. Hours into their first night, however, the men were shouted awake and told to "ruck up." The 2nd NVA Division was attacking throughout Hiệp

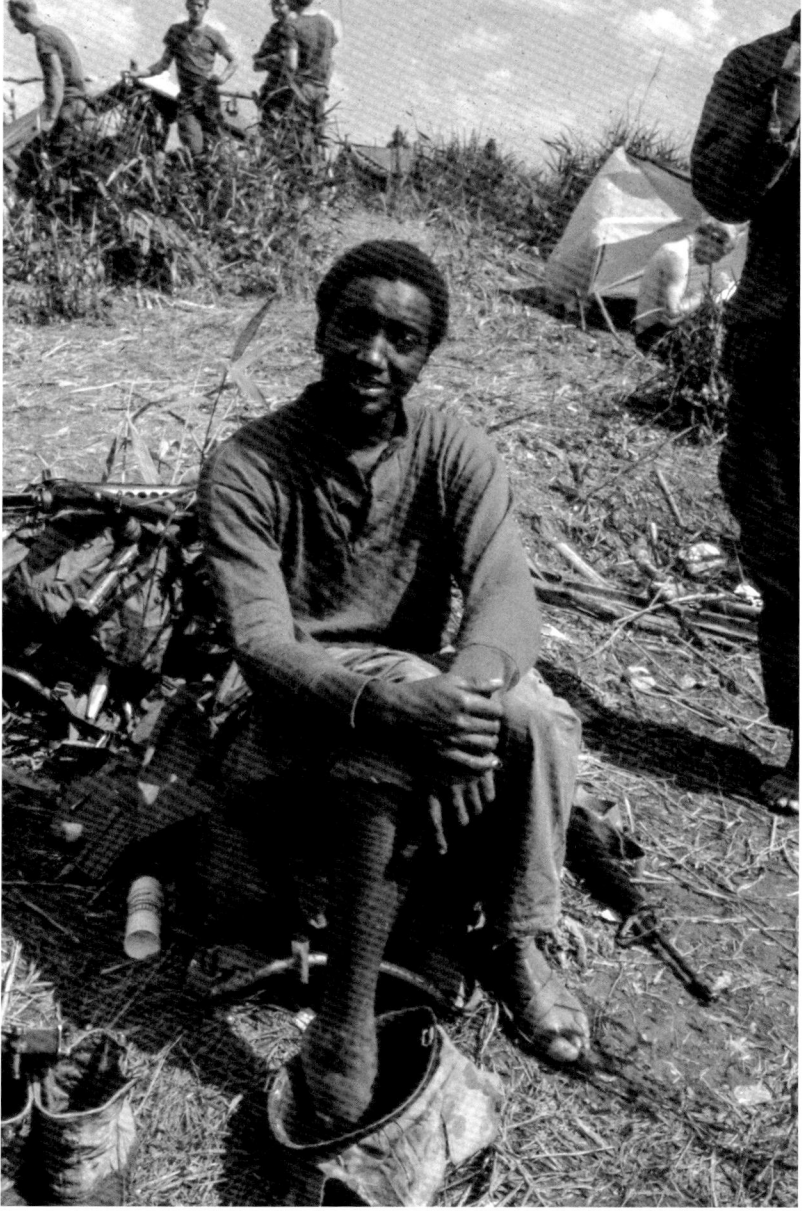

CP ("Chicago Pimp") soaks an injured foot in his steel pot. Neither Logue nor other Alpha veterans recalled CP's name. A company roll for that period is missing.

Dúc Valley, beginning a two-month struggle the Army labeled "Task Force West." Alpha veterans still call it the "May–June Battle."

Along with wrecking pacified villages and murdering civilians, the enemy attacked Americans with small arms, machine guns, and—what Alpha feared most—82mm mortars.

"If it hits in your hole, you're dead. If it lands a foot or two off to the side, you're alive. The closer they come down to you, the louder they get. So you have your last thoughts. You start realizing what's important in life," Phil remarks.

After each round, he'd think, "Okay, I lived and I never came up with a reason why I wanted to live. I didn't have a girlfriend. I didn't have kids. I didn't have anything. Everything I'd done in my life I screwed up."

Beneath raining steel, the man convinced he'd die there hungered for a future.

"I wanted to change. I'd think, 'I'm going to be different.' I never had a girlfriend. 'I'm going to get a girlfriend.' I never studied. 'I'm going to study,'" he recalls.

Death descending brought him a greater clarity of life in what he calls "the best thing that ever happened to me. Everybody needs to have end-of-life experiences, and all of the things you find out about yourself, and all of the things that are important and that are totally insignificant," he says.

Time and again came the plaintive cry, "Medic!" Time and again Phil raced through fire to render aid. Ask any Vietnam combat veteran: the bravest among them were point men, medics, and medevac pilots.

"Pruett. I liked that guy," Perry Stemen of Whitehall, Michigan, would say. "I remember one time when somebody was hurt and he only had a .45 on him. I remember him running out in an open area and somebody shot part of his boot off. He was definitely a guy you'd want on your side. He was a good doc."

In the night laager of 10 May, all heard the dreaded coughs of enemy mortar rounds.

"When a hole got hit, you could hear the screams. Then you would hear 'Medic!' One thing I learned was, before you get out of your hole, make certain they have room in theirs. The first one I responded to didn't have room, so I laid on the ground outside the hole to work on them. I got wounded in the back," he says of earning one of his four Purple Hearts.

None, however, knew that Pruett fought one fear: freezing at the cry, "Medic!"

"I was wounded four times. How many times can you keep going out there? Your team depends on you. That was the more important thing. It wasn't losing my life. It was, 'What if I slowed down?'" he says.

Another fear he fought was rendering incorrect treatment that might cost a man his life. Marching north of Hiệp Dúc on 14 May, NVA pinned down Alpha's point element. Running forward in the fire, Phil, bleeding from a round to one leg, reached the wounded Michael Kangas. He started an IV and wrapped a pressure dressing around the wound, but Kangas continued to bleed.

With moments to spare, Phil agonized over a life-or-death decision. Applying a tourniquet beneath the wound would cut blood flow to the lower limb, saving a life but likely causing amputation. Better to keep a life than a leg, Phil thought, so he applied the tourniquet. Later, the surgeon who treated Kangas praised Phil for his actions. "Doc" earned another Bronze Star, another Purple Heart.

He could not save them all, though. On 4 June some forty men, all who remained of Alpha, dug in for another night laager.

Phil and "the only person I got close to," David Flynn of Muncie, Indiana, were shoveling out a foxhole when mortars began raining down. In the night, NVA broke through the perimeter, where firing was point blank and fighting was hand-to-hand.

Flynn went down with a head wound. Just as Phil reached for him, more wounded fell into their foxhole, screaming for help but pinning Pruett to the bottom.

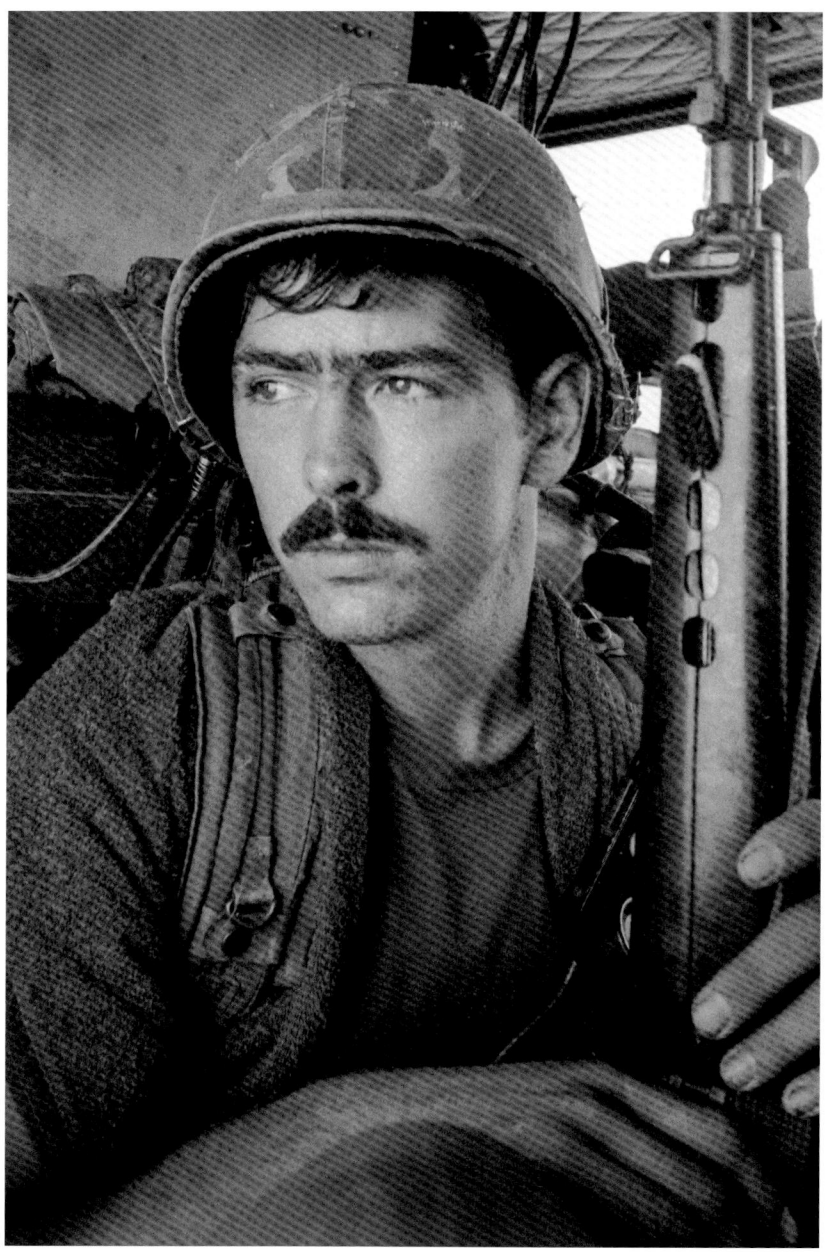

David Flynn, RTO (radiotelephone operator), waits pensively aboard a UH-1 Huey. In-flight noise of wind and rotary blades made conversation impossible.

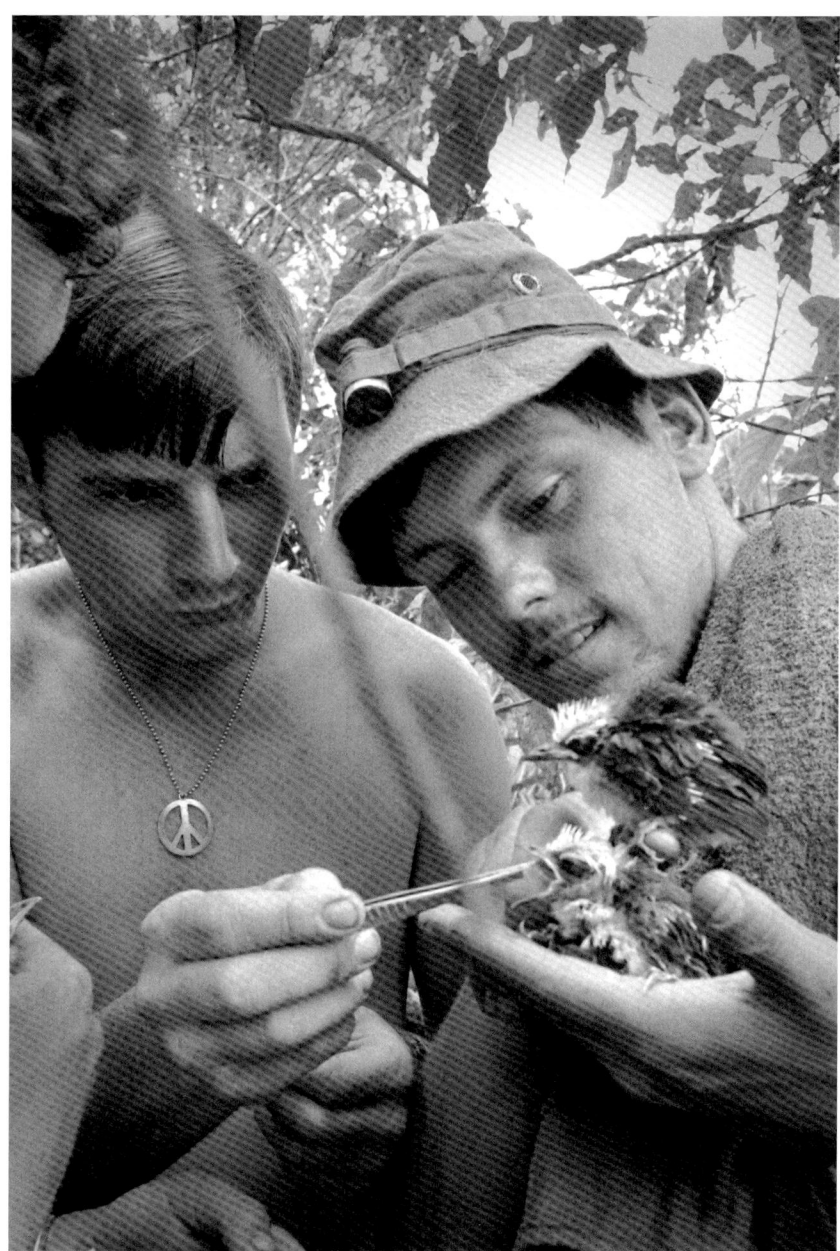

Medic "Doc" Pruett, wearing peace symbol necklace, loans his tweezers to this soldier who feeds newly born birds that have fallen from their nest.

"Mortars are coming in. People on top are hit and yelling for me to help them. They're bleeding on me. I couldn't move. I wanted to scream," he says.

A dust-off squeezed into a small clearing. While fighting continued, Phil helped Flynn aboard the medevac. Phil's voice breaks as he remembers: "The last thing he said was, 'Are you going to be all right?' *He's* going on the medevac and he's asking *me* if *I'm* going to be all right. That was the last time I saw Dave. We were real close."

Occasionally, the smallest things whispered to him the fragility of all life. Once, someone found newborn birds orphaned from their nest. Jim Logue snapped a photograph of Phil and others feeding the downy birds with tweezers, providing a chance for life for even the smallest creatures in these killing fields.

By then, Phil was fighting another enemy: fatigue that seeped into brain, bone, and sinew.

"There wasn't anything that I experienced in the Army, as far as physical endurance, that was difficult for me. The thing that brought on stress more was not a firefight. It was the fatigue. It was months of being tired. Never getting more than two hours of sleep; just walking and walking and walking.

"Your mind is wasted. All the life's been sucked out of you. You're far too tired to fight. But you do. I remember falling asleep, standing up or walking. You take a break. You stand there. You fall asleep. Somebody hits you. You wake up and you walk some more. If they gave you five minutes you fell asleep. As a medic, it was everybody getting hurt. Constantly. It wears on you, day in and day out," he says.

Finally, in mid-June, this big, strong man broke.

"I couldn't keep my hands from shaking. I couldn't talk. Finally, I told Lieutenant Erwin Esterling, 'I can't do this anymore.' I hadn't been afraid before. And I don't know if I was afraid. I think I was just worn out," he says.

In Vietnam, medics, like front-line officers, remained six months in the field. Phil had served nine.

"My body and spirit had reached its breaking point. It was the only time I ever quit at anything. I felt like a broken man. I've found it hard to respect myself since then. I have still never forgiven myself for leaving," he says.

First Lieutenant Esterling, temporary commander of Alpha, released Phil for duty on LZ West as NCOIC (Non-Commissioned Officer in Charge) of battalion medic station. There, he dreaded approaching medevacs. The ashen faces of the dead he scooped from chopper bays into body bags still appear in his recurring nightmares.

Finally, Phil boarded a plane to the States, fully expecting the airliner to splash into the Pacific. Instead, in Seattle, he processed out at Fort Lewis and slipped into a new Class A uniform. He bloused his dress trousers into combat boots, a privilege accorded only airborne soldiers. On the left side of his chest glittered his airborne wings, Combat Medic Badge, Silver Star, Bronze Star with V device for "valor," and Purple Heart with three oak leaf clusters for his four wounds.

When he paused in an airport bar, some civilians, brimming with whiskey bravado, threw down a bar napkin gauntlet and challenged him to fight. Their reason: He wore a military uniform.

"What the hell, man? I just want to go home," he replied.

"I had been up three days. I hadn't slept. I can't do this," he recalls thinking. The barstool toughs kept up their taunts, but Phil, who could have mopped the floor with them, stoically sipped his drink.

He shrugs.

"They yell at you. They cuss at you. Fine. Whatever. I'm going home."

In September 1970, he began pre-med studies at the University of Central Missouri. For exercise, he chose not football (because of its militaristic organization) but a sport in which he could still smack opponents.

"Rugby," he says with a grin. "It gave me that outlet of a kind of unorganized sport, but you still go out there and hit people."

Realizing he was cramming for tests but not learning, he moved to Tallahassee, enrolled at Florida State University, joined the rugby squad, and made First State Team.

He also met Rebecca Ann Short, at first a friend, then fiancée, then, on 5 July 1980, his wife. Phil grins and compares his heart's journey to dialogue from the film *Forrest Gump*: "It just snuck up and bit me."

He earned a master's degree in industrial hygiene. While working for Monsanto in Fayetteville, North Carolina, he played for the Fort Bragg rugby team. He was named coach, captain, and president. He made North Carolina Select Side (rugby's version of an all-star team), then Eastern United States Select Side.

Later, living in the northeast, Phil and Rebecca bought a 200-acre horse farm where they also raised greyhounds. The dog-racing circuit collapse, however, "kind of took us down with it," he recalls.

The couple sold their farm and home—a financial and mental blow to both. Then, Phil remembered what he learned under enemy mortar fire: only life matters.

"I said to Rebecca, 'Only two things we need: our health and if we love each other. The rest of the stuff doesn't make any difference.'"

They returned to Florida, where, through the years, Phil remained silent about his service. Then he watched the military masterstroke, Operation Desert Storm, under the leadership of General Norman Schwarzkopf Jr., a Vietnam veteran. He grins.

"It made me so proud that we kicked butt for a change. I went out and got a Purple Heart license plate," he remarks of the first public notice he made that he had served.

Concerning today's military, he advocates universal service for *all* young Americans.

"People need to get out there and be told what to do; to be yelled at; to be punished a little bit; to be organized; to learn to take care of yourself; to take personal responsibility. You get a work ethic. You get used to getting up in the morning. You get used to making your bed. Women ought to go, too. A woman can pull a trigger as well as a man. There are some tough women out there. The whole nation needs to toughen up."

All day he talked about Vietnam until he cried out in late afternoon: "I'll be so glad when this is over! I haven't slept in two or three nights, just thinking about it."

As when he was a hunter, athlete, then medic, Phil had performed magnificently. In a way, Jim and I had cried "Medic!" and "Doc" Pruett ran again into the fire of memory. The worst of his nightmares is a "conversation" with "families" of the three young females he killed.

"I tell them, 'I'm sorry, but they ran.' They tell me, 'Of course they did. They were women who ran into some strange men in the jungle.' They would ask why I would shoot a little girl. I would say 'I don't know.' They would say, 'When you go hunting, you can tell the difference between a buck, a doe, and a fawn. Why not a little girl?' I still haven't found an answer, just that I'm so sorry."

He also dreams of bodies he pulled from medevacs on LZ West. To talk about them, he says, is to release them from behind a locked mental door where he placed all of his Vietnam memories.

"If I open the door to put one more in, all of those are going to come out. I don't want to open that door. I don't want to go looking at another dead body and remember it all."

In late afternoon, Phil thanked us for coming and wished us well. A few days later, he called Jim. There was more he remembered.

To rid himself of a fear of heights and small places, Phil had once climbed a tower and squeezed into a chest that got locked behind him. On this day, he faced down the fear of his own voice.

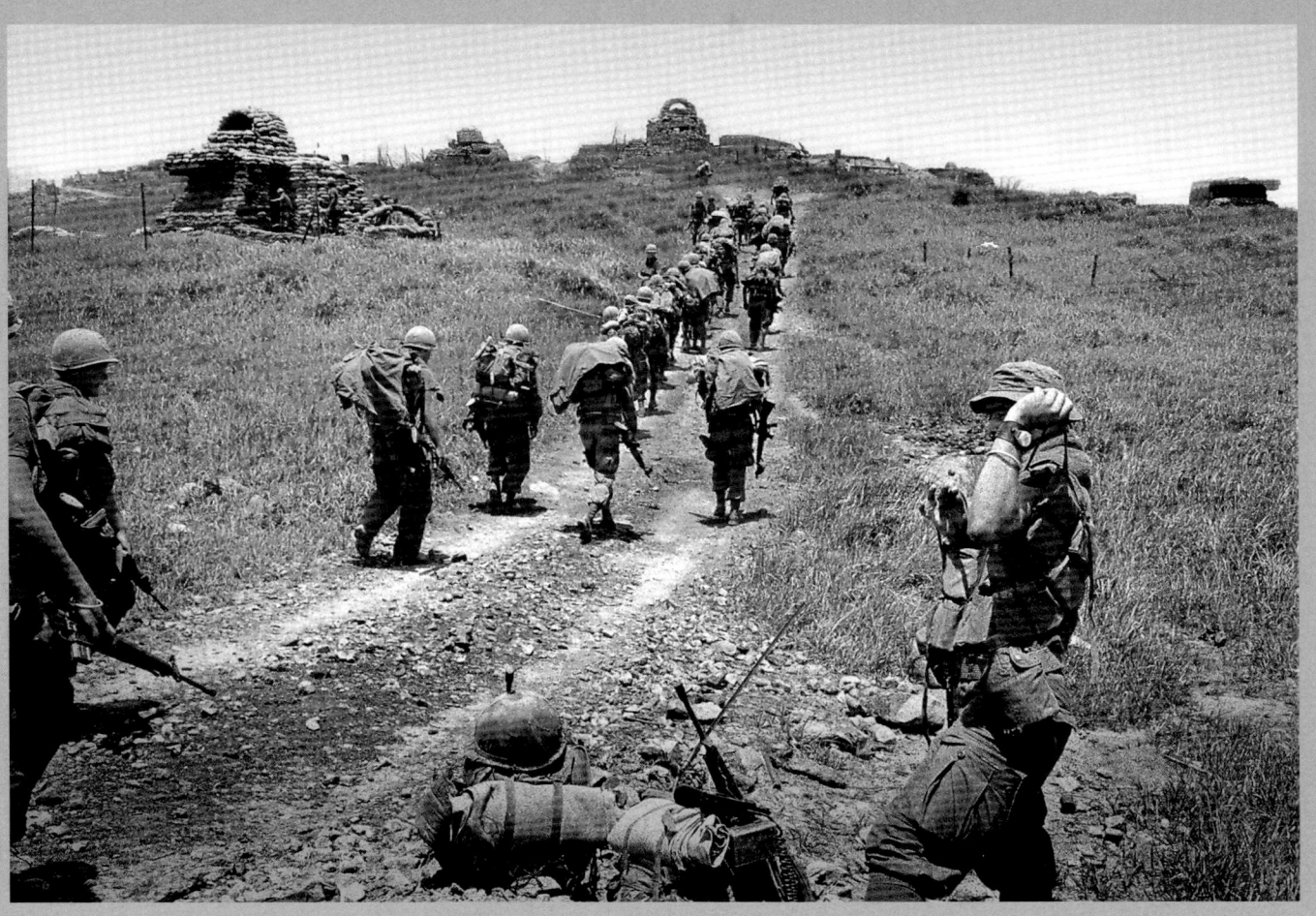

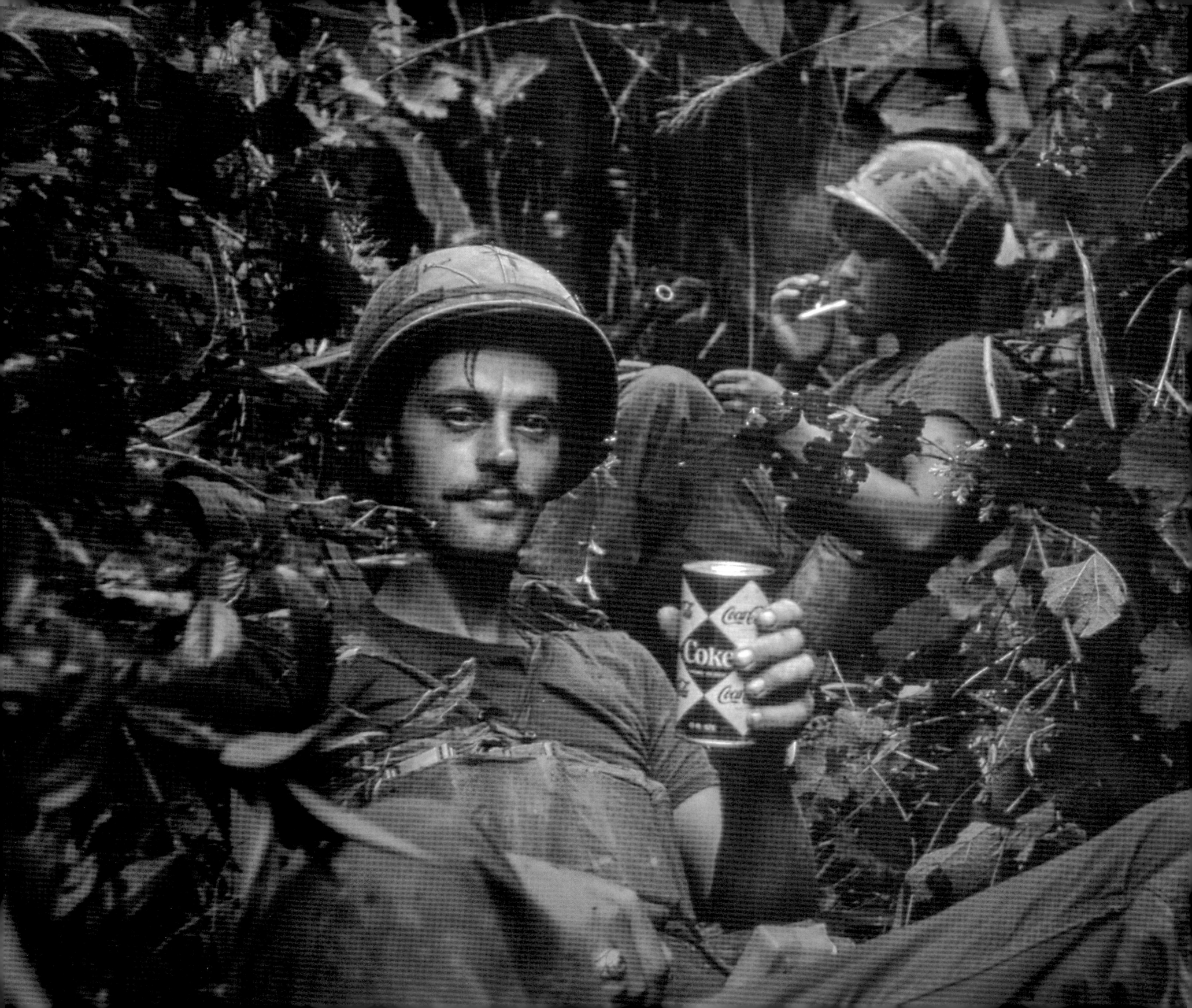

Chapter 5

I Must Go and Write My Princess

Sergeant Keith Alan Lochner (KIA)

HE JUST WANTED TO BE A FARMER.

Even as a boy, he knew his life's work was with soil and seed, and home always was Fairmount in Grant County, Indiana. By high school, he knew he would marry Cheryl Hethcote and they would raise their family and farm these fields that feed America.

"The day he was born everyone was thrilled that it was a boy. He was going to be a farmer. And as a little boy he wanted to be a farmer," remarks Betty Lochner, Keith's mother, a pretty, petite lady with sparkling eyes.

"Dad had Mom drive tractors with cultivators. When she'd come to a gate, she'd get off the tractor and let that five-year-old kid wiggle the tractor and cultivators through the gates," states Cheryl "Sherry" Davenport, of her younger brother, Keith.

It's a Sunday afternoon in late summer 2014. A two-lane road cleaves an asphalt furrow between fields of tall, green corn from Fairmount to Greentown, where Jim and I meet Keith Lochner's mother, Betty. There, too, are Keith's sister, Sherry; younger brother, Dean; and Cheryl Bockman, née Hethcote, who said "yes" when Keith asked for her hand.

We speak of these dwindling weeks of summer, once called "laying-by time," when crops were high and green and farmers could step away and let their fields flourish in sun and rain. Soon farmers harvest, then leave the land to sleep under snow until planting time, traditionally, in Grant County, on 20 April. Such were the rhythms of the seasons for farm families like the Lochners, who knew that Keith, too, would cleave to these old ways of work, worship, and family.

Cleaving. The Lochners embody this contronym, a verb with two, opposite meanings: one, to cling together, the other to part. With their plows they cleaved the earth, while spiritually they cleaved to their older-time religion of Wesleyan Methodism. The sect honors traditional wedding vows of a man and woman who cleave together as one.

Even Fairmount seems a contronym, as birthplace of Keith as well as of screen-star rebel James Dean and cartoonist Jim Davis, who created the cool cat Garfield. In town spread the grounds of the 120-year-old Wesleyan Methodist Camp and its Bethel Tabernacle, with seating for 1,500. The shady grounds and venerable structures are filled during Family Camp, held in late July.

Left: After hacking through triple-canopy jungle for 200 meters, Alpha halts to rest. Rick Knowlton enjoys a Coca-Cola.

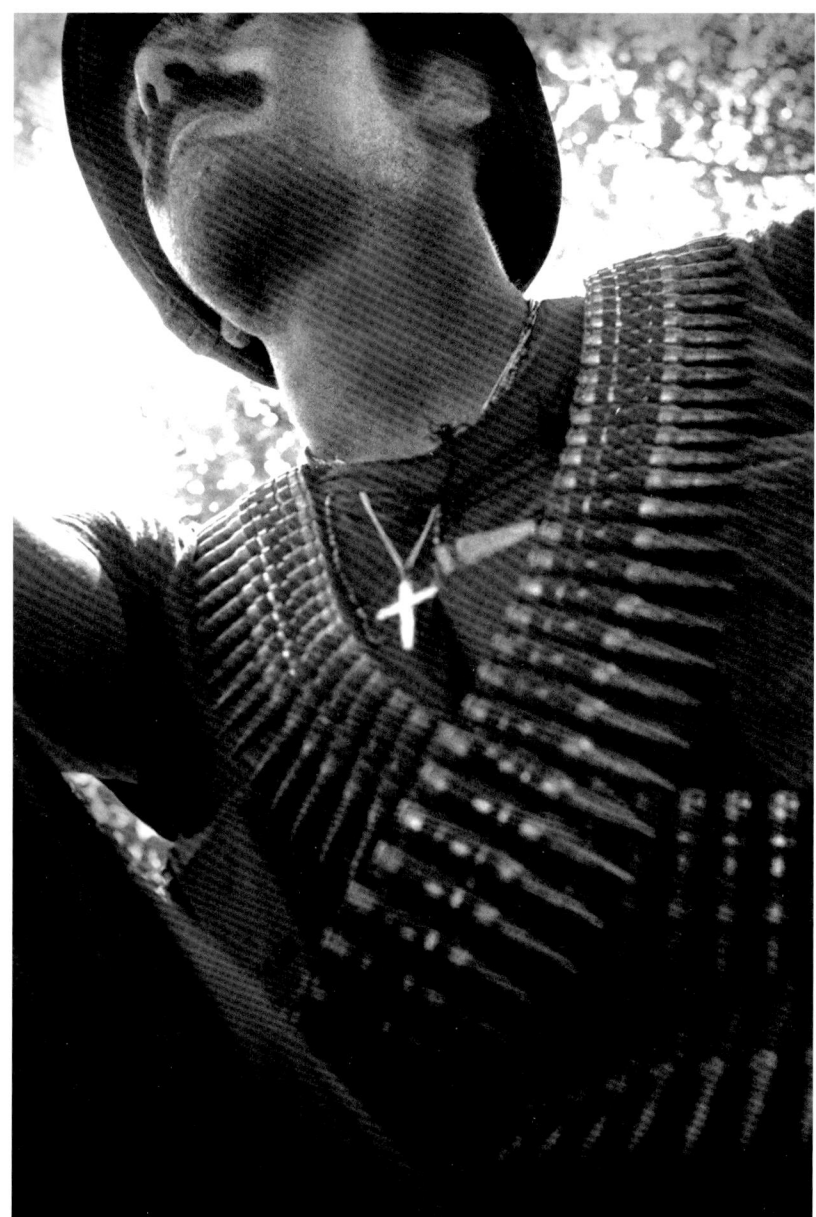

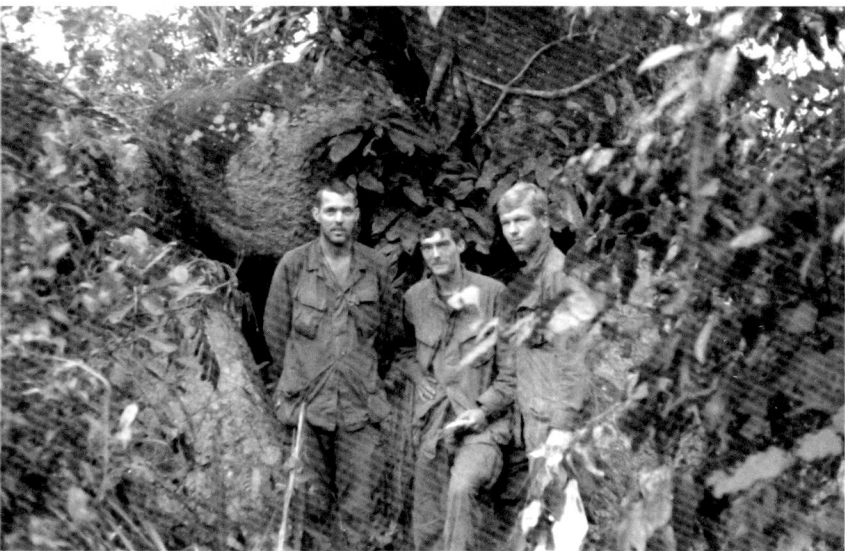

Three leaders in Alpha's 3rd Platoon include platoon leader First Lieutenant Donald Pettit; Sergeant Charles ("Chuck") Mann, a schoolteacher; and Sergeant Keith Lochner.

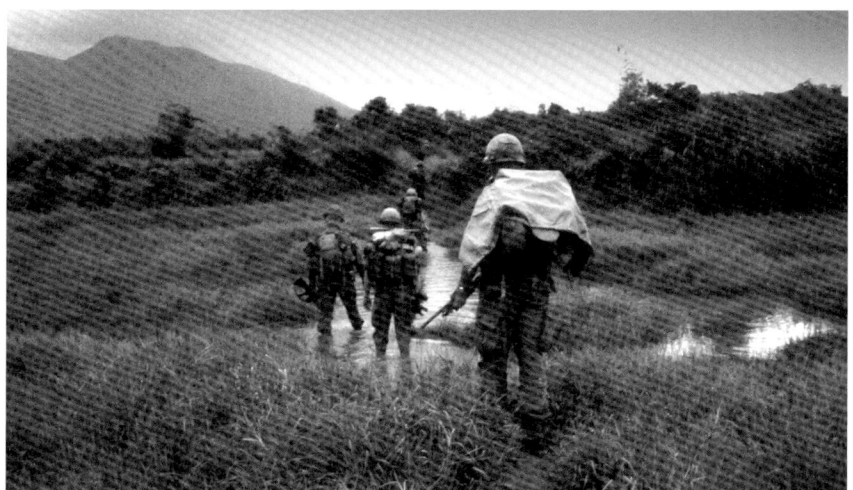

John Young wears two crosses: a necklace pendant and bandoliers of M60 ammunition. Over six feet tall, he towered over all in 4th Platoon (which others dubbed "Midget Squad" for the height of many of the men).

In rainy weather, infantrymen covered rucksacks with ponchos to keep contents dry. Walking in streams kept soldiers safe from enemy booby traps.

On Sundays as a boy, Keith squirmed on church pews, eager for the last "amen" and another week of work in the fields with his father, the now late Jacob Lochner. As Keith grew older, neighbors learned he was handy with a wrench. Spotting a farmer with stalled machinery, Keith would wriggle beneath the engine for a quick fix. When rain stopped fieldwork, farmers summoned "Jake's boy" to their barns for equipment repairs. Keith loved cars, too, and eventually bought his pride and joy, a Ford Galaxy.

"He chased the girls down with his Galaxy," Dean remarks with a grin.

For one girl in particular, Keith waited patiently. He was sixteen and watching television at a friend's house when he met Cheryl Hethcote.

"How old is Cheryl?" Keith asked later.

"Fourteen," his friend said.

"When she turns sixteen, I'm going to ask her for a date," Keith replied, and turned back to the television.

Cheryl's voice is soft.

"That was my first meeting with Keith. I thought he was cute. The summer after I turned sixteen, he called me," she remarks.

On their first date, he held the car door open for her and treated her to dinner at Custer's Last Stand, once a Marion culinary landmark. In rural Grant County, there was little else to do.

"I don't recall going to movies. We spent time together visiting people. We'd hang out with families. My parents loved him," Cheryl says.

I ask a question. She smiles and shakes her head.

"No, I don't think he kissed me on our first date," she responds.

Keith graduated in 1967 from Fairmount High School but gave college no thought. He had a wonderful family, friends, work, and, most of all, a woman he loved. He wore a bulls-eye on his back, however. His induction letter from the Selective Service System came on 11 February 1969. Betty was devastated.

"I was fixing his breakfast, and he saw me crying. I didn't want him to go. A lot of kids didn't go because their dads were farmers. He said, 'Mom, don't cry. I'm not a coward. I'll go,'" she says.

In basic training at Fort Knox, Kentucky, he met another Grant County farmer's son, Gary Himelick. After advanced individual training in infantry at Fort Lewis in Washington, both qualified for the twelve-week NCO School at Fort Benning, Georgia. Keith, Gary recalls, saw the school as a way to delay going to Vietnam.

"Who knows? We thought the war could end while we're there," says Gary, now a resident of Panama City Beach, Florida.

On leave in June 1969, Keith asked Cheryl for her hand. She said "yes." He took her shopping and let her pick out her engagement ring. Typical of his wry sense of humor, Keith also gave her a two-dollar bill, on which he wrote the date of their engagement. She still has both bill and ring.

Keith and Gary completed NCO School and then helped train troops at Fort Polk, Louisiana, until their orders for Vietnam arrived.

Granted 21-day leaves, the two men drove home in January 1970. There, Keith served as best man at Gary's wedding. Gary still owns a color photograph taken during that winter in a friend's parlor. In it, Cheryl sits in Keith's lap, her brown hair shining like the light in her eyes.

Keith and Gary reached Vietnam on 3 February 1970. Hardly were they assigned to platoons (Keith in 3rd, Gary in 2nd) when Alpha Company hit Chu Lai for stand-down. Teetotaler Keith captures the essence of the event in a letter to his parents: "The whole company comes in, eats, drinks, and acts like fools."

The two farmers quickly experienced the weather of the war: monsoon in late fall and winter; heat soaring into the hundreds in spring and summer. At least sunny skies provided Keith a trendy opportunity for this generation raised on banal beach movies of the 1960s. He wrote: "That is the only thing that is good about Nam. I will be able to get one awful good tan."

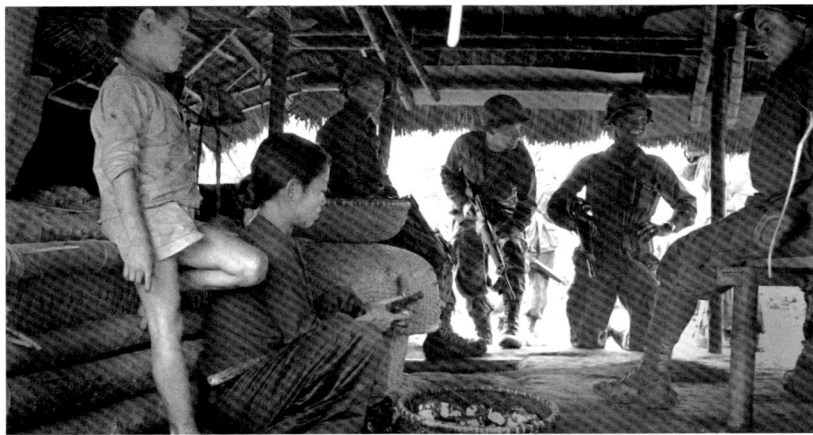

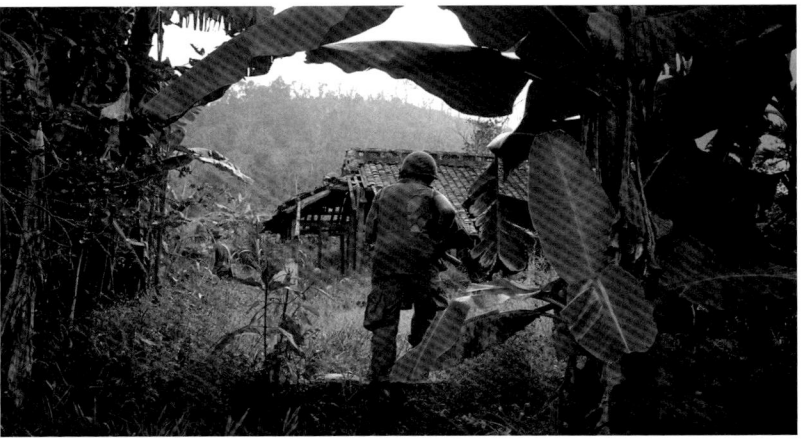

If Alpha found that outlying hooches contained enemy supplies, the Zippo Squad burned the structures. Families were sent to Hiệp Dúc. If nothing was discovered, GIs enjoyed the shade and shared candy with youngsters.

Upon approaching this hooch, an Alpha point man killed two NVA soldiers. Such hooches, hidden in thick jungle, served as aid-and-supply centers for the enemy.

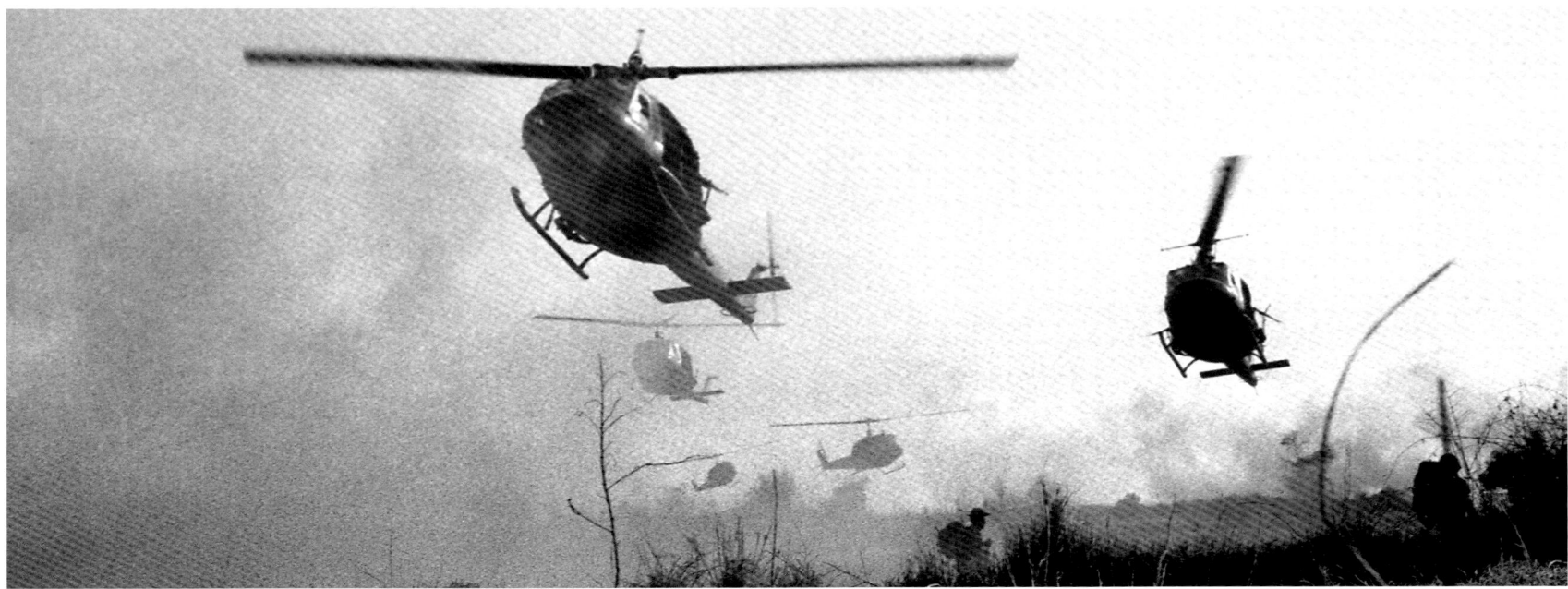

An "Eagle Flight" soars above grasslands. These one-day flights delivered Alpha to a contested area and picked them up after completion of operations for return to LZ West.

Meanwhile, he was learning to lead a squad composed mostly of short men and one giant, six feet, two-inch John Young, an all-state football player from Buffalo, New York.

John remarks, "He was a great guy, fun-loving. One of the things I liked about Keith, he would always listen. And he would take advice."

This so-called "Midget Squad" included Kent Green, of Clarksville, Indiana; Ron Hottman from Toledo, Ohio; Mark Klever of Milwaukee, Wisconsin; and Rodney Guyette of Walnut Creek, California, who became a close friend. Rod recalls:

He and I set up tents together. He was a very religious person and carried a Bible; just one of those people that was absolutely straight arrow, the kind you could respect. You knew that he would have your back and you'd have his. I remember the nights where he'd have his picture of his fiancée and the letters. He reread those letters I don't know how many times.

Scrapes with Viet Cong were scattered early in 1970. Climate, rucksacks, movement, topography, and vegetation took their tolls, along with heat exhaustion and malaria. Knives of elephant grass sliced skin, often leading to inflammations such as jungle rot. On 3 March, Keith wrote:

Last few days been busy. 27th and 28th walked about 5 to 6 thousand meters each day. I got a big blister on my right heel. I also have some of that crazy stuff they call jungle rot. 2 places, the 1st one I got is healing but I've got one on my knuckle that is sore and just won't stop. The problem is I can't wash often enough. I guess I'll survive.

Feet suffered, too. Alpha Company commander Captain John Wilson preferred walking in streams: safe paths free of land mines but hard on feet. On 26 March, Keith wrote a letter similar to those from muddy battlefields of two world wars and Korea:

I put a new pair of socks on the 16th & it is now the 26th well they are almost ready to rot off of me. I got some more in my ruck but I'll get the best out of these first. If I would pull them up real hard I'd rip the tops off. I have 8 holes in my left sock and 5 in my right.

Squad leader duties left him little time to respond to all correspondence. He wrote:

I'm giving up trying to answer all your letters. I've been getting 11 letters of yours at a time. Also on the 21st I got about 1 doz letters. Yesterday I got 19 letters and a package. Wow!

He always shared with his squad the culinary largesse from Fairmount kitchens, first handing goodies to his men before he indulged:

Right now I'm on top of 441, a big Mt. We got CA'd [combat assault] to the top of 381 yesterday about 5:30. We then went down in a valley and right back up this Mt. . . . The men settled down for the night so I got my can of nuts the Foreign Legion sent me, opened it up & passed it down the line. When it got to me I had about 2 handfuls left.

Such additional provender helped energize men subject to the feast-or-famine conditions of unreliable resupply in the field. Keith wrote:

I don't think I told you about being out 9 days and only having 8 meals, did I? Well we left West the 17th 5 meals in our ruck. On the 21st we got 3 more meals until the 25th so we were getting sorta hungry . . . . Wow! The package yesterday was real nice. I got soap, wash cloth, handkerchief, fingernail clippers, paper & envelopes, felt pen, dice, cards, shoe string potatoes, cheese, nuts, Jiffy Pop corn, devotional book, assortment of candy, Life Savers, Saltine crackers & Start [a powdered drink mix].

Keith began each morning opening a gift from Cheryl: a "promise box" containing 365 slips of paper, each with a daily Bible verse. In a letter to Keith, Mrs. Lochner cited the verse she had plucked from her own promise box that morning: "'Blessed be the God & Father of our Lord Jesus Christ who hath blessed us with all spiritual blessings in heavenly places in Christ.' Eph 1:3 . . . . I saw the devotional book like Cheryl sent you and ordered one for us."

In the same letter she wrote: "I got a kick out of what you said in regards to memorizing your M. [marriage] vows: 'How can I say No with those eyes looking in mine?'"

Jacob, Sherry, Dean, and others wrote him, too. So did the Hethcotes, who mailed him a twenty-first birthday card.

Meanwhile, Keith, despairing of answering such voluminous correspondence, devised a system that included his replies as well as preserving mail from the home front to the battlefield. On letters from home Keith penned responses, added comments, and returned the marked-up letters to the senders.

In March, he lost his only flesh-and-blood contact with Grant County. Gary Himelick was stricken with cellulitis, his leg swollen "twice its size," as the latter recalls. A medevac lifted him to away to treatment.

"I had a high fever. They gave me penicillin. Keith helped me onto the chopper. Told me to take care of myself. I said, 'You take care of yourself out here, too.'" Gary pauses, gathering himself. He speaks in a whisper, "I just remember seeing his face."

On 21 April, a week before stand-down, Keith wrote his family, closing with these words: "I must go and write my Princess. Trusting in God, Keith."

Certainly, Cheryl was on his mind, but so was soil. He knew the day before that Grant County farmers, honoring that traditional plowing day of 20 April, were cleaving the rich loam into long, straight furrows, renewing a year's covenant between farmer, seed, soil, sun, rain, harvest, and the long, snowy sleep of winter. For the first time in his life, Keith missed a year's opening of the earth that nourished body and soul.

The next day at noon laager, 3rd Platoon soldiers were finishing rations, catching catnaps, and looking around. Where was Keith?

John Young recalls the company had been airlifted near a rice paddy at the base of 441, the formidable mountain all dreaded to climb.

> Keith got separated. To this day I don't think anybody knows how he got separated. We are all just sitting around. Made some coffee, looking at the mountain, saying, "Oh, this is going to kick our butt, because it always did."
>
> We heard an explosion. Everybody grabbed their weapons, hit the dirt, got ready. Nothing happened. We started chuckling. Charlie was setting up a booby trip for us and probably tripped it. So a few of us got together. We started walking around the area . . . . We were walking on top of the rice paddy dikes. I happened to look down. It was Keith.

John believes Keith tried to lift himself onto the dike at precisely the wrong place, where death lay hidden in the grass: "It was a can with a frag in it; you know, one of our frags because it was a C-rat can. We all took it hard. Losing somebody hits everybody. You know these guys. Three-hundred sixty-five days a year you're with these guys."

Rodney Guyette recalls that Keith had been at the infirmary with a fever:

> We were headed towards 441 and we were kind of all strung out and actually 3rd Platoon at the time was in the lead. So we had a helicopter drop. We were just at the base and Keith was brought back to the field that day and he was in the back of this long procession. He triggered a booby trap. There was a hooch there with a woman and maybe one or two kids and they had a little dike and they had booby trapped it right off from where their hooch was. And for whatever reason he came over the top of that dike and he triggered it. The only reason I know that for sure is because as I said, I was all the way at the other end of our procession, but when I heard what happened I

actually went all the way back. I put him in the body bag. I had retrieved all of his personal items, a Bible and a picture of his fiancée. When we were back on stand-down I mailed all that back to his parents.

In a 6 May 1970 letter to Betty and Jake Lochner, Captain John Wilson stated that Keith was an outstanding soldier whose compassion for others and his concern for their welfare endeared them to him. He added that a memorial service for Keith had been conducted on 30 April.

Back home, Cheryl was leaving for her job as a nursing home aide when the telephone rang. Her father answered. It was Jake Lochner.

Keith was gone.

Cheryl was 19.

Keith Alan Lochner had blond hair. He stood six feet, one inch tall and weighed 155 pounds. He had blue eyes. You can see them in a color photograph he had made and sent home. It captures his face in three-quarter profile, his eyes lifted.

"He always used to say, 'Keep looking up,'" Betty recalls.

Two weeks after his friend's death, Gary left the hospital and reported to company headquarters in Chu Lai, where he heard about Keith.

"A clerk told me. Just shouted it out," he exclaims in disgust.

He also learned the Lochners had requested him to accompany the body home. Gary recalls, "It was a graveside service at the Gardens of Memory. There were endless cars. There was the 21-gun salute. Taps. They folded the flag and gave it to me, and I gave it to Betty. It sprinkled lightly. At the end of the service, a rainbow appeared. It was all very hard on Cheryl."

Gary pauses, then says of Betty Lochner, "She always treated me like a son. I still talk to her on the phone. It's hard."

While serving the rest of his tour in Vietnam, Gary often wrote Mrs. Lochner. In one letter, he assured her Keith cleaved to his faith while fighting a war: "He held on to his faith over here, as hard as it is, and inspired so many people. He was truly the best friend I've ever had."

On 22 April 1970, 3rd Platoon lost its squad leader. Gary Himelick lost his best friend; Betty and Jake, their son; Dean and Sherry, their brother; and the former Cheryl Hethcote, her first love and fiancé.

And on 22 April 1970, the nation lost a farmer.

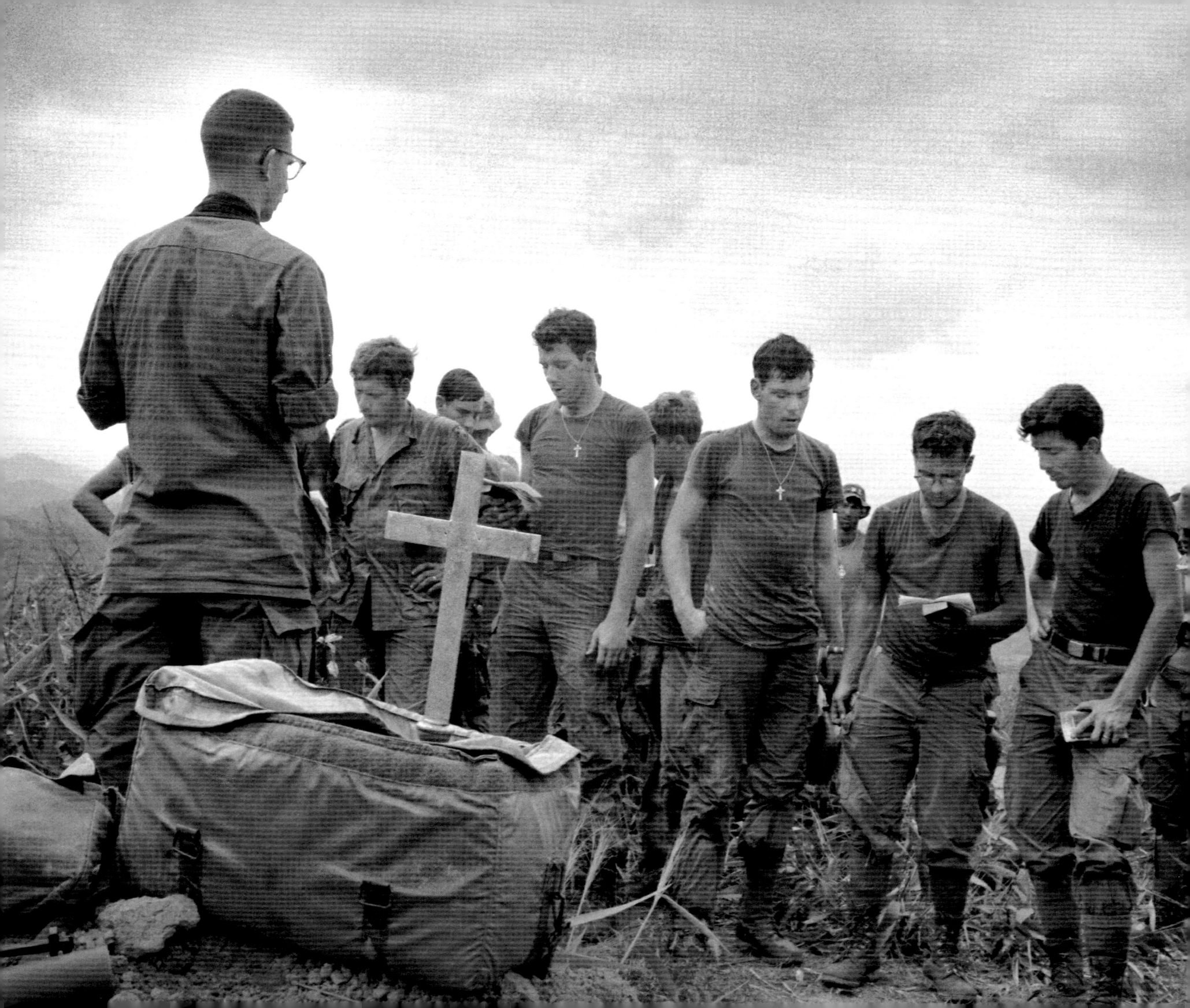

Chapter 6

Send Out The God Squad!

Captain Donald Wilson
Private Andrew Wommack

AS SOON AS CAPTAIN DONALD WILSON REACHED LZ WEST IN summer 1969, he stood at attention before Lieutenant Colonel Cecil Henry, battalion commander of 4/31.

"He said, 'Chaplain, the whole battalion is surrounded by the NVA. Charlie Company has been hit bad. I want you to go out there and raise their morale,'" Colonel (ret) Wilson recalls. He grins sheepishly.

"I said to myself, 'How do I do that?'"

Toting his chaplain's kit, Captain Wilson boarded a resupply chopper to the battlefield and took a leap of faith from the skids into sharp elephant grass.

Soon firing died out. Charlie Company scaled a mountain and set up a laager.

"That night we got hit three ways, with NVA firing RPGs [rocket-propelled grenades] and AK-47s in support of sappers who infiltrated the perimeter, and began their killing, 'walking among us,' throwing hand grenades," he recalls.

This was no place for a preacher, some may say, who was armed with only his Bible and crosses on his collar. Wilson, however, knew his destiny was here, with young Americans fighting for their lives.

"As the light began to come up it was over. The guy lying right by me was dead. We started picking up fingers and arms and putting them in bags. That was my introduction to Vietnam," he says softly.

Thus began Wilson's "war" of fighting for souls. Soon the men came to admire this chaplain who shared their dangers and matched them stride for stride on long humps. They didn't know he should have been dead.

Born on a family tobacco farm near Buffalo Junction, Virginia, Donald as a boy suffered rheumatic fever. He would walk again, the physician told his parents, but he would never be able to run and play and likely would die before age 30.

Now, with a wry smile, Colonel (ret) Donald Wilson, 75, a Southern Baptist chaplain of 4/31 in 1969 and 1970, drops to

Left: Donald Wilson, chaplain for 4th Battalion, conducts services, including singing from hymnals. In a "field-expedient" communion, he served crackers and Coca-Cola. The men called Wilson and chaplain's assistant Andrew Wommack "The God Squad."

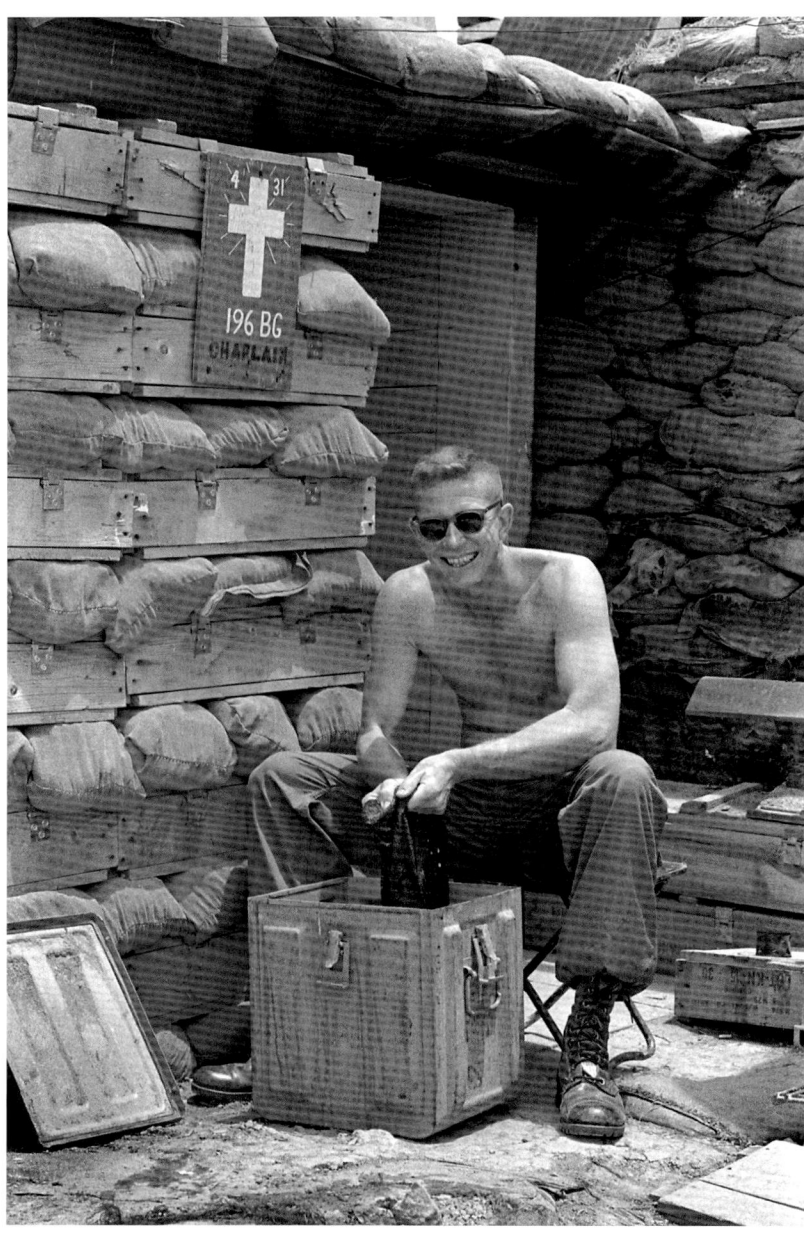

Chaplain Donald Wilson washes clothes at his hooch. Note the cross beside the doorway.

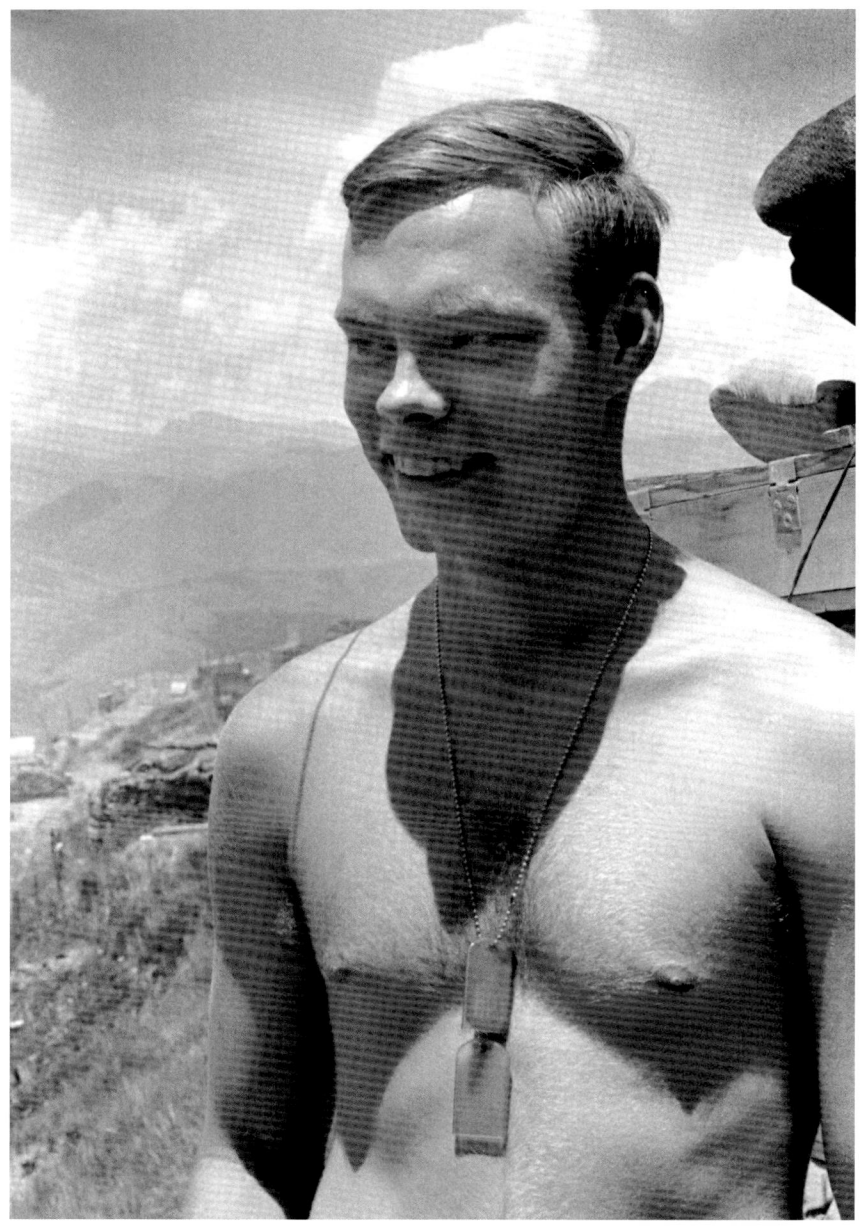

Andrew Wommack's fiancée died while he served in Vietnam. Today, Andrew Wommack Ministries, which includes worldwide television, is based in Colorado Springs, Colorado.

the floor and knocks out "airborne push-ups." Jim and I gape as Wilson stands, dusting his hands and smiling.

On this gray winter day, we sit with the soft-spoken Wilson—whose call sign in Vietnam was "Sky Pilot"—in his grandfather's home on the old family tobacco farm that he and wife Mary Lewis Wilson restored. Later, in Colorado, we would see his chaplain's assistant, Andrew Wommack. In 4/31, the call sign for the two of them was "The God Squad."

When Donald was a boy, this earth around the home grew green with tobacco, a crop that made young people old in a hurry.

"It was work about thirteen months out of the year," quips Wilson, a lifelong non-smoker. Planting, hoeing, suckering, cutting, stringing, and drying tobacco demanded dawn-to-dark work.

Young Don recovered from rheumatic fever and returned to school, determined to join classmates playing baseball. Soon he could hit and run bases, but with an odd gait—a lifelong effect of the fever.

Upon graduating from Bluestone High School, Don yearned for a future far beyond the farm, but what and where? Eventually, his pastor and football led him from mule and plow to eagles on his shoulders.

On autumn Saturdays, young Don listened to radio broadcasts of college gridiron games, including those of West Point, starring All-American William Stanley "Bill" Carpenter, the famous "Lonesome End." Soon, the word "Army" began whispering to Don.

"It's known as a 'calling' in our church. I just felt this is where I was supposed to go," he says of a military career.

At Bluefield College in Bluefield, Virginia, he earned a bachelor's degree through a work-study scholarship, then his master's from the University of Richmond. While attending Southern Baptist Theological Seminary in Louisville, Wilson was pastor of Plum Creek Baptist Church in Taylorsville, Kentucky. There a retired Army chaplain in the congregation suggested military service.

After Don married seminary classmate Mary Lewis Linthicum of Roanoke, Virginia, he enlisted and completed basic training at Fort Dix, New Jersey. He chuckles.

"I was twenty-nine or thirty and going through basic training with eighteen-year-olds," he says.

By then, Wilson felt another "calling," not only as a chaplain but also as one serving alongside men in combat. The Army offered slots for chaplains in major faiths, with only three in 1968 for the Southern Baptist denomination. Wilson got one.

Through the Summer Counteroffensive of 1969 against 2nd NVA Division, Wilson served as chaplain for two battalions of 196th LIB: 4/31 and 3/21. This he learned quickly of his fighting "flock": "They need you after [a battle]. They're more willing to listen to you."

Like the grunts, he traveled light. He stuffed his chaplain's kit with socks and small Bibles. In communion in the field, Coca-Cola and crackers substituted for the blood and body of Christ, with "church" consisting of the earth for pews and a ceiling of sky.

Wilson "preached" most sermons by example: sharing dangers and hardships. "I am with you to the end," his presence told them, even if he were equipped only with his Christian insignia and the invisible raiment of the sixth chapter of Ephesians. Although Sky Pilot would fire a weapon to defend himself and others, he sought no sobriquet as "fighting chaplain"; he considered himself to be simply a servant placed where men needed him most: beside them. He was also in high demand.

"I might be in another company but over the radio would come, 'Delta is in a fire fight. Send the 'Sky Pilot.'" Wilson grins. "Now that's one of the best compliments you can ever get."

Sky Pilot once accompanied the battalion's Recon team when it stumbled across an NVA company in formation. The enemy spotted the vastly outnumbered team and launched a night attack. Recon, fortunately, was within range of the 155mm howitzers on LZ West. With the enemy pressing against his perimeter, the Recon team leader called in artillery on his own position.

"Those guys were all over us, killing us, and there was no other option," Wilson says, of friendly fire bursting among friends and foe. "That is the most effective artillery the world's ever seen. The earth jumps. Your ears are terrible. Everybody's screaming one prayer: 'God, let me live!'"

Wilson pauses. His voice is a whisper.

"Some of us lived," he says.

Wilson would soon have help in his ecumenical duties. In the field one day, an RTO handed him the PRC-25 radio receiver.

"It was the division chaplain. He said, 'We'd like to send you a chaplain's assistant. He's a little too religious for us,'" Wilson remarks. He chuckles and praises the assistant's biblical knowledge.

"Andy probably knew about as much as they did," he remarks of Private Andrew Wommack, then of Arlington, Texas.

Chaplain and assistant made a good team, The God Squad, although with separate missions. With Wilson in the field, Andy remained at West, holding services and counseling soldiers.

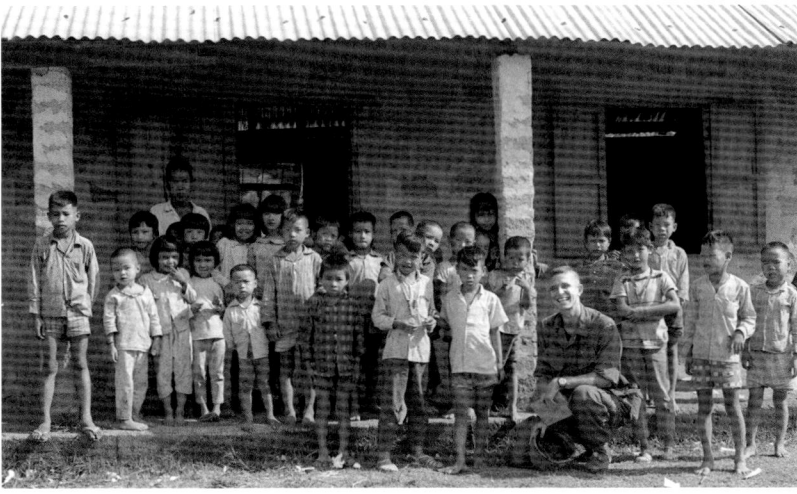

Logue photographed these children at a church orphanage in An Son, a village near LZ West. Wives, mothers, and sweethearts of men in Alpha sent clothing, food, and toys to the youngsters in 1969–1970.

Meanwhile, back in Virginia, Mary Wilson and many other Baptists helped to uplift the lives of scores of Vietnamese children. In Viet An, a village near LZ West, Don had begun assisting a Baptist church and adjacent orphanage. Mary helped organize efforts in sending to the orphanage clothing, shoes, and school supplies.

Alpha's captain, John Wilson, enlisted his mother's help as well. Soon similar manna was arriving from Alabama Methodists.

Jim Logue, out of the field by late summer 1970, accompanied Chaplain Wilson and Private Wommack to Viet An and produced a feature about the orphanage and church in the battalion newspaper he edited.

Wilson completed his one-year tour and was driving a jeep from LZ Hawk Hill to Chu Lai when he stopped to spend his last night "in the field" in a tent. As he drifted off, a man with a rifle barged in, screaming.

"He's lit up. He knows I'm the devil and I have to be killed. I do the best I can, talking with him. I know that's all I can do. There's nobody else around," Wilson recalls.

Through the night, unarmed, the chaplain lay awake, listening. Again and again the man burst into the tent, screaming death threats. Wilson lay awake, waiting for his executioner, until daylight.

He again thought he might die the next day. He was afoot in Tam Ky, where children often slipped live grenades into soft-drink cans and tossed them at Americans. Suddenly, a boy flung a can and hit him in the stomach.

"I knew that's bound to be a grenade." Wilson sighs in relief. "It wasn't."

Thus, on both his first and last day in Vietnam, Wilson twice nearly died.

Back home, the chaplain graduated from US Army War College at Carlisle Barracks, Pennsylvania, completed airborne training at Fort Benning, Georgia, and served as deputy post chaplain at Fort Bragg, North Carolina. In tours in Germany and Korea, he played mandolin in a band of officers called the "Over the Hill Gang." Stationed in Korea, he met his hero, Major General William S. Carpenter, West Point's "Lonesome End" and a decorated combat veteran of Vietnam. Wilson completed his career as senior military chaplain at US Military Academy.

A civilian again, he served seven years as a pastor in Virginia Beach before retiring. Wilson and his wife came to Buffalo Junction to restore the old home and preserve the family farm and historic outbuildings. The rheumatic boy who, a doctor said, would likely never run and play now summarizes his life in uniform: "I ran with the best of them."

ONE OF "THE BEST" WAS THE CHAPLAIN'S ASSISTANT WHO SPENT his youth as an introvert. Now, he speaks to millions. Colonel Wilson often watches broadcasts of his Vietnam assistant, who founded Andrew Wommack Ministries of Colorado Springs, Colorado.

To reach Andy, Jim and I climbed towards the sky to Woodland Park, Colorado, to the Charis Bible College that Wommack founded. Andy met us in attire similar to that he wears for his worldwide television broadcasts: long-sleeve shirt open at the throat and trim trousers. He speaks softly, as he does in broadcasts and in live appearances in America and abroad.

Born in Marshall, Texas, Andy grew up in Arlington as a Southern Baptist until, at eighteen, he "had an encounter when I got caught up in the presence of God. It was like waves of liquid love. It totally changed my life," he recalls.

He "found his voice" in that experience, as well as a passion to share the word of God—as he did in his freshman year at The University of Texas at Arlington—"making a pest of myself," he says, in "witnessing" to fellow students. He passed all his classes but dropped out that summer and was reclassified 1-A and drafted.

Drill sergeants called him "preacher" in basic training at Fort Bliss, Texas. In his barracks, other trainees were "cursing and blaspheming God. The lights went off and so I just started

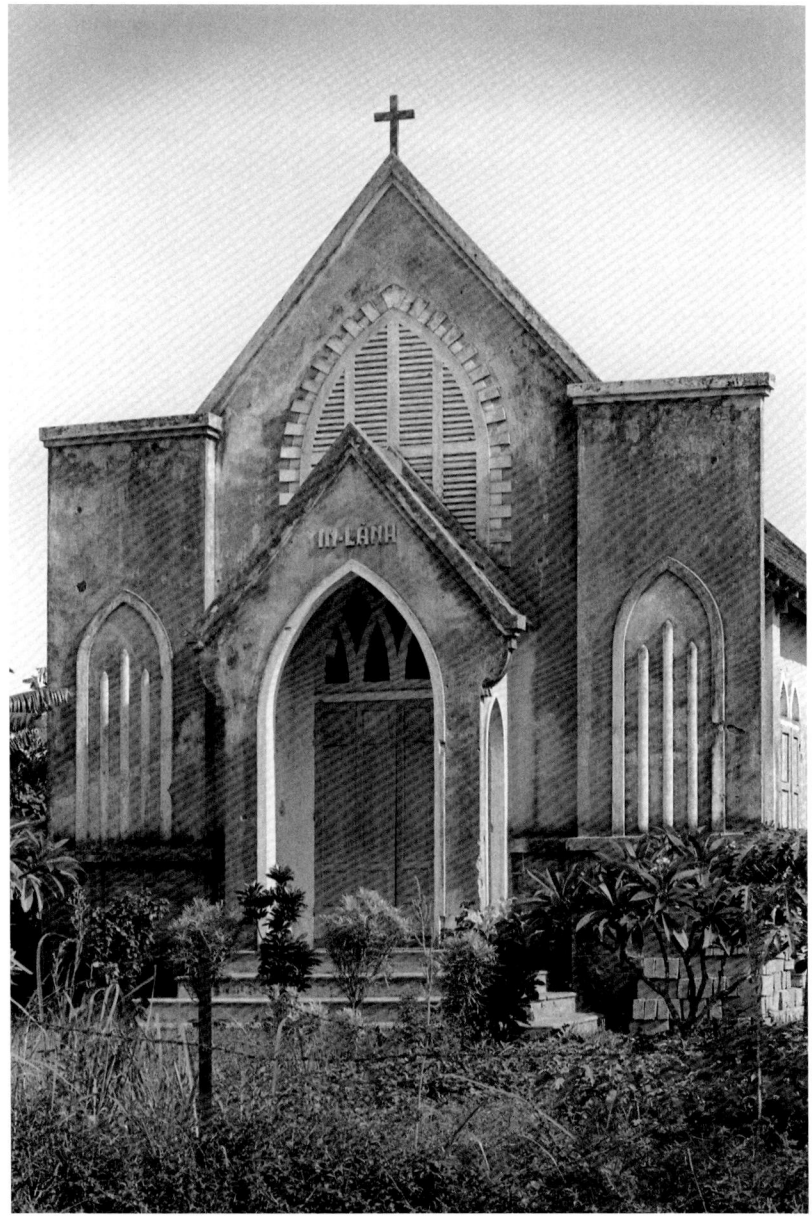

In 1970, Logue photographed the An Son orphanage and church. Communists burned the church after the war. The edifice, later rebuilt, again displays inside the same banner, bearing the Bible verse John 3:16.

preaching to them. They'd say, 'Who's saying that?' They'd turn the lights on. I'd get quiet. They'd turn the lights off. I'd go to preaching. They all got mad at me," Andy recalls, chuckling.

After chaplain assistant school at Fort Dix, New Jersey, Andy arrived in Chu Lai and began "witnessing" to chaplains of field-grade rank. Andy grins.

"They wanted me out of the way," he says, of why he was sent to Wilson. The two made a good team, with Wilson in the field and Andy at LZ West. The chaplain kept him there, Andy believes, for one reason: "I think he was protecting me because they told him not to get another chaplain's assistant killed."

When Wilson led services at West, Andy accompanied hymns on a pump organ. He also rebuilt and strengthened his bunker three times, burrowing into it on his twenty-first birthday in 1970. The bunker, that day, took twenty-one "direct hits" from NVA mortars.

"I counted them. I thought, 'Well, that's quite a birthday present,'" he says.

Andy accompanied Wilson twice to the field. The newly built artillery base, LZ Prep, was under attack when its commander urged Wilson to come and hold services. Wilson and Andy, The God Squad, flew through ground fire to the base.

"We took one hundred and seventy mortar rounds inside the perimeter during the three or four hours we were there. We held service and it was under heavy fire. We got fired at as we left," Wommack recalls.

Back home, a young woman whom Andy had been dating was fighting leukemia. As her condition worsened, her parents requested of Army authorities that her "fiancé," Andy, be allowed a last chance to see her. Andy flew to Texas and spent two days with her before she died.

Back in Vietnam, he felt "forgotten" when Wilson returned to the States. So he studied his Bible "fifteen hours a day, and prayed to die and go to heaven to be with Debbie."

Instead, he finished his tour, went home, and was discharged on 21 February 1971, still a buck private. That autumn,

he married Jamie Ann Harris and joined a church he describes as "Bapticostal," a fusion of Baptist and Pentecostal faiths.

Like disciples, the Wommacks began wandering across the Southwest, trying to establish permanent churches. Andy worked multiple jobs to feed his family and "nearly starved to death for a few years," he recalls.

In Childress, Texas, he broadcast his first message on a radio station that played country-and-western music. It was no fiery sermon, crackling through remote regions of AM radio. He didn't even "preach."

"I'd just sit down and teach in front of a microphone," he said.

Eventually settling in Colorado Springs, he incorporated his ministry and added television to expand his broadcast outreach. Today, Andrew Wommack Ministries reaches 3.2 billion worldwide on radio and television broadcasts. His programs are neither screed nor jeremiad nor happy hustling of "prosperity gospel." He doesn't plead for offerings. Andy thinks in souls. The dollars, he believes, will follow.

AT LENGTH ANDY STOOD, APOLOGIZING THAT HE HAD TO END our interview for a scheduled meeting. He shook our hands and summed up his life: "I've done a lot of dumb things. God saved my life so many times."

At least, thanks to Jim, Wilson and Wommack met again. Jim learned that Wommack was appearing in North Carolina, so he contacted both men and arranged a meeting for the two. They talked for hours; then, at the service that night, Andy invited Wilson to join him on stage. They described their experiences in Vietnam to the audience, then Andy turned to Wilson: "Chaplain, why do you think the Lord allowed us to survive Vietnam?"

"At first, I didn't know what to say," Wilson recalled. "Then I just nodded to the audience and said, 'Andy, I think we both know why we came back.'"

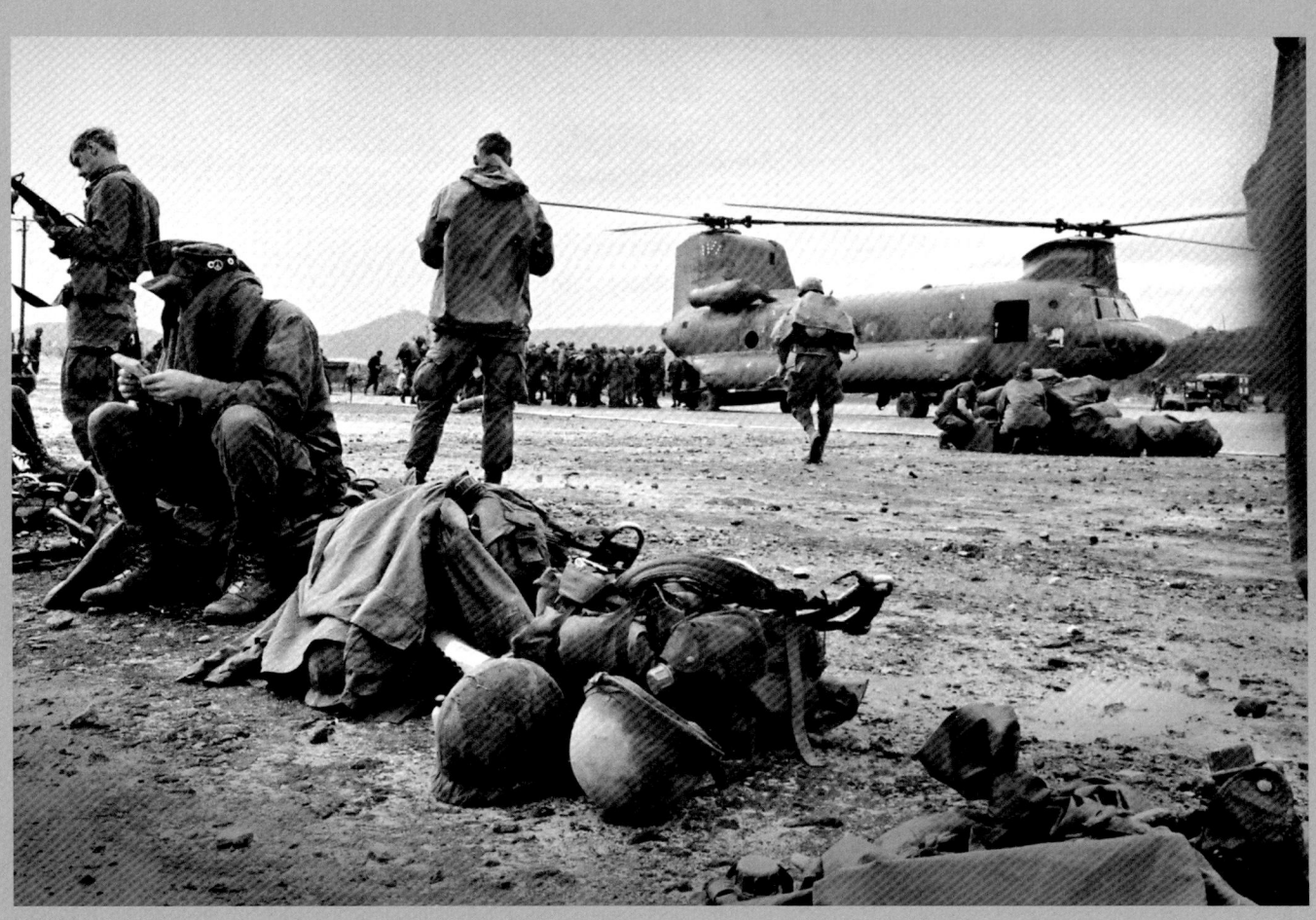

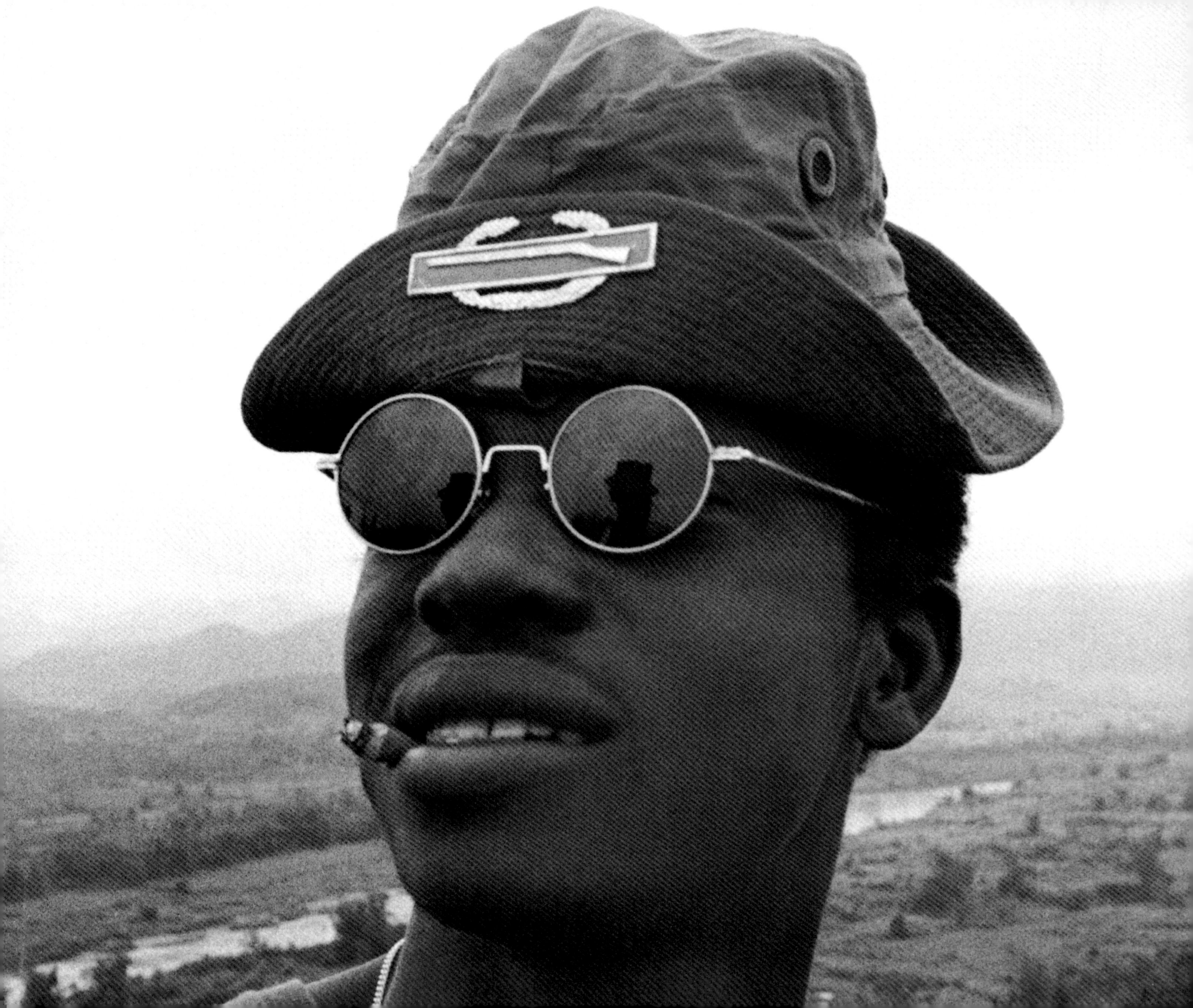

Chapter 7

Nate Is Still Walking Point

Specialist 4 Nathaniel Donaldson

AS HE DID IN VIETNAM, NATE STILL LEADS THE WAY.

Jim and I follow the long strides of tall, lean Nathaniel "Nate" Donaldson along a footpath in the Coral Gables neighborhood of West Coconut Grove, Florida.

Jim nudges me and speaks in a stage whisper: "Nate is still walking point."

Nate laughs.

He remains as thin as in his initial Vietnam days, with only faint lines in his face and closely cropped graying hair marking time's passage.

Soon we reach the home of Michael and Erika Philip, Nate's neighbors. They work with Kristy Wallace, who leads Urban Resurrection/InnerCHANGE, a non-profit Christian-based organization in this predominantly African American neighborhood. For them, one might say, Nate walks point for this group's community work. He encourages neighbors to join programs that improve health, lend hands up to better careers, and lift quality of life. Kristy quickly learned of Nate's good standing among neighbors—that if Nate says it's okay, then it's okay.

We settle around shaded tables where Nate and others gather for Bible study on Thursday nights. Erika brings out coffee and cookies, and her young children join us.

Nate was born nearby in 1949 to Felt and Essiemae Bryant Donaldson, third of an eventual fourteen children. His dad, a World War II veteran and gardener, and his mother, a housekeeper, toiled day and night to feed their family. Nate quit George Washington Carver High School in the 11th grade and got a job to help.

He soon was one less mouth to feed. Drafted at nineteen, he stood six feet tall and weighed 150 pounds.

At Fort Jackson, South Carolina, Drill Sergeants Adams and Greenburg "rode" him hard. He didn't understand why at the time, but Nate now realizes his drill sergeants sensed his leadership qualities and challenged him to strive for excellence.

"In five months, they made me from a street kid to a soldier," Nate recalls.

When he left Fort Jackson, his 150 pounds had soared to 189 of sculpted muscle.

He arrived in Vietnam on 10 September 1969, another replacement for a company shot up in the summer campaign against the 2nd NVA Division. He was placed in 1st Platoon, where squad leader Richard "Dick" Oswald of Nebraska "took

Left: All knew Specialist 4 Nate Donaldson for his abilities as point man and for his customary attire: love beads and sunglasses, the front brim of his boonie pinned with his Combat Infantry Badge.

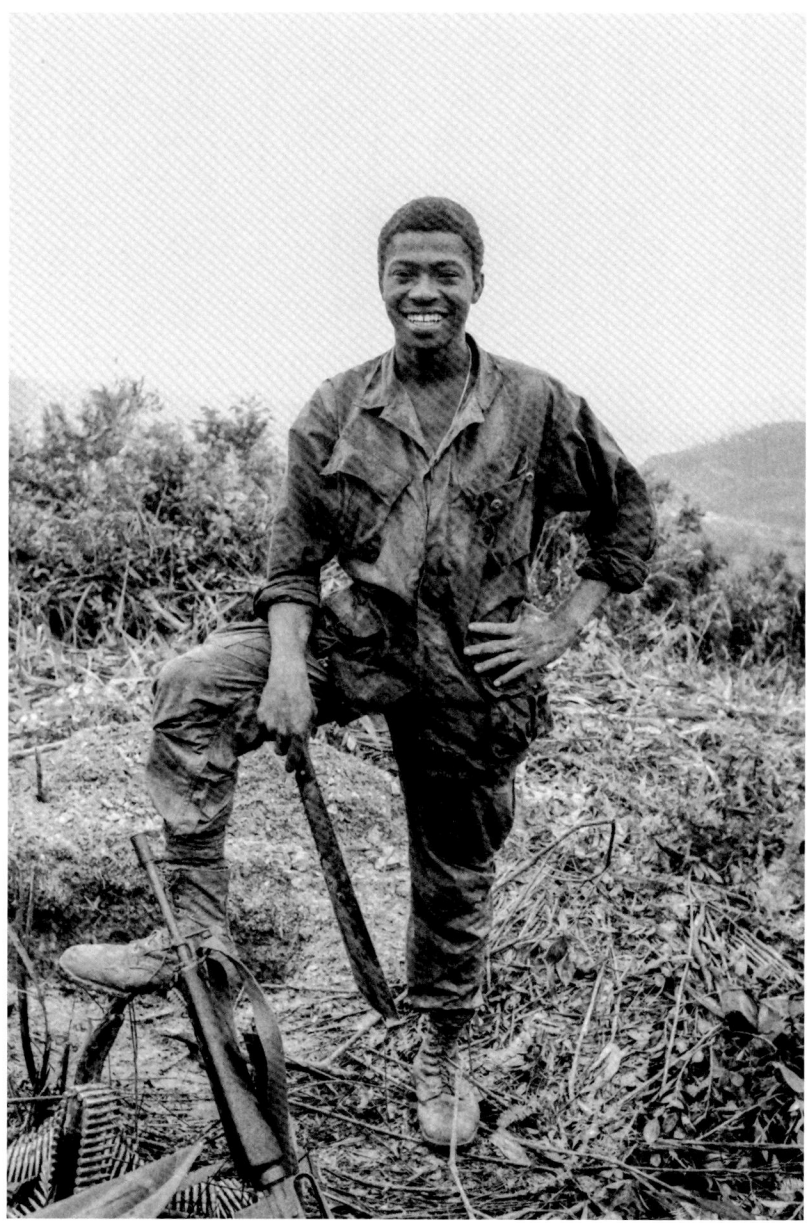

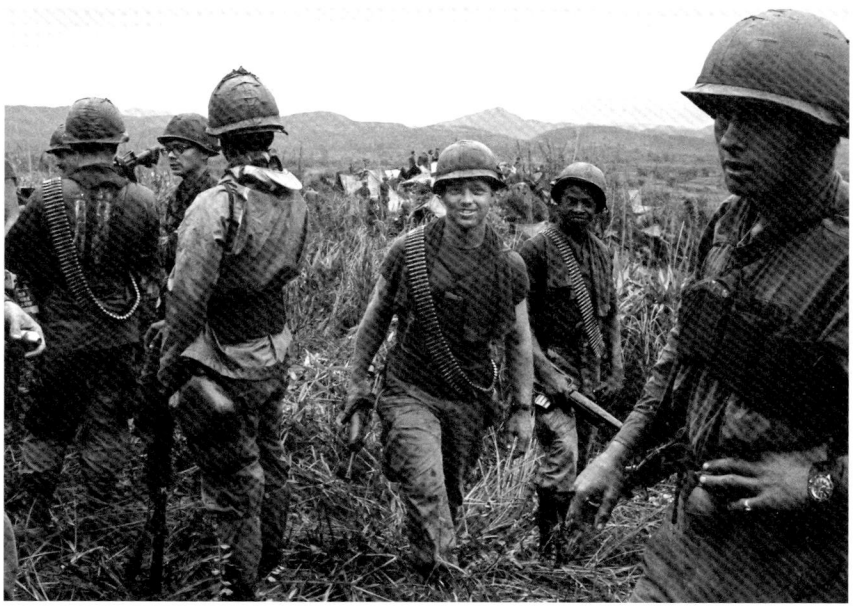

Men in Logue's squad include Ron German (center); Dan Simmons (far right); and Nate Donaldson. Left (in glasses) is 1st Platoon leader, First Lieutenant Erwin Esterling.

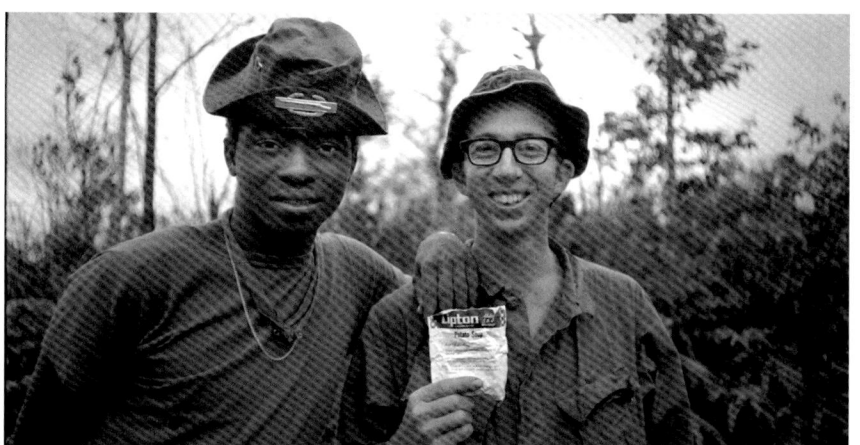

Alpha was proud when the 15 May 1970 issue of *Stars and Stripes* featured Nate Donaldson and his actions in the "May–June Battle" against 2nd NVA Division. With his machete, Nate hacked through jungle.

Nate Donaldson and Staff Sergeant Cecil Edward Milburn Jr., a Texan, display a packet of condensed soup from home. Men shared foodstuffs sent them: cookies, cakes, candy—anything that survived journeys from home kitchens to Vietnam.

me under his wing."

Others he remembers include Montanan John Oiestad; Ronald "Red" Hill of Texas; Pennsylvanian Dave Gould; and two "brothers," Ronald Hicks of St. Petersburg, Florida, and L. C. Gatewood, a good soldier Nate and all others remember only as "CP" for "Chicago Pimp." That was his nickname, not his occupation.

"We called him that by the way he walked," Nate says.

The south Floridian remembers his first day in the field.

"Fear," he says. "That was the biggest thing."

He means not only fear of the enemy but also of G.I.s around him: "Some of the guys didn't take Vietnam seriously because we weren't under fire every day. We were in a Controlled Fire Zone. Because of the villages out there we had to be careful."

The enemy was out there, too. In one night laager, he was reclining on his air mattress when all heard the coughs of enemy mortar rounds leaving tubes. Someone yelled, "INCOMING!" Nate dived for his foxhole, just as a round exploded a few feet away. Dazed and deafened, he was bleeding profusely, with a metal shard imbedded in an arm.

"I pull it out. My ears are ringing. I can't hear anything," he says.

He recovered at 91st Evacuation Hospital in Chu Lai. For the wound he earned a Purple Heart.

Dick Oswald was happy to see him back. He appointed Nate to what became his full-time assignment and the most dangerous job in Vietnam: point man. Behind him as slack walked CP.

"You and CP were always in front. We didn't trust anybody else," Jim remarks.

"*I* didn't trust anybody else," Nate emphasizes.

All in Alpha breathed easier when 1st Platoon was designated "point platoon." Officers may have c*ommanded* the men; Nate and CP *led* them.

Nate was armed with two weapons: his rifle, which he

nicknamed "Lucille," and his nose.

"I could smell them," he says of the Vietnamese. "I don't know if it was their diet or what. If they were in the area, like from here to that house over there, I could smell them."

He cut a distinctive figure, especially in hat, hairstyle, and sunglasses. In one of Jim's photographs, Nate wears round sunglasses, front brim of his boonie turned up and Combat Infantry Badge pinned to the crown.

Day by day, he grew savvier as a soldier. On night sweeps, he never fired his rifle. Tracers reveal a position. Instead, he threw grenades, one in a way he learned at the movies.

Swashbuckling Errol Flynn, in an old war film, blasts the enemy with hand grenades rolled down from a height.

"I lay in my foxhole and pulled the pin and let the grenade roll down the hill in front of me. Boom!" He grinned. "Just like Errol Flynn."

As days crawled by, Nate struggled to hold on to some semblance of humanity. From the soft flesh of civilian life he formed a hard chrysalis of body, mind, and soul in Vietnam. It was kill or be killed, shoot first or die, and, when hit, hit the enemy harder.

Yet he clung to his faith and family. He wrote home often and was always delighted to see mail postmarked "Miami." He kept a prayer cloth in his ruck, a talisman his father had sent him. Packages from home contained sardines, Spam, and cookies, all a sweet relief from day-after-day C-rations.

Along with his correspondence, he shepherded his pay, devoting half to savings bonds and sending the rest to his mother. When "the eagle screamed," in Vietnam-era parlance, he handed his payday money to another African American soldier. First Sergeant "Top" James Smith saw that Nate's monthly pay and savings bonds went home.

Although he counted several whites and Hispanics as friends, Nate and other black soldiers gravitated to each other. They dubbed Nate with a nickname drawn from his choice of cigarettes. He grins.

"Cowboy," he says, because of his preference for Marlboro, known for its western theme of advertising. "All the black dudes smoked menthols. Salem. Kool."

Cowboy dealt with racial confrontations like Wild West showdowns. Since the Civil War, black soldiers have fought on two fronts: in battle and at home for equal rights and the decency of fair play. Still, prejudices existed.

"Some guys from Southern states made wisecracks: nigger this, nigger that. I walked around the corner into one conversation. Got into a fight. He was bigger than I was," Nate says.

"I'm sure you straightened him out," Jim says.

"I did," he responds, chuckling.

Another black Alpha soldier, however, recalled few confrontations between races, especially in the field. In St. Petersburg, Ronald Hicks reminded us of how all soldiers were equal in one way. He smiles wryly.

"Everyone had a gun," he states.

An awkward incident with a white soldier that Nate doesn't remember is recalled by Ron German of Garland, Texas, a college graduate who later would found Ron German, Consulting Engineers. While the two were digging a foxhole, Ron uttered a remark common among Southerners in warm weather and directed to no one in particular: "Boy, it's hot." Nate heard it and swung at German with his pick, thinking the Texan had addressed him as "boy" instead of using the term as a filler word.

A much larger threat waited in a mid-April 1970 air assault. Nate, with L. C. Gatewood as slack, stepped onto sandy flats alongside the river, Song Thu Bon.

"I got halfway across and an AK-47 opens up on me. I hit the ground. Nobody else was out there. I was the only one that they could shoot at from across the river. My steel pot falls off but I've still got my rucksack. So I've got to make a decision with bullets bouncing all around me: 'Get up and run.'"

Nate relives the race of his life through enemy fire to cover.

"I make it to the other side. By that time, we've called in gunships and helicopters. They come in shooting." Bullets are still coming, cutting down the elephant grass, hitting the adversaries but denying Nate a chance to contribute.

"It made me mad. I couldn't see [the enemy], and I couldn't shoot back," he says.

In walking point, he lived life one second at a time, especially during the May–June Battle, an offensive 2nd NVA Division began in late April. As Nate and CP rounded a bend in the trail, they surprised three NVA soldiers. As in an Old West shootout, life and death came down to the speed of reflex.

Cowboy was faster. He killed one and wounded another. A third fled.

In its 15 May 1970 edition, *Stars and Stripes* published a feature about the incident. The story reveals what was found in one of the enemy rifles: a chambered round seared by the firing pin, a round that might have killed Nate or CP.

"I keep that shell as a souvenir. That's the only way I ever want to have one," Nate comments.

One day before the article's publication, Nate was starving. After tramping far west in its sector of operations, Alpha had just settled into its night laager when an enemy mortar attack drove the company from the hill. Captain John Wilson received orders to march to Hiêp Dúc, a four-day hump. With resupply spotty, all were famished, many were hurt, and no help from the heavens was in sight. Alpha stumbled ahead to reach Hiêp Dúc four days later where resupply choppers should have been waiting.

They weren't.

Exhausted soldiers dropped into spots of shade, asleep when they hit the ground. Nate, however, spotted a hen, caught it, and cooked it. The owner, an elderly woman, raised a ruckus, yelling at Nate, 1st Platoon leader Erwin Esterling, and Captain Wilson. To placate her, Nate forked over two dollars. He grins.

"That scrawny old bird hit the spot," he recalls.

That afternoon, in a driving rain, Alpha fought off an ambush, with several wounded and one killed.

Into June, casualties mounted. Nate winces in recalling one

night ambush when the company hugged high ground on the edge of rice paddies near a hamlet. Before sunrise, they heard movement in front of their position.

"I threw a hand grenade out of my foxhole and somebody else threw about three grenades. We heard them moaning and when the sun came up we walked out there."

He pauses and swallows.

"It was two old Vietnamese women. They tried to sneak into the village at night. They had a big investigation about it. They cleared it up," he said.

After R&R in Japan in late July, only five weeks remained in his tour. As a short-timer, he hoped for a safer job in the rear. Instead, he was ordered to the field for three weeks. Alpha, with scores of "new guys," needed experienced leaders.

Finally came the chopper to take him from the field. Nate begged his friends not to tell the pilot he was returning to Chu Lai to begin his journey home.

They did.

As was custom for G.I.s leaving for the states, this pilot gave Cowboy a ride as if he were atop an airborne bronc.

"They call it the 'jolly ride,'" he says of a soldier's last chopper flight before he leaves the country.

Soon Sergeant Donaldson boarded a commercial flight home. A black flight attendant, he recalls, made him comfortable. When the wheels lifted above the tarmac, Cowboy once again was just Nate.

He was also a proud American. In Seattle, he stepped down the ramp, dropped to hands and knees, and kissed the ground.

Without telling his family he was back in the States, Nate took a taxi to his boyhood home.

"All of a sudden here comes all of my family. Man, I . . ." His voice drops. He pauses and looks away, then smiles wanly. "My mom was crying."

For her son, Mrs. Donaldson spread a South Florida homecoming feast, a blend of the sea and the South: fish, cabbage, and collard greens.

Nate married Carolyn Murray on 23 March 1973. They would have two children, Marc Terrance Donaldson and Sheila Donaldson, and now have one grandchild. Today their daughter lives in Switzerland, while their son owns a fitness studio in Broward County.

Over his career Nate worked at two hospitals, was employed by Florida Power and Light, and retired as a postal carrier. He also purchased a home and paid Carolyn's expenses in earning her college degree. She recently retired from a career with Johnson & Johnson and now with Nate devotes time to missionary work.

Like all Vietnam veterans, Nate, for decades, dwelt in the anonymity of civilian life. Now, he is grateful and humbled when strangers learn of his service.

"It means a lot. The words 'Thank you for serving' didn't apply to us for many years. The first guy who told me 'Thank you for your service' was a cop. He had pulled me over and was writing me a ticket and I told him I was a veteran and he thanked me."

Nate pauses and grins.

"He still gave me the ticket."

Along with caring for his family and neighbors, Nate's work with UrbanResurrection/InnerCHANGE helps fulfill *him*. Kristy, Erica, and Michael, he notes, "have had a profound impact on my life." In turn, Nate has strengthened theirs.

"We were each other's mentors. I come from one side of town. You're from that side of the tracks and I'm from this side of the tracks. Fate is something that you can't control but thank God I'm glad they came into my life," he remarks.

Today his health is good except for the twin tolls of age and war. He wears hearing aids. His eyes water. His joints ache. He limps from a chipped bone after leaping from a helicopter during a combat assault.

I ask what he thinks of his time in Vietnam. He pauses for a while.

"I was a good soldier. We were all good soldiers. That's one thing about my squad," he says.

That squad, and other friends, have "returned" to his life. Earlier, he told Jim he lost all his Vietnam memorabilia—including photographs of him that Logue took—in Hurricane Andrew in August 1992. Jim handed him new copies of all those photographs and a selection of others. As he and Jim leaf through them, the years drop from Nate's face and, for a moment, he is Cowboy again, walking point.

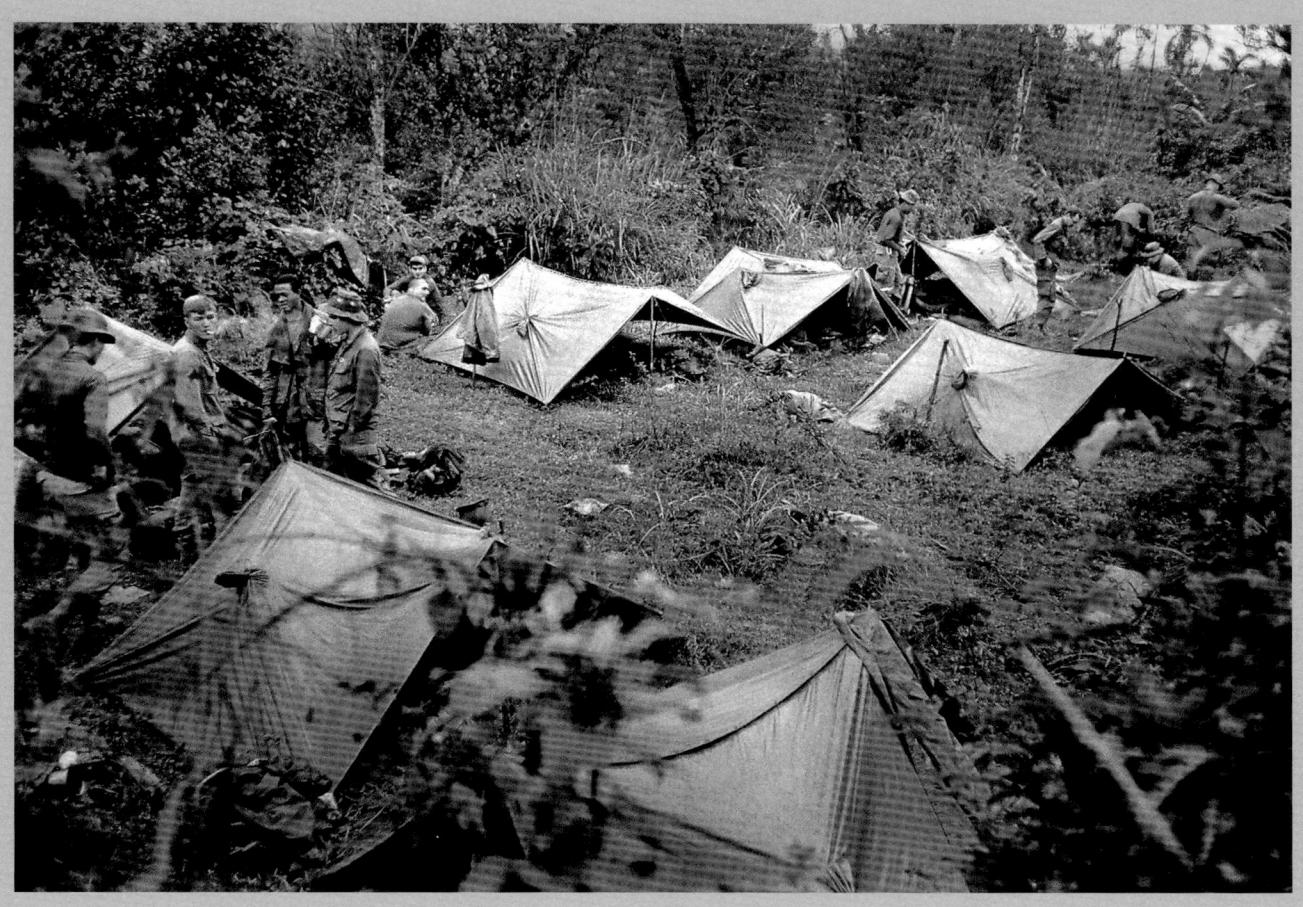

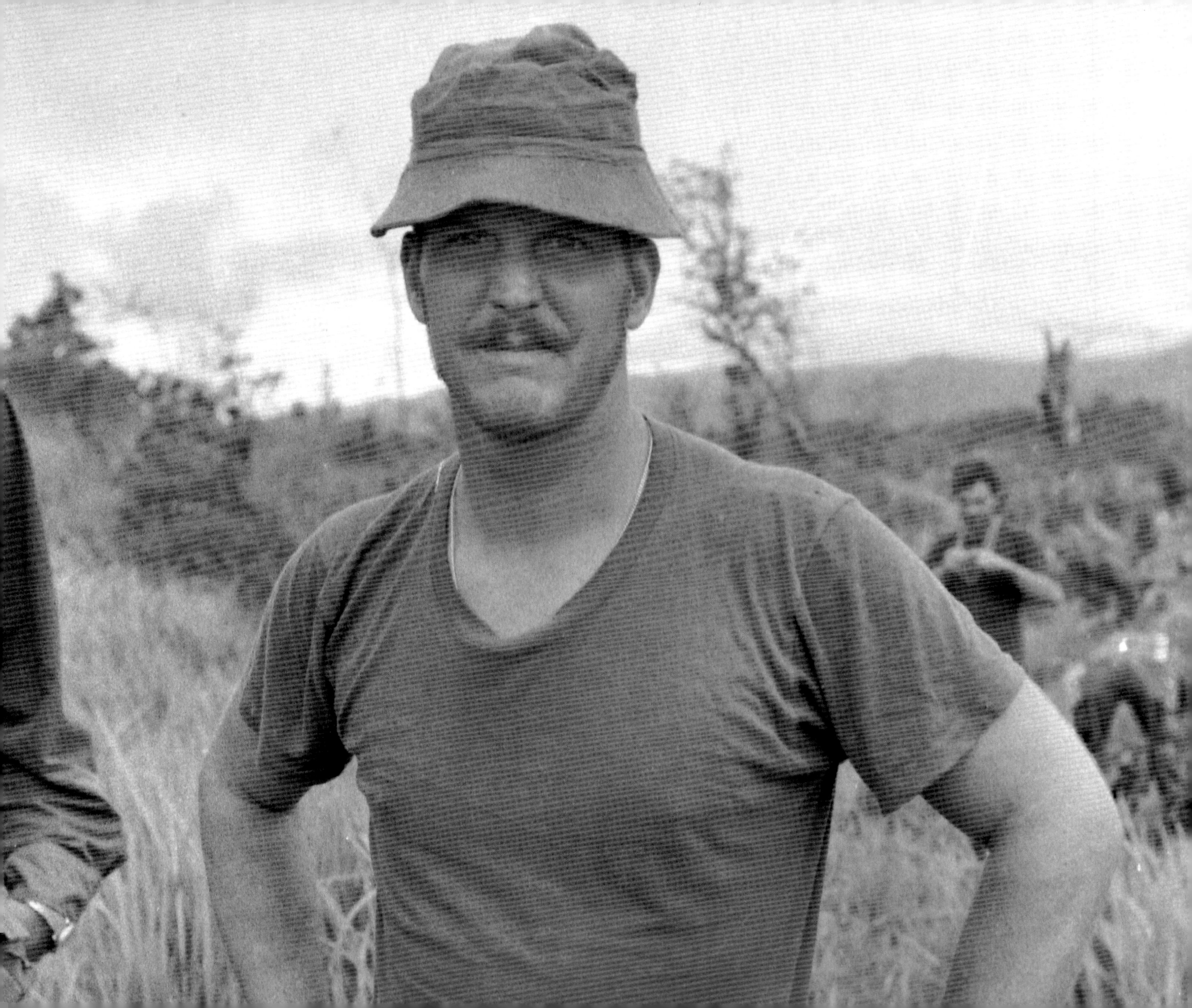

Chapter 8

His Eyes Were Open, But He Didn't Know I Was There

First Lieutenant Ross Joplin

THEY AWOKE WITH SPIRITS HIGH. AFTER TWO WEEKS IN THE field, Second Lieutenant Ross Joplin (his rank at the time) and his 2nd Platoon walked south-southwest, soon to ascend LZ Siberia. There for a week they'd guard the small artillery base high above death in the valley.

Sergeant Aldo "Mondo" Bastinancic took point. Some remember him as a professional vocalist before the draft sent him to war, where he proved as accomplished a soldier as he was a singer. All breathed easier when Mondo, an Italian word for "large," walked point.

"Saddle up!" Joplin called out at 0625. Soon 2nd Platoon led Alpha Company through this CFZ (Controlled Fire Zone), where most citizenry lived in protected villages such as Hiêp Dúc.

As part of "winning hearts and minds," American S5 units (civilian affairs) worked to improve living, health, and education standards for citizens. Many locals reciprocated in gratitude. A day earlier, Lieutenant Colonel Kenneth Skaer, battalion commander of 4/31, had written Americal Division headquarters praising locals for leading his men to caches of enemy supplies.

"This shows the effect of the cooperation between the Vietnamese people and this command. The Vietnamese families working rice fields in this CFZ were considered 'friendly,'" Skaer wrote, happy to pass to higher headquarters his battalion's success in "Vietnamization" efforts.

Alpha knew better. Joplin knew better. Many locals in such "pacified" villages as Hiêp Dúc supported the VC and NVA.

Ross watched Mondo follow a turn in the trail and veer into elephant grass. Ross tensed.

"Mondo hits that booby trap and he knows what he's done. He turns with his weapon sideways and he's trying to push everybody off this dike. Reaction time's too slow. Booby trap goes off, hits him right in the shorts. There were several guys hit with shrapnel. I dropped my ruck and ran up there and got a medic. We rolled Mondo over and put him on a poncho. He was in shock."

A dust off from Siberia, only about 200 yards away, lifted away Mondo and five other wounded. Ross watched the medevac rise, then turned to his men and froze. Murder blazed in their eyes.

Left: First Lieutenant Ross Joplin, a Texas Tech University graduate, served as 2nd Platoon leader. After hospitalization from severe battlefield injuries, he completed his tour as battalion air assets officer on LZ West.

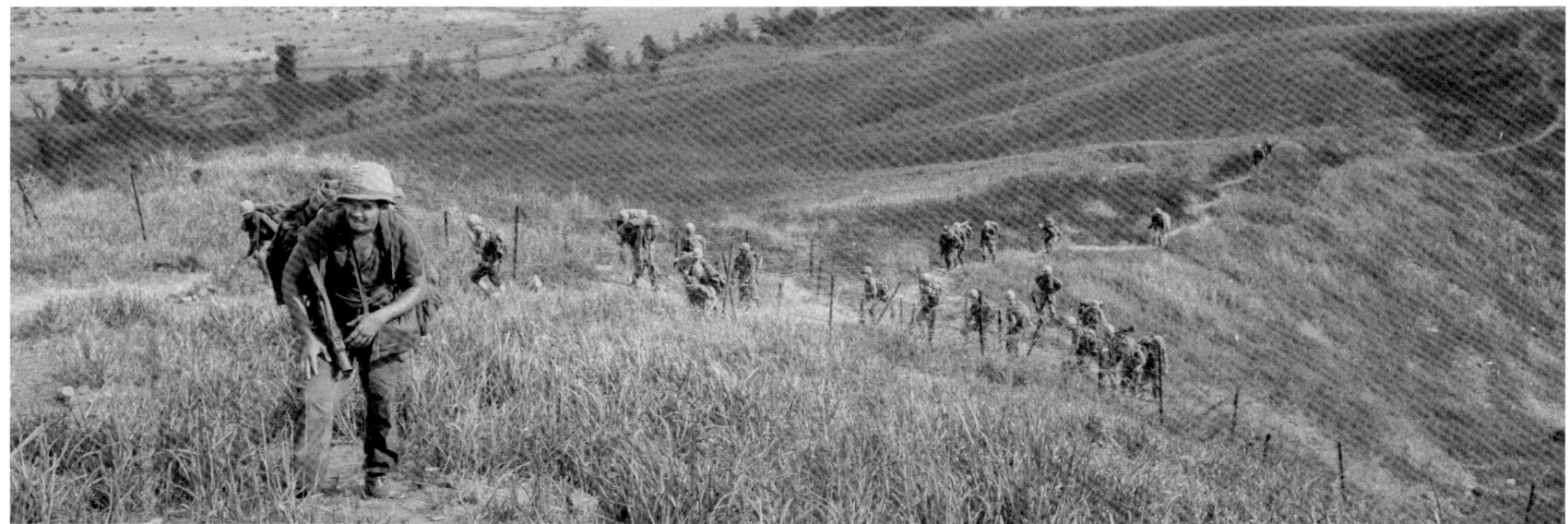

Ray Stark climbs up to LZ Siberia, where his platoon will guard 105 mm howitzers of C Battery, 3rd Battalion, 82nd Artillery. Each platoon spent four days every two months guarding Siberia.

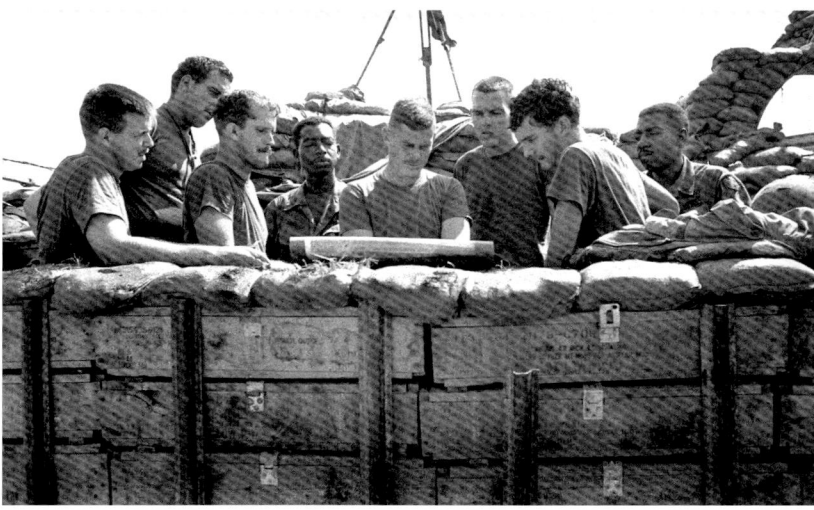

Logue calls this photo "The Last Supper." On LZ West, Alpha cadre flank Captain John Wilson (center) in reviewing objectives for the mission, Task Force West.

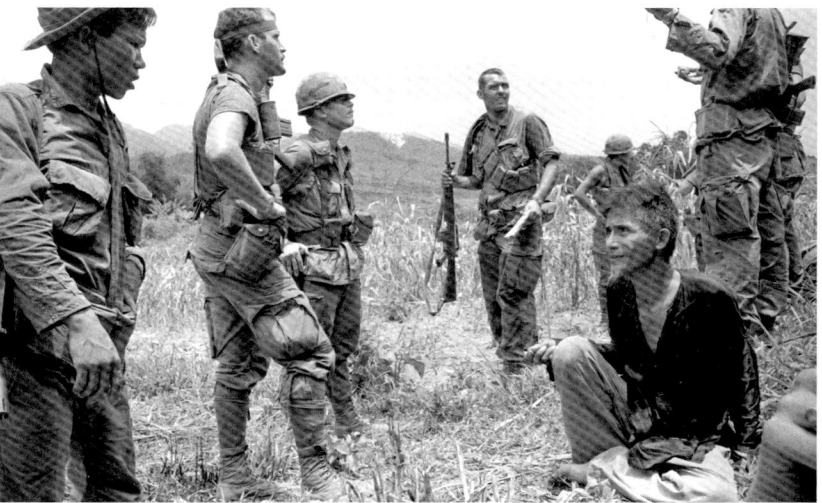

In a battlefield conference are, left to right, Ngo, a *chieu hoi* scout; Ross Joplin in headband; Captain John Wilson, and First Lieutenant Donald Pettit. A Viet Cong prisoner is seated in foreground.

Ross knew the next few moments would determine whether scores of civilians would live or die, and if he and others would spend years in an Army prison. Yet, Ross was prepared. The land back home had taught him well.

IT IS NOON ON A COOL, SUNNY FEBRUARY DAY IN THE eponymous Levelland, population 13,000, in the Texas Panhandle. Ross and wife, Nancy, serve Jim and me ribs he smoked in a pit, along with vegetables from the couple's backyard garden. Outside sweeps land that shaped him—soil and sky, as far as the eye can see. This land can nourish you, and it can kill you.

In the 1500s, Spanish conquistadors trekked across this flat, treeless sea of grass so devoid of features they supposedly drove in stakes to mark their route. In the Llano Estacado, or "Staked Plains," air itself is pleasant one moment, deadly the next when "blue northers" howl down from the northwest.

"There's nothing between here and Canada except a barbed wire fence. And it's down," quip West Texans about the severity of winters in this region.

These things Ross learned from his native heath: watch closely; listen; expect the unexpected.

Ross Eugene Joplin was born in 1945 to Howell Russell Joplin and Catherine Shields Smalley Joplin in Amarillo, Texas, where Howell was serving as a pilot in the US Army Air Forces. After World War II, the family moved here, twenty-eight miles west of Lubbock, where Howell joined his father as partner at Levelland Grain Elevator.

Now, as then, Levelland comprises modest neighborhoods, a small downtown, and rows of corn and cotton stretching from back doors to the horizon. Such crops demand hard work, a custom Ross learned early.

"As a teenager, I'd start chopping cotton at 6:30 a.m. in summer and it would be 65 degrees. By 10 a.m. it would be one hundred. It's that kind of work that makes you want to go to college," he comments.

In his spare time, he hunted and played sports: football, basketball, baseball, and track for the Levelland High School Lobos.

"I had a little bit of speed and a whole bunch of anticipation of plays and could keep my head in the game pretty well," he recalls.

Parents, teachers, coaches, employers, and later the Army taught him this: *Do Your Job*. It became his life's guiding philosophy.

Ross entered Texas Tech University in Lubbock, as a financial administration major. He enjoyed the campus atmosphere, including the beauty of co-eds in an era when college women still "dressed up" for classes. He smiles.

"They would *not* go to class without doing their hair and putting on a full dose of makeup. They always looked 'to the nines.' I guess they felt competition was a little stiff," he says.

After graduating in 1967, Ross enlisted for Officer Candidate School. In basic training at Fort Dix, New Jersey, he noted especially the marksmanship of soldiers from rural America.

"We had all grown up with firearms," he recalls. "It was just natural."

After completing OCS at Fort Benning, Georgia, Second Lieutenant Joplin arrived in Vietnam in mid-January 1970. As XO (executive officer) and pay officer for Alpha, he flew out to the field for the first time to pay the men.

"They had shot and killed a Viet Cong and his body was laying there. The platoon leader and his squad leaders were looking at maps. A *mama-san* came up with a piece of cardboard and covered the man's body. There was no emotion on that woman's face. And no emotion from anybody else," he remembers.

In his clean fatigues, Ross felt out of place among men who had been "crawling around in the mud. Beards. Filthy," he recalls.

He soon looked the same. Assigned in February as 2nd Platoon leader, Ross arrived at Alpha's day laager and asked Mike Menser, 2nd Platoon sergeant serving his second tour in

Vietnam, if they could talk in private. Settling in nearby shade, Ross looked Menser in the eyes.

"Tell me what I need to know, Sergeant," he said.

Menser was startled, he recalled later. Many new "butter bars" arrived with a swagger and a big mouth. Not this one. Mike talked; Ross listened. They walked over to the men, who sized up the new "LT" in deadpan silence.

"I'm Second Lieutenant Ross Joplin. I'm an OCS graduate, and my job is to get you and me home in one piece," he announced. Then he told them he would follow the advice of Sergeant Menser "and yours. You know the ropes. I don't."

The men, silent, turned back to their rations, letters, and naps. As for Joplin, they would wait and see. At least he was not a "lifer." And he had said that magic word: home. This new "LT" might be all right.

Thus, he went to war with a role likely the toughest in infantry: platoon leader. In his book *Not a Gentleman's War*, drawn from his doctoral dissertation, Ron Milam, an infantry platoon leader and professor at Texas Tech University, asserts that most platoon leaders were cut from the same civilian cloth as their men in life experience, age, and wealth (or lack of it).

During his second day of leading 2nd Platoon, AK-47 rounds, fired from mountains across the Song Thu Bon River, whizzed by. Captain John Wilson tasked Joplin's platoon to destroy that position. Ross first called for artillery to soften up the enemy.

"Rounds out," a red leg forward observer soon radioed back.

"I got everybody on the horse, and we moved," Ross recalls. "About the time we hit high gear, the rounds started landing on the side of that mountain."

They found no bodies, but Ross inspected an NVA's foxhole design: a hole with a man-size recess in one side that increased chances of survival through air and artillery strikes.

Ross leaned on his men's advice while growing familiar with their characters, the countryside, and the habit of command. He bantered with them good-naturedly yet kept friendship at arm's length.

"You have to get close to the guys, but not too close. If something happens, I might not be able to make decisions that need to be made. I didn't want to have to bring that home," he says.

As for his relationship with Captain Wilson, the Texan and Alabaman got along well.

"I liked Wilson a lot. Had a quiet mannerism about him that gave you a sense of confidence. Wasn't trying to be Rambo; just trying to do his job. He was a good man. Still is a good man," Joplin says.

Ross now resembled all in his platoon: unshaven and filthy but affecting a single sartorial accent. In one Logue photograph, Ross sports a headband, as if in homage to the Comanches who once stalked the Staked Plains. Ross chuckles at the image.

"There I am, looking like I know what I'm doing," he remarks.

Monsoon passed. Temperatures and humidity hovered in the humid high 90s on 12 April when 4/31 launched Task Force West to locate the NVA. The battalion made its way to "the gap" between mountains above the Song Thu Bon, but the enemy, seemingly, had vanished. They were there, Ross knew. The Llano Estacado had taught him well.

"Growing up in West Texas, you look for things that aren't normal. A rabbit will stare at you with round eyes. Dark eyes. And you learn to look for things like that. If you spent a lot of time hunting, you start understanding," he says.

Indeed, the enemy was watching the Americans, perhaps even within feet. Meanwhile, matériel and manpower were traveling the Ho Chi Minh Trail into Quang Tin Province. In late April, NVA forces launched another spring–summer attempt to wrest away the province.

Death came in firefights large and small, even man-to-man, above and below ground. One day, Joplin noticed movement along a trail intersecting the Son Thu Bon. To reach the river unobserved, a recon platoon threaded through a ravine Ross describes as "dark and covered, an ideal place for ambush."

"The next day we hitched up our horses and literally ran back in there, a half of a mile," he says.

The platoon reached the north side of the river and entered "a small village of old women. Some chickens. Rough-looking people," Ross says.

Captain Wilson ordered him to scout a footpath meandering from the village. Ross and Menser exchanged worried looks.

"We knew this wasn't going to be patty cake," Ross says of a trail as a likely site for an enemy ambush.

Along the footpath, they spotted a head above elephant grass. Joplin raised his rifle, but the Vietnamese ducked into a hole. They approached warily, tossed grenades down the hole, then called Captain Wilson.

"He said, 'I want you to go in.' Menser volunteers. I said, 'Mike, you know what you're getting into?' And he said, 'Yeah.'"

"He goes in feet first with his M16. I'm on the opposite end of the hole. In a few seconds I hear a muffled gunshot, maybe two. Then I heard Menser's weapon on automatic. Dirt flies, then here comes Mike. He says, 'That MF just tried to kill me!'

"I start to laugh. We're in this football game for keeps, and I said, 'What did you *think* he's going to do?' You're deadly serious, but your comrade is safe and he comes out with that and you can't help but laugh."

ON 18 APRIL, THE DUST OFF ASCENDED WITH MONDO AND other wounded. Ross turned back to his men, who were seething in rage. Villagers *they* were protecting, fighting the enemy for *them*, aided the VC and NVA. Such turncoats, they believed, either planted the booby trap or knew of it.

"Without naming names, we had a machine gunner who literally wanted to go into Hiêp Dúc and kill people. I had to physically restrain him. And no one helped me," Ross recalls. The former football player tackled the gunner, while screaming at others to stand down. He knew he was fighting not one man, but two. The other was Second Lieutenant William Calley.

Ross fought to prevent a tragedy like that of 16 March 1968, when Calley's platoon of 198th LIB murdered more than 300 unarmed civilians at the village of My Lai. Calley was convicted in a trial at Fort Benning, Georgia, and restricted to house arrest. The incident sickened the nation and contributed to the rise of the epithet "baby killer," spat at any American soldier in uniform.

The gunner relented. Tension eased. The words "Hiêp Dúc" would not be written in blood alongside those of My Lai.

Ross caught his breath, then roared at his platoon: "We are *not* going to go to court in Fort Benning, Georgia! Is that clear?" Silence. A few mumbled, "Yes, Sir." Others turned away without a word. All continued on to LZ Siberia.

"The machine gunner calmed down. We never got along after that," Ross said.

Soon he flew to 91st Evacuation Hospital in Chu Lai to find Mondo heavily sedated.

"His eyes were open, but he didn't know I was there," Ross says. Neither Ross nor any whom Jim and I interviewed know of Mondo's ultimate fate.

At Alpha's stand-down on 28 April, Ross was ready not to carouse but to cook. His father had sent him ingredients to prepare dishes of the Lone Star State's beloved blended cuisine, "Tex-Mex." Ross began soaking beans overnight for the next day's meal preparation.

The Tex-Mex meal, perhaps the first in Chu Lai, was not to be. The next day Ross left his beans soaking to return to battle. As it had a year ago, 2nd NVA Division launched its spring offensive.

On 5 May, with 2nd Platoon leading the company, Alpha pointed north of Hiêp Dúc to its destination, Million Dollar Hill, where the enemy was dug into its base. Wilson selected 2nd Platoon to lead the attack across expansive rice paddies—a flat, open ground to the foot of the mountain.

First artillery was to hit the enemy. Elsewhere, however, the decision was made not to fire because of the proximity of ARVN forces, Ross recalls. Someone, likely an artillery ("red leg") forward observer on his first day in the field, did not cancel the fire mission called in to artillery on LZ West.

"I tell everybody to pull off their rucks, that we're going to wait until the artillery stops. I step in front of the platoon, about 100 feet. All of a sudden two rounds come right over my head from LZ West and splash down out there, too close. I knew right then we were in trouble," Ross recalls.

He sprinted toward his RTO as rounds screamed down, each packing 15 pounds, 9 ounces of TNT.

"I took the handset and was hollering 'cease fire' instead of 'check fire.' And the next rounds that came in hit me and killed this boy."

Ross was blinded and in agony from what appeared to be a serious wound in his left leg. Still he continued barking orders "like a wounded dog. I reach up and grab that rucksack, and realize that the frame and the radio were cut to pieces," he relates of the RTO equipment.

After ten rounds, "friendly" fire ceased. With limited vision, Ross saw his left leg was a bloody mass of meat, metal, and cloth. "Doc" Philip Pruett was working on him with "a worried look; the kind of look that if you're the one getting worked on, it's not going to help anyway."

Despite protests from Pruett and others, Ross gritted his teeth, walked to a medevac, and eased onto the metal floor. Nearby on the floor lay one boot.

"Had a foot in it. I knew who had been killed," he remarks.

At LZ Hawk Hill, headquarters of 196th LIB, medics rushed him into triage where a surgeon saw that the leg wound was an impact of the flesh and bone of another person. At 91st Evacuation Hospital, surgeons cleaned and treated Ross's wounds, including that of his right eye, through which he saw only a trace of light.

His sight returned. His wounds healed. Ross went on R&R in late May. His six months in the field fulfilled, he returned to LZ West to serve as night duty officer, then as S3 for battalion air assets.

THE TEXAN LEFT VIETNAM IN DECEMBER 1970. IN LUBBOCK, he stepped off the plane to see a friend with a welcome-home present—a six-pack of Coors beer. Ross spent his first night in Texas in a Lubbock motel room, alone with his Coors and his thoughts.

The next day, he borrowed his friend's car and drove the final twenty-eight miles home, reveling in the "breathing room" of land and sky. Splendid in his Class A uniform, with Combat Infantry Badge, Purple Heart, two Bronze Stars, and airborne wings, Ross stepped into his dad's granary and whipped off his service cap. There stood a customer, discussing with his father the price of milo.

"Dad looked up and saw me and kind of smiled. When they got through doing business, he said, 'Mr. So and So, this is my son, Ross. He just got back from Vietnam.' The man said, 'Glad to meet you,' and turned and walked out. Dad said, 'I don't think he realized that you had *just* got back from Vietnam.'"

And with that, Howell Joplin grabbed his son in a bear hug. They drove home. His mother wept. Her son was home, whole and safe.

Ross spent much of his career in Houston in the housing industry and insurance and printing businesses. He worked hard, holding himself and his employees to his three-word mantra: "Do your job."

He and his first wife had two daughters. In 1990, he married Nancy Musselwhite, a Levelland native. When both were ready to retire, they came home.

Today, Nancy creates exquisite quilts in her home studio. In his home library, Ross dips into tomes about Vietnam's long and troubled past. To him, his own history with the country is clear.

"I was glad then that I was doing what I was doing, and now happy that I did it. I would really hate to think I had to do it again, or would hate to think that my grandchildren would have to live through something like that. But it was certainly an experience that I wouldn't take anything for," he remarks.

He and LTC (ret) Mike Menser of Sandy, Utah, stay in touch. Otherwise, he'd had no contact with other Alpha soldiers until Jim Logue called.

Of his service in Vietnam, he says much of it was simply waiting: "I can tell my war stories in five or six minutes. The rest of the time I was getting ready for, or watching out for, or trying to keep people from getting us. Ninety percent of the time the boredom can be the killer. It *can* do you harm."

As we leave, Ross and Nancy step outside with us into the afternoon's sunshine and urge us, with Southerners' ubiquitous invitation, to "come back and see us." In West Texas, they mean it.

THAT NIGHT, A "BLUE NORTHER" SWEPT DOWN THE PLAINS, spreading ice and snow across the Llano Estacado. Far north, winter's white blanket also covered a small Minnesota town, where 5 May each year brings sorrow to a family and a former fiancée.

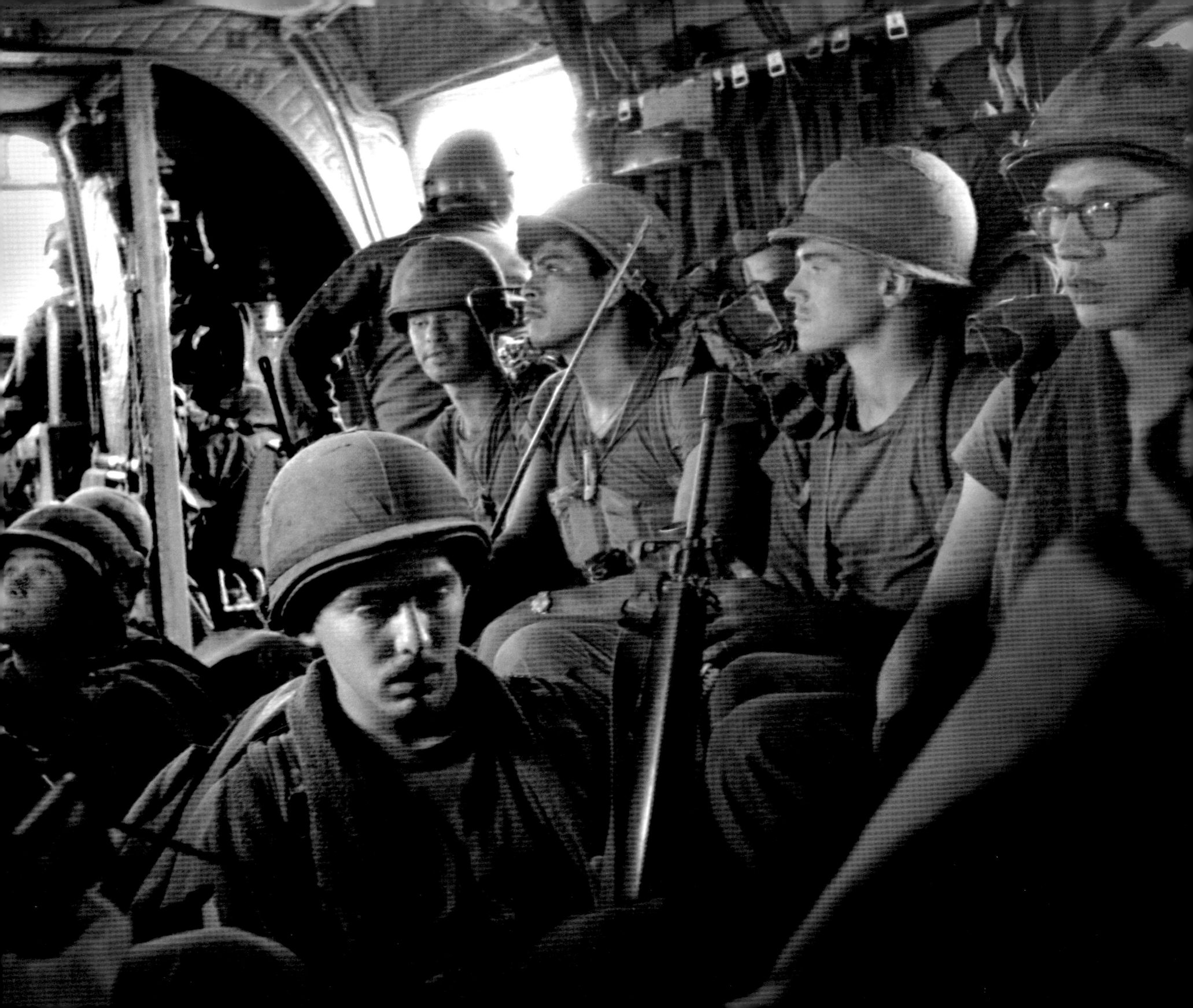

Chapter 9

I Haven't Taken My Rifle off Safety

Sergeant Duane Arvid Peterson (KIA)

IF HE WERE THE SAME AT HOME AS IN VIETNAM, HE WOULD be reserved and would tend to stand apart. Friends, however, found him genial and an excellent raconteur.

"Duane was not unfriendly; he was just extremely quiet. When you could get him into a conversation, he was a lot of fun. But he was kind of off to himself a little bit," recalls Robert Scott of Virginia Beach, Virginia, who served with Duane in 2nd Platoon.

Duane often stepped away and sat alone with his thoughts, and with good reason.

He was smitten.

Before he left his hometown of Isanti, Minnesota, population 679, in 1970, a young local woman named Diane Nelson had said "yes" when he asked for her hand. He was a lucky man. Diane's heart matched her beauty, those who knew her say. Her engagement photograph in a local newspaper portrays a young woman of fair, flawless complexion, her blonde hair perfectly coiffed, and with bright eyes and a smile to turn a man's knees to jelly.

In July 1970, she was to meet Duane on R&R in Hawaii, where they were to marry and spend their honeymoon beside the lap of the ocean. By May, Duane was counting every minute until their wedding.

In Vietnam, it's likely Duane felt no less crowded in his two-man hooch than he did at home. His father, Arvid, had bought an abandoned summer kitchen and expanded it into a one-bedroom home for himself and his bride, Clarice Linder Peterson. Eventually, the household swelled to seven children: Duane, Darrell, Darlene, Deanna, Debbie, Donald, and Dean. Area families, Clarice says, often use alliterative naming customs.

It is to this same home where she welcomes Jim and me on a summer morning. We sit at her kitchen table with her daughters, Deanna Hanson and Darlene Ewart, and son, Dean, who was a toddler during the Vietnam War.

In Duane's childhood, the Peterson family awoke early each day. All were hard workers, an example Arvid set. The son of a Swedish immigrant, Arvid was a World War II veteran, founder of Peterson Concrete Company, and chief of Isanti's volunteer fire department.

The girls helped Clarice while the boys worked with dad, their young stomachs hungry for mom's cooking: her chicken chow

Left: David Flynn, foreground, and others fly to the field aboard a Chinook on 29 April 1970 to halt the 2nd NVA Division. The flight cut short the company's stand-down in Chu Lai.

mein and homemade donuts and bread pudding. Clarice's cooking, work, and sports sculpted Duane's six-foot frame. So did long walks; after football practice at Cambridge–Isanti High School, Duane hitchhiked home, often walking the entire six miles.

In winter, he zoomed across glistening Minnesota snow aboard snowmobiles Arvid sold, specializing in the Scorpion brand. The family enjoyed competitions at Rum River Track during snowmobile season, which may span three to seven months, depending on snowfall, Dean says.

Duane graduated high school in 1964 and, with brother Darrell, entered St. Cloud Technical College to train as a machinist. After completing courses, Duane returned to work in Isanti, where he spent leisure time with friends, such as Douglas Nelson (no kin to Diane).

"He and I were alike. We had a good time, drank some beer, never got rowdy," remarks Nelson, a US Air Force veteran, who still lives in Isanti. "When I think of Duane, I remember one day we were in a bar and he started singing 'Pop a Top (Again),'" he recounts of the song Jim Ed Brown made famous in 1967.

Duane at this time was also dating Diane, two years his junior. The family doesn't remember when the couple became engaged, but they grew to love her, too, and found her temperament much like Duane's: "Very quiet, reserved," Darlene says. A teller at Cambridge State Bank, Diane often lunched with the Petersons.

Soon after their engagement, Duane was drafted, likely in late summer or early fall 1969. His timing could not have been worse. He was in infantry AIT on 1 December 1969, when the first Vietnam-era draft lotteries were conducted.

In a nationally televised drawing, an official extracted capsules, one by one, from a clear glass container. Each capsule contained a slip of paper with a draft number assigned to one day of the year. Men whose birth dates were assigned lower numbers, one to 195, were drafted in the order they were drawn. The large container was nearly empty when the official broke open a capsule and announced the number of Duane's birth: one in the

high 300s. Had he not already been in training, Duane would have married Diane and perhaps never left Isanti.

He wrote several letters home during basic and AIT training at Fort Campbell, Kentucky, and from NCO School at Fort Benning, Georgia. They read like his personality: informative and friendly, but brief. He came home on 30-day leave in December 1969, then was to return to Benning before a flight to Vietnam.

"He said, 'I'm not going back,'" Darlene remembers. "He had gone over and talked to Grandma Peterson. He told her, 'I cannot shoot anybody.' She told us that she prayed with him and that he had accepted Jesus."

He changed his mind soon thereafter and decided to go. First, though, he purchased a new Scorpion Super Stinger. Manufactured in Crosby, Minnesota, the sleek vehicle zoomed across snow upwards of fifty miles per hour. With thoughts of the next winter's snow, Duane parked his Scorpion and reported for duty.

By 9 February 1970, he arrived in monsoon-soaked Vietnam and was assigned as a squad leader in Alpha's 2nd Platoon. Perhaps he had neither more nor less trouble than those around him in adjusting to war. The man who told his grandmother he couldn't shoot anyone also mourned for the tattered, shattered lives of civilians.

"In one of his letters, he did tell me that it broke his heart to watch the little children eating out of garbage cans," Darlene remarks.

In a letter dated 15 April 1970, he hoped to calm his family's fears with a deft use of the word "safe": "You keep asking me if I'm in a safe place and have I been in any fighting yet. Well, one place is as safe as the next over here, and I haven't taken my rifle off safety yet. Haven't fired a shot."

Surely he was also corresponding with his betrothed, who often sent him letters and food packets, including his beloved peanut butter. Even his future mother-in-law wrote.

Meanwhile, Duane fit in well, says squad member Greg Moeggenberg of Mount Pleasant, Michigan.

"When he got there, he was really cool. Even though he was

an E5 he didn't start throwing his weight around. He hung back and he learned, which is really smart," Greg remarks.

"He was smart enough to ask questions and to listen to the older guys," recalls another squad member, Roger Marksch of Delaware, Ohio.

Few incidents occurred in winter and early spring as Alpha searched for the enemy, hoping AK-47 gunfire or 82mm mortars would not find them. A booby trap did, Duane noted in a letter dated 20 April 1970, referring to the wounding two days earlier of five in 2nd Platoon. He wrote: "The worst I've seen was what happened the other day when the point man tripped a booby trap and five G.I.s were wounded."

Thus far, engagements with the enemy were few and small. He wrote: "When we do get into it, we do most of the shooting before they even have a chance. And like I said, I haven't fired a shot yet."

Perhaps he wrote Diane on 28 April when Alpha arrived for stand-down in Chu Lai. The respite, however, lasted only a day before the company raced back to the field to block the advance of 2nd NVA Division. From LZ West, choppers lifted Alpha into the field northwest of Hiép Dúc.

That night Duane, like everyone footsore and exhausted, settled into his night laager. At 11 p.m. he was either asleep or pulling his two hours of guard duty, staring into the black night as the calendar turned from 4 to 5 May and marking his 85th day in Vietnam. Likely he was thinking of two dates: July in Hawaii, when he would marry Diane, and 9 February 1971, when he would "sky up" and return to his cold, clean, snowy country, glistening white in winter sun.

Thirteen hours earlier, it was morning in Isanti when Clarice sat at her kitchen table and began her letter:

May 4, 1970

Hi Son:

Monday Forenoon, 10 o'clock. I'm going to get a few lines off to you. Weather is fair, going to be about 65 today. Wind is always cold.

Looking out her kitchen window, Clarice watched little Dean in Duane's new snowmobile, pretending to drive. She mentioned it in the letter, and continued:

I guess Diane is going to send you some film & Darlene got some Lipton soup & orange drink. I'll get some cookies made to send you . . .

I hope you are fine & haven't had any more Booby traps or anything like that. They won't send you guys to Cambodia now, will they? I hope not. I hope they start sending you guys home pretty soon . . .

Hope this finds you OK & be careful now [don't] take any chances. Remember we love you and miss you very much. God bless you. Write often, please.

Love always
Mom, Dad & Kids

Time in Vietnam oozed like muck in rice paddies. If Duane were home, May to July would seem to pass as quickly as any two turns of calendar pages. In Vietnam, however, days lingered as long as Minnesota winters.

That morning of 5 May 1970, the Virginian Robert Scott carried an M79 grenade launcher. So did another soldier Scott remembers only as "Fly," who was returning to the rear for special training. Scott recalls:

We decided that we couldn't let him take the M79 back; it was too valuable a weapon. He was going to have to trade weapons with somebody, so he traded with Peterson. There was a vest that Mike Roberts had stolen from a Marine somewhere, mesh vest, and it had all these little pockets where you put all your rounds.

When you moved out everybody had a position, almost like on a football team. You have a point man. You have a slack man. And then you have the radioman and the gunners. And you usually had one 79 in front and one 79 in back, and we used to switch off every day.

So I said to Peterson, "It's my turn to walk up front." He said, "No, I'm walking up front today." I said, "We ought to do

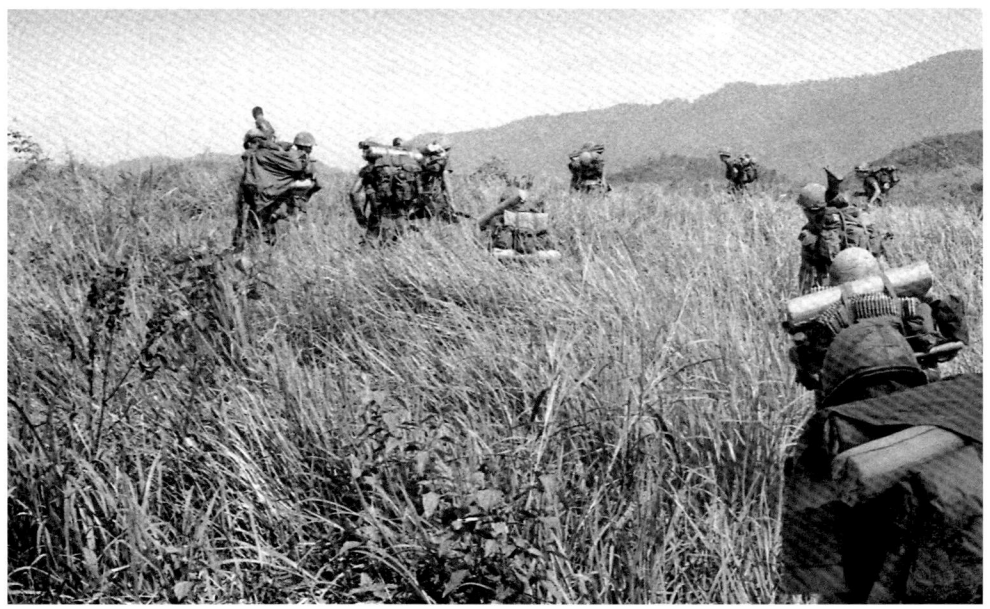

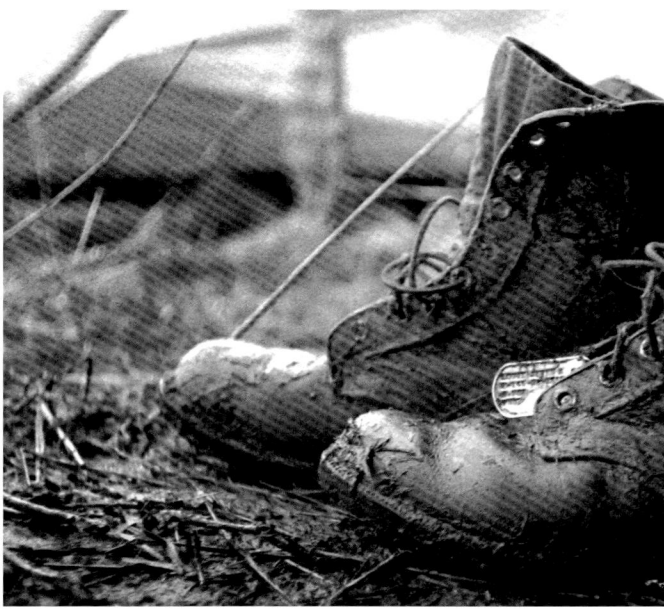

On 8 May 1970, these soldiers hump equipment toward battle. Soldiers carried seventy or more pounds in rucksacks, along with extras including additional ammunition for M60 machine guns.

To help with body identification, soldiers wore two dog tags: one around their necks, another in a boot.

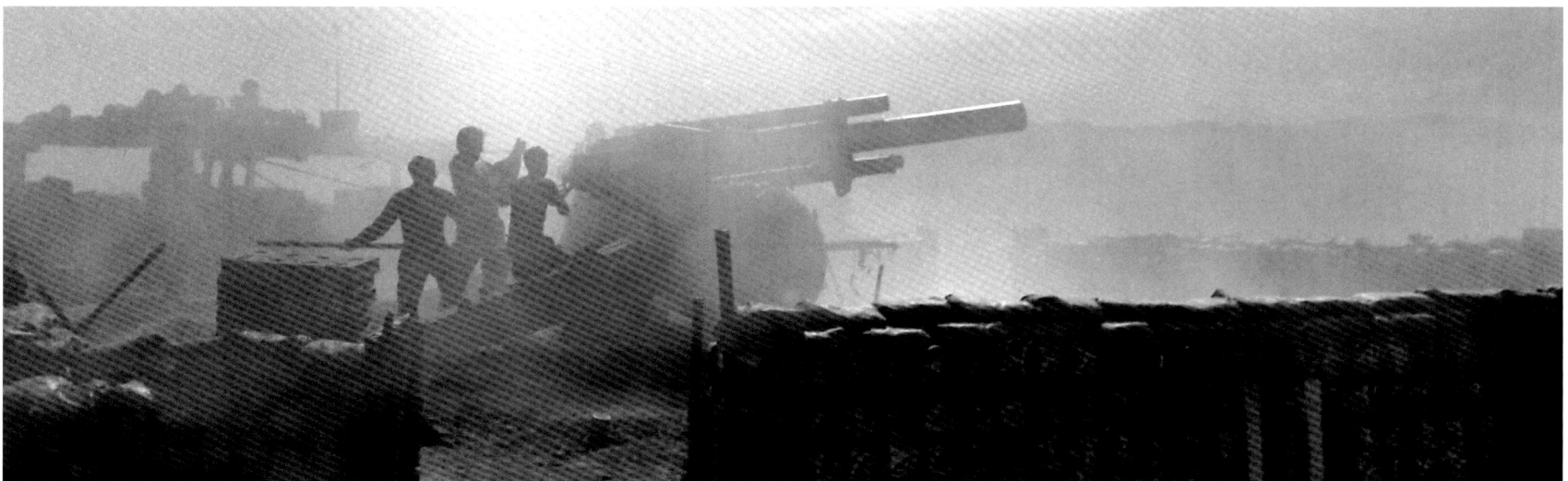

On LZ West, 155 mm guns provide supporting fire for 4th Battalion soldiers in the field.

this the way we have it laid out. By our normal routine I should be walking first." He said, "No, I want to go first." So I said, "All right." We all lined up and walked through the jungle.

When they stopped, Second Lieutenant Ross Joplin gathered his platoon around him. Scott remembers:

Lieutenant Joplin said, "You're really going to have to have your stuff together today because something is going to happen. This is going to be bad." And the rumor was that they had a machine gun up at the top of the hill waiting for us. We were supposed to go through the jungle, then there was a couple hundred yards of elephant grass before you got to a stream. We would cross the stream, and then there was the hill right on the other side. It wasn't a very tall hill, thirty or forty feet. We were supposed to get to the edge of that grass and call in artillery.

An artillery forward observer, on his first day in the field, called coordinates of the enemy to artillery on LZ West. When shells exploded beyond them, the platoon would burst from the wood line and race towards the enemy.

Meanwhile, men smoked nervously and drank from canteens. At any moment, high-explosive rounds, each packing fifteen pounds of TNT, would come screaming above and beyond Alpha and strike the enemy. Duane gripped his M79, knowing that over the next hill the rest of his life waited: Hawaii, Diane's soft hand in his, repeated vows, and, next February, his ultimate deliverance from monsoon to Minnesota snow.

And then hell rained down in eight short rounds from LZ West.

Scott recalls, "I'll never forget the sound of those rounds coming in. We'd been mortared plenty of times before. But this was a freight train and it was deafening before it even hit you."

As the first shell descended, Scott dived for cover beside a fallen tree, along with Jerry Jones, a Texan who had transferred into the company from 1st Division, and Jim Edwards, a sergeant from Kinston, North Carolina.

"The rounds had started coming in and they were screaming up at the front of the column," Scott recalls. "Our radioman, Jim Flatt, got the radio blown right off his back. So we had a lot of trouble calling in to get them to 'check fire.' Finally we did and I remember putting my head up. Jerry Jones' rifle was bent in half. His rucksack was torn in pieces. Flatt and a couple other guys were hurt."

Moeggenberg's ruptured eardrums upset his equilibrium, recalls Marksch.

"He was just chattering, not making any sense at all, just going around in circles. There were other guys hit. One was to the right and another to the left of me. I don't know how in the world I didn't get anything out of it," Marksch says.

Scott and others were surveying casualties when he stepped over what he thought first was debris. Then he looked again.

"I said, 'My God, it's a body.' There were no legs, just a torso and a head, face down. We didn't even know who it was. We found a helmet lying by the side. All of us had these line numbers written on our helmets and we picked up the helmet and it had a line number on it and I said, 'It's Kimball.'"

Then, to Scott's astonishment, there stood Robert Kimball, a popular, fun-loving Louisianian.

He came walking "right in the clearing. He says, 'Hey guys, how're you doing?'" Scott remembers.

Scott looked down again and recognized the corpse.

Casualties were identified in four ways. The first two methods involved dog tags (either worn around the neck or fastened in a boot shoelace). A third means was found around the waist: name and social security number penned on a small white rectangle of paint on the underside of the belt. Finally, a soldier's line number was written on his helmet cover. The underside of Duane's belt bore his name.

Likely, Peterson died instantly when a howitzer round set off his M79 grenades.

Back home, hours later, Diane Nelson awoke on 5 May for another day at the bank, perhaps lunch with the Petersons, and then home at night to write to Duane.

A few days later, a soldier and a Lutheran pastor knocked on the Petersons' door. Darlene, living in her own residence at the time, remembers: "It was on a Saturday morning and they said he was missing in action. It was pouring rain. My dad called. He was crying. I hardly ever heard my dad cry. He said, 'Can you come home?' I said, 'What's wrong?' He said, 'Just come home.'"

Darlene put her two small children in her car but couldn't get the vehicle started. She called her dad about the engine problem and asked again what was wrong.

"All he said was, 'It's Duane.'"

THE YOUNG SERGEANT'S REMAINS WERE RETURNED TO ISANTI and into the care of Strikes Funeral Home. Doug Nelson intended to wear his Class A Air Force uniform to the funeral.

"I couldn't fit into it," he recalls wryly. So, in civilian coat and tie, Doug attended the service at the funeral home, then joined the cortège to Isanti Union Cemetery. There, in a hard, spring rain, he watched as his friend was buried with military honors, including presentation of a folded American flag to Arvid and Clarice.

Doug stood with the Petersons and beside them, Diane, whose dreams of life with Duane died half a world away.

In days to come, the Petersons rarely saw her. They believe the Nelsons thought it best if she avoided contact with Duane's family. They understood.

Drawing from his last letter on 20 April, Duane had yet to fire his weapon. Perhaps, as he said to his grandmother, he may have killed no one in Vietnam.

Family members eventually put some 5,000 miles on Duane's snowmobile. Years later, Dean restored it and gave it to his brother, Donald.

Diane, they say, returned to work, even perhaps finding herself in the bank on that July day when she should have been standing by the sea, beginning the rest of her life with her soldier.

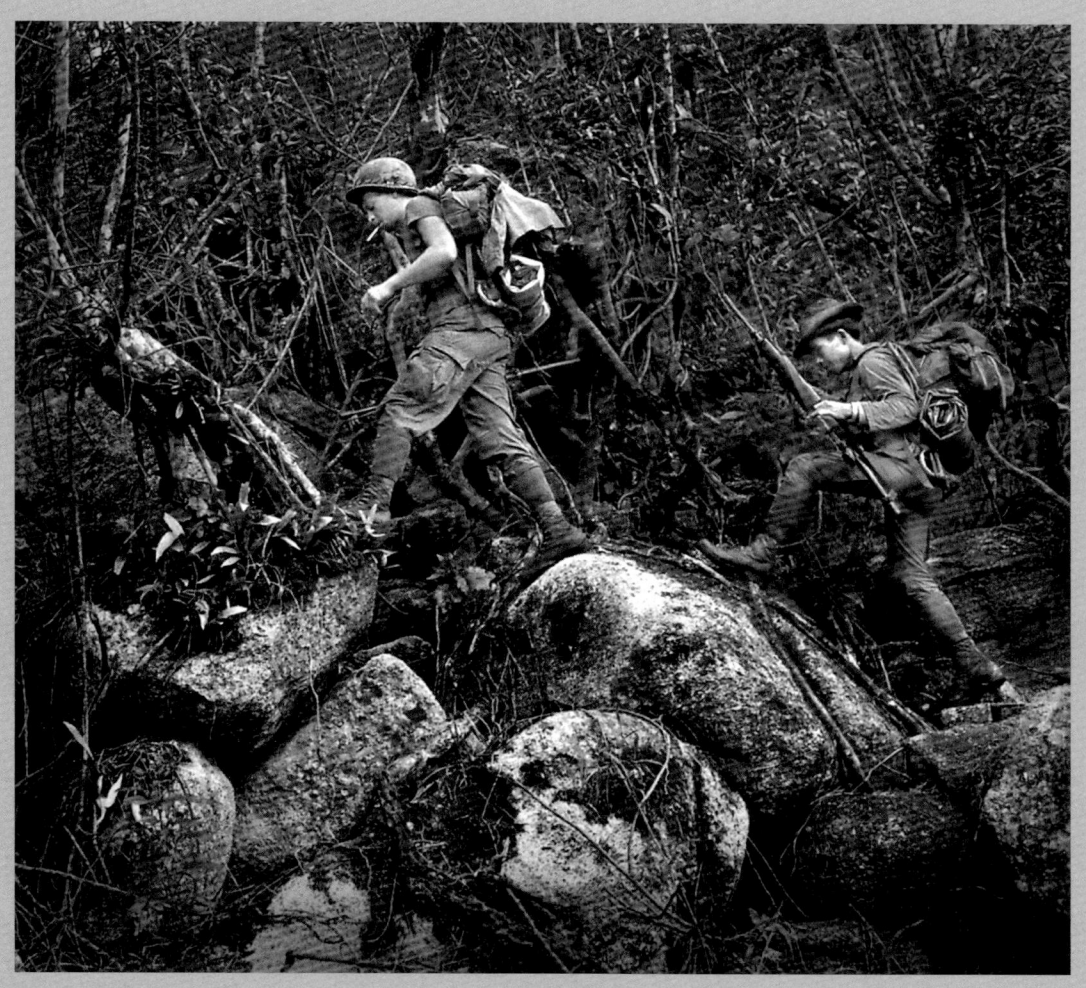

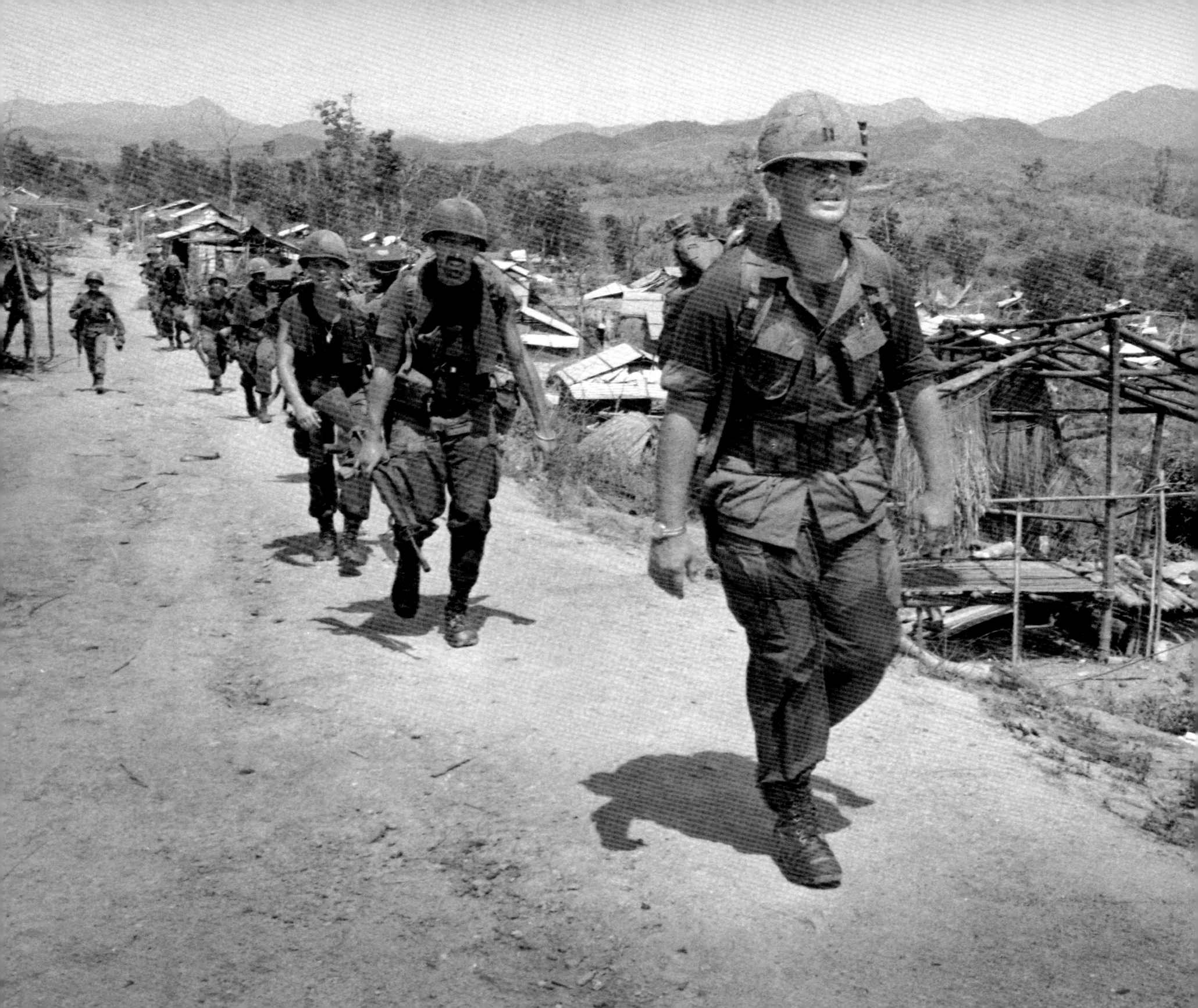

Chapter 10

I Do Not Know How I Am Alive

First Lieutenant Michael Keeble
Sergeant Donald Gary Kuzilla (KIA)

IN THE HOT SUN OF HIGH NOON, 14 MAY 1970, ALPHA TRUDGED into Hiêp Dúc village, filthy, hurting, hungry. With no resupply since 8 May, food in rucks consisted of mere crumbs and canteens were light with the last few sips.

Some ate while on the march. A *chieu hoi* (VC defector) had taught Edward Bachelor of Norfolk, Virginia, how to find snails in rice paddies. Another Virginian, Al Merryman of Fredericksburg, finally opened a can of yams his wife had sent him. She didn't know he despised the tuber; he kept the can in his ruck as a last resort. This was the last resort. He ate some and shared the rest.

"Those things tasted great," he recalls years later.

John Atholl Houchins III had known hunger. The West Virginia native who grew up in Tampa, Florida, quit school in the 11th grade and left home.

"I lived on streets, sleeping in my car a lot. Three or four of us guys would get together and rent a little house somewhere. We had the world by the tail, but it was beating us to death and we didn't even know or care," he recalls.

The "Summer of Love" siren song lured him to California where life, he quickly learned, was not all flowers, music, and sunshine.

"I couldn't find work. I was down to one hundred and seventeen pounds. I didn't know I was starving to death. Didn't care. I stayed in a crash pad that was run by the Hell's Angels. The drugs were free. The women were free. The good times were being bad," he remembers. Getting drafted, he said, probably saved his life.

Houchins' best friend in Vietnam, Kenneth Leavell, knew hunger, too. In 1969, the Santa Maria, California, native graduated high school and left home. He "survived a year with the flower children on the bank of a river, living off the land. Sleeping bag. Poncho. Fished, like Huck Finn," he says.

So Leavell enlisted, joining Alpha's 1st Squad, 1st Platoon in mid-April 1970. Soon he and Houchins were friends.

As Alpha reached the village, Jim Logue jogged to the front of the column, turned, and snapped his shutter release.

Left: Captain Wilson leads Alpha into Hiêp Dúc on 14 May 1970 after a four-day march without food. Resupplied, the company marched east and into an NVA ambush. One American, Donald Kuzilla, was killed.

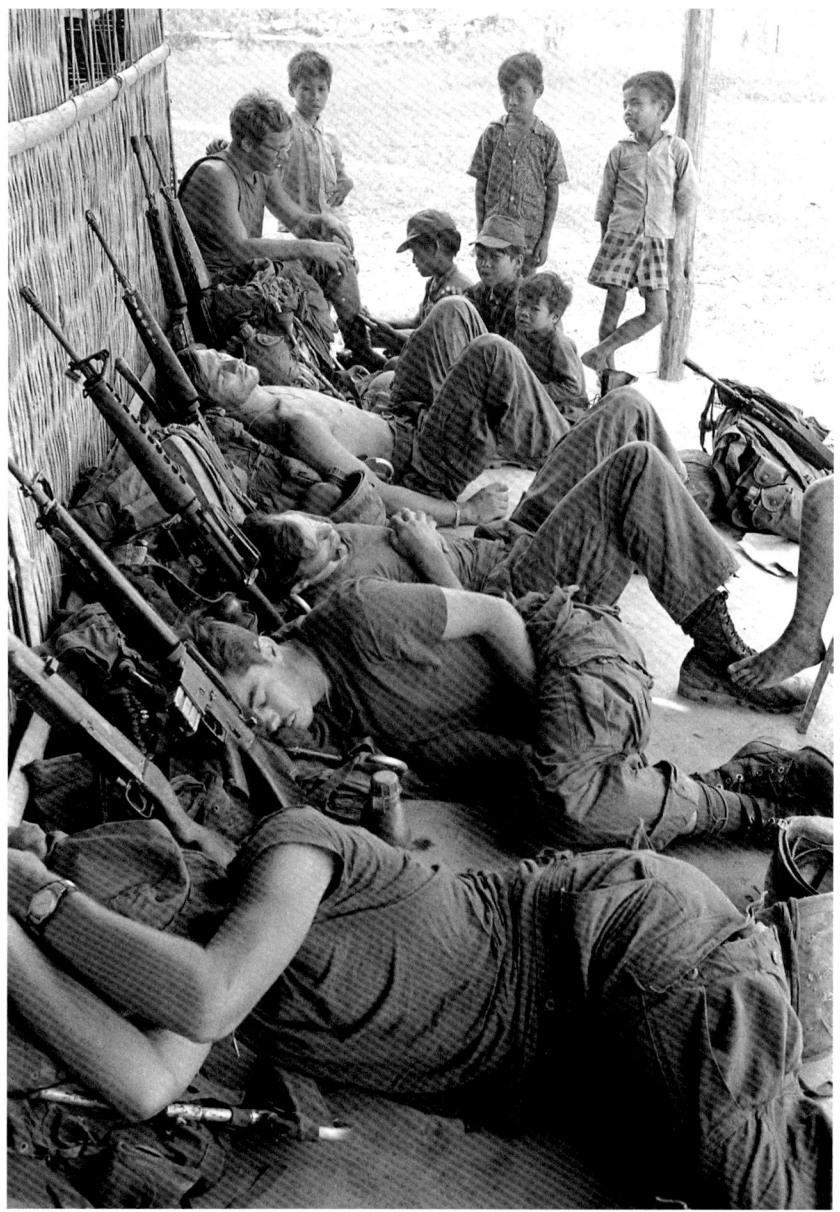

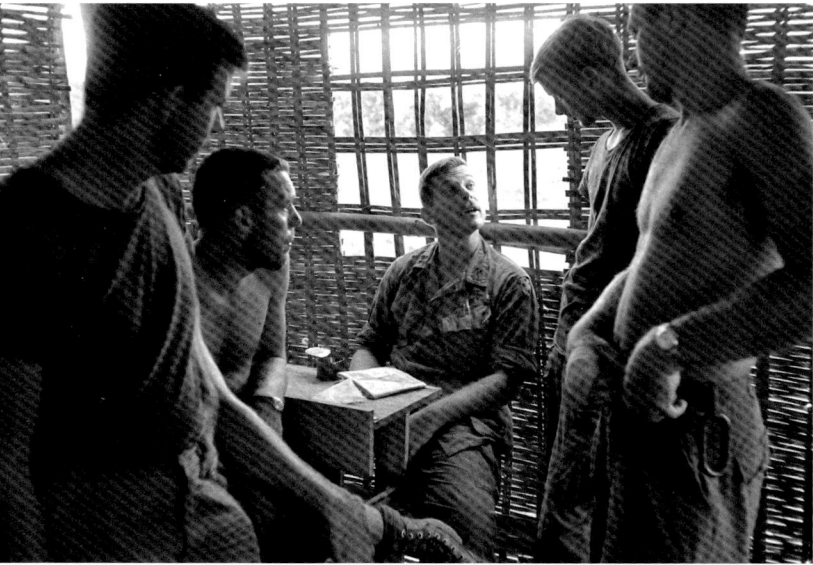

At this conference in Hiêp Dúc are Captain Wilson (back to window); Sergeant Perry Stemen and First Lieutenant Michael Keeble (right); and First Lieutenant Donald Pettit (seated). Man in foreground is unidentified.

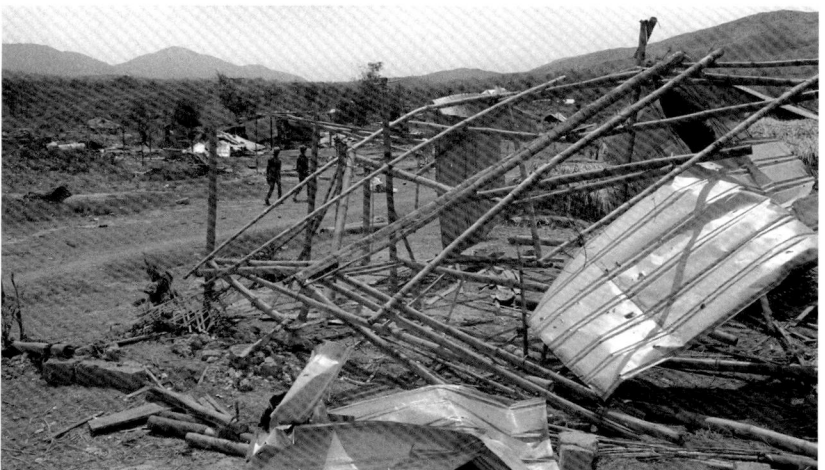

As soon as Alpha reached Hiêp Dúc on 14 May 1970, exhausted soldiers dropped and slept until resupply choppers arrived. They shared rations with villagers before "rucking up" again and heading east.

The NVA attacked Hiêp Dúc in late April 1970. They murdered several village leaders, took others prisoner, and destroyed structures including the American-built school.

The image reflects bright sunlight, a string of soldiers bent under rucks, and the soar of hills behind them. Leading all, Captain John Wilson, bone-weary as well, forces himself to walk tall, helmet low on his brow, the image of confidence and command.

So few remain. Two weeks of near-constant conflict have thinned "Alpha Battalion" to fewer than fifty.

All squint up at the sky, still empty of resupply choppers promised to be there at the company's arrival—another Army promise as empty as their stomachs. They sprawl into the first shade and soon sleep.

Logue, however, roamed the village, documenting scenes bearing descriptions from the 4/31 *Daily Staff Journal* of 10 May, concerning NVA destruction and murder of civilians:

> Of the 7 village chiefs and 14 hamlet chiefs in the Hiep Duc CFZ, 1 village chief . . . and two hamlet chiefs have been murdered. One other village chief and one hamlet chief have been severely wounded and medevacked. Two village security chiefs murdered. Many village officials missing. At least 50 civilians have been murdered . . .

Jim clicked away, documenting the damage. Faces of starving villagers peered from their hooches. The NVA also had confiscated food.

Soon, Jim, too, settled down with the sleeping soldiers, including "new guys" such as First Lieutenant Michael Keeble, new 1st Platoon leader. Keeble grew up in Fairfax, Alabama, a cotton mill village. At Auburn University, where ROTC was then required of all male students, he starred on the school's golf team until he graduated. In Vietnam, Keeble could judge distance not only in "klicks" but also in golf club choice.

"Shake-and-bake" Sergeant Donald Gary Kuzilla of Radford, Michigan, was spending his 75th day in country. Donald loved ROTC at Radford High School, ignoring sneers from classmates. No "cool guy" in that anti-war era wore military uniforms and "white sidewall" haircuts if they wanted to date.

"Girls *do* with guys who *don't*," went the wisecrack.

Richard Thimmig of Sparta, Illinois, believes Kuzilla volunteered for Vietnam "to see some action. He was a good guy, a nice guy. He wanted to be there," Thimmig recalls.

In the same platoon, PFC (Private First Class) James Neldner, a native of St. Francis, Wisconsin, grew up with a wrench in his hand. By age 16, this son of a World War II veteran and mechanic was following his father's profession.

SUDDENLY, SEVERAL AWAKENED, SENSING BEFORE HEARING helicopter rotors. Seconds after the bird landed, the men emptied it of C-rations, soft drinks, ammunition, medical supplies, and mail. They gulped down the C-rats, stuffed favorites into rucks, and left the rest to famished villagers.

Logue ate, then, in a wrecked schoolhouse, snapped a photo of Wilson informing his lieutenants of new orders he had received: to move north to a new AO (area of operations) and set up at least five ambushes. The lieutenants looked grim; the day had grown longer and more dangerous.

Rain had begun by 1610 when Alpha moved north in columns on both sides of a dirt road. Instead of hunger, now fear gnawed at bellies. Youngsters who usually scampered alongside departing troops had vanished. One boy tugged at Houchins' shirt.

"'GI, no go! No go!' he said," Houchins recalls. "I said, 'What do you mean?' He said, 'NVA.' So Gary [Stripp, squad leader] talks to Lieutenant Keeble. He gets on the horn to the CO and tells him that there's an ambush down the road and we should go a different way. Wilson says, 'We don't have time. Get your element moving.'"

Houchins stepped out as point man for Alpha, with Leavell as slack. Logue glanced back at a solemn barefoot boy beside the road, arms crossed. Understanding the portent of the boy's dark stare, Jim snapped his picture. All in Alpha who saw the photo echoed Logue: "He knew."

Houchins squinted into the downpour.

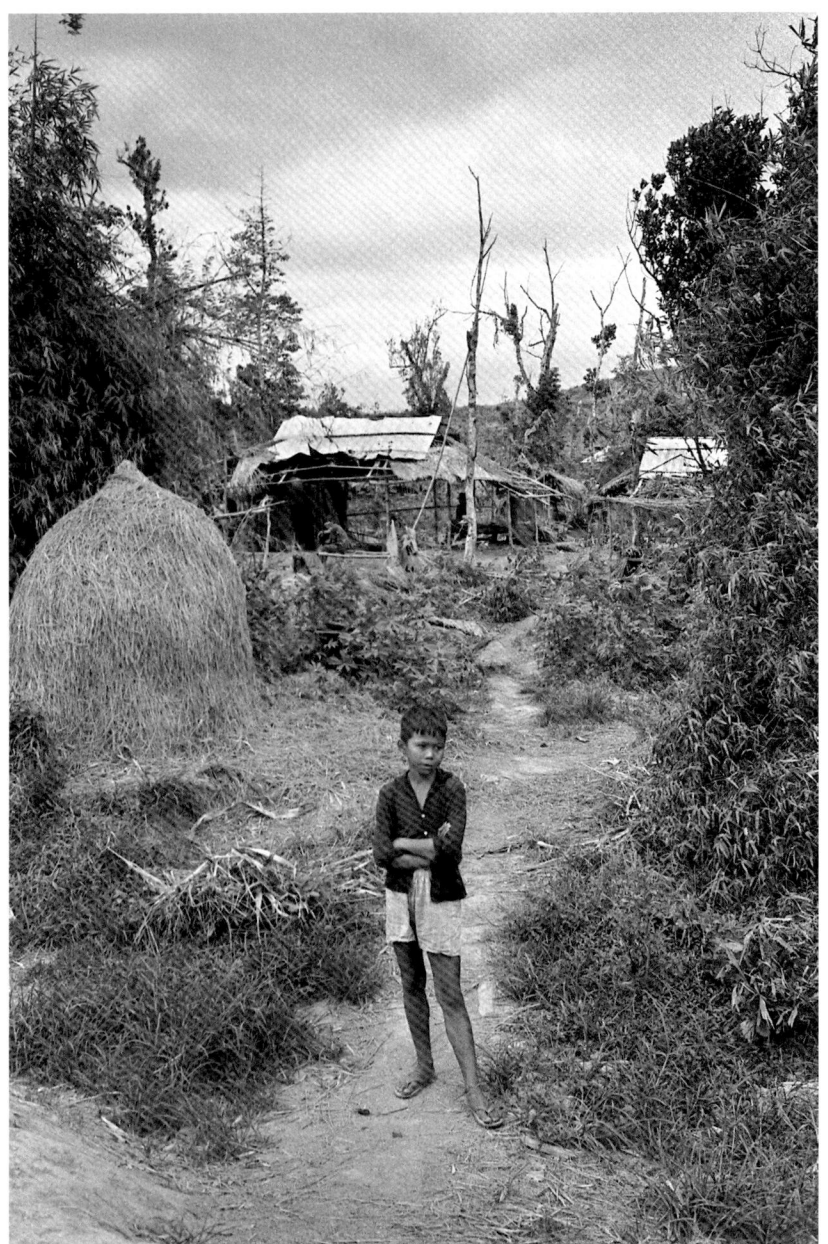

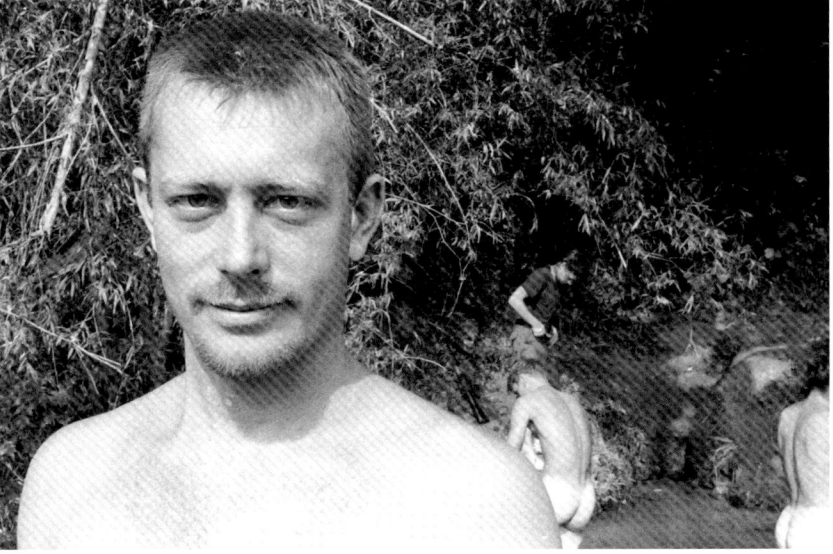

First Lieutenant Michael Keeble worked in a cotton mill and played on the golf team at his alma mater, Auburn University. Gravely wounded on 14 May 1970, he earned a Silver Star for his actions.

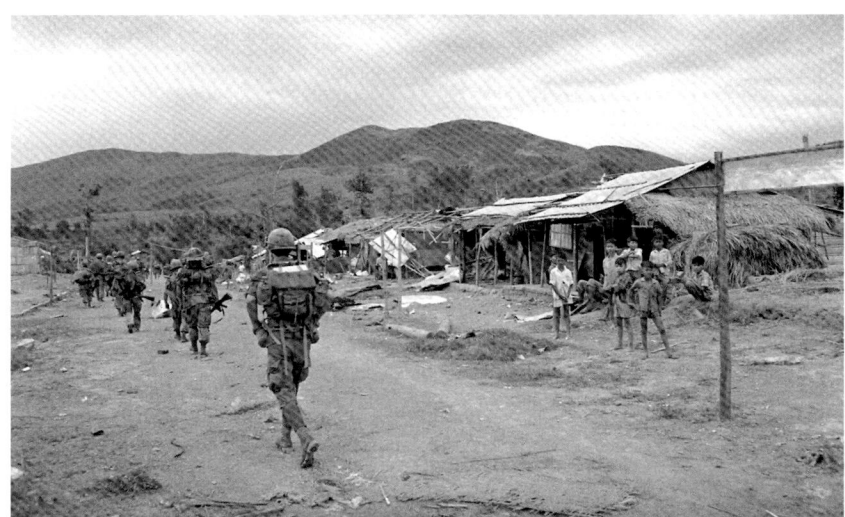

Leaving Hiêp Dúc, Logue snapped this photograph of a boy, arms crossed. "He knew," Logue and others said, of the NVA waiting in ambush up the road.

Alpha departs Hiêp Dúc in files along left and right sides of a road. Much of the village was damaged in an earlier NVA attack.

"You're looking ahead. You're looking down. You're looking up. You're looking left. You're looking right. You're looking everywhere because you don't know where it's coming from," he explains of walking point.

Another admired point man, Nate Donaldson, was near the front, too, as were Neldner, M60 gunner Thimmig, assistant gunner Dan Simmons of Glendora, California, an M60 gunner remembered only as "Laboo," and the latter's assistant, Kuzilla. Lieutenant Keeble walked in the middle of the platoon with his RTO. All scanned rice paddies to the west and a woods line to the east. All tensed for an eruption of gunfire.

It came in a sudden fury. Houchins recalls, "They turned loose on us with a machine gun from the other side of the rice paddies. So I rolled over off the trail and was returning fire and didn't know where to shoot."

Muffled by battle and rain, Keeble was shouting to his men when gunfire whizzed around 1st Platoon. All went to ground. Keeble dived behind a large rock.

Simmons, packing extra M60 ammo for Laboo, remarks, "We found a berm. Don [Kuzilla] found a spider hole. We ran out of ammo. I grabbed all the ammo from another assistant gunner. They were shooting RPG rockets at us."

Thimmig's M60 chattered back. Near him, Neldner and Kuzilla leapt into a small hole, while Laboo and Simmons jumped behind an adjacent berm.

Thimmig: "I just opened up. I figured, 'If I melt the barrel, I melt the barrel.'"

Neldner: "I remember Thimmig crying out, 'Get me some more ammo!' so I crawled back and went to every guy and took his ammo and I clipped it on just in time."

Neldner noticed Kuzilla popping up to shoot instead of raising his M16 just above the lip of cover to fire.

"I don't know where he learned that. I said, 'Get down! Don't get up! Get down!' Then he got hit."

Neldner screamed for a medic, who crawled up and quickly shook his head.

With Laboo low on ammo, Simmons scrambled to others, gathering belts of M60 rounds, and made it back to Laboo.

"He got one barrel red hot and started another," Dan remembers.

Simmons turned to Kuzilla.

"He was alive. I'm pretty sure he got it right between the eyes. He was breathing sporadically, so I held him up between my legs. In about fifteen minutes I felt him take his last breath. He just kind of heaved and that was it. So we decided to get out of there. I had Don's M16 and mine. When they wrote that Bronze Star thing up they had me coming out of the hole, two guns on my hip, shooting," Dan recalls. He shakes his head. "When I pushed myself up out of the hole, both of them just went off."

Leavell was lobbing M79 CS gas grenades towards the enemy, but the wind turned against them and "the gas was coming back on us," Houchins states.

Soon Stripp and his assistant gunner were wounded. Houchins grabbed each by one arm and "dragged them back where it was safe."

Leavell had left his M79 to help the wounded. With Houchins, he crawled back into fire, grabbed the weapon, then scrambled back.

More writhed from wounds. In front of Keeble, Michael Kangas lay in the open, unable to move because of a massive knee wound. Keeble knew the NVA wouldn't bother Kangas until someone came to his aid and then would kill both. Still, he and Leavell knew they had to go.

With rounds dancing around them, they dragged Kangas behind the boulder, where Philip "Doc" Pruett affixed a tourniquet above Kangas's knee.

Then Keeble slumped to the ground. An AK-47 round drove into his face like a sledgehammer blow, he remembers.

"Right here. It just tore through and came out," he says, pointing to the right side of his face, the line of the wound now thin but still visible from right ear to chin.

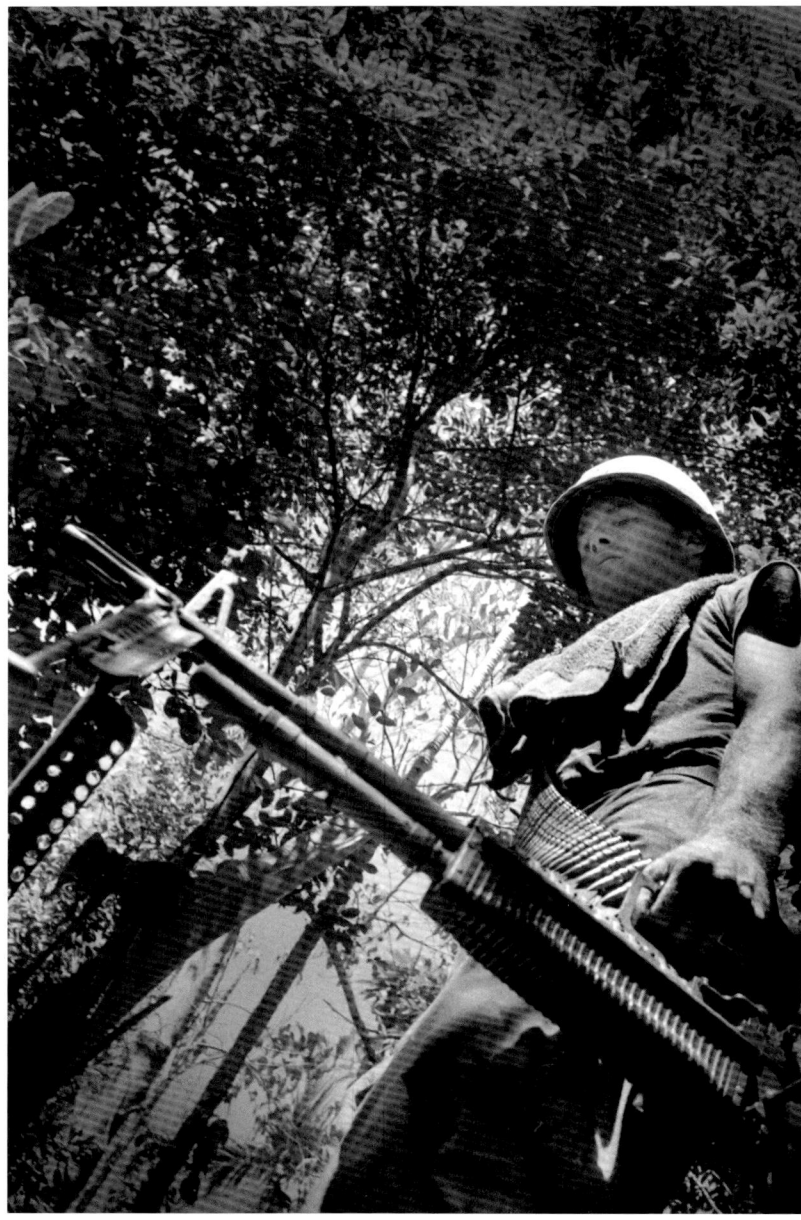

Richard Thimmig, a printer's son, provided much of his squad's firepower with his M60 machine gun. He earned a Bronze Star for bravery in action on 14 May 1970.

His head was pounding, "ringing like a gong. I thought: 'Well, I'm dead. It's over. I've got no will to live.'"

Keeble chuckles in recalling another thought as he lay, his life leaking away: "Oh, God, I hadn't been to church in ten years and it's too late now. Well, twenty seconds go by and I'm alive."

The enemy leapt from woodlands to deal Alpha a death blow. Already, 2nd and 3rd Platoons had formed a perimeter. Instead of sprinting to its safety, Simmons, Laboo, Neldner, and Thimmig turned to face the NVA.

"We knelt, shooting NVA soldiers crossing the trail on the run. It was more NVA than we ever saw at once during our whole tour," Neldner recalls in his handwritten account of the battle.

Jim Gregory, pilot of dust off #615 of 236th Medical Detachment and now of Roy, Washington, swooped down, enemy rounds thunking against his bird while Leavell loaded Kangas and Keeble. With five aboard, Gregory lifted off. It was 1720. In sheets of rain, a Cobra gunship swooped down, pouring fire into the enemy, a mere fifty yards from Alpha.

Laboo, Neldner, Simmons, and Thimmig were nearly out of ammo, with the NVA "coming after us about 100 yards back." In a deadly foot race, the four men leapt into the safety of the perimeter, Neldner recalls.

Firing sputtered out. Except for the pelting rain, silence settled over the fields. Men, muddy and soaked, drank from canteens, lit cigarettes, and waited for another attack. Meanwhile, Kuzilla's body still lay outside the perimeter.

"We tried to get our wits about us. We knew the day wasn't over. We had to move and set up a night laager. No one wanted to encounter the NVA again," Logue recalls.

Alpha pulled back east of the village. The next day, 4/31 *Daily Staff Journal* reported at 1225 that "Co A reports they have recovered the body of the US KIA of 14 May '70."

No one in the company, however, had recovered Kuzilla. To avoid enemy fire, someone gave two mama-sans a fifth of whiskey to bring him back. Kuzilla was lifted aboard a resupply to begin the journey home to Radford.

Keeble's recovery began with triage at LZ Hawk Hill, followed by surgery at 91st Evacuation Hospital in Chu Lai, post-op treatment at Camp Zama in Tokyo, then long weeks at Walter Reed Army Medical Center in Washington, DC. For weeks he took sustenance through a straw, underwent a tracheotomy, and battled a staph infection. On American Red Cross stationery, Keeble wrote his mother: "I do not know how I am alive. I was hit by a bullet slightly below the right ear and the bullet was removed from the right part of my neck. After I was shot, which felt like a brick hitting me at 500 mph, I thought I was going to die . . ."

Keeble was promoted to captain and awarded a Silver Star. The citation reads in part:

> With complete disregard for his personal safety, Lieutenant Keeble crawled forward . . . and pulled his fallen fellow soldier to safety . . . . Lieutenant Keeble maintained his strategic position and engaged the hostile element with several well-directed hand grenades . . . . He kept the enemy force pinned down

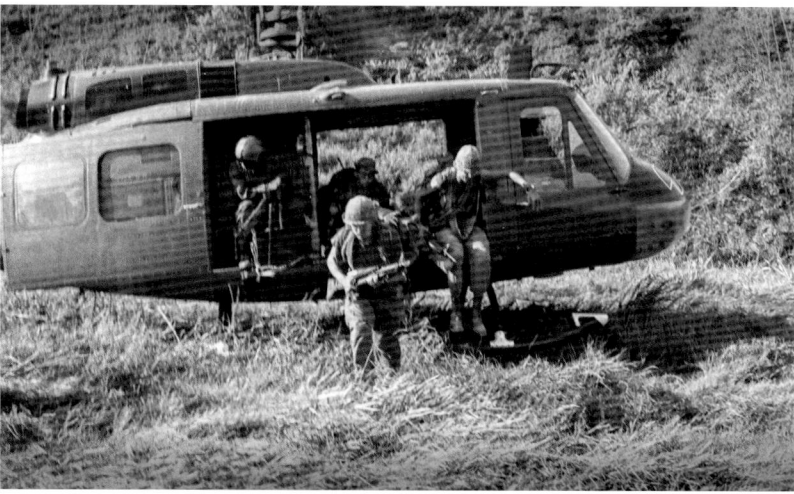

By summer 1970, LTC Thomas Breen, new 4/31 battalion commander, initiated "Eagle Flights." In these helicopter assaults, men hit the enemy quickly, then flew back to LZ West when a day's mission was completed.

while other friendly casualties were extracted and the remainder of the company moved against hostile emplacements.

Several others earned decorations that rain-soaked afternoon. Houchins, Leavell, Neldner, Simmons, and Thimmig received Bronze Stars with "V" devices (for valor).

Keeble, after nineteen months of recovery, considered remaining in the Army, but his injury gave him 40 percent disability for life. He spent a career at Delta Air Lines in Atlanta and in his free time played golf courses around the world.

For all in Alpha and for his Michigan friends and family, only memories remain of Donald Gary Kuzilla. Some are posted on tribute pages of a Vietnam Memorial internet site. Writes a relative, Laura Golden: "Oh, cousin, how I wish to have known you! The very subject of you brought such emotion from my dad. Even now, I well up at the thought of how much my dad would cry."

Classmate Katherine Helm Rose wrote of Donald as a serious ROTC leader with a great sense of humor: "I will remember you and your smile always, from our days at Radford High School and the Class of 1968."

Recalls another classmate, Tom Taepke: "We called him 'Kuzy.' He was my drill sergeant when I started ROTC."

On a misty, gray October day, Jim and I found Holy Sepulchre Cemetery in Southfield, Michigan, and wound along cemetery lanes beneath autumnal hues to find Kuzy's flat stone. Someone had placed beside it a small American flag and flowers. I wondered if any of Donald's classmates who had sneered at his ROTC uniform ever stood here and puzzled over the etched letters "SS" and "BSM" and "PH," for Silver Star, Bronze Star Medal, and Purple Heart, awarded posthumously.

If they learn the meaning of those letters, they may realize how one man in one day granted so many men life after war. On 14 May 1970, Sergeant Donald Gary Kuzilla, seventeen days short of his twentieth birthday, died in a ditch in the rain to grant the gift of longer lives to friends around him.

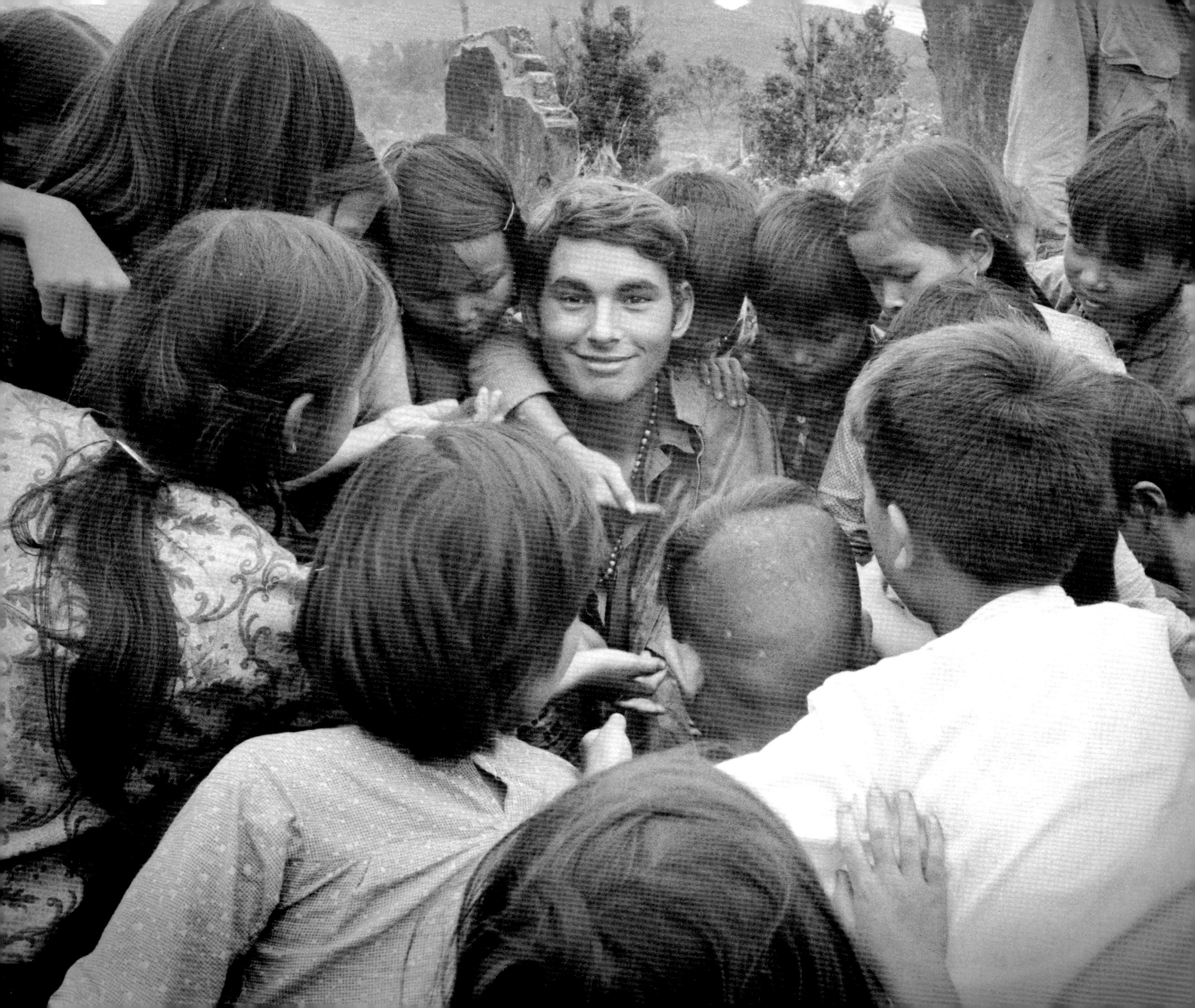

Chapter 11

That Was One Helluva Thing We Went Through

Specialist 4 Daniel Simmons
Specialist 4 William Powell

HE IS SPEAKING OF THE DAY DONALD KUZILLA DIED IN HIS arms when he falls silent, looks away, and pushes back his chair.

"Excuse me," Dan Simmons murmurs.

This big man, still strong from a life of hard, physical work, disappears down the hall of his home near Prescott, Arizona, where windows frame murals of desert and the distant peaks of Granite Mountain. Among the Alpha veterans we visited, Dan's is not the first home with views overlooking large swaths of countryside. The ghost trail of the Butterfield stage line, near which Dan spotted our car's approach earlier, is visible from the house.

"Sorry about that," he says when he returns, with an embarrassed chuckle. He sits and rubs roughly at his eyes with a tissue.

In his career, the Phoenix native specialized in constructing tall, concrete walls. The first he built after coming home was a mental mausoleum in which he locked up Vietnam forever.

Memory, however, seeps through even an iron will to forget.

Dan is speaking of 14 May 1970. He, hooch mate Bill Powell of Salem, Oregon, and the rest of Alpha were moving again, aware of reports of numerous enemy sightings. All hoped the afternoon portended an uneventful walk, but perhaps none more so than Bill, the son of a banker, and Dan, the son of a baker. Both are "short," Bill with four months and five days, Dan with three months and two days.

Dan was born in 1949 to Wallace Daniel Simmons and Lois Rowena Hicks Simmons. The family moved to Glendora, California, where Dan, by age 12, was working in the family business: Mrs. Simmons' Pastry Shops, founded by his grandfather, a World War I veteran.

Dan's was a boyhood of school, family, hot ovens, and Friday night lights. In autumn, he played lineman for the Glendora High School Tartans, then showered and by 11 p.m. joined his parents, an older brother, and two sisters at the bakery for work through the night.

Left: These youngsters have just "cleaned out" Dan Simmons of candy. Note his love beads necklace. Many GIs wore two necklaces: love beads and the cross.

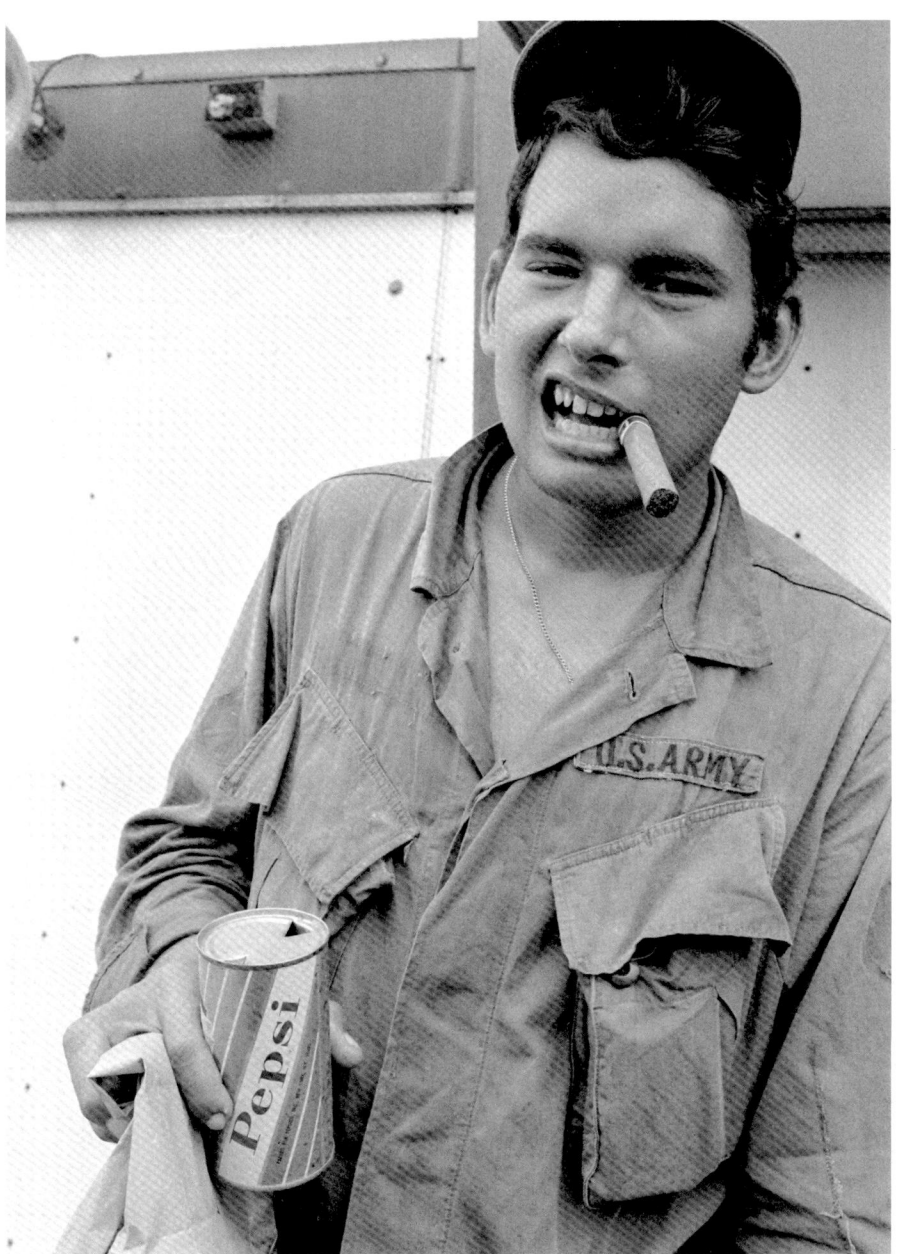

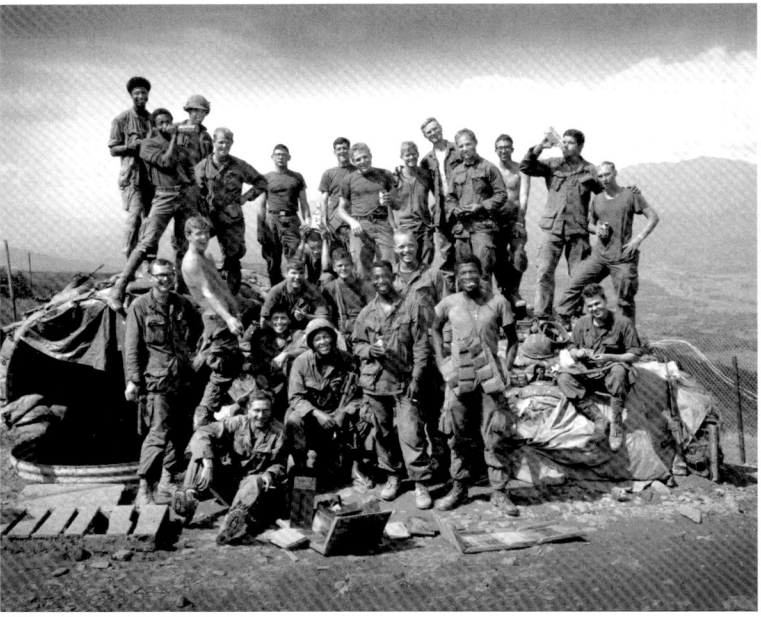

Logue snapped this informal group portrait of 1st Platoon at LZ West. Some "ham it up" for the shot.

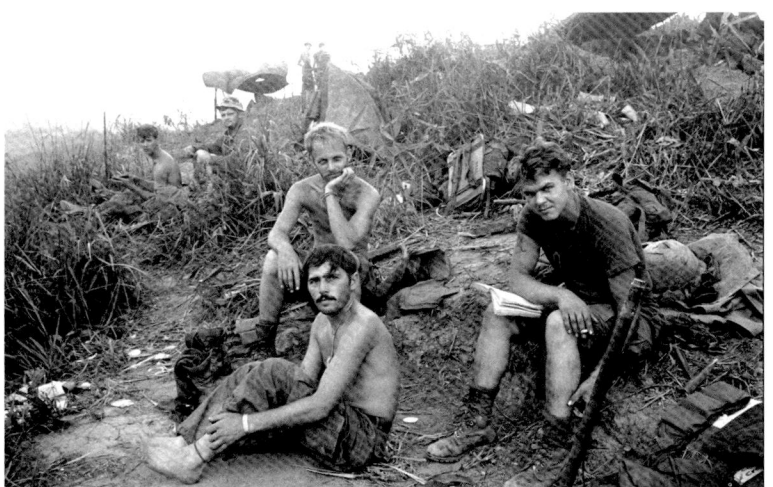

Specialist 4 Dan Simmons enjoys a cigar and a Pepsi at stand-down, February 1970. Sergeant Donald Kuzilla would die in his arms in the firefight on 14 May.

With foxholes dug and daylight remaining, these three relax. They include William (Bill) Powell; Gerry Conlon (left), and William Nadler (right).

In Salem, Oregon, Bill Powell knew no such close family ties. His dad paid him little attention. His mother spent her days at the local country club. Older siblings didn't include him in their games, so Bill turned to more solitary pursuits, devouring books about animals and caring for fish in aquariums.

"I feel like I raised myself," he says. "I don't remember any conversations with Mother and Father. They were very distant, but I had everything I needed."

Soon, he found a game he loved. Each Sunday, he caddied for his father's foursome. As a "country club brat," he combined play with work, honing his game while earning money in course maintenance. In Vietnam, Bill—like Lieutenant Michael Keeble—could spot a hooch ahead and say you'd need a seven iron to reach it.

Bill lettered in his high school's golf and gymnastics teams. He entered Portland State College but "flunked out" after one year. Several months later, he "raised his right hand."

"Volunteered. I was very naive. Didn't have a clue about current events. I knew about the draft. I just expected that's what we all do. I didn't think about being in the infantry, walking around in the boonies," he recalls.

In Glendora, Dan graduated high school in 1967 and entered nearby Citrus College. With the draft hanging over him, however, he enlisted, arrived in Vietnam on 2 September 1969, and was assigned to 1st Squad, 1st Platoon.

Bill joined Alpha on 5 October 1969. He and Dan quickly struck up a friendship. The reason? Bill shrugs and smiles.

"We were West Coast boys," he says.

Most in Alpha were tagged with nicknames. Bill's came from a C-ration he loved but that nearly all others despised. When opening cartons of rations, all tossed cans of ham and eggs to "Little Billy Gross."

"Lieutenant Esterling gave me that name. Now the world knows the story I've kept secret for forty-seven years," he says, chuckling.

Contacts with NVA and VC in the monsoon-soaked autumn were rare. Constant movement, however, punished bodies. Alpha walked "ten to twenty klicks per day," Dan says, or approximately six to twelve miles, across fields, through jungle, and up mountains. They slipped in mud like brown ice and staggered from exhaustion in blinding heat. Now Dan grins.

"I'm still not a walker. My wife is the walker. I tell her, 'I did it for a living for one year in a hot place with people shooting at me.' She says, 'That excuse is *way* too old.'"

At stand-down in December 1969, Jim snapped his first photograph of Dan. He clutches a can of Pepsi, a thick cigar clenched between his teeth, the bill of his utility cap folded back, looking like a gruff, cigar-chomping motor pool sergeant.

In a softer image, without cap and cigar, he smiles beatifically, kneeling among a cluster of children who had just cleaned him out of candy. He laughs. "That was forty years and sixty pounds ago."

Jim snapped a shot of Bill sitting alone in the night laager of 10 May 1970.

"My goal was not to be a target. I stayed away from officers and large groups of guys, and away from command bunkers," Powell explains.

Seconds after that photo was taken, rounds from enemy mortars arched down.

BILL WROTE HIS MOTHER ABOUT THE NEW COMPANY commander, Wilson, and other events, including killing the enemy's early-warning systems (dogs) and their beasts of burden for military supplies (water buffaloes):

We have a new captain and he's a great guy. He's kinda giving us a little time off this morning and he even sent for a chaplain to fly out here. I spoke too soon—our platoon just got back from chasing a few dinks . . . . Now we're back and in the process of popping some popcorn. 272 days and I'll be home. Everything is pretty quiet and I'm fine so no need to worry.

Happy Holidays. Love, Bill.

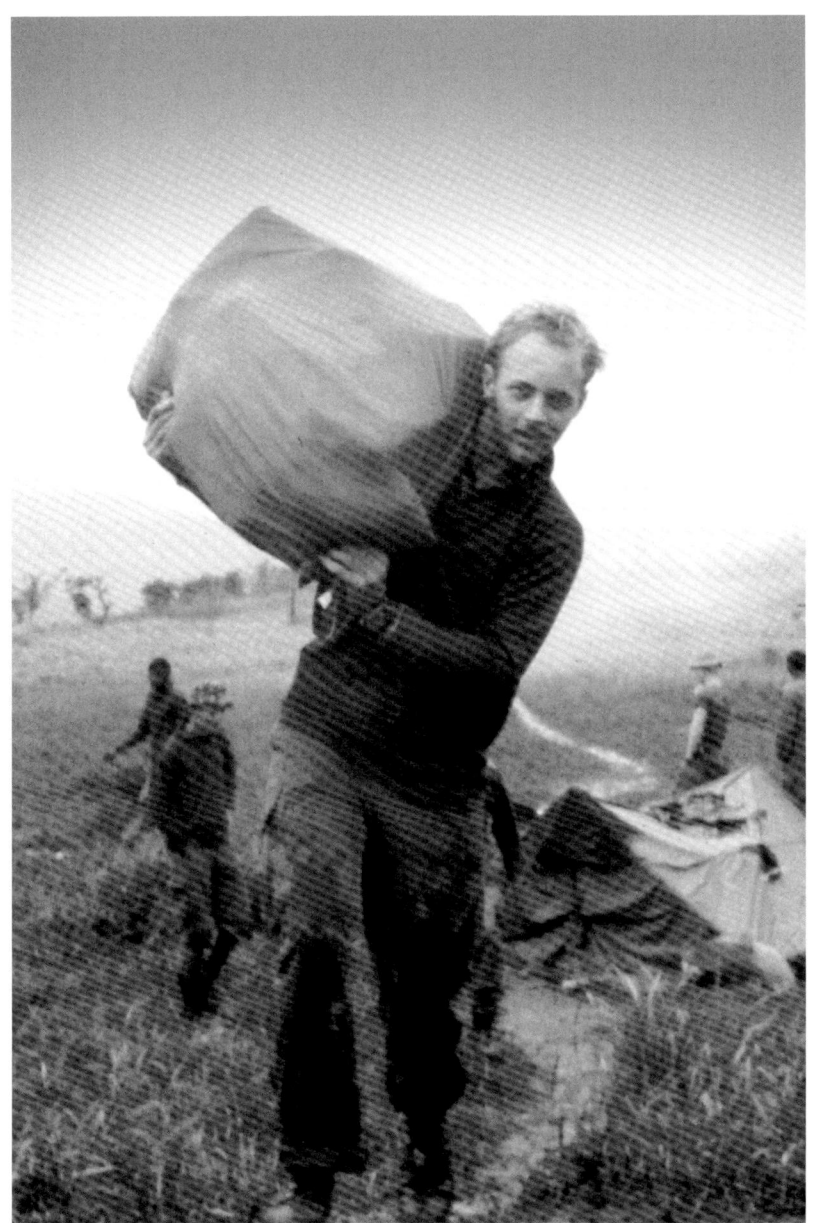

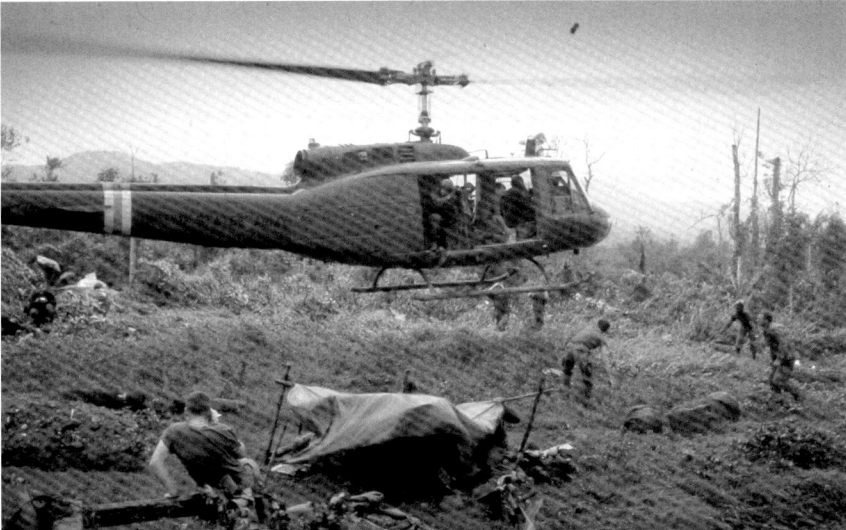

A chopper brings in mail and other welcome items on Christmas Eve. That night, men sat on Million Dollar Hill, like shepherds keeping watch. Logue hung on each hooch socks filled with C-ration pound cake.

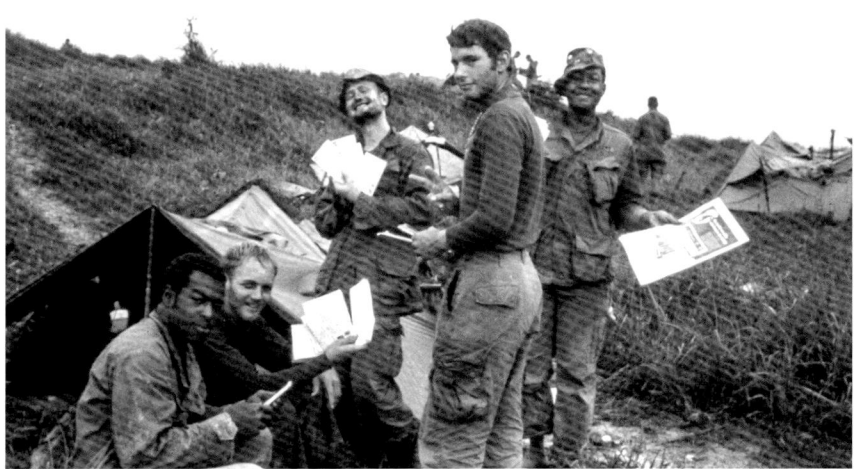

On Christmas Day, "Santa's helper," Bill Powell, totes a red mailbag stuffed with letters and goodies from home. Choppers flew in Christmas dinner. True to form in Vietnam, it rained while the men dined in the open.

Left to right: a soldier remembered only as "Laboo," Bill Powell, Ron ("Red") Hill, Dan Simmons, and Elbert Howard open cards, letters, and packages from home. Notice Simmons, foreground, delivering his Christmas "salute": peace.

In another December letter, Powell mentions Logue:

One of the guys in our company used to be a professional photographer when he was back in the world, and he has taken a lot of pictures . . . you should be getting an envelope with some pictures of me in it . . . . One of the 8 x 10s is of the 1st Platoon of A Co., 4/31 196th LIB standing on a bunker on LZ West on New Year's Day. The other, with me and all the little kids, was taken in the refugee village of Hiep Duc, located in the Que Son Valley . . . . Hiep Duc has about 3,500 people in it. I was passing out candy at the time, a couple of weeks before Christmas . . .

On Christmas Day, Logue photographed Bill and Dan at their hooch they decorated with a red-and-white stocking. Several soldiers cluster around them, all proudly displaying packages from home. Dan flashes the peace sign.

Bill soon earned a three-day, in-country leave to Da Nang. Upon his return, a female dog protecting her litter charged out and bit him. At LZ West, medic William "Doc" Allen of Napa, California, examined the bite.

"Doc says, 'You've got two choices: bandage it up and be on your way, or stay on the hill for two weeks and come here once a day and get a shot in the belly.' I said, 'That's a no-brainer. I'm staying,'" Bill remarked.

Each morning's injection was a small if painful price to pay for two weeks of safety and sleep. Between shots and naps, Bill plunged into *The Hobbit* and watched the clock. After six months, he was counting even minutes of his time remaining in country. On 12 March he wrote: "In 2 1/2 hours I'm over 'the hump' and on the downhill side of my tour, with 182 1/2 days left to go."

Between May and mid-June, keeping alive seemed as much a fantasy as was *The Hobbit*. Bill wrote home only twice, never hinting about combat and incidents such as one in the black, new moon night of 2 May, when a large enemy force walked by Alpha's laager.

"Jim Neldner and I were in a bunker. We heard canteens clanging. It took a long time for them [the company officers] to allow us to shoot. We might have been in a controlled fire zone, another reason we lost the war. We finally opened up for two or three minutes," Bill recalls.

Alpha ceased fire. An eerie silence fell. Night passed. First light revealed a badly wounded enemy soldier on his stomach outside Powell's and Neldner's bunker.

What occurred next still haunts Bill. No one touched the wounded soldier, who refused to answer questions. Finally, with orders to move on, Captain Wilson gave the order to shoot him. A soldier nicknamed "Recon Rick," Bill says, stepped forward and fired one round.

Many remember the incident with varying sentiment—some with repugnance, others with cold, hard reasoning. Often, the enemy placed beneath their badly wounded explosive devices to detonate when bodies were moved. That morning, Wilson was taking no chances.

After long months in the bush, Dan and Bill earned safer assignments. Bill took up duty on LZ West and went on R&R twice, first to Bangkok, Thailand, then to Tokyo, a trip financed in part by a $150 loan from Jim Neldner.

"I feel bad I haven't paid him back," he remarks sheepishly.

Dan's new duty was guarding the headquarters of 196th Light Infantry Brigade commander, Colonel Edwin Kennedy, at the sprawling compound, LZ Hawk Hill. Dan slept in barracks, browsed goods at a PX, and enjoyed pizza and *cold* beer and soft drinks. Once, he returned to West with Colonel Kennedy.

"He knew that I was from there and asked if I wanted to go," Dan recalls. Dan eagerly jumped aboard, but as the slick (Bell UH-1 "Iroquois," a transport helicopter) flew west, he looked down at the green killing fields and, like all of them aboard, grew frightened. He enjoyed seeing friends such as Bill and Jim but yearned for the safety of Hawk Hill.

"I was scared to death. I'd been out of the field for a month or more. I was so glad to get back on that chopper the next day," he recalls.

Bill watched his friend go, his own excitement mounting as his time in Vietnam ticked away. Then, with seventeen days remaining, news from home staggered him. A brother had drowned near his mother's vacation beach home in Neskowin, Oregon.

"Doc Allen told me. I was just a blubbering fool. I said, 'This can't be.' He said, 'Come on, Bill, we've got a helicopter. You're going home.' He walked me out to the pad. I got on a loach."

The "loach," or LOH (Light Observation Helicopter), lifted. Bill looked down at his friends preparing for another walk through the shadows of death. They were tearing into C-ration cartons, all likely tossing aside cans of ham and eggs. The bird then turned and from his sight vanished men with whom he had shared hardships and found friendships closer than those of his own siblings.

"They were my people. I couldn't say goodbye to anyone," he recalls.

Back home, he learned his brother had been swept off rocks and into the sea. Another brother, a US Coast Guardsman familiar with ocean currents, tapped a map.

"The ocean's going to give him back here," Bill's brother said, and there, the body soon washed ashore.

IN CALIFORNIA, DAN EARNED AN ASSOCIATE OF ARTS DEGREE at Citrus College and met his future wife, Karen Lynn Miller. He was waiting tables at an Italian restaurant but yearned for the silence and solitude of somewhere "out there."

"That was when Colorado called to me," he said.

So the couple left California, humming along to John Denver's "Rocky Mountain High," and began married life in a house on an island in the Blue River near Silverthorne, Colorado. Ever after, they have lived "out there." Along with a good woman, solitude soothes a warrior's heart.

"Since 1974, I have stayed in rural areas, out away from town, away from people," Dan says.

Early in his career, Dan began work with a company specializing in building concrete walls. No one out-worked him. He had been inured by the long, hot hours of a baker's life, toughened by a brutal war, and strengthened by the "nervous energy I brought back from Vietnam. I just worked and worked and worked, often 60-hour weeks," he remarks.

He credits Karen, a 32-year postal employee, and her accounting skills for the couple's comfortable life.

IN OREGON, BILL ALSO CRAVED SOLITUDE. HE LIVED SEVERAL months in Thoreau-like isolation in his mother's beach house. Without that house, he says, "I would have gone to hide in the woods to get away from people."

Seclusion calmed him. He began a 35-year career with the US Postal Service, all the while fearing the violence of Vietnam lurking inside his soul.

"I was afraid I was going to hurt somebody. I was afraid I didn't have any control," he recalls.

Bill wed and fathered two sons. The marriage was short-lived. He took custody of his sons and raised them as a single parent.

"I was working ten hours a day, then doing laundry, cooking. Never had time to date. Never got a night off. I was not a good father. From my parents being totally uninvolved with me, I went the other way. I was kind of a drill sergeant. They were my new squad," he remarks.

At night, he helped the boys with homework, cooked, washed, and cleaned the house. Often Bill awoke from nightmares on sweat-soaked pillows, then faced a day's work. Finally, seeking a truce between past and present and hungering for peace of mind, he joined other Vietnam veterans for "rap sessions" (a reference from leftover parlance of the 1960s). For twenty years, he sought help at veterans' centers, including a three-month, in-house counseling program at a VA hospital.

"What was so important was realizing I wasn't the only one. A lot of guys were having recurring nightmares and night sweats.

My self-esteem was real low. I thought I was a bad soldier. Vet centers were the biggest help to me. I wasn't insane. I wasn't a loser," he states.

During our interview, Jim gave Bill Jim Neldner's address. Later, Bill sent the latter a $150 check in payment for his long-ago R&R loan. Then he called, and the two talked for a long time. Neldner never cashed the check.

Bill now lives in downtown Portland, where he strolls to shops and restaurants. He must drive to indulge his passion, golf, a game he especially enjoys with his sons, one of whom claims a two handicap.

"Taught him everything he knows," Bill says with a grin.

Now he seems to have come to a truce, if an uneasy one, with the war. In his apartment hang framed photographs from Vietnam, including one Jim took. He also takes quiet pleasure when his sons introduce him to their friends.

"They introduce me as 'My Dad, a Vietnam combat veteran,'" he remarks, and beams.

The Simmonses have a son and a daughter and one grandchild. Empty nesters now, the couple camp in luxury compared to the condition of Vietnam laagers. The garage houses a spacious, well-equipped camper and, beside it, Dan's super-sized pick-up truck. It bears a bumper sticker, "Not Fonda Jane," a reference to the actress who posed for propaganda photographs with NVA soldiers, earning her the lasting enmity of Vietnam veterans. Dan grins sheepishly. "I wanted that bumper sticker that says, 'Jane Fonda American Traitor-Bitch,' but my wife wouldn't let me."

Dan's only physical ailment from the war, he believes, remains a virulent strain of asthma, stemming from an attack that occurred "two weeks after I got back from Vietnam. I swore it was from Agent Orange or Vietnam or something," he says. Neither Colorado's altitude nor Arizona's arid climate has helped. Otherwise, he remarks, "I'm actually pretty healthy."

We step out into brilliant Arizona sunlight to leave. As always, Jim offers an Alpha veteran his hand.

"It was an honor to serve with you," he says.

Dan grabs him in a backslapping bear hug, then defines war as only a combat veteran can.

"Thanks, buddy; you too. That was one helluva thing we went through."

YOU CAN LAY DOWN A DEAD MAN BUT NEVER THE BURDEN OF a broken heart. This is so for the friends and family of Donald Kuzilla. So it is for another soldier's widow far to the east. For her, it is always the afternoon of 16 May 1970, two days after the 14 May fight when Kuzilla was lost. Captain Wilson needs volunteers for a patrol. Sergeant William David Menscer volunteers to lead it. Others include David Gould, John Houchins, Kenneth Leavell, Bill Powell, and Dan Simmons. Each checks his gear, then in the steaming, breathless afternoon they step off through tall grass. For a moment, all is quiet.

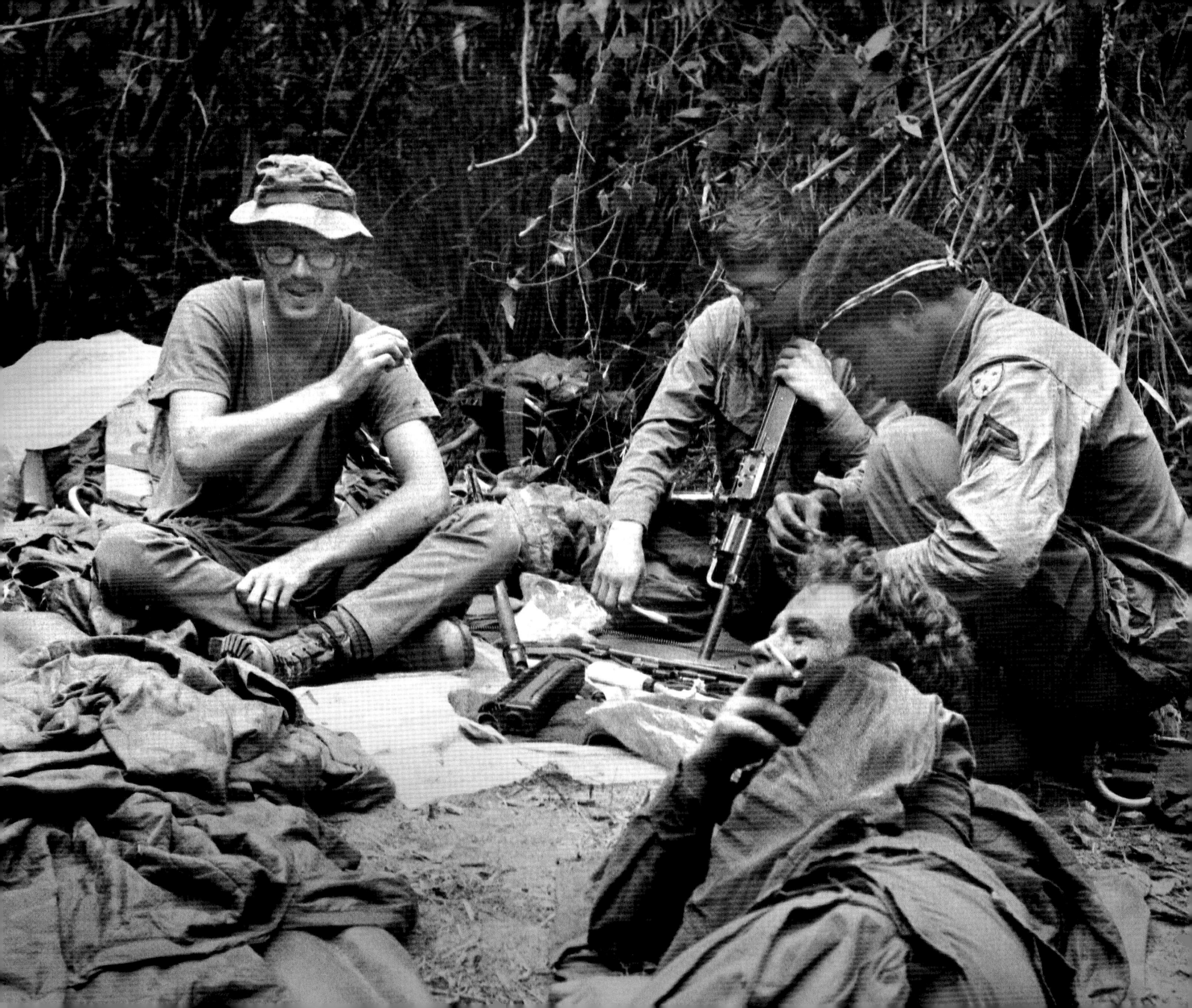

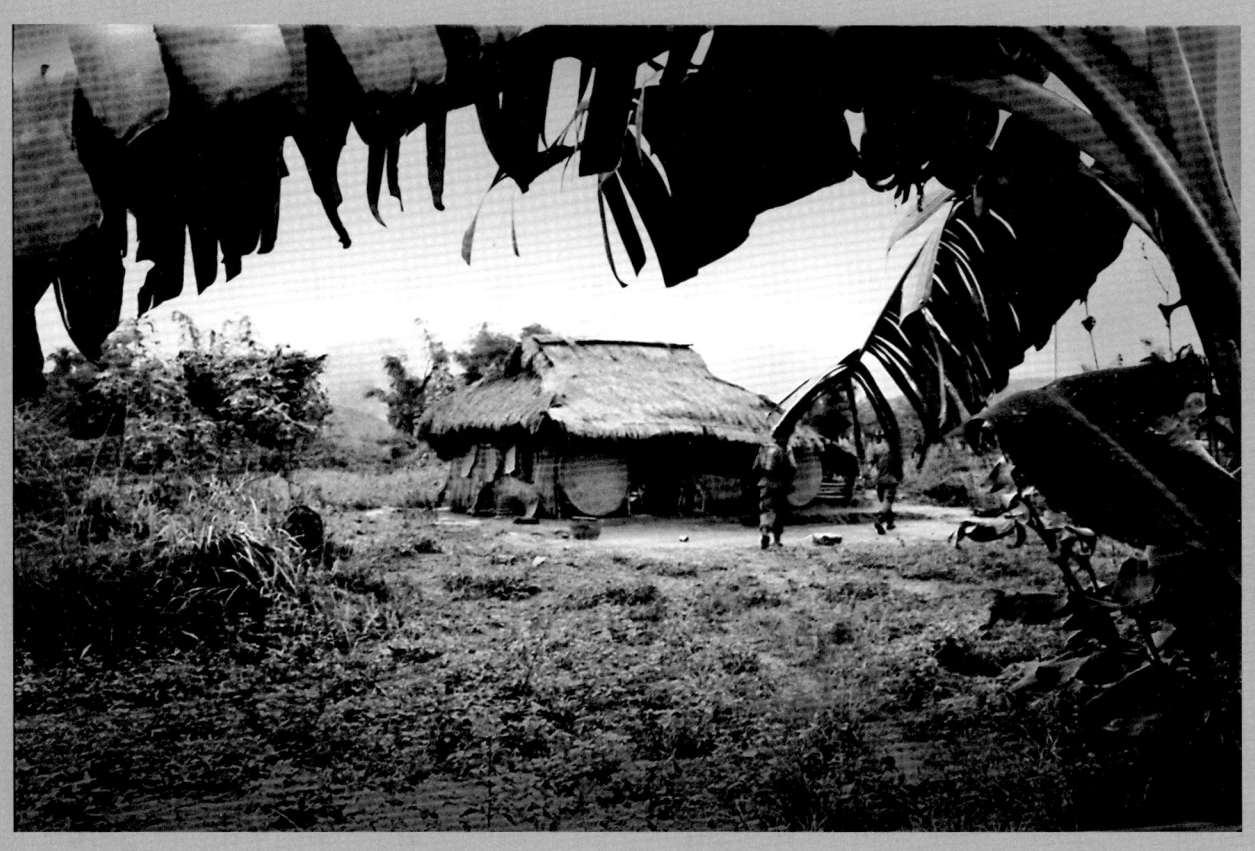

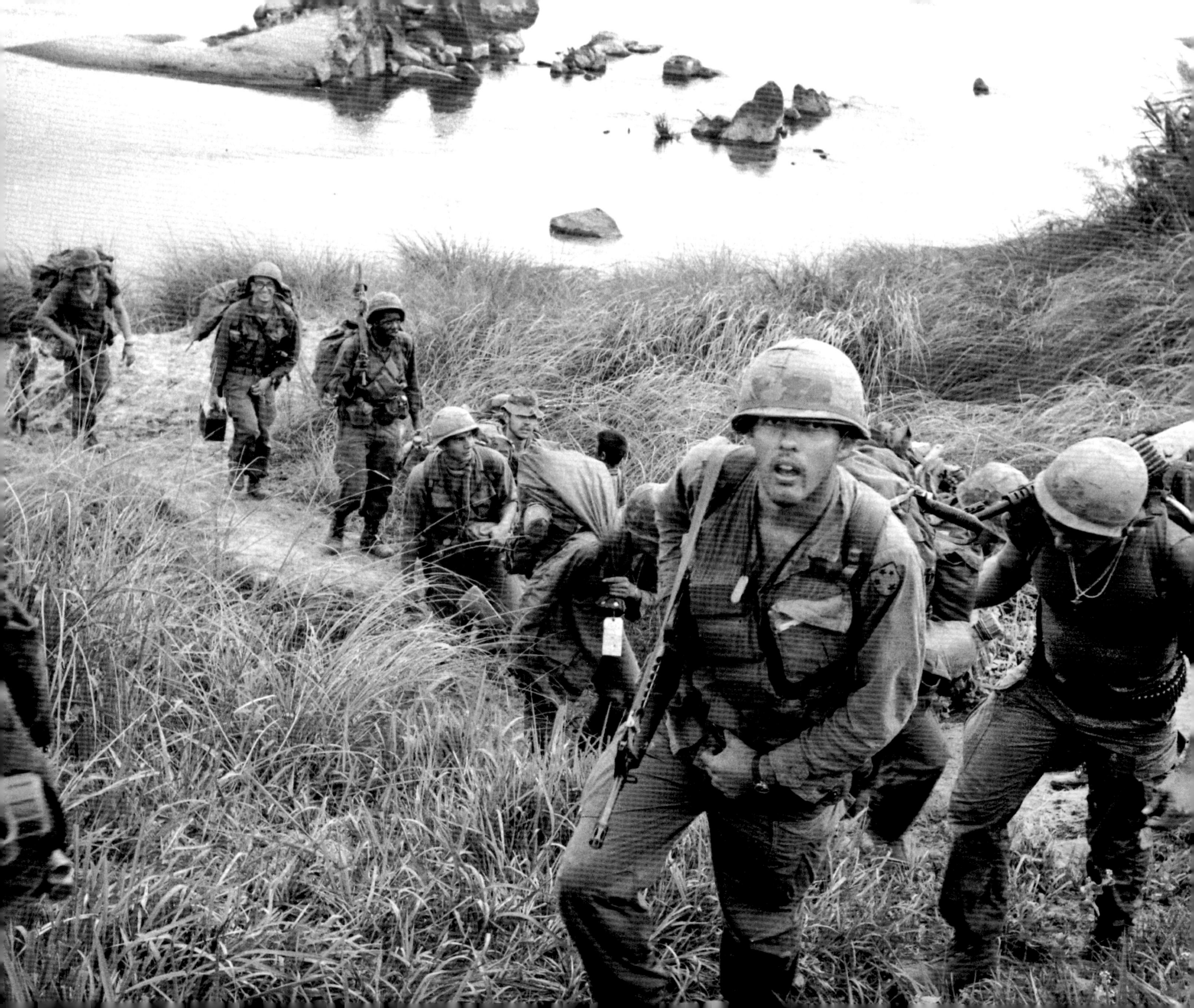

Chapter 13

We Traveled Hard and We Traveled Fast

First Lieutenant Donald Louis Pettit

"Just a moment," don says, and disappears down the hall. His wife, Barbara, shrugs, also wondering what her husband will bring forth in their Greensboro, North Carolina, home.

Soon he returns, holding combat boots he wore nearly fifty years ago. To them clings red clay of Vietnam, some perhaps from among boulders where he crawled in destroying an NVA nest of snipers.

As we dine on sandwiches from Stamey's, the legendary Greensboro barbecue restaurant, Donald Louis Pettit speaks of his red clay childhood. Born to Jasper and Beatrice Thompson Pettit, he grew up in tiny Columbus, where he roamed among hills, forests, and streams, listening to the whispers of the wild.

"I think the good Lord was looking after me back then. I fished and I wandered through the woods and acclimated myself to the outdoors. I learned if you're in tune with yourself, you know what's going on around you. You know when birds stop singing and when animals get quiet, that things are not right," he recalls.

He had just articulated the perfect résumé for war in the highlands of Vietnam. First for him, however, there was boyhood, with baseball, hunting, fishing, and work that began from the dirt up. He mucked out horse stables and swept out the Columbus post office.

Such after-school, weekend, and summer jobs helped provide for the family. Beatrice certainly had to cook—*a lot*. Her son grew to six feet, five inches, a hulking presence on athletic fields. After graduating high school in 1963, he entered Appalachian State University in Boone, North Carolina. Married, he worked nights and attended classes by day.

Then, one fateful day his mother called.

"She knew some people on the draft board and my number was up. So I could either wait for the draft to pull me in or I could shop around and see what the services could offer me," he recalls.

They offered him Officer Candidate School. After basic training and AIT, he entered OCS at Fort Benning, where he learned a leader's first, hard lesson in a blazing Georgia summer: how to force your brain to work when you've pushed your body beyond exhaustion. A body in superb condition keeps the mind clear. OCS honed both.

Left: First Lieutenant Donald Pettit leads 3rd Platoon up LZ Siberia. Platoon members recall Pettit's stringent rules, strength, and woodland skills learned from boyhood. He would earn a Silver Star.

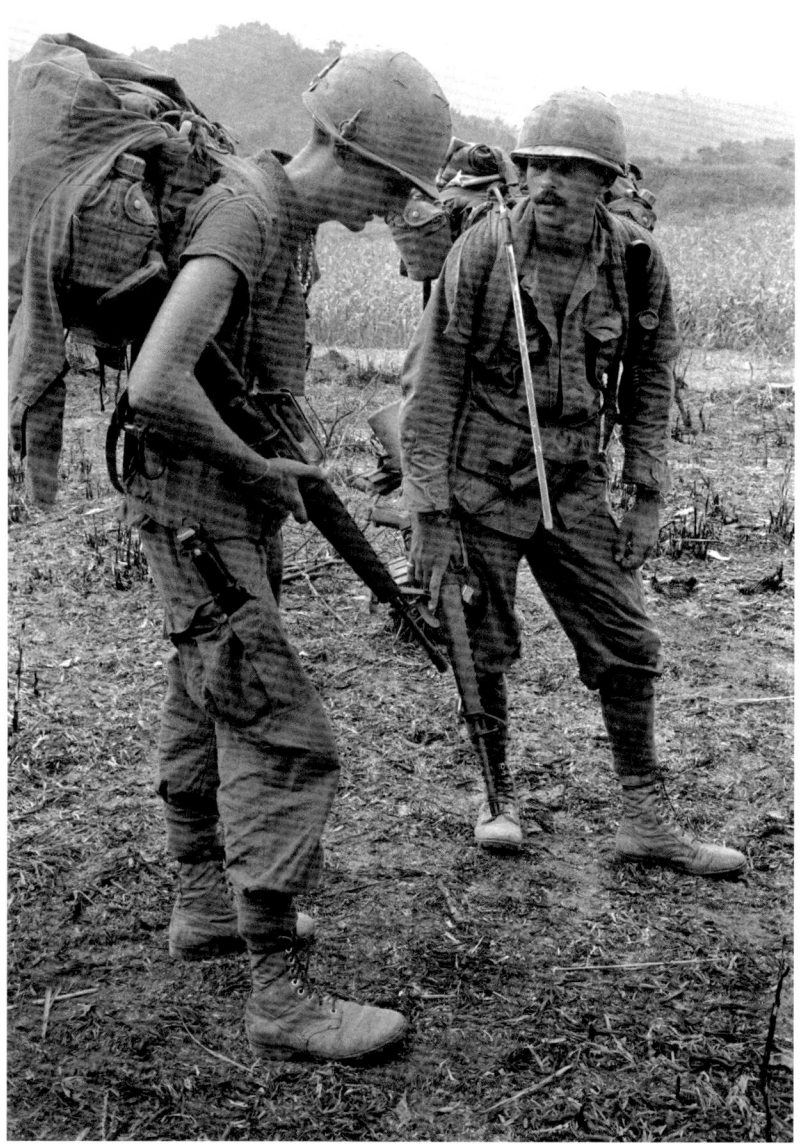

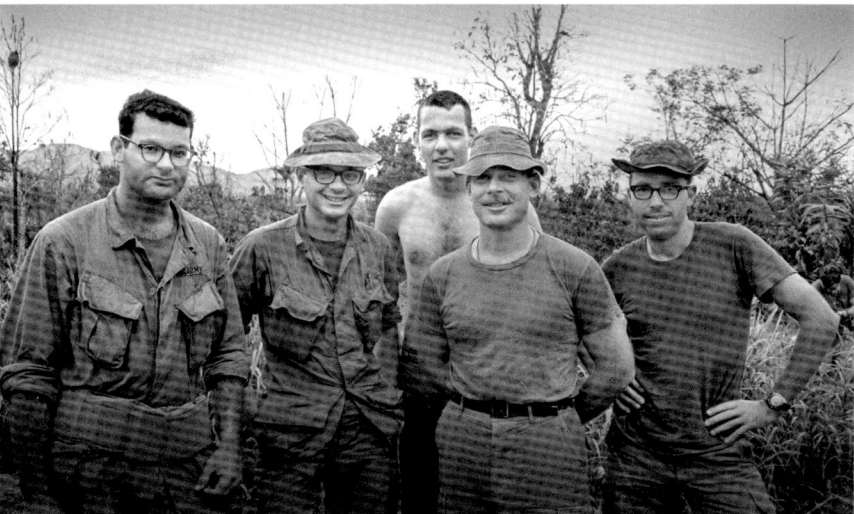

Captain John Wilson (center) poses with platoon leaders. From left: First Lieutenant Marvin Kay; First Lieutenant Erwin Esterling; First Lieutenant Donald Pettit; and First Lieutenant Charles Jacob, artillery forward observer.

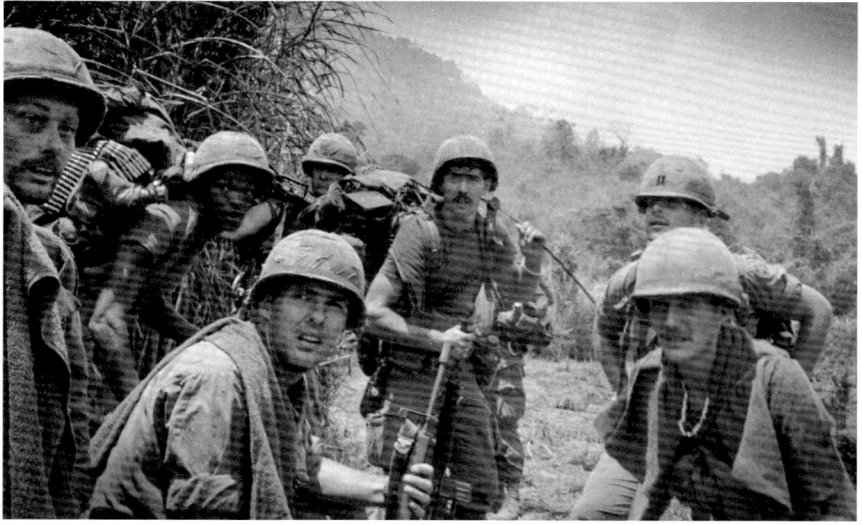

Sergeant Charles ("Chuck") Mann, a schoolteacher with a master's degree, chats with RTO Robert Nelson. Snipers often targeted RTO operators to cut off a unit's communications.

RTO David Flynn (standing center) winces at nearby fire. In foreground are, from left, First Lieutenant Mike Keeble; First Lieutenant Donald Pettit; and Sergeant Charles Mann.

Don graduated, served in the caliche dust of Fort Hood near Killeen, Texas, then completed survival school in Panama. When he arrived at LZ West in October 1969, he gazed across topography similar to that of western North Carolina, of peaks and valleys and wending streams.

"I could navigate mountains. I knew what I was doing in mountains," he said. Accustomed to the high lonesomeness of the Appalachians, he was assigned his perfect task: leader of the reconnaissance unit of 4/31. "It was a small unit. We traveled light and we traveled hard and we traveled fast. We were looking and seeking, not engaging. If I needed artillery, if I needed gunships, I could call in. I was my own boss out in the field.

"The people I had were a volunteer group, a Puerto Rican, a couple of American Indians, and blacks. They couldn't get along with anybody in the rear; not even with themselves sometimes. But put them in the field, they were like a well-oiled machine. You would not believe how smoothly they operated. They could just about tell what each other was thinking," he says.

Risks were high. In fading day, Recon was walking back to LZ West when a booby trap injured one man. The RTO called for a medevac, but Don had no way to mark the team's location. Even knowing light would alert the enemy, he burned his only map to guide the bird that lifted away the casualty.

Don's roving freedom would not last. When Captain John Wilson took command of Alpha, he assigned Pettit as 3rd Platoon leader.

"I was not a happy camper. In recon, I was the dude calling shots. I was my own destiny to some extent," he says.

One order from Captain Wilson was to cure "Third Herd's" penchant for being late. Under Pettit, tardiness ended the next day. For an early-morning combat assault, he told his platoon the time to be ready. Near daylight he found many still snoring in their bunkers. He upturned bedding and sent men tumbling to the ground. He grins.

"My people were there half an hour early," he recalls.

Third Herd was never late again.

Don knew many in his platoon cared little for this taskmaster with no patience for sloth and incompetence. He kept firing underperforming platoon sergeants until Charles "Chuck" Mann, a Pennsylvanian, lived up to Don's high standards.

Mann was no swearing, shouting NCO. A husband, father, and college graduate with a degree in American history, Chuck was the only male teacher among a faculty of nuns in a parochial school. Drafted, he proved a tough, smart soldier, earning outstanding trainee in basic and honor soldier in NCO school. Offered Officer Candidate School, he declined and arrived in Alpha as an E-6 (staff sergeant). He won the platoon's respect by soliciting advice from experienced men of any rank.

"You had to prove yourself, more or less. I thought, 'Listen to the Pfcs. Listen to the Spec 4s. Listen to the guys that have been out in the bush for a while.' They're the ones who know what this is all about," remarks Chuck, who lives near Denver, North Carolina.

Pettit, helped by Mann's guiding hand, molded Third Herd into a good platoon. As for its devotion to him, Don shrugs.

"I would say most of them didn't like me. I think they respected me," he says.

He laid down two rules: "Don't be wandering off by yourself, and watch where you walk. I had a few who were pretty sharp guys and they learned quickly. The kids who were ready to take the knowledge and their training and adapt it to the situation did well," he recalls.

Although Pettit drove his men hard, he measured their physical limits by his own. He was in excellent shape, so when he grew tired, he knew his men were exhausted.

"New guys," remarks Jim Logue, thought Pettit had some "crazy traits." Don grins at Jim and nods.

"But that kept me and my people alive," he says. "One of the secrets over there I learned real quickly: Do not be predictable. If you get predictable, then you're in trouble."

Among better soldiers, he found, were those from rural backgrounds who "had a little advantage in marksmanship." They came from places similar to western North Carolina where, he says, a rifle hung above front doors in many homes.

Alpha needed good marksmanship in spring 1970, when 2nd NVA Division attacked throughout Quang Tin Province. Although Pettit already had spent six months in the field, the usual tour of a line officer, he remained with Third Herd. They survived the friendly fire incident of 5 May, the mortaring on 10 May, and the 14 May fight in the rain along the dirt road north of Hiệp Dúc. Pettit's platoon was second in line of march.

"Next thing I knew there was firing in front of me in the lead platoon. On the left were open rice paddies for maybe a hundred yards. On the right were bush, jungle, and dikes. You always follow the path of least resistance but something in my brain said, 'Don't do it. Don't do it.' So I went through the bushes. Later I found out they had 51-caliber machine gun units over there in the wood line. Had I gone out there my whole platoon would have been caught in the open," he recounts.

Before a night laager two days later, Captain Wilson sent out an area sweep. Minutes later firing erupted, in which fellow North Carolinian, Sergeant William David Menscer, was killed in action.

"My platoon started down there to retrieve the body and to find out what was there. We got the body out. Of course, we were laying down a whole lot of fire, but we still didn't know what we were firing at and where. We were under the crest of the hill, which meant they couldn't see us. If we'd gone forward, they would have seen us, so we would have been wiped out or taken a lot of casualties."

Alpha had just set up its night defensive position across from a small hill where, atop it, NVA dug in beneath large boulders. To silence the enemy position, Wilson orchestrated air assets, including spotter planes, the fury and fire of Cobra gunships and jets with napalm. On the ground, two platoons, with Wilson directing, coordinated a pincer movement to clean out the nest.

Jim Logue, near Wilson, had a seat for the action, photographing men in this pincer movement. As 2nd Platoon wormed its way towards the boulders and enemy foxholes, Pettit's Third Herd swept behind the rocky stronghold. Jim snapped a photograph of Wilson with a phone, choreographing the movements. 2nd Platoon's Sergeant Perry Stemen of Whitehall, Michigan, inched nearer the foxholes, his grenades ready.

"I saw a dink's head pop out underneath. He had a thing on it, a flap door," recalls Stemen of the enemy's foxhole. "So I took a hand grenade and threw down and it blew the trap door off."

He then tossed a grenade toward another sniper hole.

"This is hard to believe but he had a rice basket. He caught it with the rice basket, popped it out and threw one and got me in the back of my leg. But I got him the next time."

His wound earned Stemen his second Purple Heart.

Still, enemy remained among the rocks. The pilot of a Helix 19, a spotter plane, confirmed what Alpha knew: enemy spider holes nestled among massive boulders, one ten feet high. The platoons were pulled back; in came a jet with napalm and 250-pound bombs.

"We were so near the targets that metal fragments fell on us like snow," Logue recalled.

Don knew he had to act: "At that point it was kind of like, 'Tag, you're it.' I got the football. What am I going to do with it? My folks used to tell me, 'You got yourself into this mess, get yourself out of it.'"

At the lieutenant's request, the Helix pilot flew once more over the enemy position and radioed back that the NVA "is right in front of you, on the other side of the boulders."

"He said, 'Please don't ask me to fly over again. They were about to hose me down,'" Don recalls.

The Carolinian knew what had to be done but would not ask it of his men. He needed several grenades, but how would he carry them? "And why in the world it happened I don't know, but one of my guys had a sandbag in his pocket," he recalls.

Men dropped grenades into the sandbag and Dan gathered his courage. He speaks of what he did next and why. "I knew officers who went over there to get hero medals, but that was *not* my intention. I was just trying to take care of my folks. I know a lot of them didn't like me too well but as long as they respected me, that was the main thing," he says.

Clutching his bag of grenades and his M16, Don inched his way up the hill behind the enemy. He crawled from one hole to the next and with three grenades "neutralized" enemy positions, then pressed against the hill's largest boulder.

"At the fourth hole I did the same thing. Imagine my surprise when my grenade came back at me with one of his. My mistake was not allowing the grenade to 'cook off' before tossing it. I ran behind one of the boulders."

Again he pulled himself up the boulder and cautiously peered over the top to see the barrel of an AK-47 "looking right at me. I fell off the rock. I didn't jump. It would take a split second for my muscle to react and that might be too late. I just relaxed and dropped," he says.

AK-47 rounds chipped at rock near where he had lain. He saw an enemy soldier scramble out of his foxhole, but he did not see where he went until Don's men pointed out his position. Don clawed his way up again, pulled a grenade pin, let it "cook off" a few seconds, and threw it over too far. The next he tossed too far, as well. Finally, he pulled the pin on a third grenade, waited, then placed it on top of the rock and let it roll down. It exploded. All was quiet. He slid from the rock, exhausted. David Menscer was avenged.

With such heroic action, Captain Wilson knew, Pettit had accomplished much more than did most platoon leaders. Wilson thus recommended him for the Silver Star. General Order Number 8364, dated 11 July 1970, describes how Pettit earned the third highest award (behind the Medal of Honor and the Distinguished Service Cross) for his "intrepid actions" and "personal heroism . . . in keeping with the highest traditions of the military service."

For hours after the fighting, Don remarks, his high state of constant adrenaline denied him deep sleep. He dropped into his bedding in a bunker. "I slept two days and three nights. I got up, ate, and went right back to bed," he says.

Pettit remained on West as night duty officer and enjoyed R&R in Hawaii with his wife. When Captain Wilson went home, Don became Headquarters Company Commander. Back in the States, he served in the 82nd Airborne Division, then in Special Forces, completing service as a captain.

Again a civilian, he was back on the land that had taught him how to survive war.

"I think God was preparing me when I was a kid, running around through the woods, listening subconsciously to everything that was around me," he remarks.

Don earned a degree from Campbell University in Buies Creek, North Carolina. He worked many jobs, from chief bottle washer and cook at a 24-hour truck stop to supervisor in textiles to thirty-three years in a pharmaceutical plant.

Decades later, as we began our interviews, Jim found Pettit's platoon sergeant, Chuck Mann, living in Denver, North Carolina, about ninety miles west of Greensboro. Jim told Don of the proximity of his platoon sergeant.

"To get reacquainted with Chuck has been so enlightening," Don later wrote in a letter. "The common bond of combat is a feeling that you can never be mentally separated. *Ever.*"

Don has fought his own battles against enemies of mind and body that afflict so many veterans.

"Sometimes you have to laugh. Otherwise, you'll cry," he says. "That day I was crawling around in the rocks? People died that day. Not only Americans but also NVA. Not from natural causes. Not because of heart attacks, cancer. It was because man decided to kill man. I will say this: the NVA were *soldiers*. They were not just a ragtag bunch out there running around. They were *soldiers*."

So was Donald Louis Pettit. To prove it, he still has his jungle boots coated with the red clay of combat.

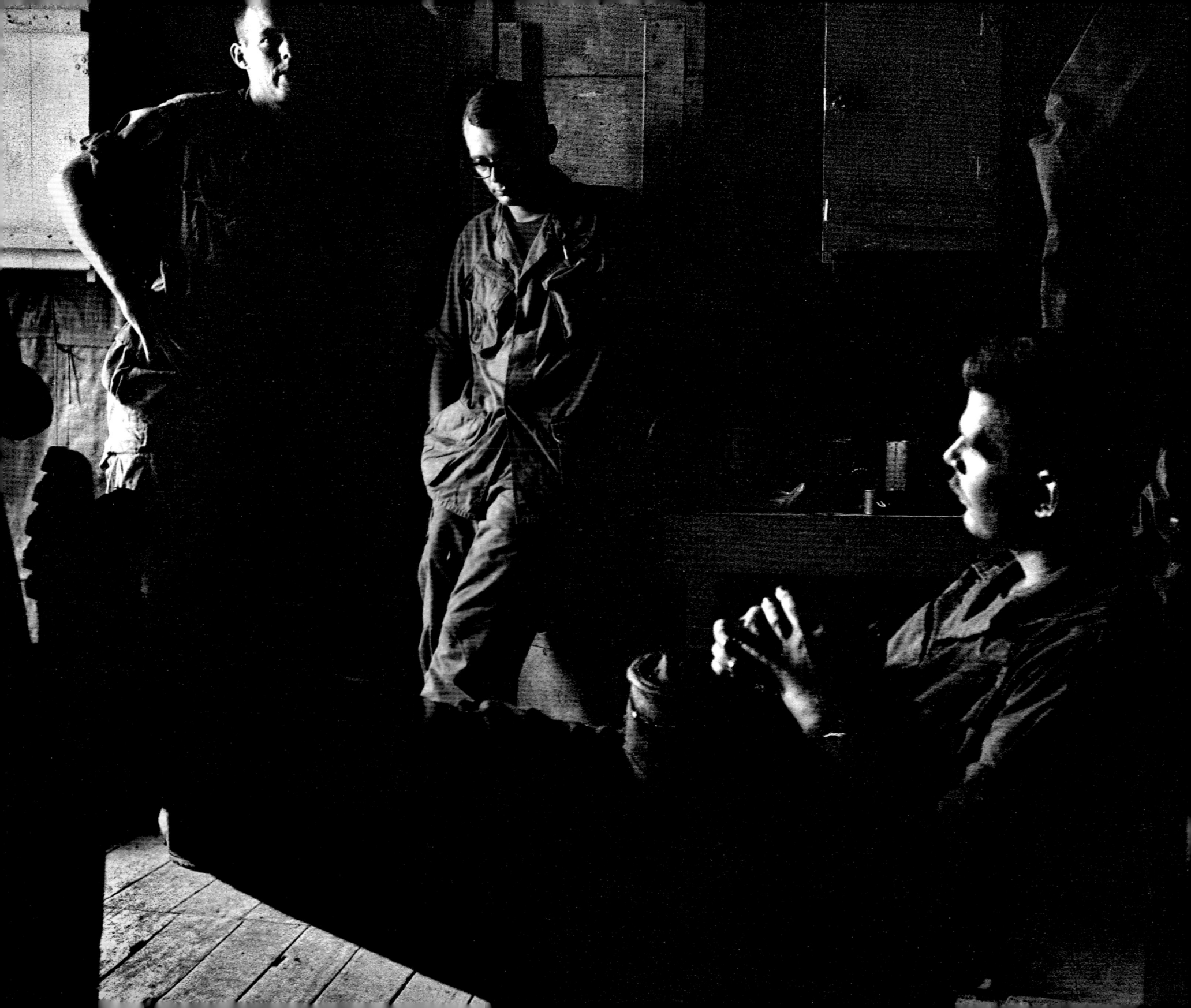

Chapter 14

Je Suis Effrayé, Fatigué, Affamé, et J'ai le Mal du Pays

Private First Class Daniel Richard LaPierre

THERE WERE SO FEW OF THEM NOW, THIS DAY OF 28 MAY 1970.

"Alpha Battalion," a name far too grand for its numbers, stepped down from LZ West into Hiêp Dúc Valley, its ranks hollow from so many good men gone—dead, wounded, ill, or home again.

Captain John Wilson had "punched his ticket" after six months in the field. Temporary command fell to First Lieutenant Erwin Esterling, leader of 1st Platoon. He'd never make a recruiting poster, with the bookish looks born of his big, black spectacles. However, there was no better soldier, many in Alpha recall. Esterling had that "it" about him, that something in someone men will follow.

He certainly wasn't above his talents in commanding this company. Platoons in Vietnam numbered about forty-eight men. This day, Alpha filed into the valley with no more than thirty-six, so small it was under operational control, one day to another, of Charlie or Delta Companies of 4/31.

All among Alpha stooped beneath the burdens of their calendar, whether as "new guys" or "short." Perry Stemen of White

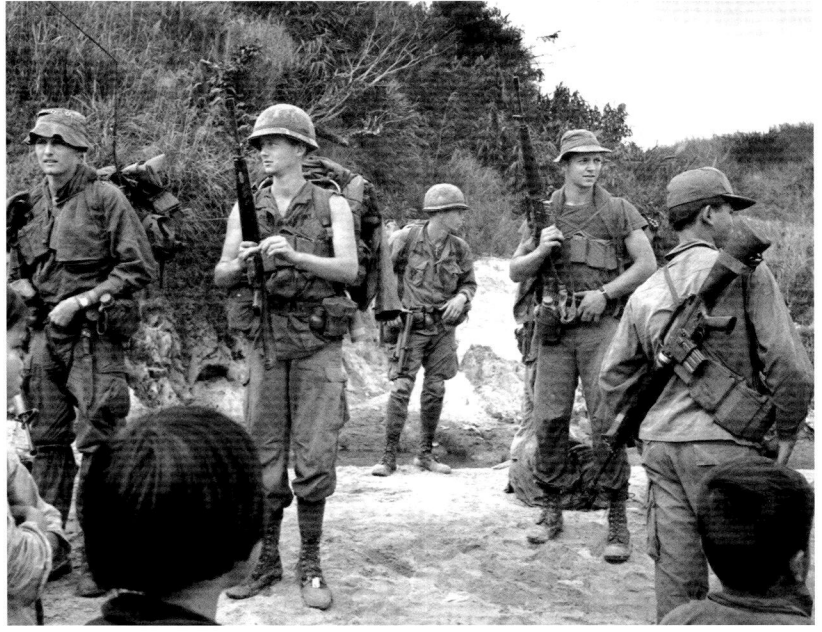

Waiting at a river crossing is Sergeant Perry Stemen, sleeveless. He would earn a Silver Star.

Left: Three chance spots of light dramatize this image. From left are First Lieutenant Donald Pettit; First Lieutenant Erwin Esterling; and (seated) Captain John Wilson on his last day with Alpha. Wilson appointed Esterling interim company commander.

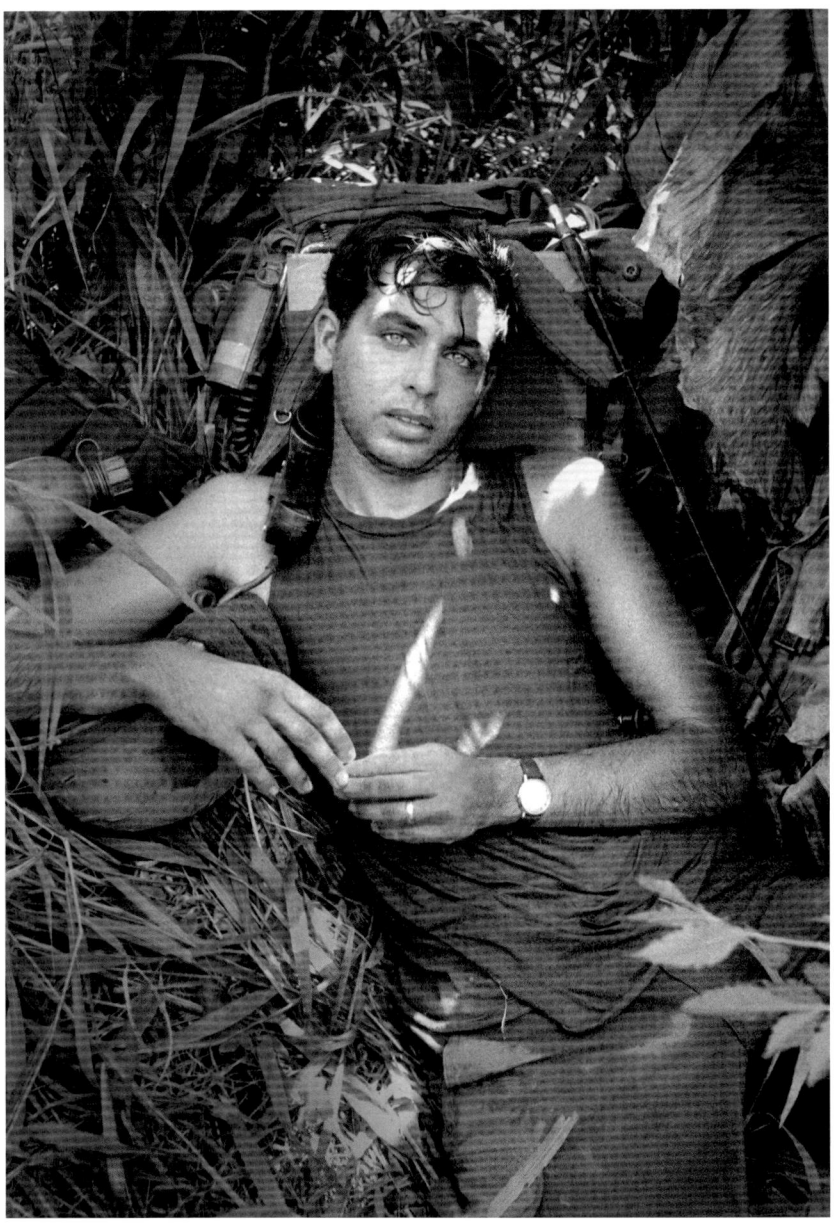

Logue remembers this soldier with expressive blue eyes as Ed Schneider. His rucksack serves as a pillow in a shady noon laager on a hot day.

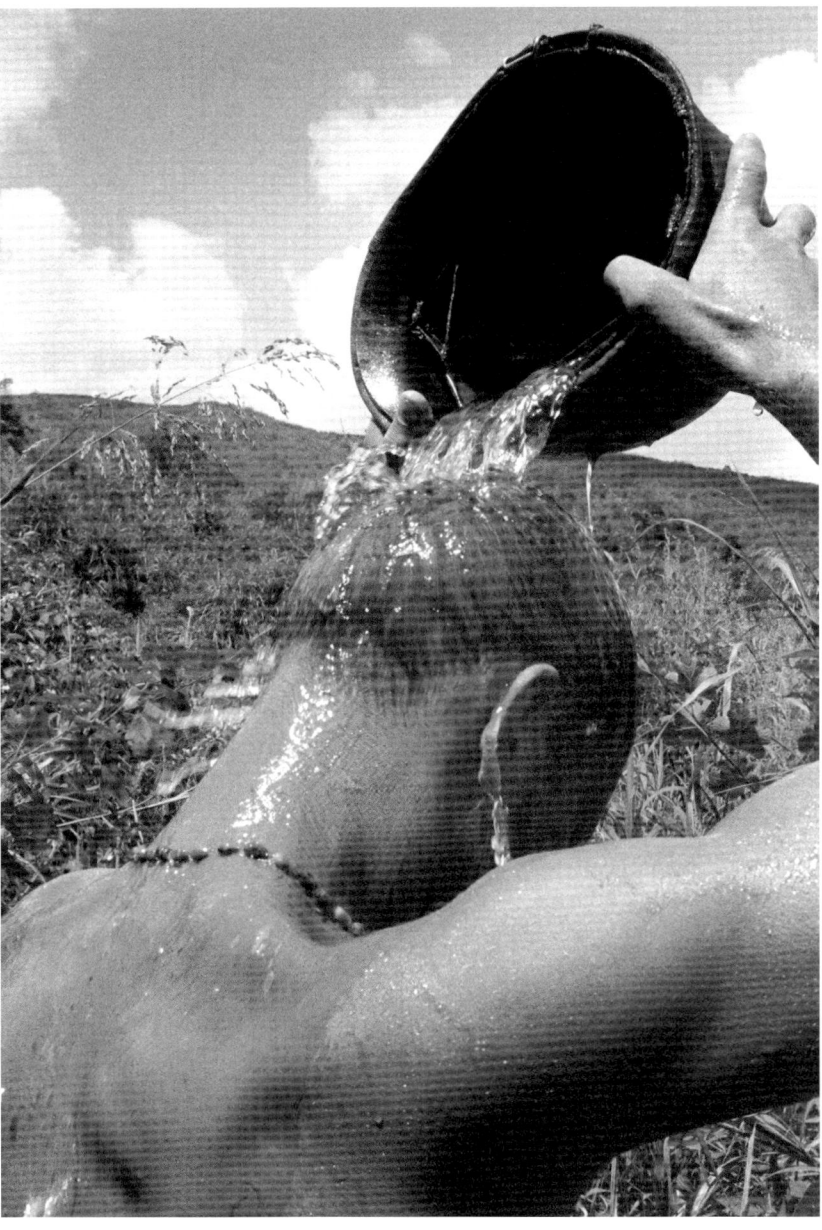

In yet another use of the "steel pot" headgear, a soldier cools down on a hot day. Soldiers filled canteens at streams, then added water-purifying tablets and packets of Kool-Aid to yield sweet, safe water.

Hall, Michigan, had less than three months to go. Michael Knutson of Norfolk, Virginia, faced nine long months. Either or both might die any second any day in this valley.

There, the 1st and 31st NVA Regiments were harassing infantry and artillery bases with mortar fire. By day, 4/31 was to find, fix, and silence those weapons. By night, they set out three separate ambushes.

Alpha had walked nearly a week when on 3 June it settled into its night laager. Except for guard duty, all slept while the calendar page turned to 4 June. Jim Logue jerked awake at the first shots at 0105.

"I heard, 'Pop. Bang. Kack, kack, kack.' You could hear explosions and the firing of small arms. You could hear them coming towards you, but who were they, our guys or the NVA? The action seems to have been in front of me. Explosions were going off inside the perimeter. You could see the flash of grenades. We were taking mortar rounds. The 'Midget Squad' was getting hit."

"All I remember is a bright flash and I went down," recalls Midget Squad member Kent Green of Clarksville, Indiana, who was weak from malaria. "When I came to, Ron 'Speedy' Hottman was pulling me into our foxhole, under fire," he recalls.

The NVA lunged into the laager, where fighting was hand to hand.

"They were right at our perimeter," recalls Chuck Mann, the Pennsylvania schoolteacher and temporary platoon leader of Third Herd. "I was blown up in the air. I heard a bunch of guys on the right side of my perimeter and I knew they were wounded. Three of the guys should've been extracted from the field, because they had, like, ten days left. They were *short*. They were seasoned veterans and they were falling apart, emotionally."

Chuck struggled to keep his own sanity.

"I had no feelings in my legs. When I heard guys crying or more or less getting excited, I crawled over to see what the situation was. I was platoon leader. You've got to find out the status of your troops."

He wriggled among his men, then towards the CP, the ground trembling from mortar bursts. Ngo, or "No-Go," as the men called one of Alpha's Kit Carson scouts, pulled Chuck into a foxhole. Seconds later, a round exploded where the schoolteacher had lain.

"I would have taken a direct hit. My guardian angel, somebody, was watching me," he says.

Logue, hugging the earth in his foxhole, shouted into the PRC-25 receiver for a medevac.

To evacuate wounded, Michael Knutson, now of Illinois, and Esterling searched desperately in the black night and found one clearing, so small only a superb pilot could squeeze into such a vest pocket of space. Worse, someone had to stand in the laager with a light and guide the pilot down. Michael grabbed a hand-held, lithium battery-powered SDU-5/E Strobe Light and, wearing a boonie, walked out into the middle of the field and held up the strobe in the crisscross of fire.

"You cannot pop smoke at night. You have to use a strobe light. So I said, 'Shit. These are my friends.' We had to get them out. I knew I was getting shot at. I really didn't care. You have to stand there with the light and he [medevac pilot] hits you with a landing light. You wind up your arm and you point a direction for him to come out," Michael explains.

As the pilot of medevac tail number #610 of 236th Medical Detachment descended into the clearing, his aircraft nearly killed Knutson.

"When he swung that tail rotor around he probably missed my head by about six inches, enough to put a little hole in my hat," he says.

While most poured a withering fire at the enemy, others hustled the wounded onto the medevac. Chuck boarded last, behind "guys who were really banged up worse than me."

With ten aboard, the pilot willed his heavy bird into flight, trails of enemy tracers whizzing past.

Alpha held the perimeter until firing sputtered out.

At 0340 hours, *Daily Staff Journal* of 4/31 listed these men medevacked to the 91st Evacuation Hospital in Chu Lai:

John Linnenkamp, hearing impairment; Stanley Falasa, fragment wounds to right leg, left arm, and hips; Edwin Batchelor, fragment wounds to right ankle; James Hogan, fragment wounds to face, wrist, and hip; David Flynn, fragment wounds to skull; Charles Mann, fragment wounds to both legs and back; Robert Hart, fragment wounds to left wrist; Richard Frain, fragment wounds to left arm; Daniel Whitman, multiple fragment wounds to left leg; Rollin Miller, fragment wounds to left arm and right ankle.

Another wounded, Raymond Stark, was treated in the field. Kent Green, malaria-ridden, remained on duty, too.

Alpha had held.

Sergeant Perry Stemen watched day approach. "I was never afraid until it was over," he remarks of firefights. "You're moving, fighting back. When things were over I thought, 'Son of a gun, I could have been killed.'"

He had been lucky as a squad leader in 3rd Platoon. When "friendly fire" artillery killed Duane Peterson, Perry stood three feet away. He was injured, earning him his first Purple Heart. His second, as well as a Silver Star, came on the 16 May attack on NVA dug beneath boulders.

Wounds sustained in the 4 June night attack earned Stemen his third "Slow Badge," slang for Purple Heart. One more would qualify him for safer duty until he completed his tour. Had he a dozen more such honors on this day, however, no chopper would whisk him to safety. Alpha, now with thirty-seven men, needed every rifle.

Stemen was thinking only, however, of the sweet hot chocolate packet in his ruck to wash away combat's acrid taste.

"I walk back to my hole and another dink sticks his head out," he recalls. "I was lucky to see him first. I dropped to the ground and we kept firing at him and he's keeping his head down. Got him with a hand grenade. He had an RPG."

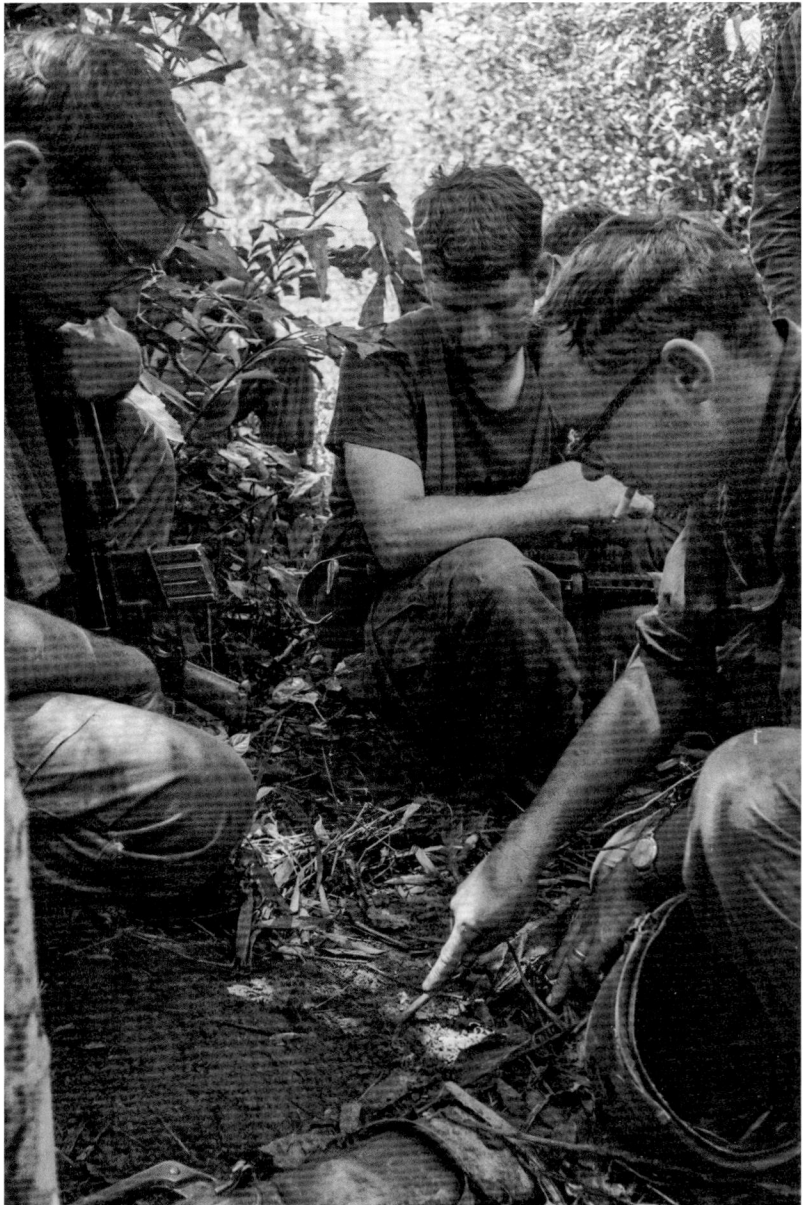

As if drawing up a sandlot football play, First Lieutenant Erwin Esterling maps strategy with Second Lieutenant Richard A. Brandeburg and Sergeant First Class Everette Caldwell.

Thus another day, the 38th since Alpha locked horns with 2nd NVA Division, began with fire.

Late that afternoon, Alpha ascended LZ West. Malaria-stricken Kent Green, who had walked all day, was medevacked with a 105-degree fever. Now the company numbered thirty-six.

The morning of 5 June, the clerk Finkbeiner typed into *Daily Staff Journal* the day's forecast: a high of 97 degrees, with 95 percent humidity. Late that afternoon, with orders to move, Esterling led the company down West once more.

At 1610, Alpha reached its night laager at topographical coordinates NDP 968252, designating a lower slope of West. All dropped their "heavies." All drank deeply from canteens. They were a pitiful sight: stick men in filthy olive drab, wraiths because of scant rations and numb from three months of fighting and moving, all set to the dirge of medevac rotors lifting away friends, among them some they'd never see again.

Night laager routines began. Patrols swept the area. Other men encircled the laager perimeter with claymore mines. All dug foxholes, looked to their feet, and opened C-rations. At least the little band had won a single victory this day. Each was alive, each one day nearer home.

"Click. Click. Click."

Logue was taking photographs. For one shot, he stood above the company's new first sergeant and two lieutenants squatting over a map drawn in the dirt: circles and lines resembling a play in a sandlot football game.

Like Esterling, newly arrived Second Lieutenant Richard A. Brandeburg wore glasses. Drafted before his senior year at Temple University, he completed Officer Candidate School and jump school. At his home in North Las Vegas, Nevada, he chuckles when recalling his arrival at Fort Bragg, North Carolina, for Special Forces training.

"'Little Ricky is going to be a Green Beret,' I thought. I walked into the orderly room with six other second lieutenants. We all had glasses on. They just said, 'Sorry.'"

Green Berets needed perfect eyesight.

As another who was transferred from 1st Division, Richard took command of 3rd Platoon. The new LT sought advice of enlisted men and spoke to them with respect. Grunts tolerated such junior officers who, like them, just wanted to go home.

None, however, cared for Sergeant First Class Everette Brent Caldwell, the new company first sergeant.

"Lifer," they spat.

Caldwell was no "cherry"; he completed one tour in Vietnam as a helicopter gunner, then trained troops as a drill sergeant in the States, while requesting a combat infantry assignment in Vietnam. He arrived at Alpha loud, demanding, and demeaning, as if he still wore the Montana peak drill sergeant hat.

"Just stay away from him," veterans advised each other. They knew distance was their best defense. Loudmouths get killed. Loudmouths get *you* killed.

Richard Thimmig, a printer's son from Sparta, Illinois, shucked off his boots to ease his painful ankle. "A sprain," medics insisted, and sent him back to the field. In the 4 June attack, he had hobbled over to Michael Knutson and sprayed the enemy with his M60 until the medevac sped away with the wounded.

"You got *some* cojones," Thimmig recalls a soldier telling him.

Cleveland Crist, now of Grand Junction, Colorado, was equally respected. Like most other enlisted men, he dreaded fighting in the war. After infantry AIT at Fort Lewis, Washington, he was so desperate to remain with wife and infant daughter he tried to break a leg.

"I propped one leg up on a set of stairs and I had one of my fellow soldiers get up higher and jump on it. I heard things go, 'Snap, crackle, pop' and thought, 'Oh, boy, I did it. I'm out of this thing,'" he recalls.

The leg was inflamed but unbroken. Cleve hobbled on crutches, then tossed them into a trashcan on the airport tarmac before boarding the plane for Vietnam. He grew into a good soldier, an excellent rifleman, M60 gunner, M79 grenadier, and point man.

Nearby, Daniel Richard LaPierre, collapsed in his foxhole, was so weary he perhaps lapsed into his native French: "*Je suis effrayé, fatigué, affamé, et j'ai le mal du pays.*" Indeed, he was "scared, tired, hungry, and homesick."

In 1842, LaPierre's ancestors migrated from Quebec to Levant, Maine. As fifth generation of his family to farm potatoes, he began each day at first light.

June was planting time back home. Later, while crops grew, Dan repaired cedar-and-ash potato barrels. Of all the civilian occupations of the soldiers, "cooper" was likely rare among those serving in Vietnam.

English was Dan's second language. In the 1950s, Maine public schools prohibited children of French-Canadian ancestry from speaking their language, just as schoolchildren in south Louisiana were forbidden to speak their French Acadiana patois.

An accounting major at Husson College (now Husson University) in Bangor, he lacked ten credits to graduate when he was drafted. In Vietnam, he instantly bonded with his squad leader, fellow farmer Keith Lochner, and with Kent Green.

Now, in his fifth month in Vietnam, Dan still mourned the loss of the Indiana farmer. One good friend from Midget Squad, Ron "Speedy" Hottman, remained. In fading light, Dan touched the blue cross on a rosary he wore around his neck.

Nearby, Mark Klever of Milwaukee, who had enlisted at 17, prepared for the night. To the men of Alpha, Mark, at just above five feet, was like a "kid brother" due to height, age, and maturity. On this June night, Mark should have been at his high school prom with his girlfriend, Rose.

Midget Squad boasted one giant. Medic Michael Janak of Buffalo, New York, stood six feet, five inches tall. He knew his height made him a bigger target.

"I don't think there was a day there that I wasn't scared," he would say later. "You never got comfortable. It was always something eating at you in the back of your mind." "Doc," in his ninth month in Vietnam, would make his rounds in the morning to watch men of 3rd Platoon swallow their daily malaria pills.

Stemen pawed through his ruck for supper. He needed the calories; months in the bush had slashed his weight from 185 to 145. To make C-ration entrees palatable, he doused them with Tabasco sauce, the Avery Island, Louisiana, condiment he first tasted in Vietnam and still enjoys.

"I'd never been homesick in my life until then," he says of his stint in Vietnam. "I guess you don't realize what you've got until you don't have it."

"TWO WEEKS. TWO WEEKS. TWO WEEKS."

Each time Specialist 4 Dennis Hogenboom gouged his entrenching tool into soil, he murmured like a mantra his days remaining in Vietnam.

The Clymer, New York, native was 26, married and father to an infant daughter. A high school history teacher, he held a master's degree and looked rather dapper as a pipe smoker. He was soft spoken, well liked, and widely admired. Younger soldiers saw him as a father figure and often sought his counsel. If they had legitimate gripes, he presented their cases up the chain of command on West. With his professorial demeanor and command of language, he often won for his "clients."

Dennis lit his pipe and dreamed of his family and future. He'd complete his PhD then choose a career: life as a college professor or in public service, perhaps elected office. Mostly, he yearned for his beloved wife, Patsy, a registered nurse, and their infant daughter, Natalie, born ten days before Dennis left for Vietnam. So very soon, he'd be clean and safe with his lovely wife and holding again that soft, talcum-scented bundle of pure innocence.

Dusk deepened. Dennis knocked out the ashes in his pipe. Except for those on first watch, all fell into exhausted sleep: thirty-six young hearts beating in the night at NDP 968252, a place with only a number for a name.

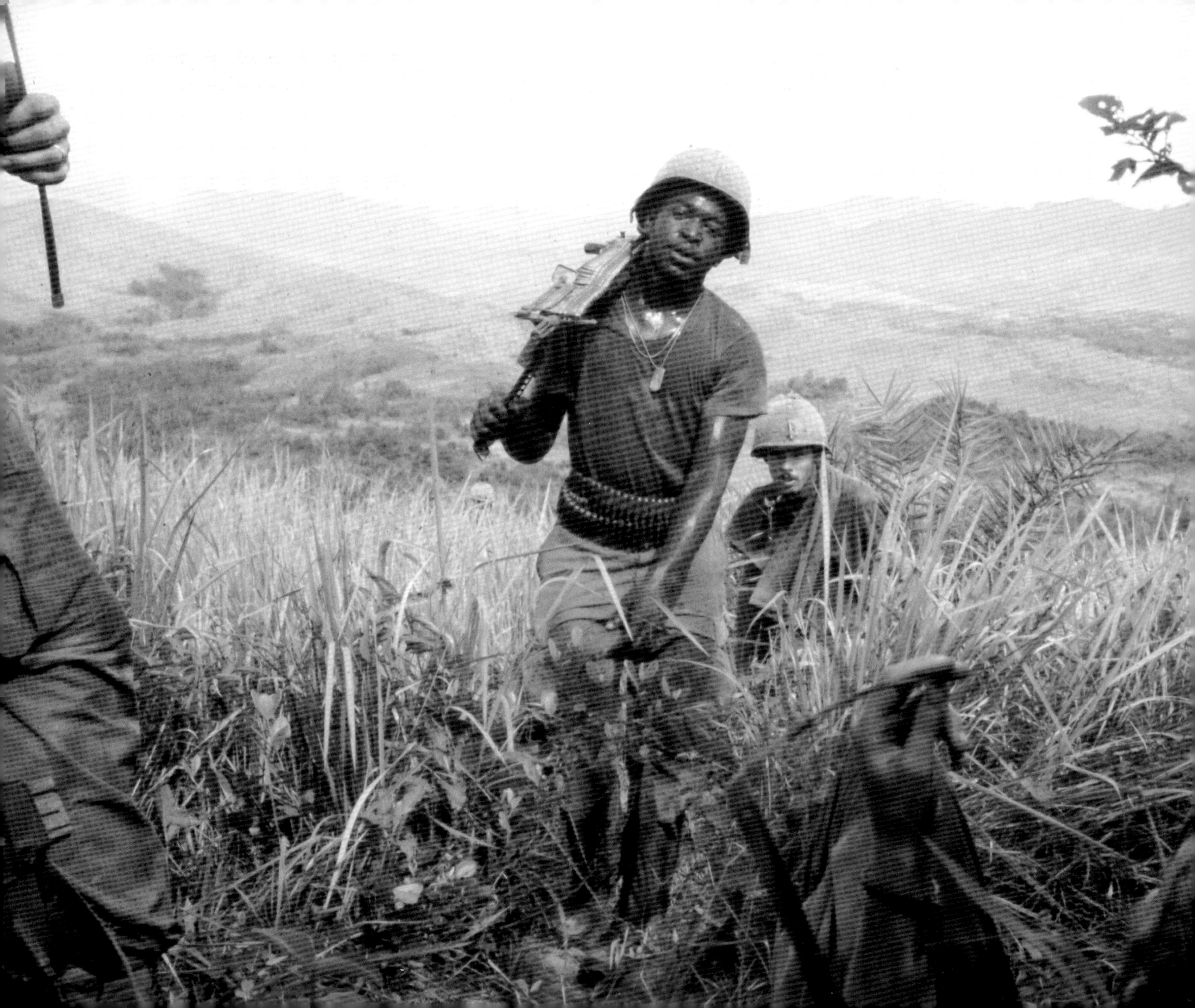

Chapter 15

That Day Was Just Pure Hell

Specialist 4 Roger Marksch

AS ALPHA SLEPT, HIGH ABOVE ON WEST, FINKBEINER TYPED OUT *6 June 1970* and *2400 hours* into 4/31 *Daily Journal*. Then he entered Alpha's destiny for that day: to *block any enemy forces coming into CFZ [Controlled Fire Zone] from LZ West.*

Nearby, another clerk rolled into his typewriter a sandwich of two pieces of blue carbon paper inserted between three white pages. Then he typed in triplicate a memorandum from LTC Kenneth L. Skaer, commander of 4/31, entitled CIVIL AFFAIRS AND CIVIC ACTION REPORTS for 29 May to 4 June 1970. Skaer had written:

> Main Force elements of the 2nd NVA Division continue their presence in the Hiep Duc Valley. However, [Operation] Golden Fleece has been carried on for the Third Lunar Harvest. 27 tons of rice has [*sic*] been harvested around the Hiep Duc Controlled Fire Zone. As the tactical situation permits, more rice will be harvested.
>
> The Medcaps have continued their daily operations. They will continue.

Soon, copies of the memo winged their way to in-boxes at higher headquarters. Skaer's note and Finkbeiner's summary of Alpha's mission description characterize America's two main efforts in South Vietnam: fight the enemy and pacify civilians.

Far below West, Alpha finished meager breakfasts and lit cigarettes. This only they knew: They would soon depart for another walk in the war, and one day nearer home.

Thirteen hours later in America, millions opened morning newspapers to a front-page story, illustrated with a grainy photograph by Robert Capa, depicting G.I.s wading ashore under heavy fire at Normandy, France.

"Oh, today is the 26th anniversary of D-Day," a World War II veteran might comment, then sip his coffee and turn to the sports pages.

Likely, none in Alpha thought in particular of this seminal date years before they took first breath. John Young of Buffalo, New York, just knew this: Once again he would look out for Mark Klever. At six feet, two inches tall and 200 pounds, John was a gentle giant to Mark, who stood a little over five feet.

Left: Days after the 6 June battle, Alpha ascends LZ West with remains of KIAs.

Mark was both pet and pest, the kid brother-type who begs to tag along with older guys but can't keep pace.

"He was a great person, but he wasn't meant to be an infantryman. Mark was really close with me. We all looked after him as the baby brother because he was so little," John explains.

Many in Alpha believed Mark had never previously been given the dangerous job of walking point. Others, such as Kent Green, said he *did* lead Third Herd on occasion. On this morning, however, the news, shouted in disbelief, swept through Alpha:

"CALDWELL TOLD KLEVER TO WALK POINT!"

All who heard pounced on the new first sergeant.

"He's too young!"

"He's too little!"

"He's too scared!"

Caldwell shot back that *everybody* had to walk point. Mark said he didn't mind. Then he mentioned it to his big friend.

"I said, 'No you're not! You let one of the experienced guys walk point!'" Young recalls. "Mark says, 'What have I got to worry about? You're walking behind me with an M60.'"

Not all got the word. Caldwell had first ordered Cleveland Crist to walk point, but the Coloradan protested that he was carrying an M60 that day, a weapon too important to fall into enemy hands from a point man.

At least the mission portended little danger. Lieutenant Brandeburg recalls that Alpha was to locate some mortar tubes so close to the laager that the men wouldn't even need their "heavies." To move quickly, Esterling announced for all to take only water and ammo and leave their rucks with a rear guard of six.

Those six were "short": Dennis Hogenboom; two Kentuckians, John Megerle of Elsmere and Harold Bays of Flemingsburg; Tom Devlin of Paradise, California; the Montanan, John Oiestad; and Leonard Maggard of Delaware, Ohio, the same hometown as that of Roger Marksch.

At 6:45 a.m., Alpha stepped off. Behind Klever came Dan LaPierre as slack, then Young with his M60, Perry Stemen, and Lieutenant Brandeburg. Jim Logue shadowed Esterling as RTO. Soon all were slick with sweat from the wet heat.

Klever splashed through a small stream, crossed an open field, and then trampled through tangled brush in a westerly direction. All knew where they were: an old Alpha laager pockmarked with foxholes amid thick, green bush.

Just as Klever stepped to the edge of a foxhole, gunfire exploded. AK-47 rounds ripped through his chest and back.

It was 0700.

Klever toppled into the foxhole, dead. LaPierre dived into a shallow trench as Young hit the ground.

"I can see Mark's foot. I was that close to him. But the bullets were digging up all the dirt and grass in front of me," Young says.

Alpha, stumbling into an NVA company, roared in reply, M60s drowning out smaller weapons.

"I opened up. I mean, *I opened up*," recalls M60 gunner Richard Thimmig.

Others rushed forward, including Crist and Bob Jurek, a Texan also with an M60, whose face was covered with blood.

"Next thing I knew they were calling for another machine gun so I went out there and started shooting," Cleve remarks from his Grand Junction, Colorado, home.

Nearby, Brandeburg—whom Crist remembers as "real tall, about 6 feet, four inches and skinny as a rail"—said, "'I'm going over and give LaPierre some support!'

"I told him, 'You're crazy. They'll shoot your ass down. You're too tall.' He said, 'I'll crouch down low.' And he took off running. They shot him in the leg and there he lay in the middle of the clearing."

Cleve screamed for more ammo. Someone threw him several belts. He tossed some to Jurek and both "just kept whacking at what we couldn't see. We knew they were in the tree line in the jungle, just past the clearing. So that's all we did; just laid down a field of fire right to left. I got that gun so hot I could light a cigarette on the barrel," he remarks.

Esterling knew that everyone in Alpha, outstripped by two times their numbers, would die. He kept screaming for his men to pull back, while Jim Logue yelled into his radio for artillery and air support. Jim was shaking so with both terror and outrage that he could not safely fire his rifle with friends in front of him.

"I was going to throw rocks at the enemy. You remember when you were a kid and got so mad that you wanted to throw rocks? That's how I felt. I was standing up to throw when Esterling pulled me down by my belt and said, 'You don't want to do that, son.' He probably saved my life."

The battle's roar worsened. Along with AK-47s, the NVA unlimbered 82mm mortars and 51mm machine guns. Caldwell, seeing that Thimmig needed ammunition, wriggled his way among men, grabbing belts of M60 rounds.

"Sarge came up and brought me some ammo, and hooked it up," Thimmig recalls. He shakes his head incredulously. "And then he put his head up. I shouted, 'Get your head down!' Caldwell screamed back, 'Hell, these sons of bitches.' And then he got up. A round hit him right under the edge of his helmet and he went over. I think it killed him instantly."

Stemen, who lay nearby, remembers Caldwell's death slightly differently. "Caldwell came down and he was lying next to me, and we were firing to keep the heads down. The lieutenant was out here," Stemen says, indicating to his right. "I can't remember the exact order of things, but he [Caldwell] ended up taking his helmet off and he had a brushy haircut that was kind of shiny. They shot him right in the head. I've wondered if it were a sniper."

All were certain: Caldwell died instantly.

Soon, in answer to Logue's radio pleas, Cobra gunships swooped down on NVA positions. Air Force jets dropped 250-pound conventional bombs and 500-pounders of napalm. The earth shook and erupted in billowing flames. Still, the enemy laid down sheets of fire.

Medics worked desperately on Alpha's wounded. The 236th Medical Detachment quickly responded, with dust off

tail number #608 zooming into the battlefield, the Red Cross emblem on its nose like a promise of hope.

Brandeburg, hugging the earth, took a deep breath and leapt to his feet, dashing for a wood line when a round knocked him down. His glasses flew from his face. He didn't need them to know how badly he was hit.

"I saw part of the bone in my thigh sticking out of my leg," he recalls.

Immobile, he yelled for an M60 gunner to lay down fire for the medevac descending.

"As I'm yelling back towards the guys, I hear an explosion and I feel pressure in my side. So I knew I'd been hit by shrapnel from a grenade," he says. Stunned from two wounds, he squinted at a fuzzy image of "my medic running to me and bullets at his feet."

Medic Michael Janak reached Brandeburg and worked feverishly on his wounds. Stemen was running to the lieutenant, too, when mortar shards ripped into his face and legs. He kept running and reached Brandeburg, whom he was sure would die.

"Janak's putting a tourniquet on my leg and it hurts like hell. I yelled, 'Stop! Leave me alone.' Janak said, 'LT, you're going to bleed to death,'" Brandeburg remembers.

LaPierre, out of ammunition, also snaked his way toward the lieutenant.

"I crawled all the way across the field and yelled to Janak to get on his belly. The lieutenant is down so he's in the grass, but the medic is on his knees," LaPierre remarks of the medic's courage.

With a dust off descending, Janak, Stemen, and LaPierre dragged Brandeburg through toward the chopper. "I'd say a good fifty feet. He was screaming for us to leave him and let him die," LaPierre recalls.

The NVA concentrated fire on the medevac, now rising and turning away from the field.

"Somebody yelled up, 'You forgot the LT!' They call the helicopter and he comes back and lands and they throw me on,"

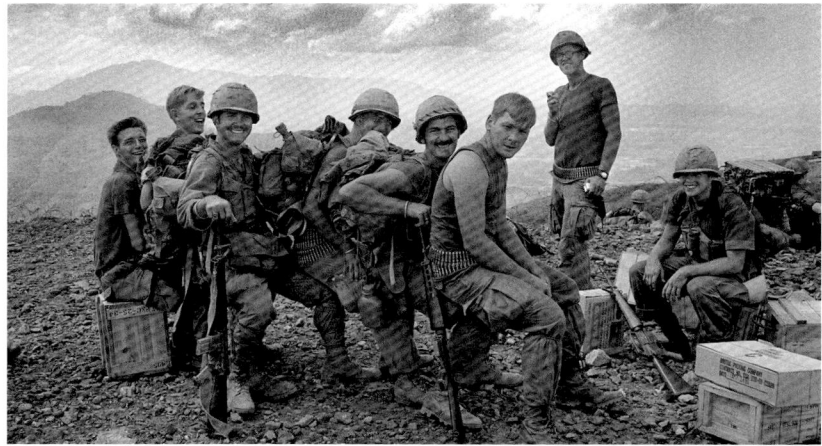

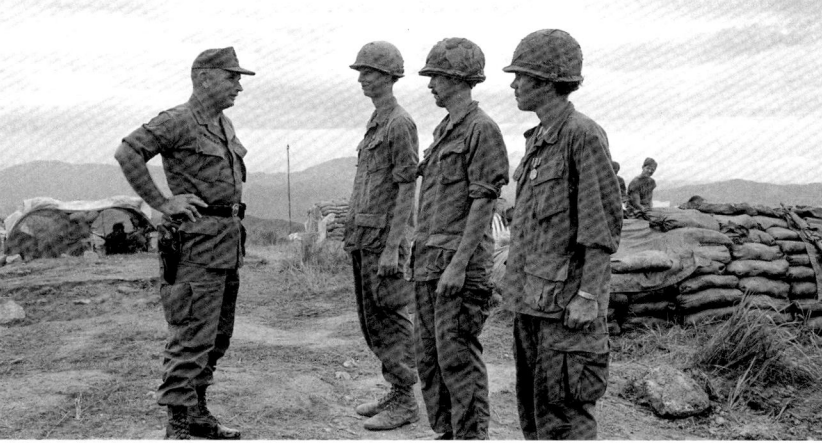

After the 6 June battle, these Alpha soldiers sit for Logue's camera. From left: Jim Hall; Ron Guyette; Cleveland Crist; Ronald Loomis; John Young; and Robert Sadler. Nearby stands Dennis Rutledge, with Dave Gould seated.

Major General A. E. Milloy presents Bronze Stars to (from left) Michael Janak and Dan LaPierre. Cleveland Crist receives the Army Commendation Medal with V for valor.

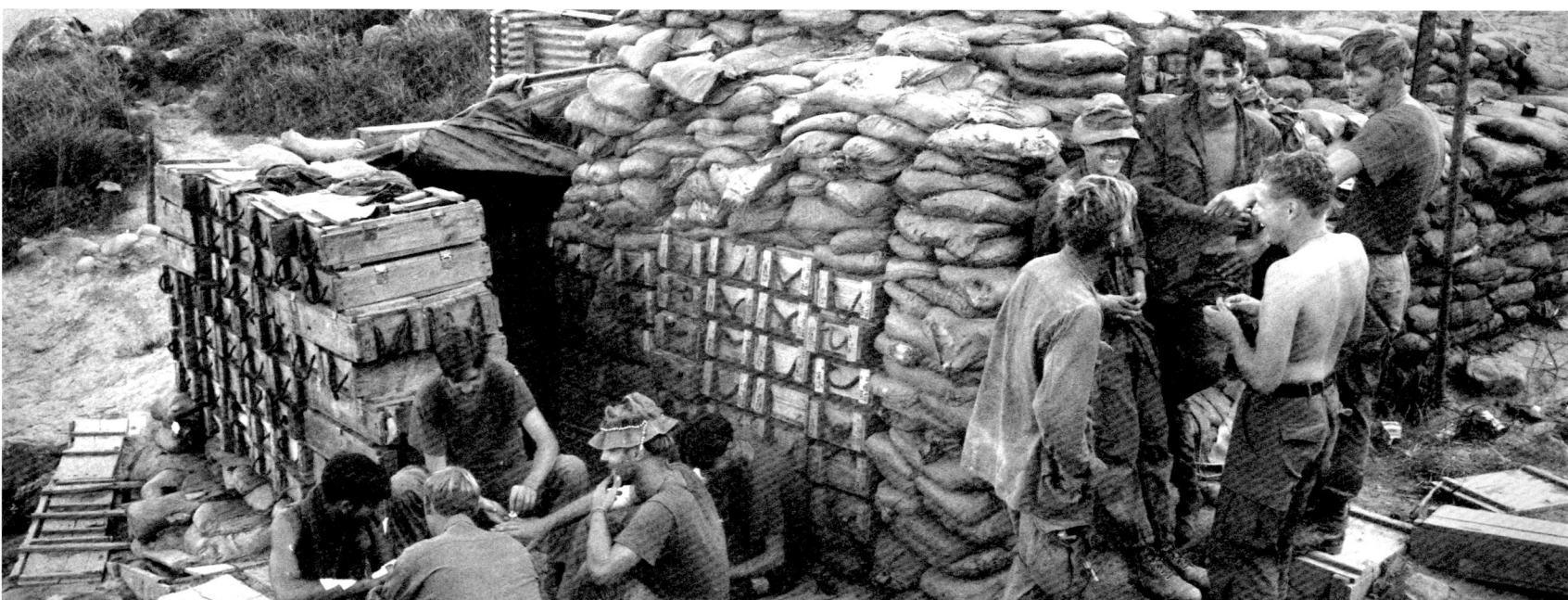

Mac ("Doc") Allen treats several men for small wounds after the 6 June 1970 battle. All are overjoyed at having survived Alpha's costliest firefight.

Brandeburg recalls, still both awestruck and humbled at the bravery of those who tended him and the medevac crew that twice flew into torrents of gunfire.

Other wounded aboard included James Kimball, Michael Roberts, Dan Ronnow, Danny Snyder, and Stemen, who had just earned his fourth Purple Heart and a second Silver Star. Bernard James was wounded but treated in the field.

One more Alpha soldier was pulled aboard to safety. Marksch watched the chopper rise with "a guy in one of those harness things. He had a steady stream of blood coming down. There were so many of us out in the open. And there are helicopters trying to get us out, and I know some of them went down," he recalls of the birds. No one we interviewed knows the name of the soldier.

Meanwhile, as D Company was rushing from the south towards the firefight, enemy gunfire roared from Alpha's right. Another company of NVA had arrived, threatening to roll up Alpha's right flank. By then, the nearly depleted company was dueling with *an estimated 70 men attempting to flank their position to the north at nearly point blank range*, as Finkbeiner wrote later in the *Daily Staff Journal*.

After three and a half hours of fighting, Esterling knew D Company was his last reinforcement. This day, he determined, would be no Little Big Horn, no Alamo, no reason to "die in these ditches." He made his decision.

"Retreat" seems a quaint word from a martial lexicon of the distant past, suggesting an orderly maneuver to extract a force from the field.

On this day, the men just ran like hell, uphill.

They streaked back through their night laager and scrambled up the mountain. Five of the six "short" guys in the rear joined them, first taking a last, anguished look back.

Hogenboom, twelve days from returning home, lay dead from the direct hit of a mortar round.

Falling and rising, running and tossing gear aside, they scrambled up, up through a gauntlet of steel from NVA rifles, machine guns, and mortars. With lungs afire and legs like rubber, one then another reached a "finger" higher up the slope where they turned, sprawled out, and sprayed covering fire for those still clawing their way to safety.

Megerle, two weeks from home, fell and drew up into a ball as a mortar screamed down and exploded nearby. He recalls: "I'm hit. Then I stood up. This guy behind me said, 'My God, I can't believe you're alive.' I said, 'I'm alive, but I'm going to get my ass up this hill.' And with that seventy-pound rucksack, I ran the rest of the way up that hill."

Meanwhile, Brandeburg lay on a table at 91st Evacuation Hospital in Chu Lai.

"They cut off my clothes and put a tube down my nose. They told me to count backwards and I woke up in a hospital bed with a cast from my stomach to my ankles," he remarks.

Atop LZ West, Logue recovered his breath and checked his Nikonos, astounded that he and his camera had survived the firefight. He steadied his hands, and once again camera, film, and light became more than the palette and canvas of his profession. With Nikonos to eye, he could banish briefly the nightmare of the killing fields below and work in the joy of his art.

Two photographs he took that afternoon signify an end and a beginning. None knew it, but Alpha had fought its last major engagement of the three-month campaign. Small firefights would flare up in the months to come; more would suffer wounds; more would fall ill; more would die. By mid-June, however, 2nd NVA Division, unable to crush the resistance of 196th Light Infantry Brigade, vanished into high, mountain mists.

In Logue's first image, Jim Hall sits on an upturned wooden box. Ron Guyette plops down on his lap; then, in the same manner, on one lap after another, sit Cleveland Crist, Ronald Loomis, John Young, and Robert Sadler. Some still wear steel pots and grasp M16s. They grin at the camera as Logue clicks his shutter.

Logue finds it curious that so many *love* this photograph. Indeed, it's a cliché. In the late 1800s, men in jaunty bowlers and women in leg-of-mutton sleeves similarly arranged themselves and smiled at big, hand-held box cameras. Even now, friends may sit lap-to-lap for cell phone photos.

Time, place, and subject, however, lift Logue's photograph to a portrait of humanity's will to survive. Those smiles, offered just minutes after a bloody battle, reveal the resilience of youth and the ecstasy of life granted in the face of almost certain death.

In another image, two groups of men have stowed combat gear and loiter among sandbags outside BTOC (Battalion Tactical Operations Center) bunker. Four sit before a medic who tends their minor wounds. Steps away stand a group of five. None notice the camera. As Logue snaps his shutter release, all break into big smiles, teeth brightly white in faces bronzed from weeks of sun. Now they are safe. Now they can laugh. Tomorrow they will see one more sunrise nearer home.

For their actions on 6 June, Cleveland Crist earned an Army Commendation Medal and Perry Stemen, his fourth Purple Heart and second Silver Star. Michael "Doc" Janak and Dan LaPierre each earned a Bronze Star with V device for valor.

For all, that day goes on and on and on. All his life Cleveland Crist blamed himself for Klever's death, not knowing, until Jim told him decades later, that Caldwell had *ordered* Klever to walk point.

For Alpha, 6 June 1970 is etched as deeply in their memories as 6 June 1944 had been for their parents.

"It's like an anniversary. We count the years. I've thought about that day all my life," Crist remarks.

In late afternoon, many pick at C-rations. Some fish out "church keys" and punch two triangular holes in tops of beer and soft drink cans. At twilight, many finish their last cigarettes of the day. Someone passes around a tin of cookies, crumbled during the long journey from a mother's kitchen to a combat zone. No one cares. Even crumbs taste sweetly of home.

Some begin first watch. A few write letters. Many fall asleep instantly. Others remain awake. Only when they hear sounds of sleep around them do they clamp hands over mouths and cry silently in joy for surviving what Roger Marksch so succinctly describes: "That day was just pure hell."

Back home, the 6 June battle earned not a mention, nor would hundreds of quick, bloody actions like it: small numbers, an hour or two of combat, a few dead. Certainly, in the next year or so, there would be larger engagements and the long-delayed heavy bombing of Operation Linebacker that nearly brought North Vietnam to its knees. Since at least 1969, however, the war had turned into dozens of 6 June battles, a long denouement marked by such small actions made large by very young men performing acts of incredible heroism for the same reason as had their fathers and grandfathers and the men of their blood long before them: not for country but for each other. And for every young man killed, a man beside him, old now, weeps in gratitude for the long life gifted him.

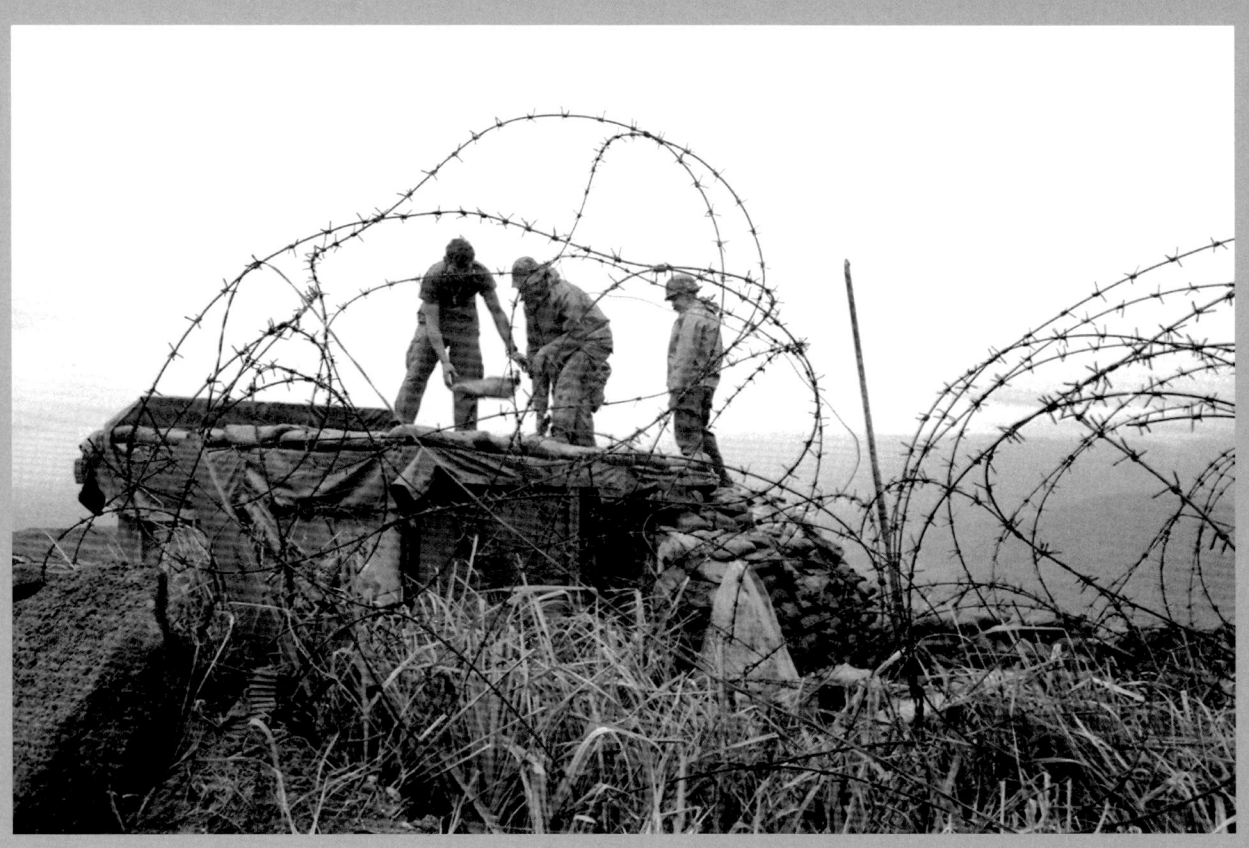

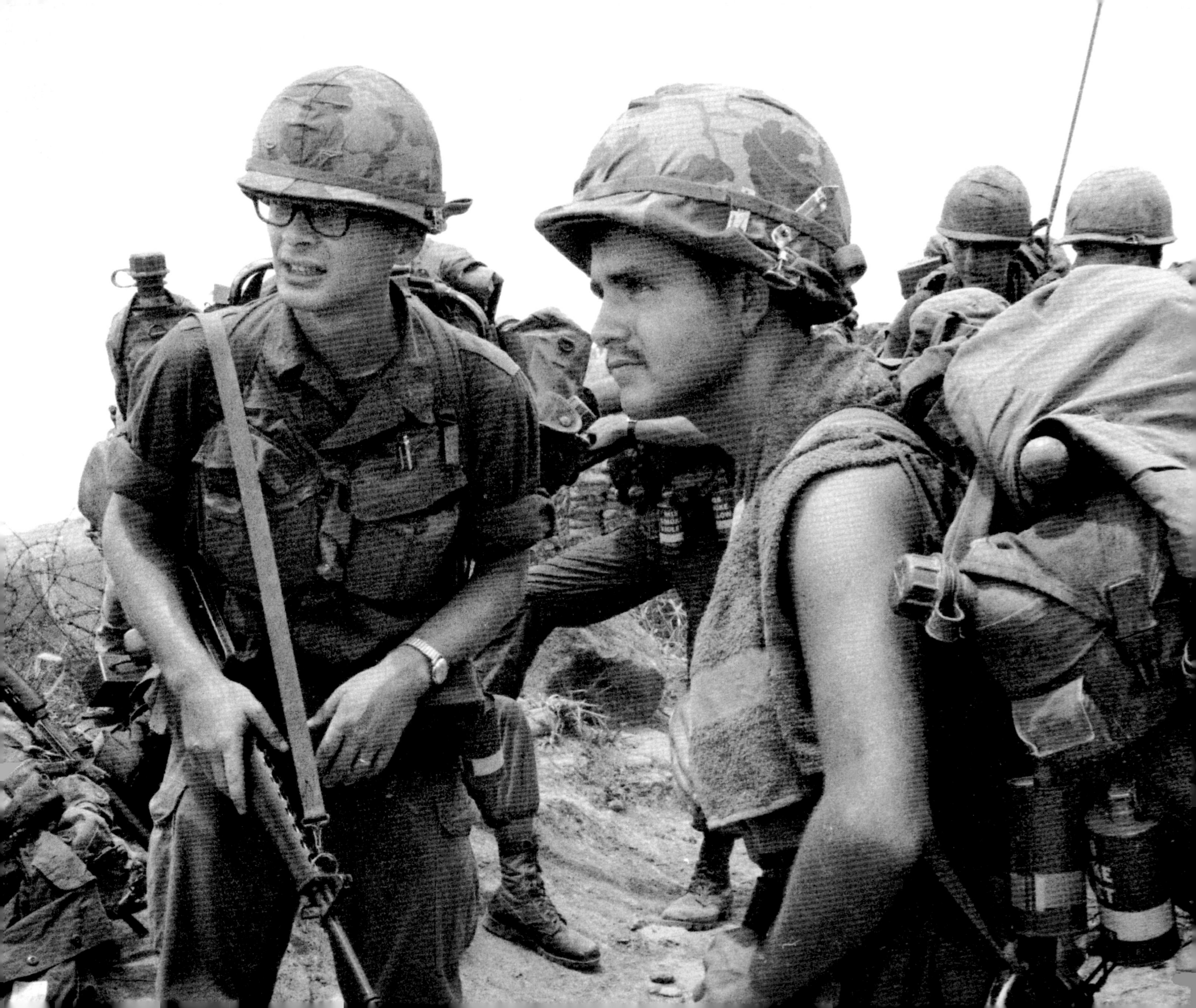

Chapter 16

Now I Know the Truth

Specialist 4 Mark Edward Klever (KIA)
Sergeant First Class Everette Brent Caldwell (KIA)
Specialist 4 Dennis Norman Hogenboom (KIA)

WHEN WE KNOCKED ON THE DOORS OF THE FAMILIES OF THE dead, Jim and I knew we were half a century late in explaining how their soldiers perished. In turn, they taught us how families shape them into such good men. So it was, too, of those lost on 6 June 1970.

Specialist 4 Mark Edward Klever — Milwaukee, WI

Most of all, the Klever family told us, he loved summer.

Each day, Mark dashed from his family's cottage near Kempster in northern Wisconsin to fish, swim, and hunt—not for sport but for food. Of seven siblings, Mark, last and least, stood only five feet, four inches. Bringing home food to feed the family helped him stand a little taller.

"We needed it so we could eat," remarks Sheila Klever, one of Mark's older sisters.

The Klevers, residents of Milwaukee, certainly were *not* a wealthy family to "summer" at their cottage. Mark's dad, Donald Victor Klever, after a week of work, spent weekends at the cottage with his wife, Mae Merrell McDonald, and the family.

Mae guided the family with a firm hand. Her word was law, we learned when we met John, Mark's older brother, and his wife, Pat, in their Wauwatosa home south of Milwaukee. Also there were Mark's niece, Gail Klever Harvancik, her husband, Gary, and Mark's sister, Sheila.

Donald and Mae Klever reared their older children amidst workaday rhythms remaining from the nineteenth century. John remembers horse-drawn conveyances of the ragman, the garbage man, and the iceman—all of which had vanished by the 1960s.

The differences in two eras caused a clash between Donald and Mae and their youngest, Al and Mark. Parents who once swooned to Nelson Eddy crooning "Indian Love Call" to Jeanette MacDonald winced as Al and Mark blasted out the Rolling Stones.

Left: Among the youngest in Alpha, Mark Klever (right) turned 19 in Vietnam. He had enlisted at age 17. He waits with First Lieutenant Erwin Esterling for orders to move out.

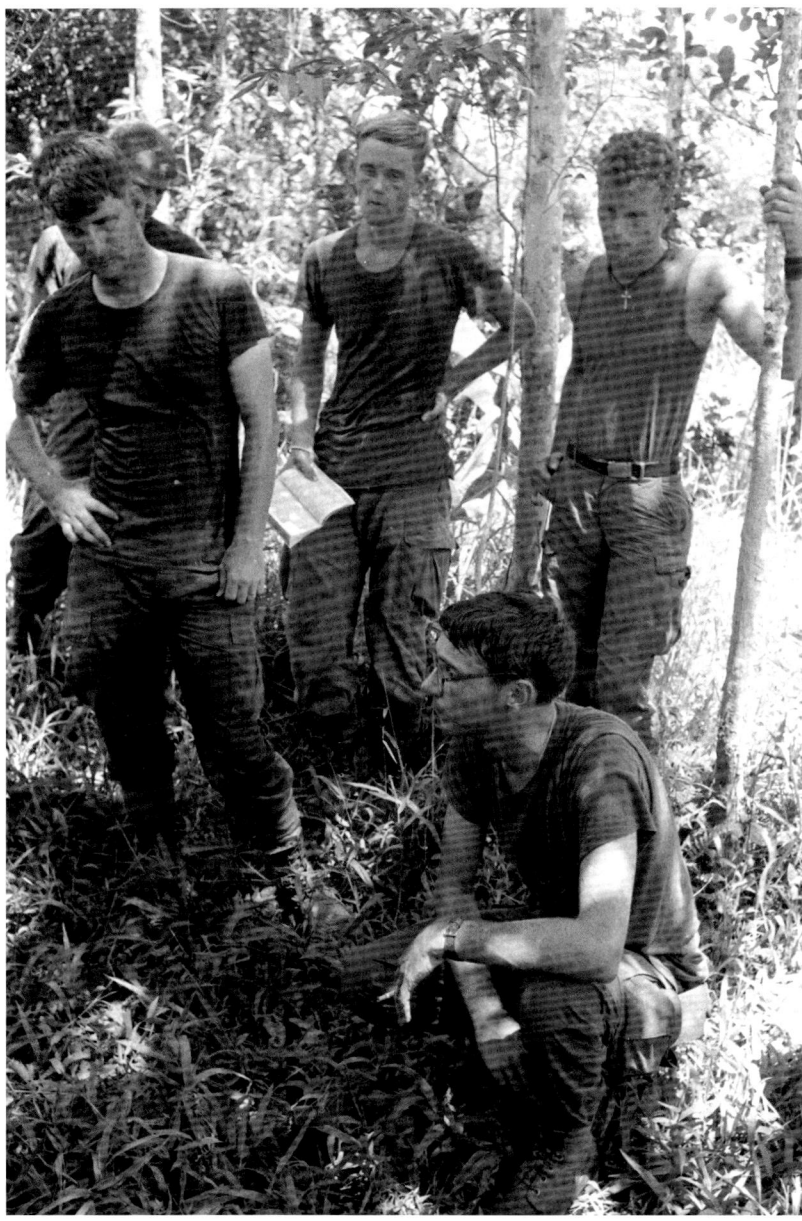

Sergeant First Class Everette Caldwell (left) listens with others to a quick lesson on setting up claymore mines. Claymores were placed around night laager perimeters against possible attacks.

Young love brewed more trouble when Mark was smitten by a girl "named something-Rose, or Rose-something," John remarks. The parents worried about consequences of "puppy love," while Mark seemed to be spinning out of control as he reached high school. Perhaps, Mark's family determined, the Army might instill discipline the boy needed, while separating lovestruck teenagers.

"I was in favor of him going to the Army," John says. He winces. "I said, 'It can't hurt him.'"

When Mark turned 17, Mae signed enlistment papers.

None remember where Mark took basic training; nearly all of his artifacts disappeared after his father's demise. One photograph portrays the young soldier beside a sign of a tiger, likely indicating "Tigerland," the infantry training area at Louisiana's Fort Polk.

The family was astounded when Mark came home before departing for Vietnam. In his Class A uniform, he carried himself with a new maturity, "like a gentleman," as John recalls.

Mark stepped onto LZ West on 21 August 1969. Veterans kept their distance from "new meats," especially this kid.

In Keith Lochner's Midget Squad of 3rd Platoon, Mark tried hard but proved inept, often humping too much and falling behind. Slowly, however, he "grew" as a soldier, learning how to pack his ruck and carry it high on his back, to maintain noise discipline, to stay alert. During the night of 5–6 June, perhaps he reread letters from his family and from Rose, stared into the black void, and counted again. Seventy-six days later, he'd be home.

For nearly two hours, Jim talked to the Klevers about life in Alpha Company. Then, he gently related the events of 6 June as Mark led Alpha into battle. Jim assured them that Mark died instantly. He received posthumously the Purple Heart and promotion to corporal.

On a July day in 1970, the family held Mark's funeral at St. James Lutheran Church. Ronald "Speedy" Hottman of Toledo, Ohio, Midget Squad member who accompanied Mark's body home, was in attendance. So was Rose.

"She was a cute little thing. She was very distraught," Sheila recalls.

The body was borne 200 miles north to Kempster, where the family buried their soldier near the woods and waters he loved.

Sergeant First Class Everette Brent Caldwell — Tulsa, Oklahoma

She says her Brent was evolving into a faithful, loving husband and father when he flew to Vietnam for his second tour in spring 1970. He was 24.

"I often wonder how things would have been had he lived," remarks his widow, Loretta May. She sits on the sofa beside her son, Everette Brent Caldwell Jr., in her home in Claremore, Oklahoma. Jim smiles at Brent.

"You look like your dad," he says. Brent beams.

His dad would have been proud of him. Young Brent played on a football scholarship as a safety for the University of Alabama and then served a career in the Navy and Air Force.

Jim quietly but matter-of-factly relates to Loretta and Brent how others in Alpha mistrusted, even despised, SFC Caldwell. They nod solemnly.

"He didn't have the greatest childhood," Brent says of his California-born father who grew up in Tulsa. In the 1950s, Everette was tossed back and forth between divorced parents. His stepfather locked the refrigerator between meals, an especially cruel act for young children so hungry after school. Everette never had proper clothing. His feet hurt from wearing shoes he'd outgrown.

When he was 15, he met Loretta Aery in church. They began dating, but soon her parents forbade her to see him. At 16, Everette lied about his age and enlisted. He was stationed in South Korea when the Army learned his true age and shipped him home to serve in the Oklahoma National Guard until he turned 17.

The young couple married when Brent was 19 and Loretta 18. At Fort Ord, California, he was serving as a drill sergeant when their first child, Kerry, was born. Trouble followed Everette. At Fort Benning, he fought a master sergeant's son and was busted from E5 to E4.

Brent was still an infant when his dad completed his first tour in Vietnam, where he earned a Purple Heart as a helicopter gunner with 120th Aviation Company, 5th Aviation Battalion. A drill sergeant again, this time at Fort McClellan, Alabama, he earned E-6, then E-7 ranks. Meanwhile, Loretta noticed, he was maturing as husband and father. He quit the bar life with buddies and came home from work each afternoon. On weekends, he treated the children to amusement parks and ice cream.

With orders for Vietnam, he was solemn and subdued in the Tulsa airport and refused photos taken of him until his sister begged for just one. In the image, Everette, wearing summer khakis, looks up at the camera with only a hint of a smile. As his plane lifted off the tarmac, young Kerry Caldwell turned to her mother.

"I'll never see my daddy again," Kerry said as his plane lifted off the tarmac.

"I said, 'Yes, you will.' She said, 'No, I won't.' And we never saw him again," Loretta says.

At age 24, Everette (the youngest SFC in the Army, he claimed) arrived on LZ West on 5 May 1970. Jim relates to Loretta and Brent the battle of 6 June: how Everette exposed himself to fire in bringing up ammunition for M60 gunners and how he died instantly from a single round.

Mother and son, sitting close together, fall silent. Then Loretta tells Jim, "I want to thank you. They told me a completely different story."

"We heard he was killed by a mortar," explains Brent, who as a young child fell asleep during his father's funeral.

Today, all the family possesses of Everette's military career are photographs Jim took of him one day before his death. Brent's stepfather, now deceased, burned all Everette's military artifacts, even his drill sergeant hat. Brent, then a youngster, was devastated and as furious with his stepfather as his dad had been with his own father.

"He did apologize to me later," Brent said.

This Jim assures them: Had he lived, Everette, like all soldiers new to ground war in Vietnam, would have learned to listen to his men and benefit from their experience.

Later at lunch we chat, laugh, and discuss the topic that arises in many Oklahoma conversations: Sooner football. As we leave, Loretta hugs Jim and thanks him for the knowledge he has provided of her husband's last day of life.

"Now I know the truth," she says.

Specialist 4 Dennis Norman Hogenboom — Clymer, New York

This peaceful countryside tucked in the southwestern corner of New York State may nurture a love of learning. Small towns rise along the drift of two-lane roads, where shoulders bloom in Queen Anne's lace and blue chicory. The village, Chautauqua, still hosts educational and entertainment programs like those it spread across the nation in the nineteenth century. This lovely country, quiet and reflective, may as easily produce professors as farmers.

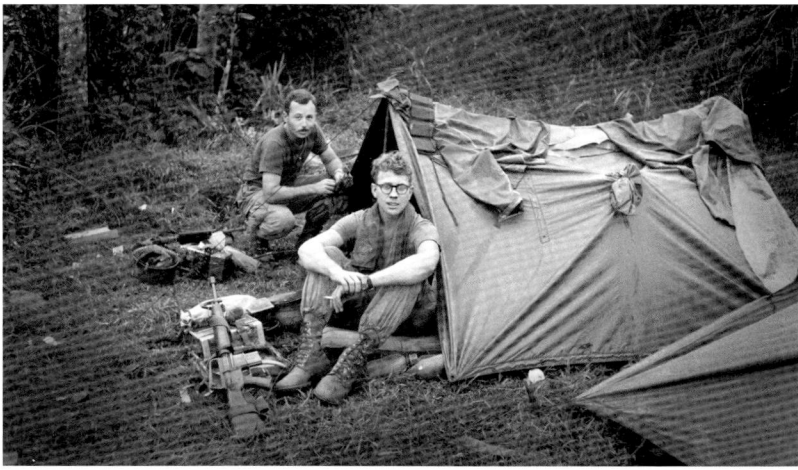

Dennis Hogenboom (top) held a master's degree in history when he was drafted. All, including officers, respected Dennis for his wisdom and generosity. Hooch-mate Leonard Maggard is in foreground.

On an August Sunday, Patsy Lane, widow of Dennis Hogenboom, meets us in the latter's hometown of Clymer, population 1,698, in the fellowship hall of Abbe Reformed Church. Here, during Sunday sermons in the early 1960s, "Denny" Hogenboom daydreamed about Patsy Hemink, who attended the nearby Methodist church. Her voice is soft and eloquent, perfect for her profession as a nurse, a field in which she earned a PhD.

"Absolutely," she responds when I ask if she lived a small-town child's life of bare feet, mud pies, and chores. In the barn, beside her grandfather, she learned to milk cows and in the kitchen helped her mother make butter and cottage cheese.

Meanwhile, Denny worked on his family's dairy farm with his father, Norman, a World War II veteran and chairman of the school board. Good grades were expected of Dennis and his sisters, Mary Ann (later Gerson) and Celia (Thompson). As youngsters, they rode their bicycles downhill to the town library, a six-mile round trip. Extensive reading helped them in gleaning knowledge for discussions at the family dinner table, ranging in topic from history to politics to world affairs.

The Heminks and Hogenbooms knew each other well. Denny, who played basketball for the Clymer High School Pirates, asked Patsy on their first date to the team's annual banquet. He graduated in 1962 (Patsy in '63) and enrolled for fall term at Hartwick College in Oneonta, New York, as a history major.

He was a graduate student in history at New York State College for Teachers (now the State University of New York at Albany) when the two wed. With his master's degree, Denny was practice-teaching high school American history when he was drafted in August 1968.

The Army sent Denny to Officer Candidate School at Fort Belvoir, which he did not complete. Patsy does not remember why. Their daughter, Natalie, was born in September 1969. Ten days later, Denny left for Vietnam.

Nearly all in Alpha, Jim tells Patsy, looked up to Dennis, who at 26 was older than the enlisted men and even some officers. As if he were a surrogate father, he grunted often when asked his advice on such topics as school, money, marriage.

In April 1970, Patsy and the baby, Natalie, met Denny in Hawaii for R&R. Already, he had told her the exciting news: He was getting a three-month "drop" in Vietnam and could return to teaching in September. Patsy wasn't as optimistic about this idea. She found Dennis "jumpy" from months in the field.

"I was very concerned. This was before PTSD had a name. I did not know how he was going to ETS at the beginning of August and start teaching," she recalls.

"Don't worry," Alpha men would have told her. When a sniper's round smacked Denny's wallet one day, all he said was: "Shot through with magic. That was the bullet meant for you!" "'Man, you got it made!'" they exclaimed.

A soldier and friend of the Hogenbooms, Fred Stacey was stationed on LZ West and tried to find duties to keep Dennis out of the bush, especially as his DEROS [Date Estimated Return from Overseas] neared. In early June, Alpha was returning to the field. Despite Stacey's efforts, Denny rucked up.

"He wanted to be out with the company. He liked the guys, knew most quite well, and had became [sic] a spokesman for them in compiling and presenting grievances, and for this he was respected," Stacey wrote Patsy.

From this letter of condolence to her, dated 6 June 1970, Stacey related an earlier conversation with Denny. He was "in fairly good spirits, although a little depressed over the size of the company and all the enemy in his area."

John Megerle of Elsmere, Kentucky, recalls Lieutenant Esterling's instructions to the men guarding the rucks in the night laager of 5 June.

"The lieutenant says, 'Megerle, Devlin, Weird [Harold Bayes], John-John [Oiested], Hogenboom, you guys stay back. You're short.' You guys went off the hill and . . . hit the shit, and we said, 'Oh no!' So here come gunships and we pop smoke."

The smoke marked to the choppers the location of the men left behind as rear guard but also likely alerted the enemy's mortar teams.

"Mortar tube on this side and mortar tube on that side," Megerle recalls of the enemy's crossfire. Down screamed mortars on the six men left in the rear. One round found its mark.

"It landed right in the hole with him," Megerle says of Hogenboom's death.

Back in the States, Patsy received a telegram that he was "missing in action," then another confirming his death. All of Clymer turned out to mourn the loss of one of the town's favorite sons.

On this Sunday afternoon, Patsy leads Jim and me up to Brownell Road, past Denny's boyhood home, a white frame, early twentieth-century two-story structure, and then to Holland Cemetery. At Denny's grave, she speaks of the interment: "The 21-gun salute, 'Taps' with a bugler. It was elegant. It was very nicely done." She sighs and adds, "The US Army certainly knows how to bury people."

Alpha men such as Perry Stemen of Whitehall, Michigan, speak admiringly of Hogenboom: "He was what you would expect of a very intelligent college professor. He was quiet, smart, a really good guy. I always felt bad because I knew he had a daughter."

Cleveland Crist of Grand Junction, Colorado, who battles his own nightmares of 6 June, remarks: "We all looked up to him. We respected him as a soldier. He didn't take a lot of chances and every day was a chance in Vietnam. He wanted to teach history and when he died I thought, 'Now he is part of history.'"

Patsy believes that Denny might have entered politics or attempted in other ways to improve the lives of Americans.

Perhaps his true calling, however, was as a history professor who had earned a greater knowledge few of his sheltered colleagues could ever know. One can picture him in a classroom, dressed in three-piece tweed faintly scented in pipe tobacco. Who better to teach students than a soldier who knew the worst of what it means to fight a war?

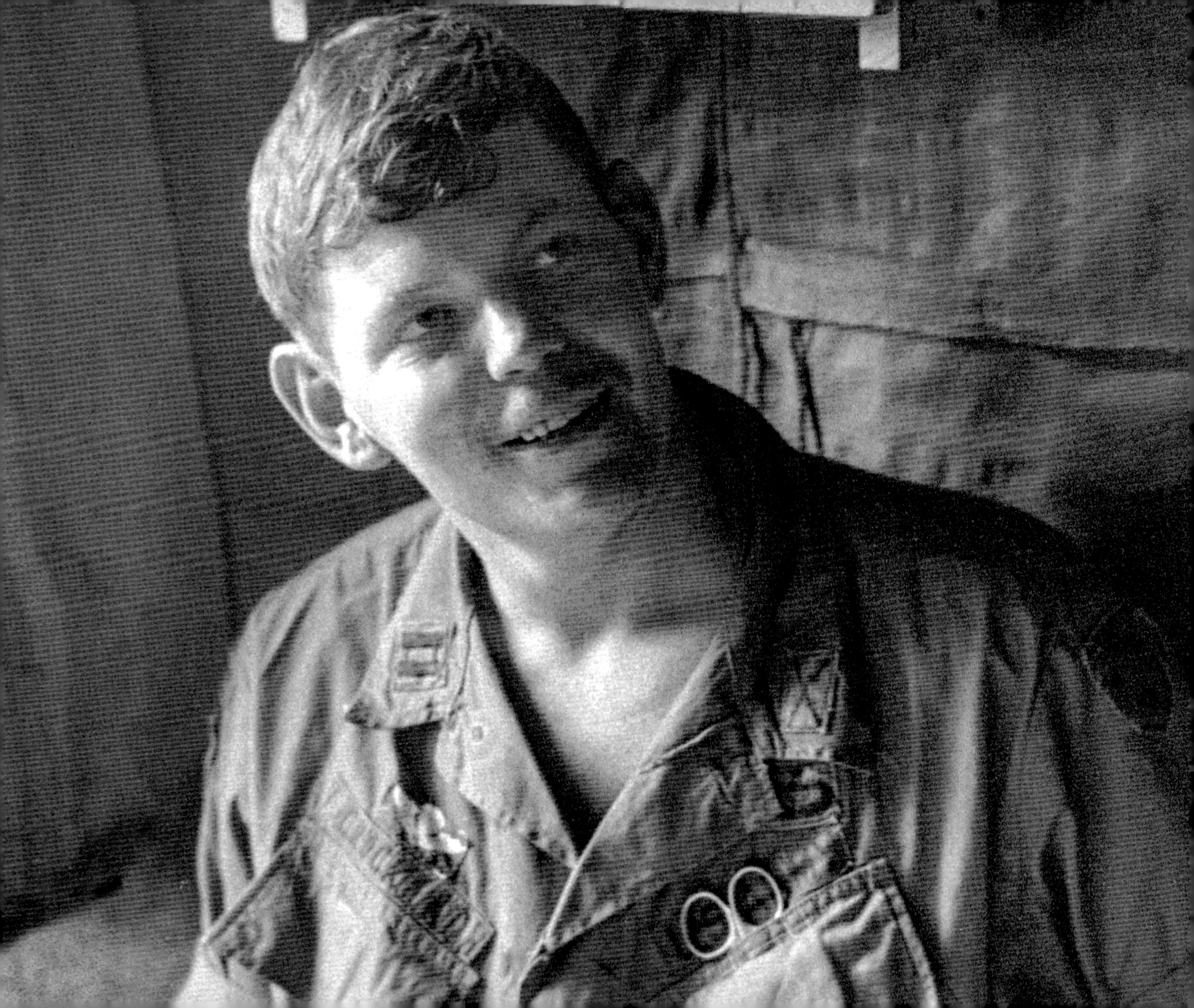

Chapter 17

Best Time in My Military Life

Colonel (ret) James Crockert

HE WAS SO STUNNED, HE STOPPED AND STARED AT THE gaggle of gaunt men huddled outside the perimeter of LZ West in the brutal heat of mid-afternoon.

"*This* is my new command?" he thought, with sinking heart.

Already, Special Forces Captain James Crockert, 25, had been disappointed when he arrived in Vietnam for his second tour on 2 June 1970. To his dismay, his orders had been changed. Americal Division desperately needed seasoned company commanders.

So late on 6 June he reported to LTC Kenneth Skaer, 4/31 commander, and Colonel Edwin Kennedy, commander of 196th LIB Alpha, at LZ West. They told him Alpha Company had fled battle that morning, leaving behind their dead and tossing aside rucks and weapons in an uphill retreat to LZ West. Worse, they had refused Kennedy's order to return to the battlefield and retrieve their dead.

Crockert's mission was to lead the company down to the battlefield, retrieve the dead, then whip this "excuse" for an infantry company into shape. He'd find them at "the finger," a protrusion one-half mile outside the fire base perimeter, bearing

the isolation of a leper's colony. As he drew near, he masked his amazement at their appearance: tatterdemalions in filthy fatigues, with skin blackened from weeks in the bush.

"This isn't a company," he thought. "It's a mob."

Crockert introduced himself and announced that the men were going to retrieve their fallen. Just as quickly they shot back that the enemy was still down there. He frowned. Skaer and Kennedy hadn't told him that.

This, however, he knew: His long-term mission was not only to shape up a company but also to raise it from the dead. That meant bringing it to full strength, bolstering spirits, sharpening abilities, and instilling a new esprit de corps. Just as important, he had to shield his little command from what he already sensed: incompetency at higher levels that had brought Alpha to its knees. After that, perhaps, he might earn their trust.

Years later, Colonel (ret) James Crockert, a kind man with a quick smile, described the divide between Alpha and the brass at battalion and brigade levels: "The animosity could be cut with a knife going both ways, and that is as kind as I can be. These

Left: Captain James Crockert served six months as Alpha Company commander beginning 7 June 1970. A Green Beret, he already had completed a tour in Vietnam. Crockert retired as a "bird" colonel.

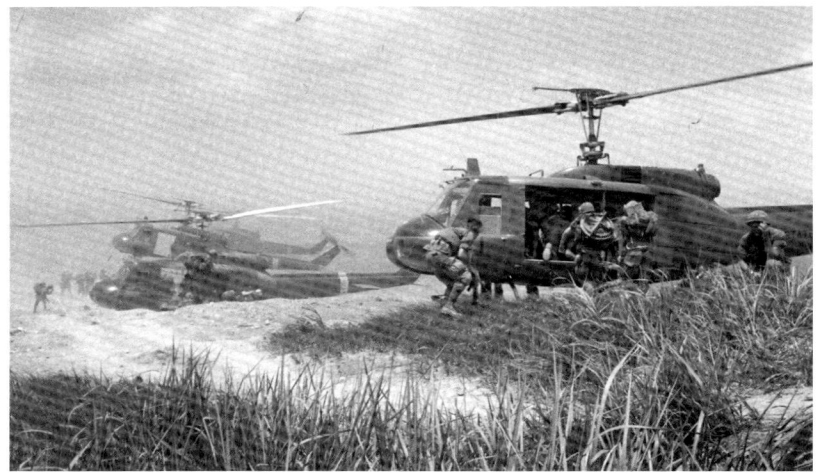

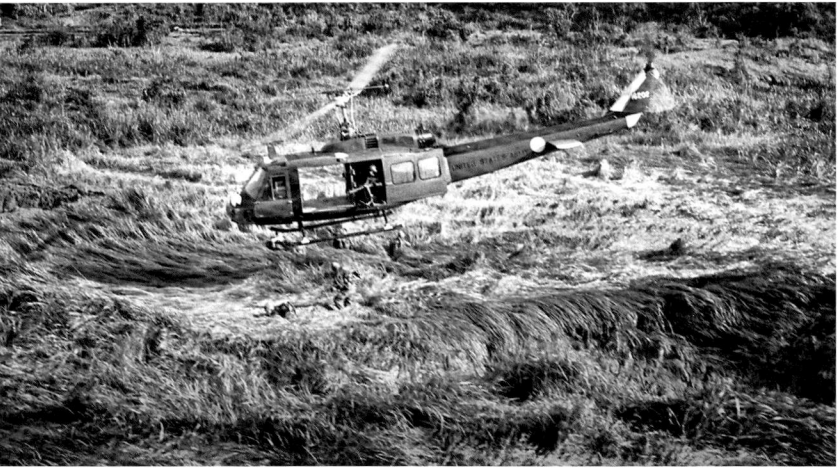

C Battery, 3rd Battalion, 82nd Artillery on LZ West "soften" an area before choppers land Alpha Company in an air assault during Task Force West.

Logue snapped this photograph from a chopper above an area that artillery from LZ West had pounded for thirty minutes.

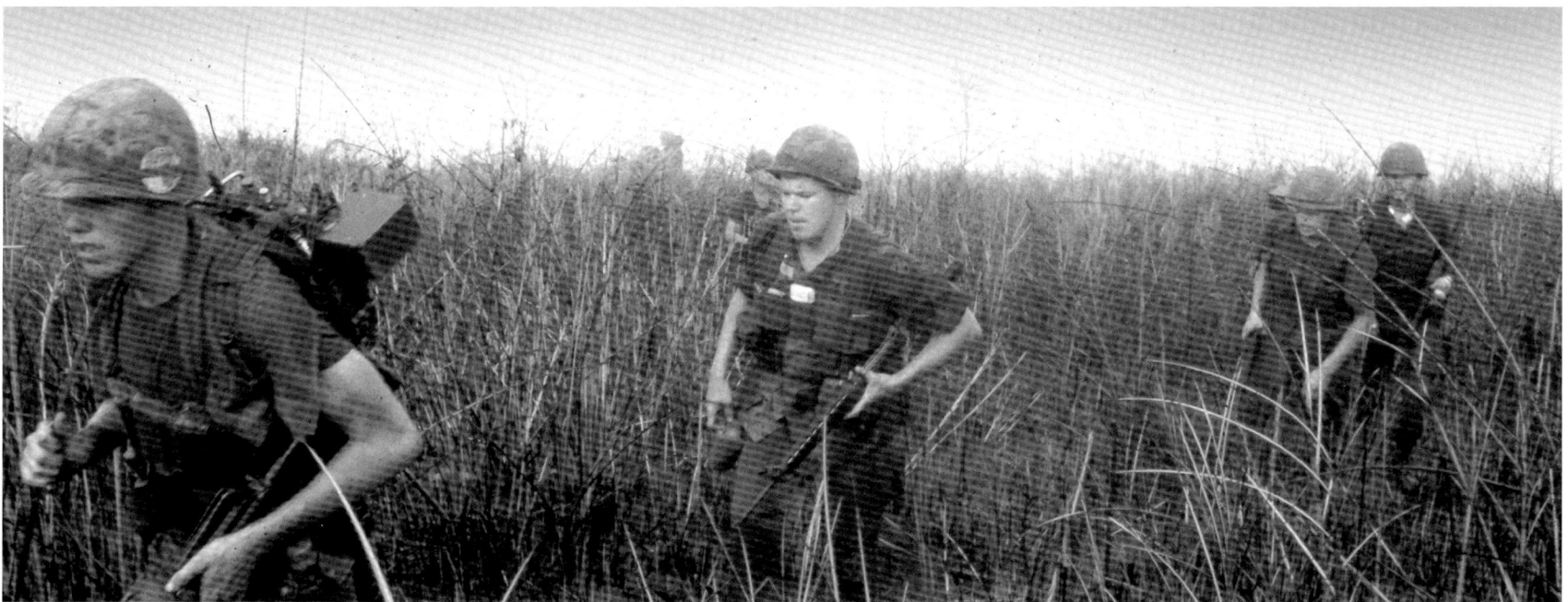

Al Merryman (left) and Captain Crockert return to LZ West after recovering soldiers' remains from the 6 June 1970 battle.

men were defiant, scared, insubordinate, battle weary, and on the verge of breaking."

This, too, he saw: They were just plain hungry.

"Some looked like concentration camp prisoners. They had been mistreated and there was no doubt about that."

First, he ordered ten cases of C-rations. The men ate. Night fell. It grew cooler. Crockert pulled from his ruck his fatigue shirt bearing a Special Forces patch, CIB, and jump wings. Someone muttered, "He's a damned lifer!"

"I was like, 'Okay, guys,'" he recalls, chuckling in remembrance.

Colonel Kennedy choppered out the next day and asked if the 6 June dead had been retrieved. Crockert said no.

"We've got some things to do first before we start. Honestly, you didn't tell me the full story before I said we'd go down," he stated.

Already, Crockert saw the men of Alpha would follow orders, but "I had to convince them I knew what I was doing, and they had to convince me that they were going to do it right. Then I told them, 'I didn't come over here to get killed. I'm not going home in a body bag.'"

ON AN AUGUST DAY IN VIRGINIA, JIM LOGUE AND I SIT WITH Crockert and his wife, Judith Sheri Bradley Crockert. A "mustang," Crockert enlisted as a private and retired as a "bird" colonel.

A New Jersey native, Crockert was raised in Dumont, where he played sandlot baseball as a kid whom everyone called "Rusty." One day on LZ West, he heard someone say, "Rusty, what are you doing here?"

Crockert grins.

"It was Billy Kitley. We played Little League baseball together," Crockert remembers of First Lieutenant William Kitley, who served as a platoon leader, then as commander of B Company, 4/31, in 1970.

After graduating high school in 1963, Crockert enrolled at Morehead State University in Morehead, Kentucky. Soon he grew restless with college classes and followed his father's advice to enlist. In basic training, Crockert sensed he had found a home. He graduated from Officer Candidate School at Fort Benning in 1967. After jump school, he reported to 7th Special Forces Group at Fort Bragg near Fayetteville, North Carolina, withstood mental and physical hardships of training, and earned the coveted Green Beret. He reached Vietnam on 18 April 1968.

Based at a Special Forces camp at Ba To in Quang Ngai Province in I Corps, Crockert served as executive officer/commander of a twelve-man team that operated under cover of darkness.

"We wanted to go in at night quietly and do what we had to do and leave. We were based on stealth," he says.

While living up to the Green Beret motto, *De oppresso liber* ("To Free the Oppressed"), Crockert adhered to more practical advice: "'Don't do anything stupid. Don't be a hero.' I heard that a million times," he recalls.

Back at Fort Bragg a year later, he was handed captain's bars then ordered to Vietnam. There he stood on 7 June 1970, learning that his new, ragged company had refused a direct order from a superior officer.

"They said no, and he told me they had said no. They had a reputation that they refused to fight. Well, they didn't refuse to fight. They had refused to go down and get these dead bodies because they didn't know what was down there," Crockert explains.

On his second day, Crockert selected two men and retraced Alpha's retreat, marked by equipment strewn along the mountain slope. Someone bent down to pick up a rucksack.

"I yelled, 'Stop! You don't pick up anything. You use a grappling hook,'" explaining that the enemy often rigged such equipment with booby traps.

So, with that command, "Rusty" began reshaping Alpha, literally from the ground up, to return a keen edge to a once-sharp company mauled, demoralized, and exhausted from a three-month running fight with 2nd NVA.

On 12 June, Crockert announced they were going down to retrieve the dead. The men picked up their rucks.

He shouted, "Stop! We're going light and fast." He explains, "In Special Forces, we didn't wear that stuff."

Grateful for burdens eased, the men carried only weapons, water, ammunition, and three body bags. From those moments, Everette Caldwell, Dennis Hogenboom, and Mark Klever began their last journey home.

Then, school began for the company once called "Alpha Battalion."

"They had never been pulled back from the field to train as a group. Nobody had zeroed in a weapon," he recalls.

Map-reading skills also were poor. Red leg forward observers relayed incorrect artillery coordinates.

For important roles, Crockert selected those "who displayed basic leadership and knew what they were doing." Sensing a silent, malevolent turmoil—specifically "a racial overtone to platoon assignments"—he reassembled platoons and reassigned duties.

Good men were underpaid, he learned. Scouring personnel files, he saw many deserved higher rank for length and quality of service. He promoted some soldiers two ranks (and two pay grades), such as from private first class to sergeant.

"In the first couple months, we were making E5s like they was going out of style," he recalls.

Meanwhile, as replacements "fresh off the farm" arrived, veterans "so 'short' they could walk beneath ants standing up" were saying goodbye to old friends.

"God love them, they were all trying the best they could do and just as fast as we were getting new men, others started going home. It was like a revolving door," he remarks.

One new soldier arrived with experience. Larry Wayne Rasey, 22, of Taft, California, had served in F Troop, 17th Cavalry in his first Vietnam tour. Months later, he "re-upped" and arrived at LZ West on 19 June 1970. The former cavalryman, however, found "humping" not to his liking.

"We don't get hot meals or clean clothes—hump the sticks for 15 days without a change of pants, shirt, or socks," he wrote his parents.

No prima donna, he was accustomed to hard work back home in the oilfields of San Joaquin Valley. Like many of their neighbors, Larry's parents migrated during the Dust Bowl from Oklahoma and Arkansas—flesh-and-blood "descendants" of the Joads, the fictional family in John Steinbeck's novel, *The Grapes of Wrath*.

"He wore a red, white, and blue bandana around his neck. Everybody had to have a nickname, and his was 'Captain America,'" remarks Robert Scott of Virginia Beach, Virginia, of Rasey.

In boosting battlefield skills, Crockert knew he must gain the men's trust as one who could and would do *their* jobs. So he humped an M60, often walked point, and *never* ordered anyone to take the dangerous position. They volunteered, and then he walked slack until he had "trained some sergeants that I thought were just as good as I was," Crockert says.

He was aware that the enemy knew Americans preferred walking trails, so Crockert issued machetes to cut paths through jungle. Like Captain Wilson, he also led them through streams to bypass booby traps.

He taught noise discipline. He taught spacing, stealth, and movements to confuse the enemy. Alpha walked one way to designated target areas and returned another. They also stopped in late afternoon to eat, then slipped away in failing light to another night laager.

They flew.

LTC Thomas A. Breen, who succeeded LTC Skaer as 4/31 commander, instituted "Eagle Flights," air assaults in which Alpha swooped down, completed missions, then flew back to West before nightfall. Eagle Flights, while dangerous, proved easier on soldiers' feet, eliminated dangers of night laagers, lessened time in the field, and often surprised the enemy.

Breen soon noticed Alpha's good work.

"If the battalion had an Eagle Flight, it was, 'Alpha Company, where are you?'" Crockert remembers.

Day by day, "Rusty" noted his men taking initiative and performing tasks without his constant oversight. "They knew what they were doing: fields of fire, backing each other up, shooting semi-automatic bursts rather than the 'rock-and-roll' of automatic fire," he says.

In November, the next battalion commander, LTC William Hammil, a Korean War veteran, accompanied Alpha on a mission. The company slipped quietly towards its destination, waited silently through the night, and hit the enemy at first light. In returning by a different route, Hammil asked Crockert where they were going.

"I said, 'We never go anyplace the same way we came.' He said, 'I'm really impressed with these guys.' I said, 'Yes, sir, they're good.'"

Crockert's voice lifts joyfully at the memory.

"I wanted to grab them and hug them all, and say, 'You finally did what I told you to do!' The worst part of it, every time he had a mission, he sent Alpha."

Crockert's six months as company commander ended on 12 December 1970. A fulfilling career notwithstanding, his time with Alpha caps all professional accomplishments.

"Best time in my military life. I enjoyed the heck out of it. I don't think I ever cursed. I don't think I ever yelled. You don't yell at people when you're in that situation. These people were scared. They'd never even been out of the United States. They'd never been in the jungle. Many had never had a gun. America owes them a great debt of gratitude. They operated in the heat, the mosquitoes, the enemy trying to kill you. The food. C-rations were terrible."

He sighs and repeats many veterans' sad refrain: "I wish I could remember all their names."

Years later, he bumped into one soldier's son. Crockert was a company commander of 45th Airborne Battalion at Fort Benning when West Point cadets arrived for training. He noticed one named Kennedy.

"I said, 'By any chance, are you related to Colonel Edwin Kennedy?'"

The cadet replied, "Yes, Sir. That's my dad."

"I said, 'I worked for him in Vietnam. Best ass-chewing I ever got I got from your dad.'"

Cadet Kennedy and Crockert laughed. LTC (ret) Edwin Kennedy Jr. (whose father retired as a brigadier general) served many years as an instructor at United States Army Command and General Staff College.

In his time with Alpha, Crockert lost only two men. On 26 July, the company swarmed a clutch of hooches suspected of enemy activity. Rasey, who had arrived thirty-seven days earlier, ducked into a hooch where two NVA soldiers waited in ambush. He died in a hail of gunfire.

IN AUGUST 2015, JIM AND I DROVE INTO TAFT, CALIFORNIA, a small town atop the third largest contiguous oil field in the nation. There Mayor Randy Miller, a Navy Seabee (from CB, for Construction Battalion) who served two tours in Vietnam, showed us around the pretty Art Deco downtown and pointed out Taft High School and Taft College, where medic Philip Pruett had played football.

In Bakersfield's Kern County Library, a 1970 Taft city directory lists the residence of Larry's parents: Charles Eugene Rasey, a native Oklahoman and oil field worker, and Mamie Maxine Best Rasey, a store clerk born in Arkansas. Jim photocopied Larry's obituary in the Bakersfield newspaper and scanned his photograph from a 1966 Taft High School yearbook.

And there, Larry's tracks disappear. His parents, an older brother, and a younger sister are deceased. I called and wrote other possible relatives, even published in the local newspaper a month-long notice for anyone who knew Larry. None replied.

On a blistering Sunday afternoon, Jim and I walked through the well-tended West Side Cemetery, grateful for its shade trees and the cool, wet mist of sprinklers. Nearby, oil field pump jacks bowed and scraped like serfs in obeisance to the subterranean king of the local economy.

Larry's small, stone marker is incised with birth and death dates and symbols of his Bronze Star with Oak Leaf Cluster and Purple Heart. When Charles and Mamie buried their son, Taft, with a 1970 population of 4,285, already had lost ten of its young men to Vietnam. Larry was eleventh and last.

One day, none will remain to tell of Larry's time on earth, marked only by his headstone's hyphen of life between dates of birth and death. The harshest cost of war, perhaps, lies in those who perish without children. With them ends the growth of generations, waiting forever in the wings of the never born.

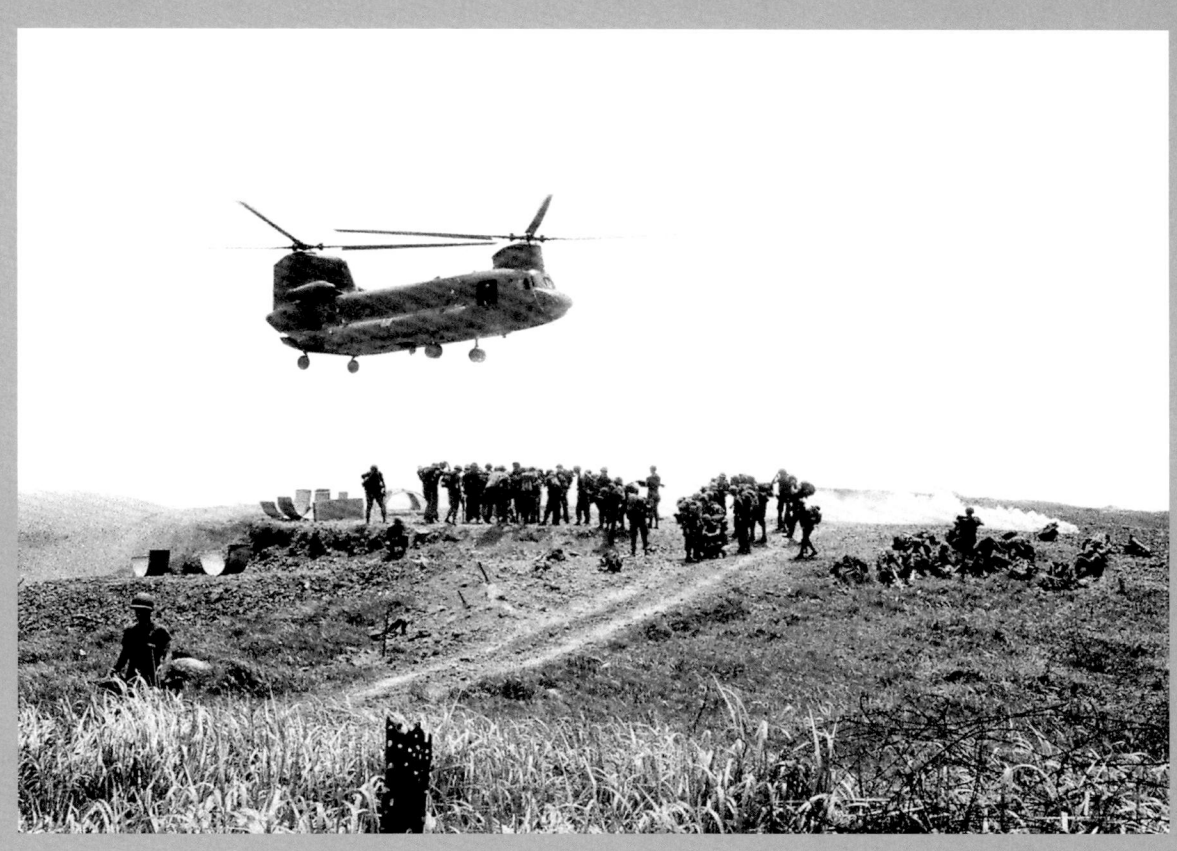

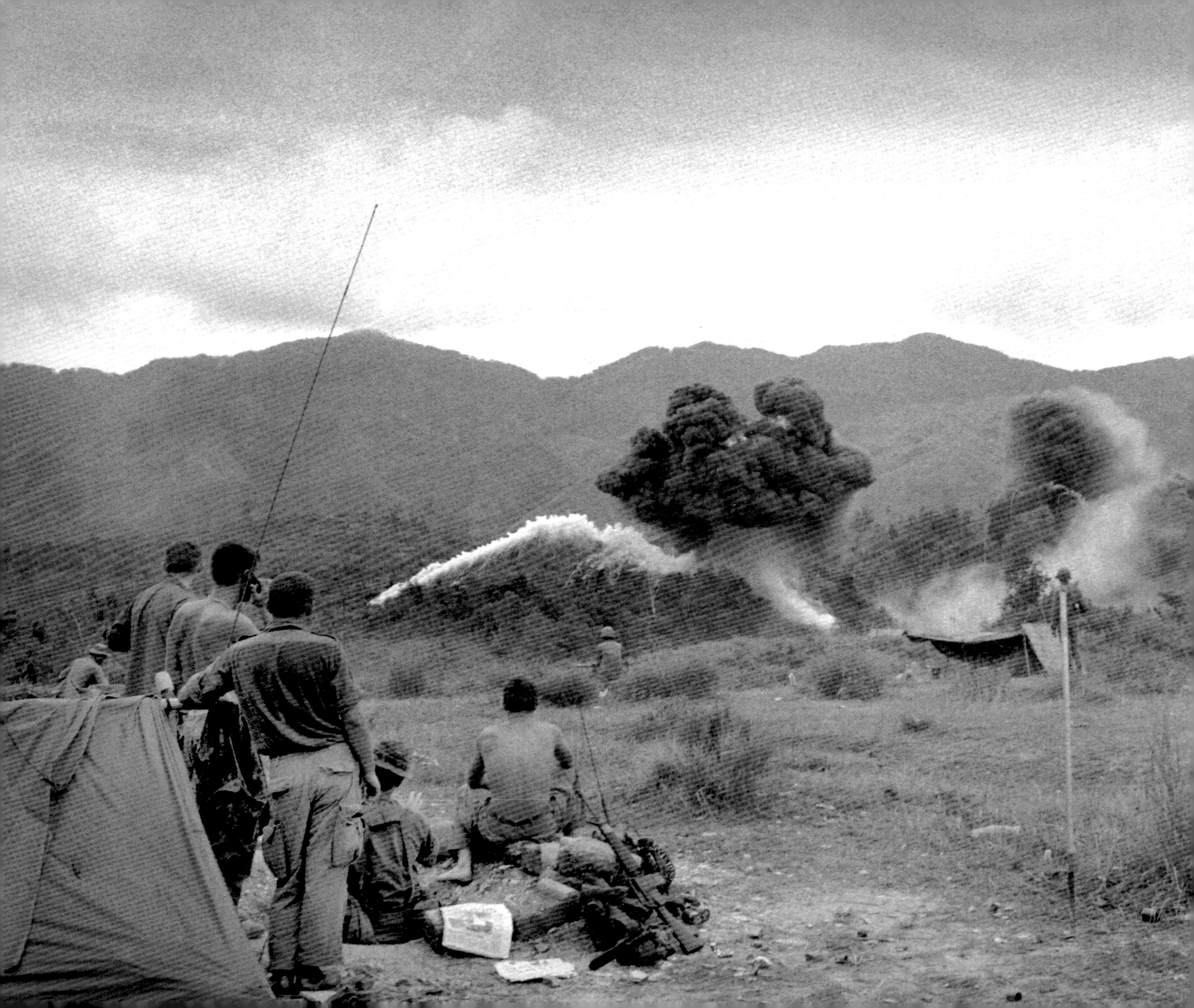

Chapter 18

I Loved Mouse. Everybody Loved Mouse.

Medic Thomas John Roberts (KIA)

EARLY SATURDAY MORNING, 22 AUGUST 1970, FLOYD Roberts sat in the shade of his backyard in Cedar Park, Wisconsin, waiting for his wife to dress for Mass. Likely, he was thinking of his eldest son, Thomas John Roberts, a medic in Vietnam.

A small, quiet, bespectacled boy, Tom spent hours in nearby forests and sailing across Brown Lake. He talked with holy men and read and wrote poetry. He liked photography. He was wise in the ways of the outdoors and the terrain of the soul and spent hours exploring both.

A tank driver in World War II, Floyd knew good soldiers came in all sizes, including small ones like his son, who often fought bigger schoolyard bullies in defending his younger twin brothers. Tom would be just fine. Floyd stood. It was time for Mass.

At that moment in Quang Tin Province, Tom was pointing his .45 Colt pistol at the backs of two captured VC. Beside him, Jim Logue, who was humping a PRC-25 radio, his camera, and his M16, was guiding the prisoners towards a shady holding area. Although long out of the field, Jim jumped aboard a chopper to cover a one-day Eagle Flight mission for the battalion newspaper he edited.

As captors and captives approached, others of 2nd Platoon watched. So did a sniper.

SEVERAL G.I.S GRINNED AND EXCLAIMED WHAT JIM NOTED AS a perfect "lead" for his story: "Look at that! Ol' Mouse captured himself a *chieu hoi*!"

"'Mouse?' I never knew he was called 'Mouse!'" exclaims Nancy Roberts Christman, Tom's older sister, as Jim relates the story. In her Grand Chute, Wisconsin, home spreads her paper trail of research to learn about Alpha Company, her brother's service, and how he died. A source she lacked, someone from Alpha, now sat beside her. Jim smiles sheepishly.

"We called him Mouse because of his height and how his ears . . ." Jim gestures at how Tom's ears stuck out. Nancy chuckles. Jim leans towards her, his voice a near-whisper.

"I want you to know that *everybody* loved your brother," he says.

Left: In "front-row seats," Alpha watches jets pound enemy positions. Logue snapped this frame just as a jet drops deadly cargo.

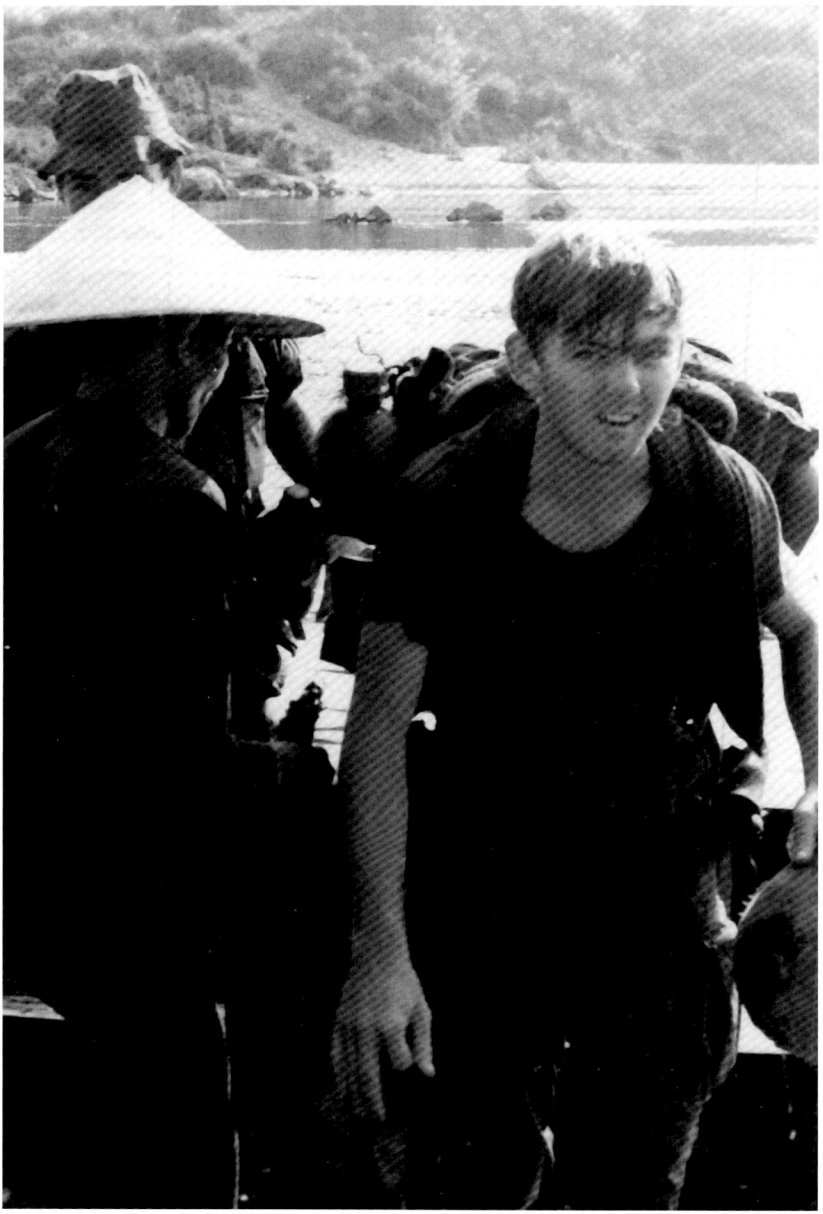

Medic Thomas John Roberts, nicknamed "Mouse," steps from a boat after a river crossing. While Alpha admired all medics, the men especially loved Mouse for his kindness and courage.

She smiles and nods. Her eyes glisten.

He assures her, too, of this: While most towered above Tom, all looked up to him as a man, a medic, and a soldier who never hesitated to help a fallen brother.

He had helped his own brothers all his life, Nancy says. After her, Tom was second oldest of eight children of Floyd Eldon Roberts, a Nebraskan, and Laura Margaret Kramer Roberts, a Minnesota native. In their children blended the blood of French-Canadian, Swedish American, and Lakota Sioux forebears.

One might have called Tom a *coureur de bois*, or "runner of the woods," an eighteenth-century term for French-Canadian hunters and trappers. On schoolyards, hunter became hunted. Bigger boys shoved Tom and his younger brothers around.

Tom stood "only five feet, three or four inches tall, a petite fellow and rather frail. They got picked on. I was always battling for them and picking up the pieces," Nancy relates of Tom and the twins.

Tom relished solitude and knowledge. He often discussed faith with priests and novitiates at nearby Queen of Peace, a Franciscan friary. As for a career, he mentioned photojournalism but may also have contemplated the priesthood. He dated little, but in the Army he wrote to a local girl nicknamed "Pinky."

In July 1969, Tom enlisted, Nancy believes, to put his body between his brothers and the war, hoping his service would keep them out of the conflict. He registered as a conscientious objector and requested service as a medic.

Soon after arriving in monsoon-soaked Vietnam on 12 January 1970, he wrote home about how much the men loved medics: "I'm getting into the swing of things pretty fast, and the guys are always looking out for me . . ."

One was a mentor Tom admired most: Specialist 4 Dennis Hogenboom of Clymer, New York. Tom often sought advice from "the professor," the 26-year-old history teacher with a master's degree. Mouse claimed Dennis as his "best friend."

The 4/31 medic fraternity included two other conscientious objectors, Dennis Mack of Salt Lake City (now deceased), and

William Allen of Napa, California. Two other medics towered above Tom: former college linebacker Philip Pruett, of Crawfordville, Florida, and Michael Janak of Buffalo, New York, who stood well over six feet tall.

As at home, Tom craved time alone to read, write, and soak up Vietnam's vivid green scenery. In a letter to his parents, Tom wrote:

> You know this is really beautiful country and I could really love it if there wasn't a damn war going on. You know this thing you hear about changing your feeling about the war if you ever really saw it. And this stuff about all the guys in Vietnam know the war must be won. And that we really are doing a lot of good. Well, 90 percent of it is bullshit. None of the infantry soldiers know why they're here or what they're here for. I believe in winning but not the war. We have to win the hearts and minds of the people. And we are going backward on that by all of the useless destruction of this beautiful country and by all of the immoral actions of the damn G.I.s. I think the Army has undone most of the good the church has done over here.

As a medic in 2nd Platoon with Pruett, Tom was tramping through monsoon-soaked countryside, bent by the weight of rucksack and his MD5 medic pack and an M1911 Colt .45 pistol to defend himself and the wounded. All saw that Mouse knew weapons and the ways of the woods and matched larger guys stride for stride. In each night laager, he made sure "his" men dried their feet and socks, and in the morning, he watched each swallow his daily malaria pill.

With little need for money, he mailed home most of his pay, earmarking some for savings and the rest to help his parents defray expenses.

By 18 April, Mouse had walked off his second pair of combat boots when point man Aldo "Mondo" Bastinancic triggered a booby trap. The blast badly wounded Mondo and four others. Pruett and Mouse worked feverishly on them until a medevac swooped down.

Those who set the trap, Mouse knew, were civilians. He wrote, ". . . a big percentage of the people . . . jumping back and forth to us, against us and back again . . . . The next nite [*sic*] they are shooting at us. The next day we shoot innocent civilians and patch them up and they still hate us."

In the May–June 1970 fighting, he related one undated engagement: "We got in a heavy firefight coming off [Hill] 441. We got the dinks pretty mad at us. We found their hospital. It was a deep tunnel complex under Hill 441. So we filled it up with C-S gas and smoked everyone out and that pissed them off, but the day before we found a rice cache on Hill 386 and we blew it a mile in the air with C-4 explosives . . ."

Through firefights and caring for sick and wounded, Mouse shivered with a fear common to medics: that he would freeze when a soldier screamed for help. He wrote, "I see a lot of scared guys around me every day and the thought of letting down my guard scares the hell out of me so I just keep my cool."

In mid-May, malaria felled Mouse. From 91st Evacuation Hospital in Chu Lai, he wrote Nancy about his illness, also noting "a tiny bit" of shrapnel for which he received a Purple Heart. He ached more, however, from malaria and the loss of another friend:

> I've patched up almost 60 guys in the last 3 weeks and four of them died. The last one was real close but I couldn't get him out in time. He was an especially great person (from N Carolina), David Menscer. Only 38 days left in country . . . . Nance, I need some extra prayers for my guys.

Fear, the grueling pace, and lives lost devastated Tom. He wrote to "Gram," his grandmother, Margaret Kramer, on 22 May 1970:

> I've had so many guys wounded this month. And four killed. I feel so sorry for their families . . . . The doctor told me that I might not be able to go back out to the field. But we need medics so bad now I'm sure I will. Besides, my guys don't do so

well out there without me. You know we had a real cool guy in our platoon named David Menscer from N. Carolina. He would always whistle at the VC or NVA to make them turn around when he spotted them while he was walking point, because he couldn't shoot one in the back. Everyone used to yell at him knowing he would get killed that way some day. Well, he was shot in the back 5 days ago. He's dead now . . . . I guess I got to know him too well, because I've gotten bitter about his dying.

In a prescient moment, he mentioned to her a condition later labeled post-traumatic stress disorder:

They come home and have a hard enough time straightening themselves out, much less contributing anything to our society. Well, I guess prayers are the only answer. We have to have peace and love among men on earth. Well, Gram, I know you are praying and a lot of people are and I am . . . . Don't worry about me over here. I'm sure God wants me alive a while yet. I've done so little so far and there is much to do before I could possibly deserve to leave this world. Take care of yourself, Gram. I'm sure your prayers have been my strength.

Always, your loving Grandson, Thomas
P.S. I'm 22 years old today and still just a child.

In the same letter, he wrote of America as a raft in raging currents:

You know, I really don't believe the world is a sinking ship. It's just a big log raft bumping into the rocks and spinning around in the whirlpool and eddies of the rock, on its way downstream. A log raft is almost impossible to steer especially in these wild, raging headwaters of humanity. I believe we are destined to reach calmer water further downstream and maybe someday our big log raft will reach the sea of tranquility.

His continuing recovery from malaria saved him from Alpha's 6 June debacle.

August came. Tom looked forward to his September R&R in Japan, where he planned to buy a camera. Late summer days were "flying by" and nights passed like "a click of the finger":

Dear Mom and Dad:

Although it's still very hot over here every day, the mornings have a distinct air of early autumn and I feel it when I wake up around 4:30. These days I'm really feeling good. Fall always seems to me like almost the end of a long day when you look around and realize how much you have or haven't accomplished all summer, or how much you have to do yet . . .

As much as he yearned for home, leaving behind friends left him blue:

I'm sure going to miss some of these guys when I come home. You know they like me and treat me better than any other group of people I've ever known . . . . Well, I'm pretty well awake now and it's 5:30 already. I never miss a sunrise anymore.

He saw sunrise on 22 August and at 1445 boarded a slick for another Eagle Flight. Soon after choppers touched down, Alpha destroyed an enemy cache of 4,000 pounds of rice. In a firefight, Mouse patched up two G.I.s. The mission was nearly complete when Mouse and Logue, on a trail teetering atop a small slope, rounded a bend and startled two armed Viet Cong.

"*Chieu hoi! Chieu hoi!*" Mouse and Logue screamed.

The VC dropped their weapons and raised their hands. Logue and Mouse nudged them towards a holding area for POWs, a circle of shade under a tall tree.

Robert Scott of Virginia Beach, Virginia, remembers walking behind Logue, along with "Dusty" Gonzalez and Danny Savage, an M60 machine gunner. Ahead of them was Sergeant Jim Edwards of Kinston, North Carolina.

From his aerie, the sniper watched the two Americans, one with pistol and the other with rifle pointed at the prisoners. Officers, he knew, carried side arms. Beside officers walked the radioman. If he shot twice, he might render the Americans leaderless and without communications. He peered through his sights, swinging his rifle slightly from Mouse to Logue, deciding which to kill first.

He fired.

Mouse fell dead.

Logue leapt into tall grass and screamed into his radio for a dust off.

With the two prisoners under guard, 2nd Platoon erupted in anguish and rage. They found and killed the sniper, then swarmed into the village that had hidden the cache of rice.

"There was a lot of anger. I remember our guys trying to burn all the hooches down, but they were too wet," Scott recalled.

Four decades later, in Levelland, Texas, the soft-spoken First Lieutenant Ross Joplin, leader of 2nd Platoon, winces in speaking of the death of this small, good man: "Of *all* of us, Mouse shouldn't have died."

Back at West, Jim dutifully wrote the story of the destruction of the cache of rice, the capture of the two chieu hois, and the death of a medic. He did his job. He reported the news but not the decision he made: never to return to the field.

To Nancy, years later, Jim relates the incidents of that day. Nancy speaks quietly: "One of the things that he said in a letter was that we should not be surprised if he did not come back from Vietnam and he did not mean that he would die. He said, 'I've fallen in love with the children here and I can't imagine leaving them without people who love and care about them and that are willing to teach and educate them.'"

She pauses for a moment and adds, "He loved journalism and photography, so I can imagine that had he not been killed he would still be in Vietnam telling stories."

Instead, Thomas John Roberts, 22, was borne home and buried in Saint Mary Cemetery near the lake and woodlands he loved.

This Jim and I heard again and again from men of Alpha Company: "I loved Mouse. Everybody loved Mouse."

Two families miss him: one of blood he shared, the other who shed blood together. Men of Alpha still lived in the giant shadow cast by this little big man who may have yet come to their aid. For the rest of their lives, seconds before lashing out in anger, perhaps they stopped when the memory of Mouse called forth their better angels.

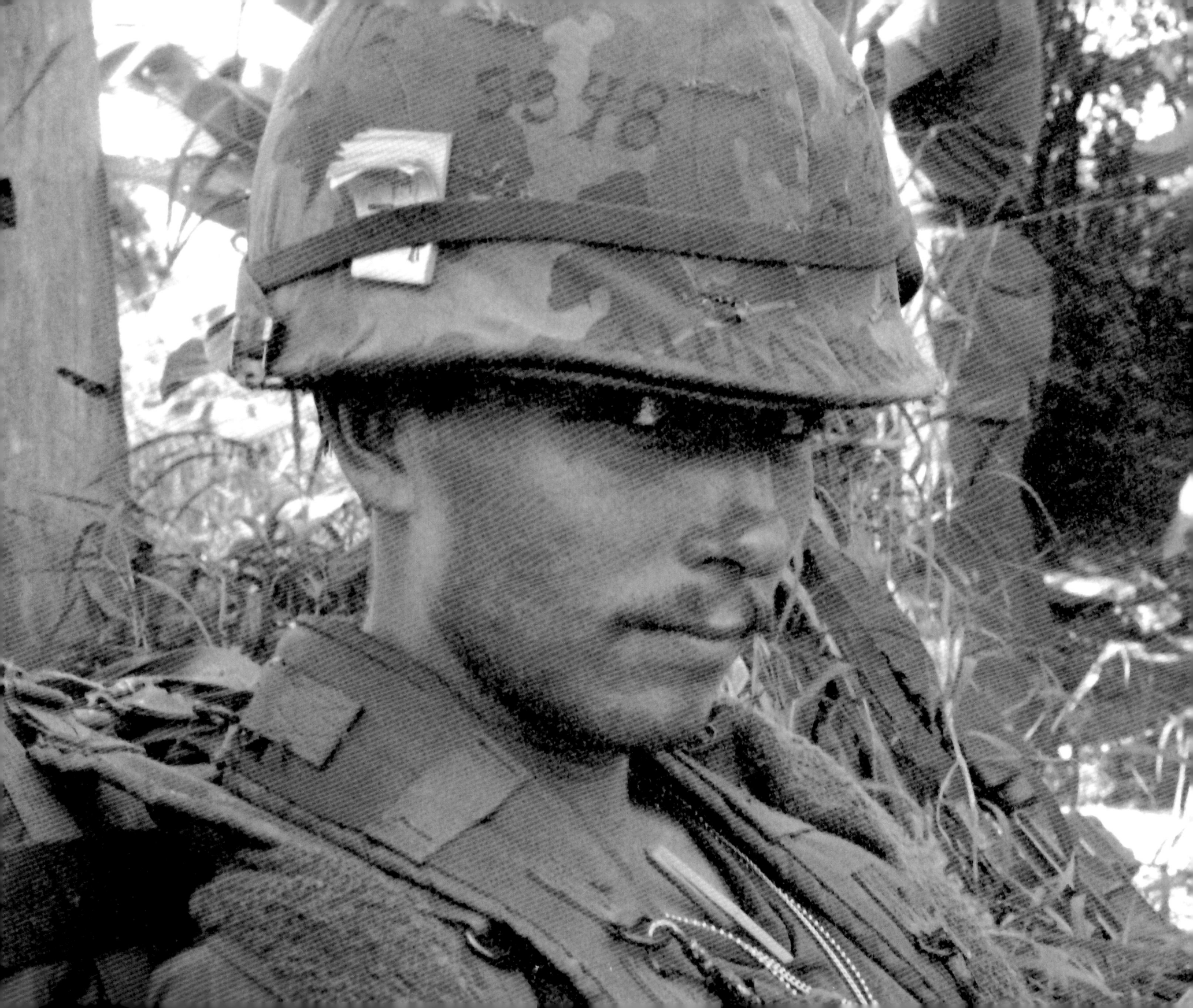

Chapter 19

Hear My Humble Cry

Specialist 4 James Frederick Lemmon

IN LATE SUMMER IN SOUTHEASTERN ILLINOIS, SILKEN BREEZES rustle among leaves and tassels of tall corn along seams of farm roads. Here and there in clearings rise homes like this one, shaded with trees and fronted with a long porch bordered with roses, daylilies, and oakleaf hydrangea.

Out bounds Buck, barking, followed by Diana and James Lemmon, who grins and opens his arms as Jim steps out. I never tire of watching men of Alpha meeting again.

We settle with coffee around a dining table, where James produces the helmet, canteen, and gas mask his father carried in World War I. William Edward Lemmon was 54 when his 32-year-old wife, Virgie Marie McDonald Lemmon, gave birth to her youngest son in 1949.

A widow by 1963, Mrs. Lemmon worked in Robinson, while James farmed after school and in summer. Meanwhile, he learned to play guitar, at home and at Prior Grove Southern Baptist Church in Hardinville, where each Sunday found mother and son.

One summer as a teen, James attended a church youth camp where, in a single glance, he learned this universal truth: To a young man no one is more beautiful, exotic, and mysterious than an out-of-town girl, although her town was only eleven miles away.

Her name was Diana Faye McCarty of Robinson.

Soon they sat together in her church and, with Diana on piano and Jim on guitar, they blended their voices in hymns sung in such rural churches in the nineteenth century and earlier. With little else to do on weekends, the couple simply drove around, happy in each other's company. Call such excursions one-tank dates. James grins.

"We'd spend five dollars the whole weekend. By Sunday night we were out of money and nearly out of gas," he says.

The rest of their lives were harmonizing, too. James graduated from high school in 1967, Diana a year later. She turned down a college scholarship, content that her life's path lay at home.

"All I ever wanted to do was settle down and have a family," she remarks.

Hardly had they wed when Vietnam tore them apart. The couple capped off James's thirty-day leave after basic and advanced

Left: Music murmurs in the heart of James Lemmon, a guitarist. Before the war, he and his wife, Diana, sang duets in church. Today, they perform in bluegrass gatherings in pristine mountain settings.

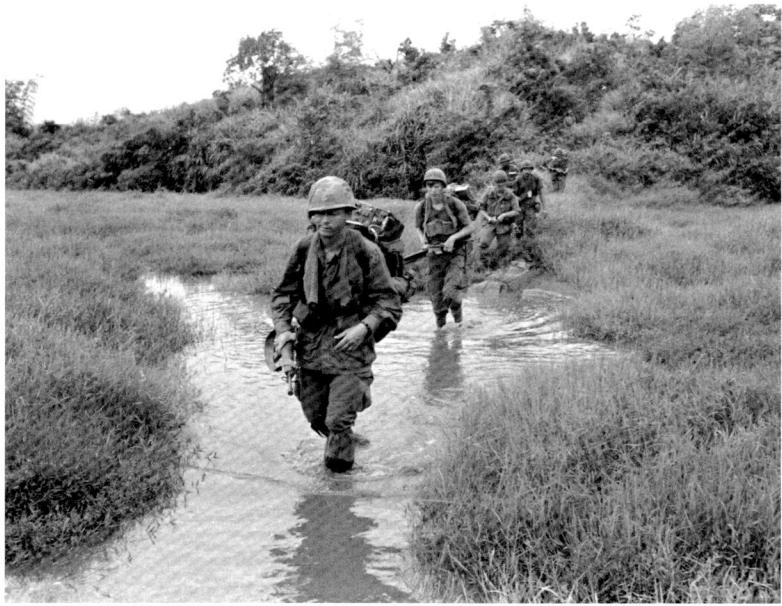

James Lemmon leads Alpha through a stream. While "water walking" diminished fear of booby traps, wet feet often led to trench foot. Socks rotted; skin peeled from soles. Medics examined men's feet most mornings.

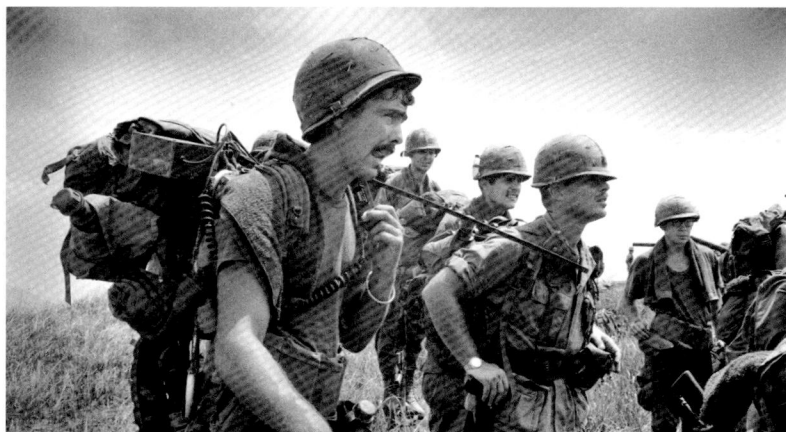

RTO David Flynn directs artillery fire from LZ West. From left: James Lemmon, Dennis ("Doc") Mack, Captain Wilson, and William Arnold watch rounds hit.

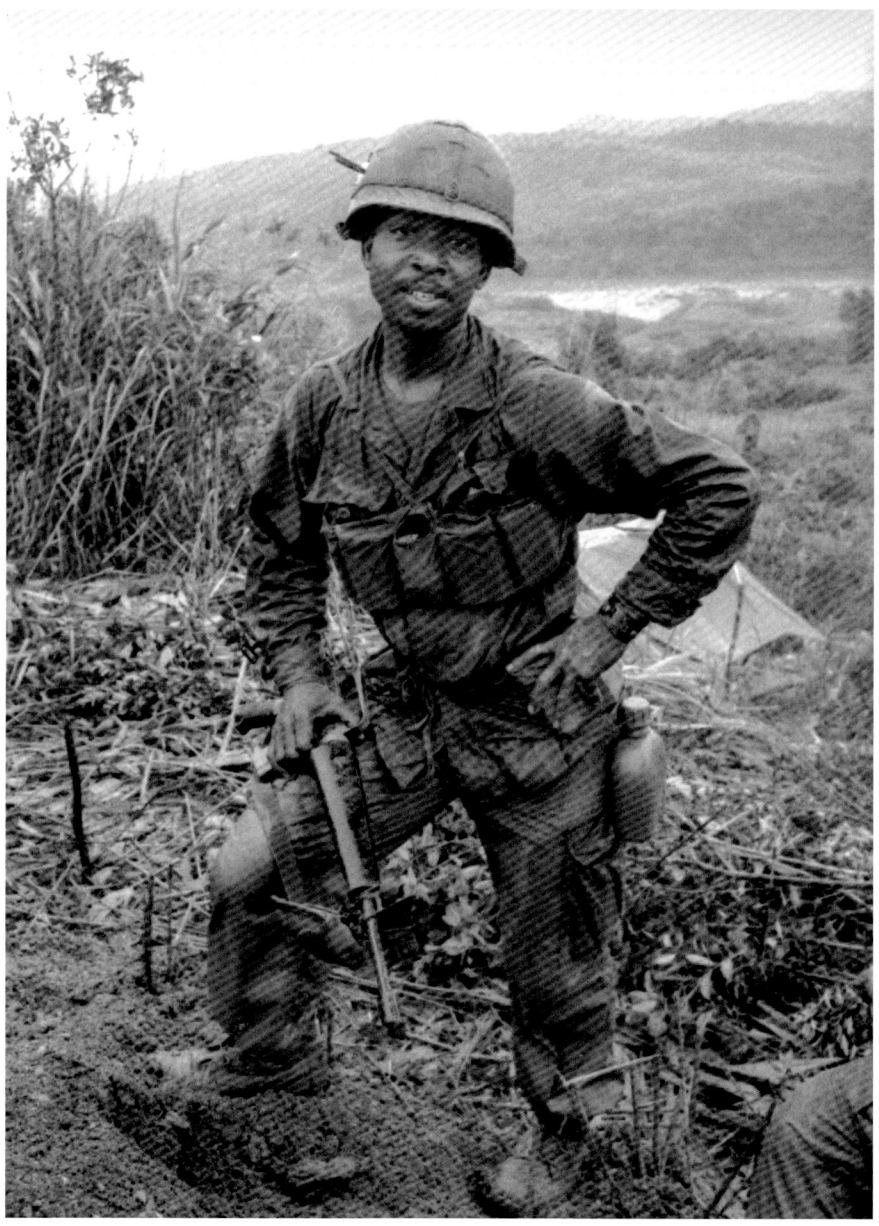

Staff Sergeant Donald Edward Yarborough survived Vietnam and retired after an Army career.

training with a lakeside vacation in Kentucky. He arrived in Vietnam smarting from sunburn.

Seventy-five of their war letters survive. In his first to Diana, dated 9 August 1969, James succinctly captures every American soldier's first impression of the country: "There's not much to tell; it's just hot & wet and dirty and it stinks awful bad."

Like David Menscer, he, too, began his war in 1st Division, slogging through flat, sodden country of III Corps with Bravo Company, 2/18. His war was one of small ambushes and combat assaults that took Bravo west towards Cambodia and Laos. For having completed thirty-eight air missions, he earned an Air Medal.

"We just kept going farther and farther and farther. It was ambush every night," he recalls.

As they lay in wait, he and those around him, with no stomach for combat, remained silent if enemy were near. As night descended on 2 November, he wrote:

> There are 11 of us out here on a 4-day ambush . . . . We are well hid in brush about 2 feet apart. We have the machine gun with us and 800 rounds of ammo plus I have 325 rounds for my M16. We don't intend to use them.

Learning Diana was in the hospital, he grew frantic to be by her side.

> Nov. 4
>
> 3:30 p.m.
>
> I'm starting my 4th month in this hellhole . . . . If you have to have anything done try and get *me home. Ask the Doc. Go to the Red Cross. Do anything to get me home. I miss you honey.*

Diana recovered while weeks of monsoon and assaults wore upon the body, soul, and feet of her husband in Vietnam. In the rain in late November he wrote:

> Last night our new CO had us playing John Wayne and we got

soaked. We were almost froze this morning. My feet and socks and boots have been wet for 3 days . . . . My boots are so big . . . my feet slide around in there and pulled the hide off the bottom of my feet . . . . This place isn't fit for a decent human. I guess we are paying our debt for being born a male American . . . fighting for a worthless cause. We're just a bunch of animals . . . trying to survive from one night to the next.

Raw feet earned James a short reprieve for treatment and a "sham"—a few days of light duty.

> Sun 23 Nov 69
>
> I am on a sham right now for three days. My feet were too wet and the skin started coming off . . . . We don't even feel human anymore. If we're not living out in the woods somewhere like an animal, I'm living in the ground like a rat . . .

Diana's letters kept him going. The brush of her hand across stationery left a faint scent of her perfume, "Rain Goddess." He scratched replies while waiting in ambush:

> Sun 30 Nov 69
>
> 1 p.m.
>
> I will see about making your allotment bigger now that I made Spec 4. My base pay is $214.20. That's not counting 13 or 14 dollars for overseas pay and $65 combat pay.

Meanwhile, he dreamed of R&R with her in Hawaii, ending a 19 December letter with a sly wink:

> Those 6 days will be so nice. To be treated like a human being for a change with clean clothes, white sheets, hot water and someone to love. Well, I hope you'll be ready for me.

James, while listening to their Sunday music in his memory, clung to one ritual of home: beginning and ending each day with a prayer. He recalls: "If you make it through the night, you

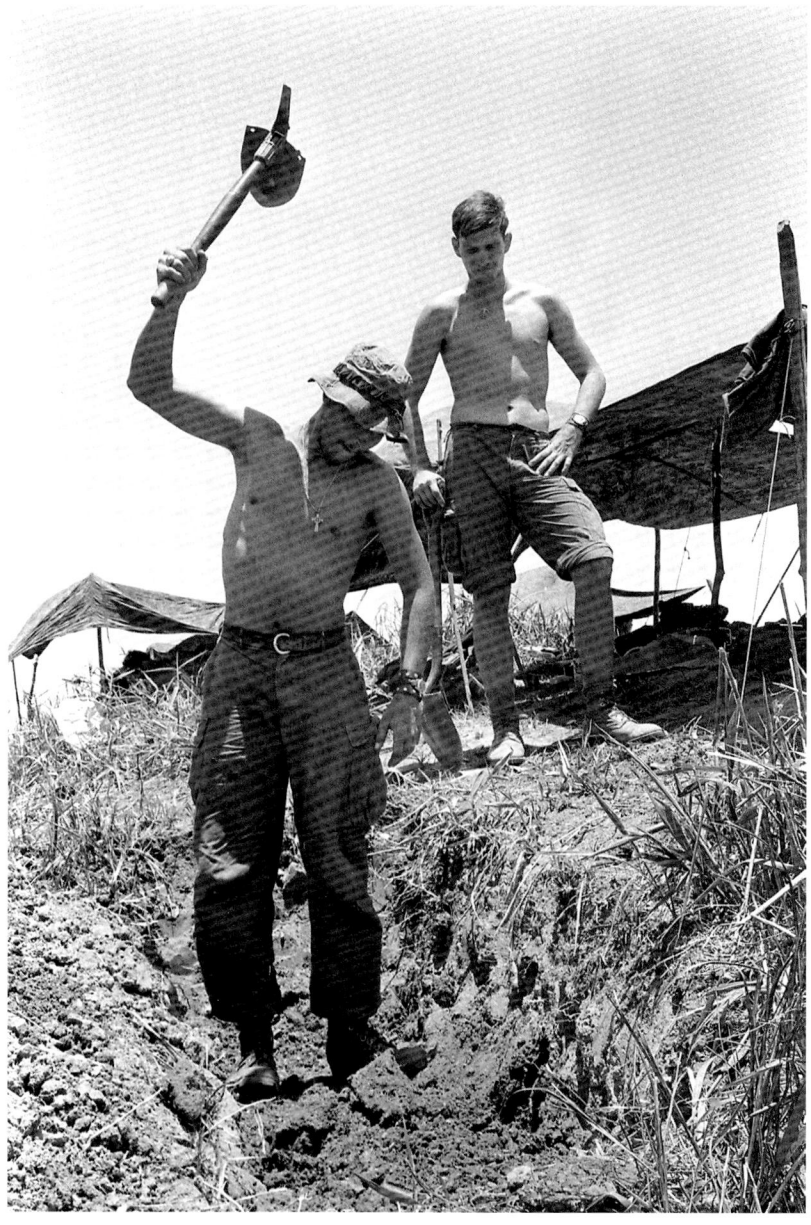

James Lemmon digs a foxhole in hard, sunbaked soil.

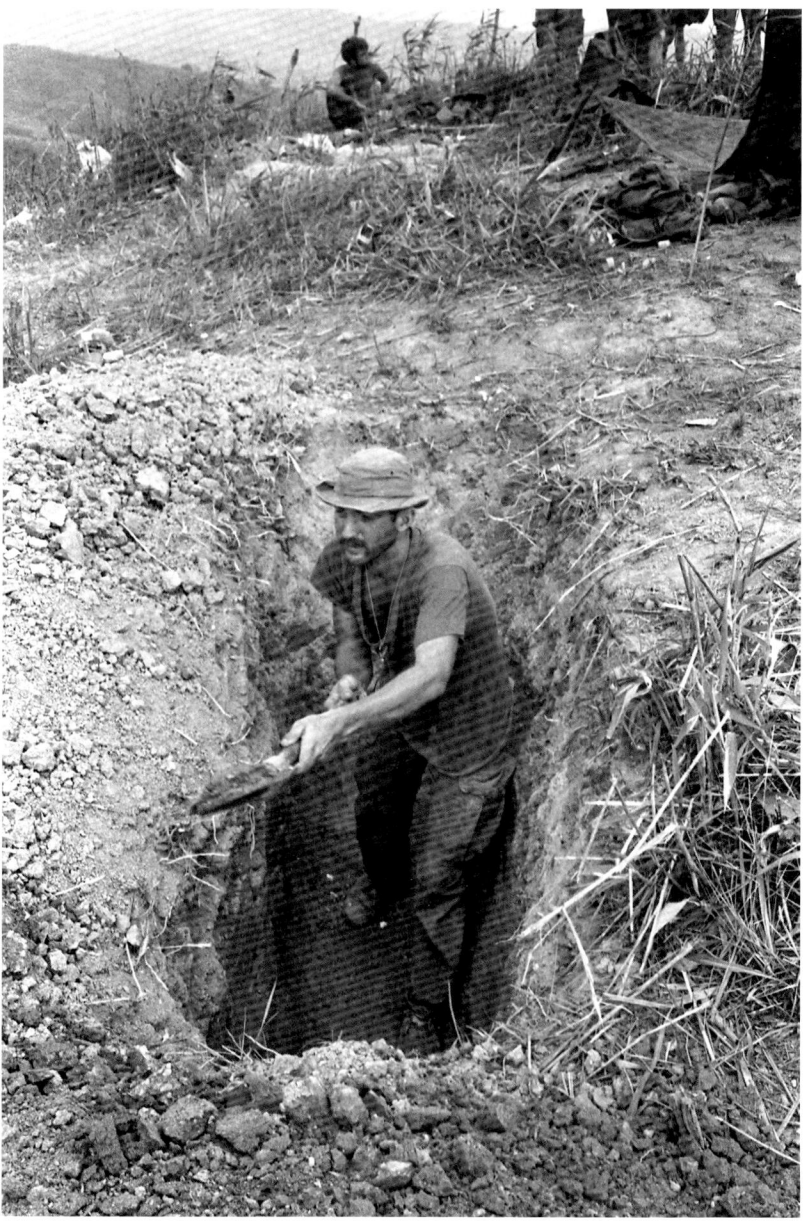

Jim Logue spelled Lemmon in completing this foxhole. Minutes later, the enemy began lobbing mortar rounds on Alpha's position. Four landed within inches of the hole.

say a little prayer. And if you make it through the day, you say a little prayer: 'Help me get through this day and this night.'"

On a sweep one morning, a nearby soldier triggered a booby trap that "picked me up and blew me back." Metal ripped into his face and body, blinding him temporarily and rupturing his eardrums. In a hospital, nurses plucked metal shards from his face and body. He worded his next letter carefully:

Tues 30 Dec.

I'm in the hospital right now. There's nothing wrong with me. I just got some dirt and stuff in my eyes and I just had to get them cleaned out . . . . I have a 30-day profile so I won't have to go back to the field for a while. My eyes are all well now and I love you.

In early 1970, he spent a week of heaven on R&R in Hawaii with Diana. His spirit soared, then crashed back in Vietnam. With 1st Division headquarters ordered stateside, all remaining personnel were folded into other units in Vietnam. With Alpha, 4/31, by March, he was humping the 28-pound cipher (voice encryption device). Beside him walked David Flynn of Muncie, Indiana; Jim Logue; Al Merryman; and Captain John Wilson.

It was a different war than in III Corps, he wrote Diana, not only in topography and duty. Now he hacked through jungle, stumbled up and down mountains, splashed through streams, and humped a ruck.

Mon 30 Mar 70

2:30 p.m.

I carry air mattress, poncho, mos. net, tent poles and pegs, poncho liner, plus my food. And I have five quarts of water . . . the last of April we get a 3- or 4-day stand down and when we come back to the field I'll be in my 10th month over here. I'm starting to get short, honey. I'll break 120 days in 2 or 3 days.

On 10 May, two weeks after 2nd NVA Division swarmed into Hiệp Dúc Valley, Lemmon and Logue, along with Sergeant Don Yarborough and "Top" Smith, were huddled in a foxhole when enemy mortar fire rained into the laager. Lemmon, deafened again, was dusted off with several others. A day later he wrote Diana:

Foxhole 8 feet deep, 10 feet long. Jim Logue in it, too. He and I, sergeant [Don] Yarborough . . . Top Smith. They were praying out loud. First time I ever heard that. Seven mortars reached within arm's length of the hole. That was the first day we really got attacked by NVA. 3 of us in the hole got Purple Hearts that day . . .

Honey I'm in the rear again. I came in last night with some other guys. I'm trying to get out on my ears. But my nerves are worse than my ears right now. I don't know whether I can take these next 82 days or not . . . . I know one thing the Lord was sure with me yesterday . . . .

The mortar attack marked Lemmon's last day in combat. Captain John Wilson released him to duties on LZ West. James wrote his beloved:

24 May

5:25 p.m.

I came back out to LZ West just now to help the guys run the CP. I don't have to go to the field anymore. The captain got me a job out here.

Time passing brought him within sixty-seven days closer to home: its tastes, games, and time with Diana.

27 *May 70*

9:30 a.m.

We'll have to stop at Ray's Market and get some peaches & apples and watermelon. And the Dog and Suds and get a gallon root beer. Cold! And the Humpty Dumpty and get some fish and French fries. And go bowling and fishing and swimming.

She replied on 3 July: "I guess we've waited so long that it seems that this 'waiting' will go on forever." Then she closed with three words that mean as much as "I love you": *I need you.*

On 21 July 1970, only thirteen days separated the couple when James sniffed "Rain Goddess" on Diana's last letter overseas. He replied, ending with this sentence: "I can smell you on your letter and you smell good."

Jim Lemmon won the war in the only way an American claimed victory: He came home, mostly whole, his Class A uniform hanging on a 132-pound wraith-like frame.

After completing service at Fort Hood in Killeen, Texas, James, like all veterans, built a mental wall between the present and Vietnam past and buried himself in hard work, holding jobs at both a grocer's and a paper products company. Few knew he had served. He shrugs.

"Nobody asked. Nobody cared. Just went on with your life. Glad to be home. Glad to get back to work," he says.

His body, however, weakened. A surgeon discovered James was host to "nine kinds of parasites they said that aren't found in the United States," Diana comments.

Physically well again, James worked by day, and by night in a community college trained for another career: extracting what lay beneath the quilt patterns of two-lane roads and cornfields. Robinson Sand, an oil-bearing geological stratum first drilled in the early twentieth century, was still an active field in the 1970s. James began a new career as a "roustabout" on oil well platforms: hard, dangerous labor in all weathers, with workdays beginning at 3:30 a.m.

Over the years while their three children, Shandi, Elijah, and James William were born and growing up, the couple bought land, raised cattle, pigs, horses, chickens, and tended a large kitchen garden. In 1990, the former roustabout started his own business, Lemmon Home Repair Service.

His mind and body, however, were betraying him. He lost sleep, lost purpose, lost direction.

"I got messed up. Two or three years I don't remember," he says.

Finally, the coiled snake of post-traumatic stress disorder struck.

On a Saturday night in 2003, he asked Diana to drop him off at a motel in Robinson. Neither knew if he would see another sunrise.

"Me and a case of beer and all the ghosts of my past. Made it through the night. Sunday morning I knew she was coming in for church so I called her and she came, got me and called Danville and they said bring me up. I've been pretty well tangled up with the VA ever since," he says.

At the VA Illiana Health Care System in Danville, Illinois, James came home again from Vietnam. He is quick to laud a counselor, Tim Kohlbacher, as "much of the reason I was able to get better."

Still, his physical condition worsened. Eyesight and hearing diminished. He struggled with short-term memory loss. To keep him busy, his nurse-practitioner suggested gardening. Now, this farmer, roustabout, and combat soldier was reduced to tending flowers bordering the front porch.

"I couldn't do anything else. I'd drag a bucket around, sit on it, and water the flowers," he remarks.

The front-porch garden blossomed under his care. With another surgery, eyesight and hearing improved. He quit smoking. Energy and strength returned. This is the James Lemmon Jim Logue met again a half-century after Vietnam.

Music heals, too. Acoustical music always soothed his soul—chords of memory that brought him and Diana even closer. James plays guitar, dobro, and mandolin. Diana accompanies him with her lilting voice and bass fiddle.

They still perform in churches. In winter, he leads jam sessions in Robinson. In warmer weather, the couple travels for weekends of "bluegrassing"—gatherings in scenic, highland settings. These are his "laagers" now, where friends keep alive the corpus of early American music.

While music helps widen the mental distance between veteran and Vietnam, Lemmon still "senses" the war. In mid-sentence, he falls silent, listening. He peers at Jim.

"Choppers," the two veterans say, before Diana and I hear the distant thump of rotary blades. Lemmon sighs.

"They always came and got us," he says of medevacs. "That's why I can *feel* a helicopter coming. Before it makes any noise, I just *feel* it."

They walk into another part of the house, chatting.

"It's hard for him," Diana says, setting the table for lunch. She pauses and looks up: "The war. It's always there, right behind his eyes when he looks at me."

She served us shepherd's pie, fresh fruit, and oatmeal-and-chocolate-chip cookies like those she sent James in Vietnam.

Then they bring out bass fiddle and guitar and break successively into two, rollicking bluegrass numbers: "Ole Slew-Foot," a Porter Waggoner standard, and "The Old, Old House," by George Jones and Hal Bynum. The last notes die away. Jim and I applaud.

"Pass Me Not?" James asks Diana. She nods.

In this waning afternoon, they raise a plaintive hymn, written in 1868 by the blind lyricist Frances J. (Fanny) Crosby. As with her other songs, she listened to the music and dictated lyrics, including this hymn's chorus:

Savior, Savior,
Hear my humble cry;
While on others Thou art calling,
Do not pass me by.

If music could take wing, "Pass Me Not, O Gentle Savior" would lift above these quilts of cornfields and take flight to the eternal laagers of Larry Wayne Rasey, Everette Brent Caldwell, and William David Menscer—whose son's life began as his own ended. It skims across Duane Peterson's Minnesota and the Wisconsin woodlands of Mark Klever and Thomas John Roberts.

It turns autumn's leaves on the flat stone of Donald Kuzilla in Michigan; glides through farm fields of Keith Lochner's Indiana; and ascends a rise above Clymer, New York, where Dennis Hogenboom rests. Finally, it drifts among ordered rows of white crosses and Stars of David above the Potomac River on the first lilt of green hills in Northern Virginia.

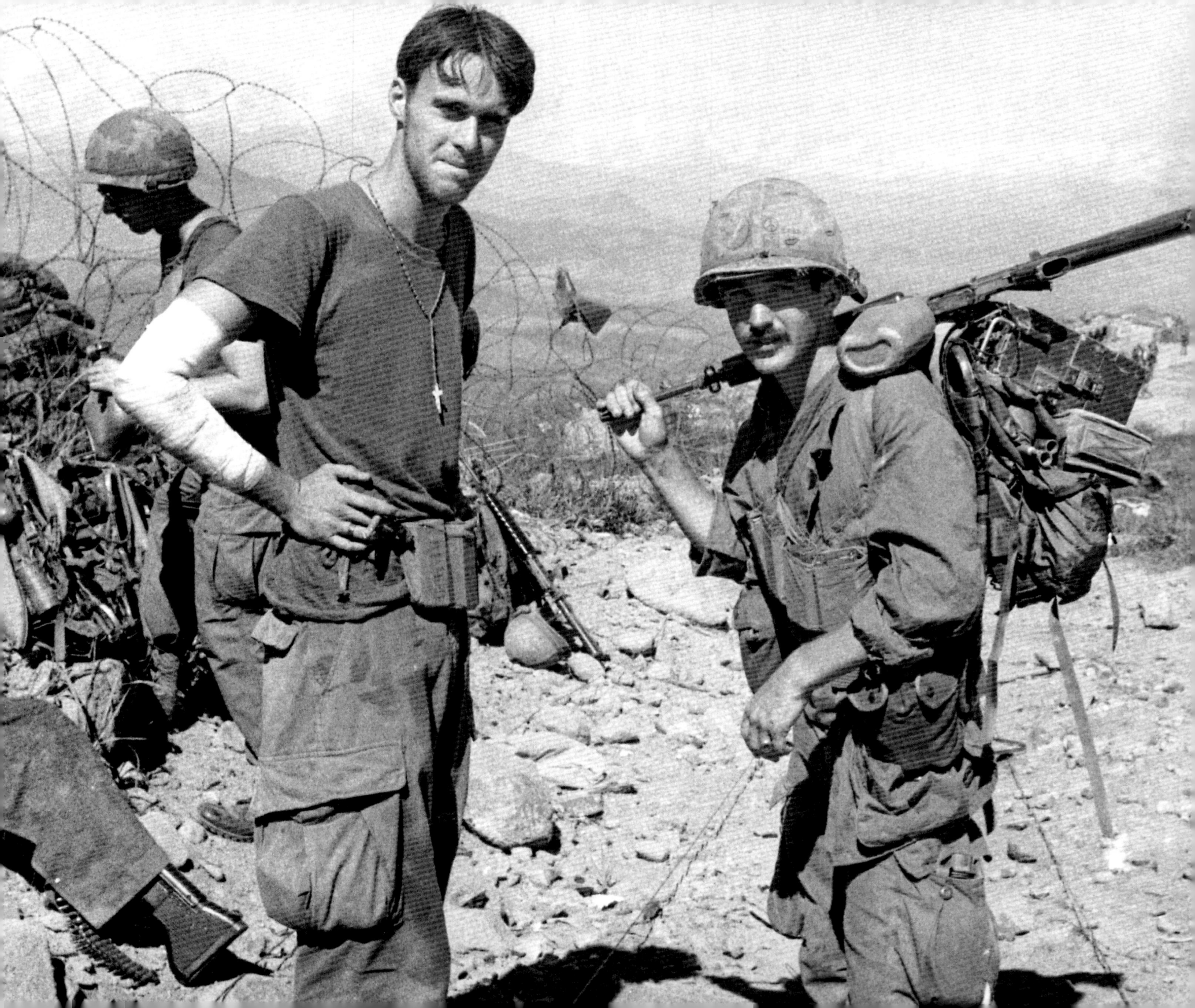

Chapter 20

It Made Me What I Am Today

Sergeant Benjamin Ellis Perry

THIS JOURNAL OF OUR ODYSSEY ACROSS AMERICA ENDS where it began—in Worcester, Massachusetts, in a restored Victorian home filled with books, art, and a crackling fire to warm a winter day. First, before all others of Alpha Company, we had to see Benjamin Ellis Perry, Jim Logue's lifelong friend during and since Vietnam.

It is 9 December 2012, cold but sunny, when Ben greets us cheerfully at his front door. Inside hangs his pride and joy: an original, signed poster of Woodstock Festival. While his contemporaries trekked to the muddy, music bacchanal in the summer of 1969, Ben was training to fight a war.

He is thinner now than when last I saw him, his voice diminished and a little hoarse. We gather around the dining room table with his gracious wife, Meg, who sets before us platters of cookies and coffee in fine china cups.

This house the couple restored is a quiet haven compared to the maelstrom of Ben's boyhood home in Worcester. Eldest of six children, Ben was born in a "three-decker" tenement house.

"That's the way the low- and middle-class lived. The neighborhood tended to be ethnic. You met kids who were not like you and you got to eat different foods. Greeks, Italians, French, Polish, all lived together. There was a real feeling of family. No one was divorced. People didn't have a lot of money. Not everybody owned a car," he recalls.

As a boy, Ben loved fast cars and showed artistic leanings.

"I just drew. I started drawing cars, was pretty good at hot rods. Since I was ten years old I was a dyed-in-the-wool 'hot rodder.'"

If art and cars intrigued him, school bored him. Never among the caste of high school gentry, he dared not ask any of the pretty, popular girls for dates. They were arm candy for handsome athletes and wealthy boys whose sleek sports cars left Ben on his bicycle in their dust.

"I was very, very shy, never a good student. I do thirst for knowledge. I have a great love of history and the arts," he says.

Upon graduating from high school, he enrolled in the school of the Worcester Art Museum that "looked neat because it was kind of 'hippyish' and I might meet girls, not the girls who want the football players."

Left: When artist Benjamin Perry (left) joined Alpha, he and Logue formed a lifelong friendship, with art and their warrior experiences as common bonds. Decades later, Ben urged Jim to print and publish his Vietnam photographs.

After an academically lackluster junior year, Ben's draft notice came.

"I said, 'What do I do with this?' Everybody who I was friendly with in art school got deferments, one way or another. The easy way was to say you were homosexual. I couldn't do that," he recalls.

A local anti-war advocate assured Ben he could slip him north of the border in a day. The artist anguished over his choices. Prison was punishment for refusing service. Fleeing to Canada meant banishment. Draft dodgers who fled America were forbidden to return. Either way, he was trapped. Ben had always sought someone who would make a decision for him. Now, only he could make this choice.

He *could not* flee north.

"I thought, 'I don't know if I can just take a pair of scissors and sever my life.' Everybody in my family had served and they all made it. So I let myself be drafted," he says.

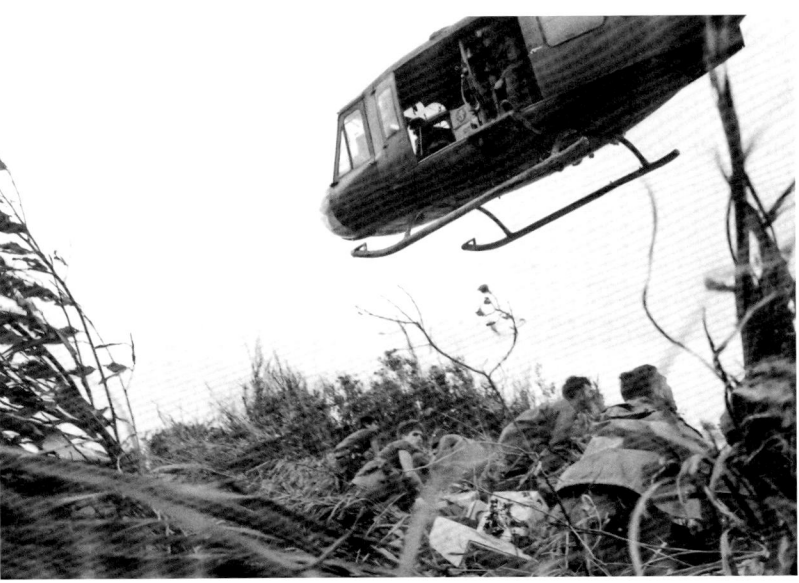

In the "bush," infantry loved most of all medevac choppers and resupply "birds." Resupply always brought C-rations and ammunition—and often soft drinks, cigarettes, and, best of all, mail from home.

After training at Fort Dix, New Jersey, and Fort Lewis, Washington, he was in Vietnam by February 1970 and aboard a slick flying resupply to Alpha in the field. As the Huey descended into a "hot" LZ, Ben peered below at crisscrossing fire of green and red tracers. The crew chief grabbed Ben by the neck and shouted, "We're not going to land. You can jump at three feet. You can jump at twenty feet. I do not care. But you're off *my* bird."

Ben throws up his hands at the memory.

"I'm sitting alone on this bird with boxes of ammo. I don't know what to do. 'Where am I going to go? Who's going to tell me what to do?'" he says.

Ben sips his coffee. His hand trembles as he returns cup to saucer.

"We got down over rice paddies. He kicked out all the ammo boxes and shouted, 'You! Out!' I was on the skid. I waited for about six feet before I jumped into a paddy and over my knees in mud. I couldn't move. I thought, 'Oh, God, I'm dead!' I hear automatic weapons fire. I smell something burning. I hear some guys yelling but I can't see anything.

"Some guy walks by, picking up ammo boxes. 'Get your ass out of the rice paddy!' he yelled. I crawled up on the dike and followed him. The Zippo Squad was burning a hooch. Those guys were all dirty. I'm clean from the waist up and filthy from the waist down. That was my first day," he recalls.

As firing died away, an armed civilian leapt from cover and dashed down a trail. A soldier fired one shot. The civilian crumpled. Ben stared down at the body.

"It was an old *papa-san* with an old rifle, and he's stupid enough to pick it up. So he got shot," he says.

Death came again hours later in a night ambush. Someone whispered, "We've got movement." Rifles and M60s erupted. Ben fired his weapon for the first time.

"In the morning we found bodies of a girl and a young man. Rigor mortis had set in. Flies. I thought, 'These people really aren't too much different than us.'"

In humping a 70-pound rucksack seven or eight klicks a day in heat above 100, the body hardens quickly. The heart hardens quicker. Ben leans towards me, his eyes intense.

"I can tell you that four months later, you don't feel like that," he states flatly.

This he learned his first day and night in war: An old man and a young girl would kill him as quickly as any NVA regular. Therefore, this artist the men of Alpha called "Gentle Ben" would survive in only one way. He speaks softly but firmly: "Kill them. Kill them all. If you don't, he's going to come back and kill you. If you don't pull the trigger first, he's going to get you."

In these first days with Alpha, Ben stood out as "new guy." None came near him. Few spoke. "New guy" does stupid things. "New guy" gets killed. "New guy" gets *you* killed.

His first ally was the rifle that brought him a comfort soldiers rarely find in weapons—a touch of home. The M16 issued to him was made at Harrington & Richardson, a firearms manufacturer in Worcester. It seemed to be a "friend," even a talisman. It wouldn't let him down, nor would Ben let *it* down. Every day he cared for his Worcester rifle with oil, cloth, and cleaning rod.

As veterans avoided *him*, Ben kept his distance from other "new guys" and filed friends, incidents, and emotions as if papers into office cabinets. From most, he preferred to stand apart.

"If they weren't in your platoon, you didn't know them and you didn't want to know them," he says. "First, you become sort of mentally responsible for knowing that person. If you cannot learn to compartmentalize your feelings and turn your emotions off, you will *not* survive. Otherwise, you either go mad or you would not be able to function. You had an emotional distance that was not even measured. It wasn't even a mile. It was eons."

Steadily, Vietnam was turning gentle artist into savvy warrior who discovered various solutions for self-preservation, as well as what little comfort war affords a soldier. Take underwear. He grins: "Commando," he says of going bare beneath. "It's too hot. You chafe. You just ask for trouble."

Sun burnished his skin. He grew stronger in endurance, yet lighter in weight. Heat, hills, and humping a rucksack carved his 170 pounds to 140. Appointed RTO for 1st Platoon leader, he strapped a PRC-25 ("prick") radio atop his rucksack.

He ticks off an inventory of his burden: "I had a steel pot, helmet liner, rucksack and frame, and that had to be six or seven pounds. The 'prick' was twenty-five pounds. The battery was five pounds and you carried two. I carried three hundred rounds of ammunition, two smoke grenades, one hand 'frag,' maybe two. Sometimes you'd get saddled with one hundred rounds of M60 ammunition. Ten pounds. M16 comes in a little under ten pounds. Each full canteen is a pound."

With food, extra socks, air mattress, poncho, and poncho liner, Ben hefted about seventy pounds.

The radio introduced him to fellow artist and soon-to-be best friend, Jim Logue, RTO for company commander Captain John Wilson. Little creative distance separates those who work with palette, brush, and canvas and those whose "paints" are light and shadow on film.

Into spring, Alpha slogged through "the bush," skirmished, and destroyed caches of enemy supplies, all while yearning for the three-day stand-down of 28–30 April.

With Captain John Wilson's permission, Jim and Ben choppered to Chu Lai a day early. Their reason (or rather excuse): to create colorful signs and murals "for morale": peace signs, daisies symbolizing "flower power," and, incongruously, a banner bearing the company's bellicose slogan: "Alpha Battalion: Killing is Our Business, Business Has Been Good."

Upon arriving in Chu Lai, Alpha made a beeline for the beer. Ben still remembers the refreshment inventory: "A jeep was parked there with cold beer in the trailer. A pallet full of beer next to it. I made sure that I knew from that day on exactly how much beer is on a pallet, which is 85 cases."

"And after three days of stand-down?" I ask.

He grins.

"Zero cases."

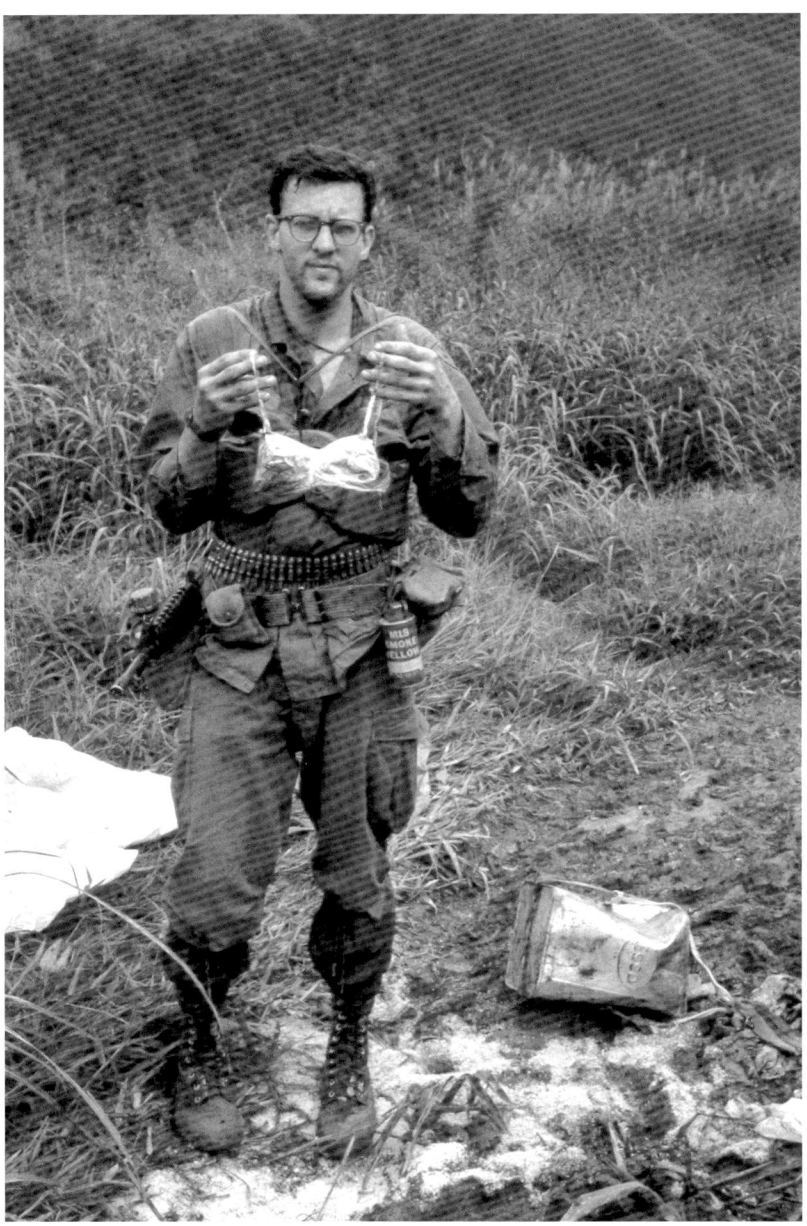

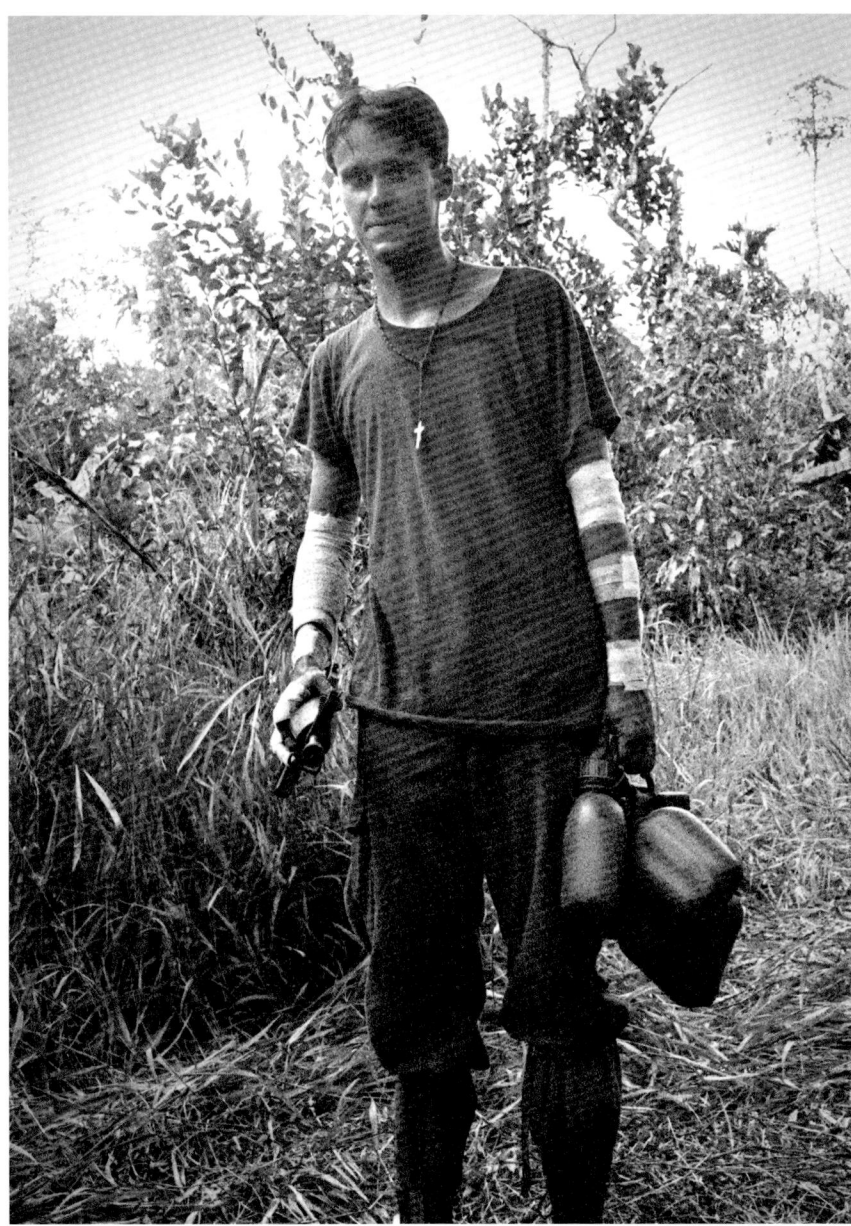

In searching a Viet Cong position after a firefight, this soldier lifts a bra from a pack, evidence that at least one enemy fighter was female. VC included men, women, and even children.

Going on a "water run," Ben Perry clutches weapon and canteens. Note his runner's physique. Most infantrymen in Vietnam dropped thirty to forty pounds a year. A size 30 waist was common.

Plenty of beer was left over this time. In the early hours, word came that the NVA was on attack. Alpha stumbled out for airlifts. Ben winces at the memory: "Hung over. Stoned. 'Jesus Christ, I can't even stand up!' People are puking on the landing pad."

Aboard a Chinook, he peered down at the countryside ablaze.

"Everywhere there was a village on fire. Hueys were down and burning. Hiép Dúc was burning. Everybody sobered up pretty quickly," he says.

Through May into June, combat bled the company in deaths, wounds, heat, disease, and feet stripped of flesh from trench foot. All were exhausted, all were hungry, all yearned for resupply choppers bearing rations, ammo, and mail.

In writing letters home, Ben gnawed at his pen. How could he describe a country that Americans, half a world away, could understand? Take weather. His family inquired about the heat.

"Yeah, it's hot. How hot is hot? The hottest day you ever experienced in your life is what is normal. It was a very difficult way to translate that type of feeling, so I ended up not doing it. Just tried to reassure my mother that everything was fine and I was getting by," he says.

On 14 May, Alpha and its walking wounded limped into Hiép Dúc, footsore and starving after humping four days mostly without food and water. Resupply choppers arrived. The men feasted, then shared rations with villagers.

Barefoot children recognized the G.I. who drew pictures for them and clustered around him. With C-ration cardboard for canvases Ben began to draw: portraits of the youngsters, of animals, and of Ben's "hot rods," the strange American cars they had never seen.

At one point, Jim snapped his shutter release just as Ben, cardboard canvas and pen in hands, looks up and into the distance with a hint of a smile, as grinning youngsters drape themselves over his shoulders.

It is, quite simply, one of the best photographs of the war—in one frame a glimpse of art bridging a peace between people locked in conflict.

Minutes later, Alpha marched north and into an ambush in which Donald Kuzilla died. Two days thereafter, David Menscer of Statesville, North Carolina, was killed. More wounded were medevacked. The next day, after slugging it out with the NVA, Alpha staggered to a hilltop night laager.

"This is what I call my 'second' first day in Vietnam," Ben says.

Knowing NVA lurked nearby, Ben Perry and Richard Thimmig of Sparta, Illinois, gouged out a foxhole in the cement of sunbaked earth. Captain Wilson passed the word: He had received orders to return to LZ West the next day. The company would steal away at first light.

"I had my rucksack crossed up with my M16," Ben recalls of his gear on the lip of his foxhole. "Soon as first light hits, we're gone."

In the dim predawn, all froze at the chilling cough of a mortar round leaving a tube. They flung themselves back into foxholes as 82mm mortar rounds rained down.

As a mortar round screamed down upon them, Ben and Dick jumped out of the foxhole. Another round hit dangerously near them. They jumped back into their hole. Two more rounds left tubes. Out they bounded, seconds before the shells exploded, ripping apart Ben's rucksack. Then he stared in disbelief to see below an NVA soldier with an AK-47 "walking" rounds up the hill.

"He's coming towards me. I said, 'You son of a bitch!'"

Ben grabbed rifle and ruck and with others fled down the other side of the hill. Alpha walked all day, then ascended LZ West. Only then did Ben peer down at his ripped rucksack and his Worcester rifle. His heart fell.

"It had a four- or five-inch mortar shard right through the bolt. I couldn't have fired the weapon," he recalls.

Soon he heard a familiar voice. "Re-up" sergeants trolled firebases when units returned after fierce fighting. Scared

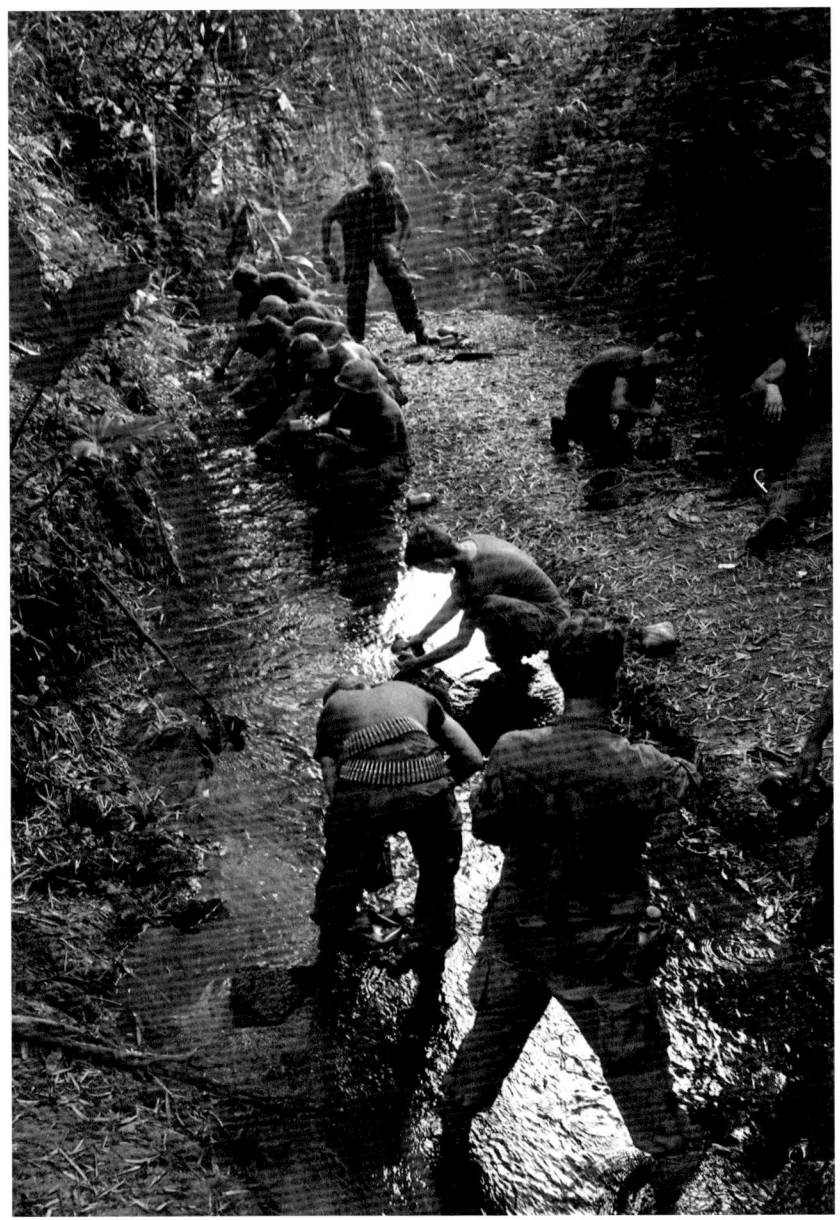

Soldiers fill canteens in a stream. At far right, medic Dennis ("Doc") Mack (with cigarette) will ensure that all will purify their water with iodine tablets.

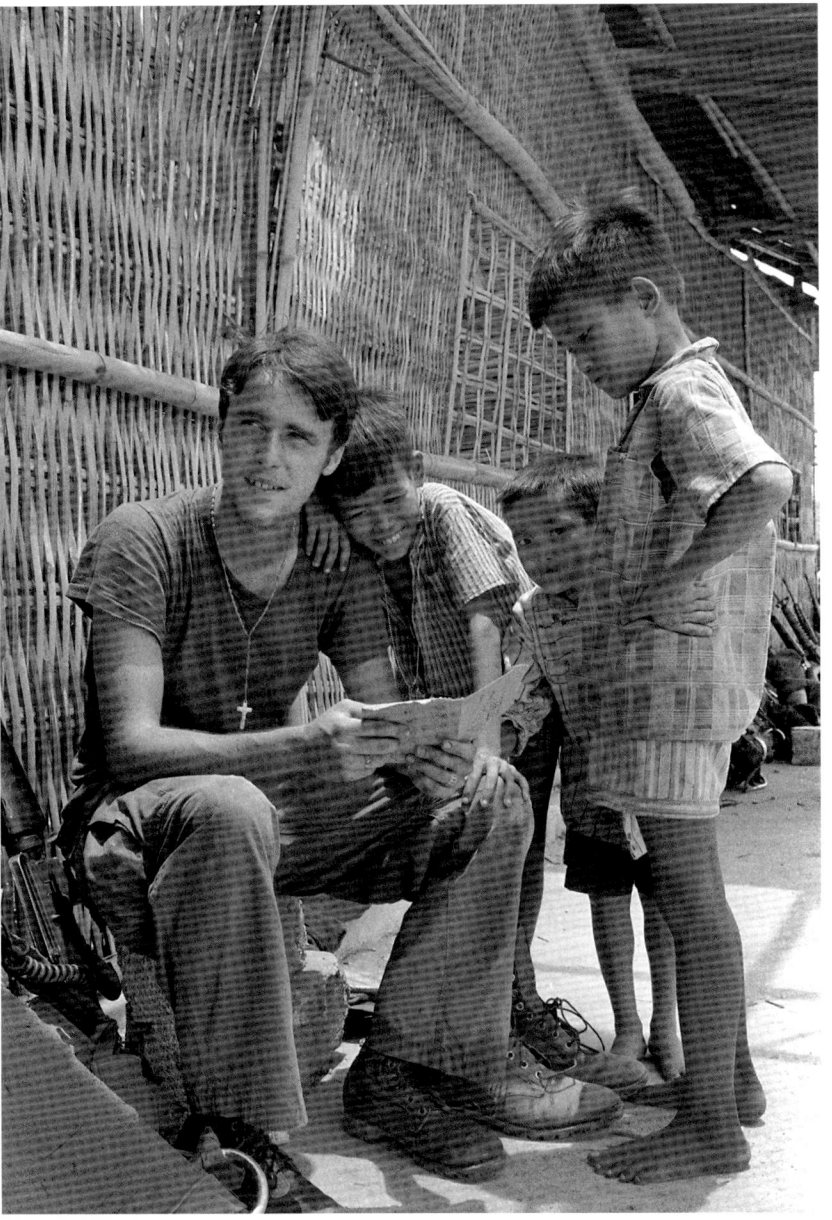

Youngsters at Hiêp Dúc watch while Ben Perry draws pictures of hot rods and other cars they'd never seen. Logue shot this photo on 14 May 1970. The child in the middle is Vo Sy.

soldiers were ripe pickings to reenlist for supposedly safer assignments. In his clean, starched fatigues and gleaming boots, the re-up sarge shouted out his mantra like a carnival barker: "Step right up. Reenlist. Get a thirty-day leave to the States and a safe job in the rear." Reenlistment, however, was a six-year commitment. To re-up, in G.I. lingo, was to "take a burst of six." The sergeant's promises meant nothing. Men who "took a burst of six" and a thirty-day leave often found themselves back in the infantry.

Ben sat, thinking not of a leave but of a "number." He had endured so many close calls he wondered if "his number was up." As men looked down at one of their dead, someone would sigh, "When your number's up, your number's up."

On 17 May 1970, Ben figured his number was up.

"My rifle's gone. My ruck's gone. How much closer do you have to get? So I went and talked to this re-up guy. He said, 'Oh, yeah, sure we can help you out. Just wait for the bird to take you to the rear.'"

As others reached West, the re-up sergeant added Ben to those who had succumbed to his siren song.

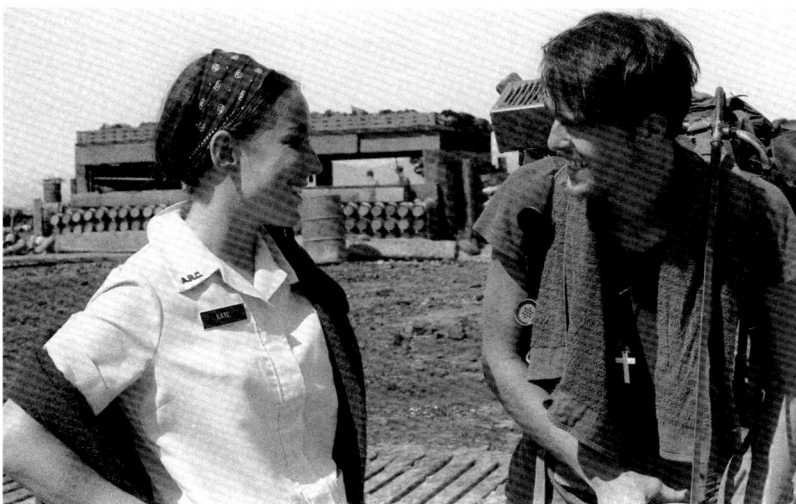

Donut Dollies often choppered onto firebases with Kool-Aid and games. Their visits gave G.I.s time to socialize with young American women. Donut Dollie Katharine Beckwith, from San Antonio, chats with Ben Perry.

"He pointed me out as the kid who was going to re-up and get out of the field. He kept saying, 'He's doing the right thing. Don't you want to do the right thing?'"

The artist had heard enough. "Gentle Ben" stalked over to the sergeant and stood an inch from his face.

"I said, 'Listen. You can go fuck yourself!' I went back to where the new mess hall was being built. Dick Thimmig was there. He said, 'What happened?' I said, 'I told him to go fuck himself.' He said, 'Good for you.'"

Ben pauses. His voice is soft.

"That guy changed my life," he says of the re-up sergeant. "I stopped being a victim. I took charge of my own life. I figure it made me what I am today."

ON 6 JUNE, REMNANTS OF ALPHA WALKED INTO AN NVA TRAP.

"Perry Stemen was in charge of 3rd Platoon and they were getting hammered. They're calling for help. I dropped my radio and went forward. The guys needed help, and no one came with me. I get about halfway there and somebody's coming towards me dragging [Everette] Caldwell. He said, 'Don't go up there. We're pulling out!'"

Caught in an L-shaped ambush by two companies of NVA, Alpha, the size of a platoon, clawed its way up the mountain under fire.

Later that day orders came: "Go back down the hill and police up your dead."

With the enemy remaining on the battlefield, the men knew it was a death trap. They refused the order.

Colonel Edwin Kennedy, commander of 196th Light Infantry Brigade, learned of the insubordination and flew to West. Kennedy had graduated from West Point, served in World War II, and earned a Silver Star both in the Korean War as a rifle platoon leader and in Vietnam as a field grade officer.

Kennedy's eyes, the color of blue ice, crackled in anger when he commanded Alpha to retrieve their dead.

"Now!"

Men shuffled nervously. To disobey this order meant possible incarceration. To go down there was to die.

Then someone stepped forward, neither an officer nor a rugged "lifer" NCO but an artist. Specialist 4 Perry nudged his way through and stood within inches of the colonel.

With his Nikonos, Jim recorded one of the most important moments in the Vietnam War. Ben Perry in t-shirt, with tousled hair and hands at his waist, stands face to face with the brigade commander, a Specialist 4 refusing a direct order from a "bird" colonel.

Politely but firmly, Ben reminded the colonel that superior enemy forces waited below. Yes, all of them wanted to bring back the remains of their friends, just not that day. All who went down there would die. When the enemy left, Alpha would retrieve the bodies. Others, stunned at courage they could not muster, nodded in silent assent.

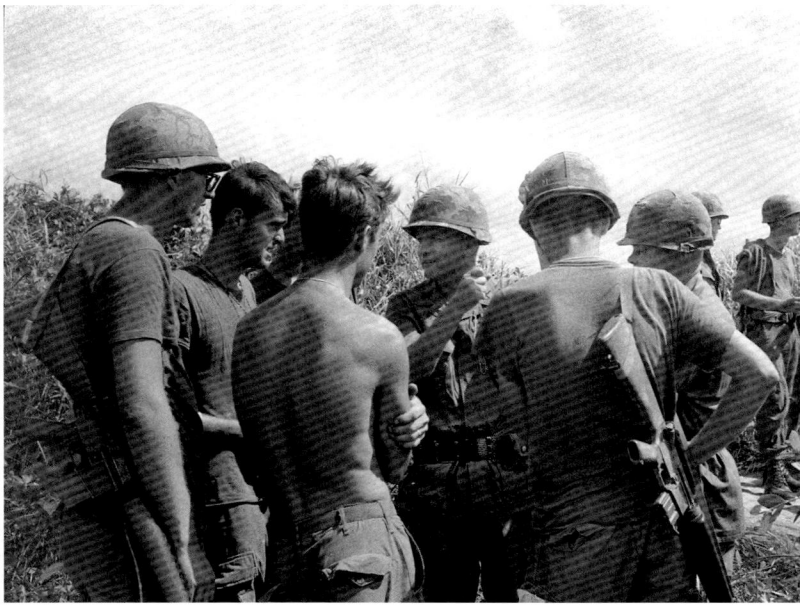

Hours after the 6 June battle, Colonel Edwin Kennedy orders Alpha to collect the dead. Knowing NVA remained there, Ben Perry, second from left, refused the order, a criminal offense. He was never charged.

Colonel Kennedy backed down.

Jim's photograph was the first of two great war images snapped within minutes. Ben trudged back to the mess hall, sat beside Jim, and picked up the photographer's Nikonos. He snapped a photograph of Jim as remarkable as the classic image *Exhausted US Marine at Côn Thiên, Viet Nam (1967)* by David Douglas Duncan. Jim huddles in a corner, his knees drawn up. He leans his head against his right hand, his dark eyes empty of light and life.

The next day, elements of 1/46 tramped onto the 6 June battleground. The same NVA forces chewed them up. Not until 12 June, when the enemy vanished, did Alpha recover the remains of their dead.

Ben had entered his fifth month in Vietnam. That summer, with Alpha's ranks bolstered with "new guys," battalion commander Colonel Thomas Breen instituted "Eagle Flights": one-day strikes at targets.

New company commander Captain James Crockert was leading, with RTO Perry just steps behind him. Ahead of them, a Vietnamese man wriggled from one hole and burrowed into another. Crockert and Perry sprinted forward, with Crockert tossing a grenade into the recess. A secondary explosion blew back on him and Ben, injuring both. Two pieces of shrapnel ripped into Ben's chest, one lodging in his sternum.

"It missed my heart by half an inch," he says.

He was treated at 27th Surgical Hospital, where he spent two months in rehabilitation. Then he and Logue enjoyed R&R in Tokyo, where they toured the Nikon camera plant.

Crockert granted Ben a new job: radio operator for LZ West. Preferring not to serve the remainder of his military time stateside, Ben extended his tour so that he would complete service when he left Vietnam.

In March 1971, his "freedom bird" reached Seattle at night. Like a time traveler from the past, he peered through the airplane window, amazed at the view below after a year in the bush.

"I saw cars with lights on! Streetlights! I said, 'Civilization!'" he recalls.

Dressed in a new Class A uniform adorned with his sergeant stripes and medals, including Purple Heart and Combat Infantry Badge, Ben boarded a Pan American Airlines flight to Boston. A stewardess beckoned him and other soldiers to follow her aft to seats near the galley. Most passengers carefully ignored the servicemen as they passed. Others, Ben recalls, looked up in open, if silent, hostility.

"At least we didn't have people staring at us," he remarks of sitting in the back of the plane. "We didn't feel too much out of place."

He smiles in recalling the flight attendants.

"They were nice to us. They whispered. That's all I wanted: to be quiet. No yelling. No screaming. No laughing. No back-slapping. I wanted quiet." He pauses. "Seems like the next day I was on my mother's porch."

Ben hung his uniform in a closet and put on civilian clothing. "And that was it," he says.

The warrior-artist returned to college. He didn't stay long.

"I couldn't do it," he states. "I was so separated emotionally from the student life after the experience that I had. I felt I was older. I had been through a real experience."

Quickly, he learned not to mention his service. A female acquaintance once chirped: "'Oh, Ben what a wonderful tan. Have you been in Florida?' I said, 'Yeah, kinda.'"

Ben and Meg married and had one daughter, Sydney. He enjoyed a successful career as a marketing agent for Brother International. He bought his pride and joy, a Jaguar, a car he drew as a kid. As Vietnamese restaurants opened, he came to savor the fare of the country.

When Jim and Ben renewed their friendship in the 1980s, Ben kept reminding Jim of his treasury of photographs. He was delighted when Jim uploaded those images onto the 31st Infantry Regiment website.

AFTER WE FINISHED A TWO-DAY INTERVIEW, BEN AND I embraced and wished each other well. Jim stayed behind, then spent several more hours with Ben the next morning. Later, as we drove through the afternoon and into night, neither of us spoke of Ben, until Jim said, more to himself than to me: "I'd like to be buried beside Ben."

A shadow had lingered while we talked in Ben's beautiful home. In 2011, physicians had discovered cancer, but Ben recovered after treatment. By fall 2012, however, the disease returned. As Jim and I began work on this project, Ben was fighting his last holdover battle of Vietnam. Still, he had wanted to talk. How humbled we were that he bequeathed to us two days of precious breath to tell his story. But is that not the greater love of a soldier who served at the point of the spear: to lay down his life for a friend?

On 13 January 2013, at Rose Monahan Hospice in Worcester, Ben died of squamous cell carcinoma, resulting from exposure to Agent Orange in the Republic of Vietnam. The family followed Ben's instructions: cremation, and then burial at the place of his choosing.

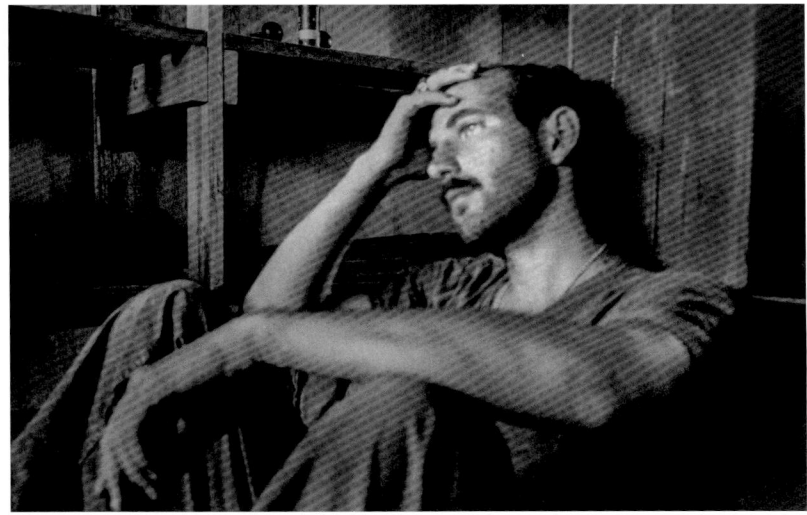

With Logue's camera, Ben Perry snapped this image of Jim. Both were bone-weary after the 6 June battle. Both nearly lost their lives. Three had died, with many wounded.

For the graveside service, Colonel (ret) James Crockert drove up from his central Virginia home. Jim flew up from Florida, joining Ben's kin and other friends. Jim photographed the honor guard as they brought the flag-draped casket forward. A chaplain spoke. Two soldiers crisply shaped the flag in its 13-fold triangle and presented it to Meg.

A 21-gun salute shattered the stillness. A bugler sounded "Taps." And then Sergeant Benjamin Ellis Perry, the artist who came within a brushstroke of fleeing from service in Vietnam, was buried beside a mighty oak in the place of his request: on green slopes above the Potomac River in Arlington National Cemetery.

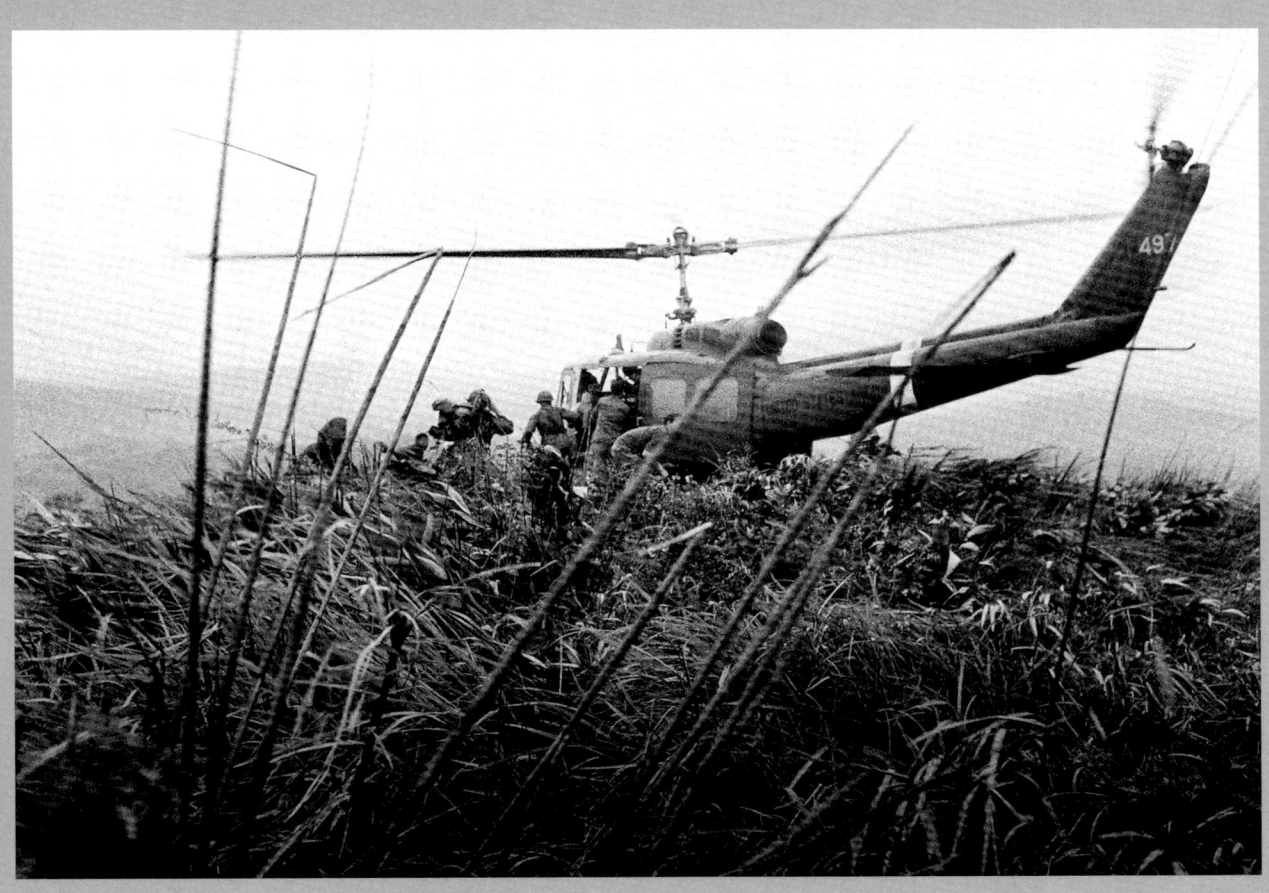

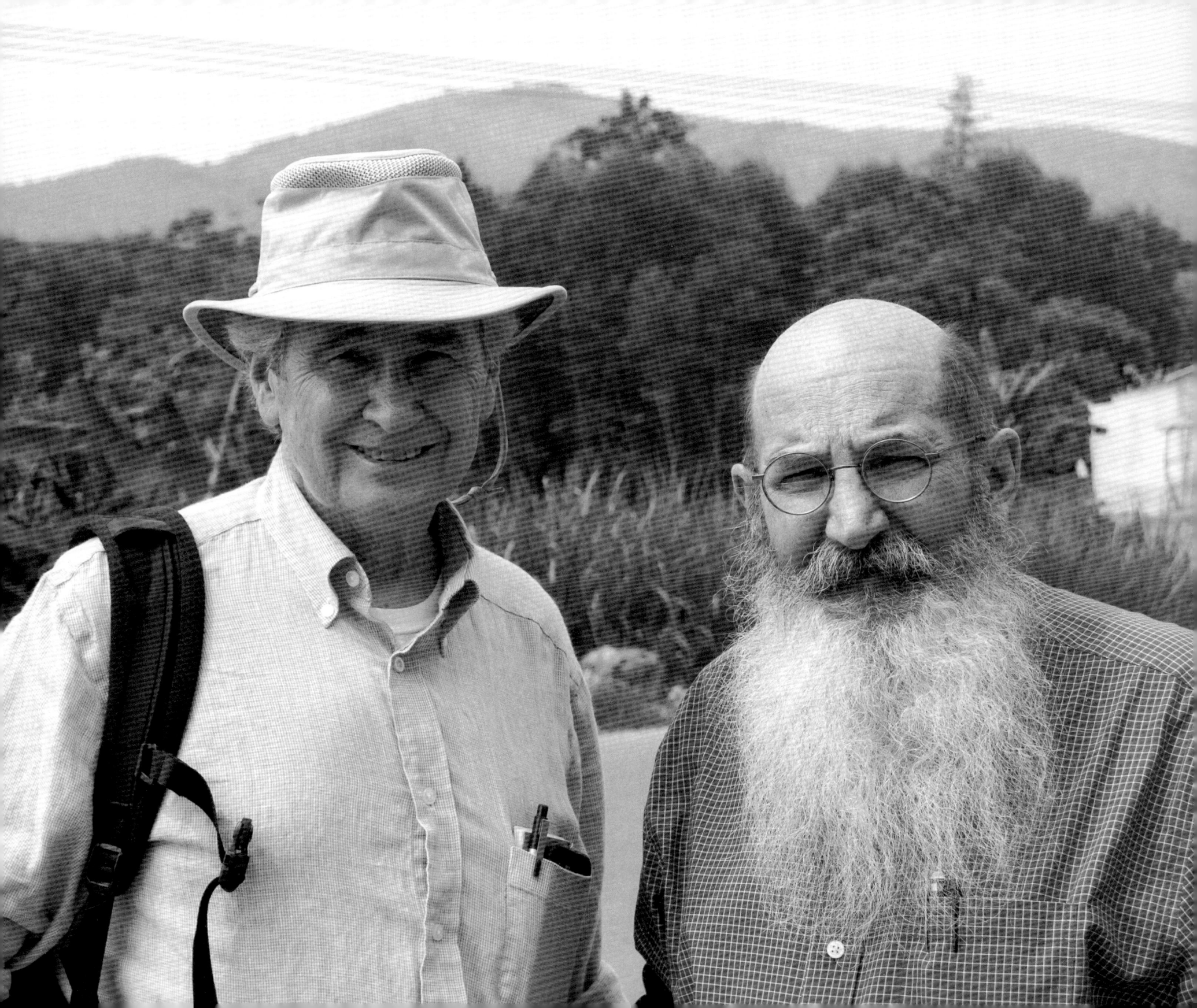

Epilogue

The Last Sweep

Hôi An, Socialist Republic of Vietnam: SO, WHAT COMES AFTER loss but a long journey? After Ben's passing, Jim and I traveled 54,000 miles across America over four years to interview seventy-one men of Alpha Company or their survivors. Now, we fly above the Pacific a day into the future to reach the distant past and tread the terrain of memory.

It's noon, and it's 113 degrees—as hot as Phoenix and as humid as Houston. Jim walks point on a trail between long knives of elephant grass in what was formerly Quang Tin Province. It's 29 April 2016, forty-six years to the day since these men of Alpha began three months of firefights, fear, hunger, heartbreak.

Only aging veterans, who have made peace with mortality, hear the whisper of old battlefields, beckoning. Old men in white beards shook hands across stone fences at Gettysburg. Doughboys walked again through forests of the Meuse–Argonne. G.I.s stooped to sift the sands of Normandy. Surely, those "precious few" who fought on Saint Crispin's Day tottered across the fields of Agincourt.

Now, Vietnam veterans return and slip through their own terrains of memory murmuring to them.

What is Vietnam like now? Stepping outside Tan Son Nhát International Airport in Ho Chi Minh City, we stagger back from the same blast of hot, humid air Jim remembers. Gone, however, was the second assault to the senses: the fetid stench of waste.

We spend ten days in luxury so far beyond Alpha's night laager dreams: fine hotels, restaurants, an air-conditioned Mercedes with chauffeur and guide, all thanks to arrangements made by Audley Travel of Boston.

Jim's brother-in-law, Bruce Delaney, who teaches in the US-based International School, Saigon Pearl, shows us around Ho Chi Minh City. It remains "Saigon" to most citizens. Many signs read "Saigon"; many residents say "Saigon," from tradition, as a vocal smirk at Hanoi, or because of the efficiency of two syllables rather than five.

The din of commerce rings beneath a skyline soaring with skyscrapers amid the gritty haze of new construction. We see America in Baskin-Robbins, McDonald's, and Starbucks, along streets that rumble with traffic, including herds of motorbikes with bleating horns.

This is not the Vietnam that existed just after 1975, when Hanoi set up its collectivist system. Hunger followed. Hanoi then closed its reeducation camps and looked the other way while citizens operated their own farms and businesses for

Left: In April 2016, James Allen Logue (right) and Gary D. Ford explore Alpha's area of operations. Behind them soars the mountain Núi Liêt Kiêm, its green crest once home of LZ West.

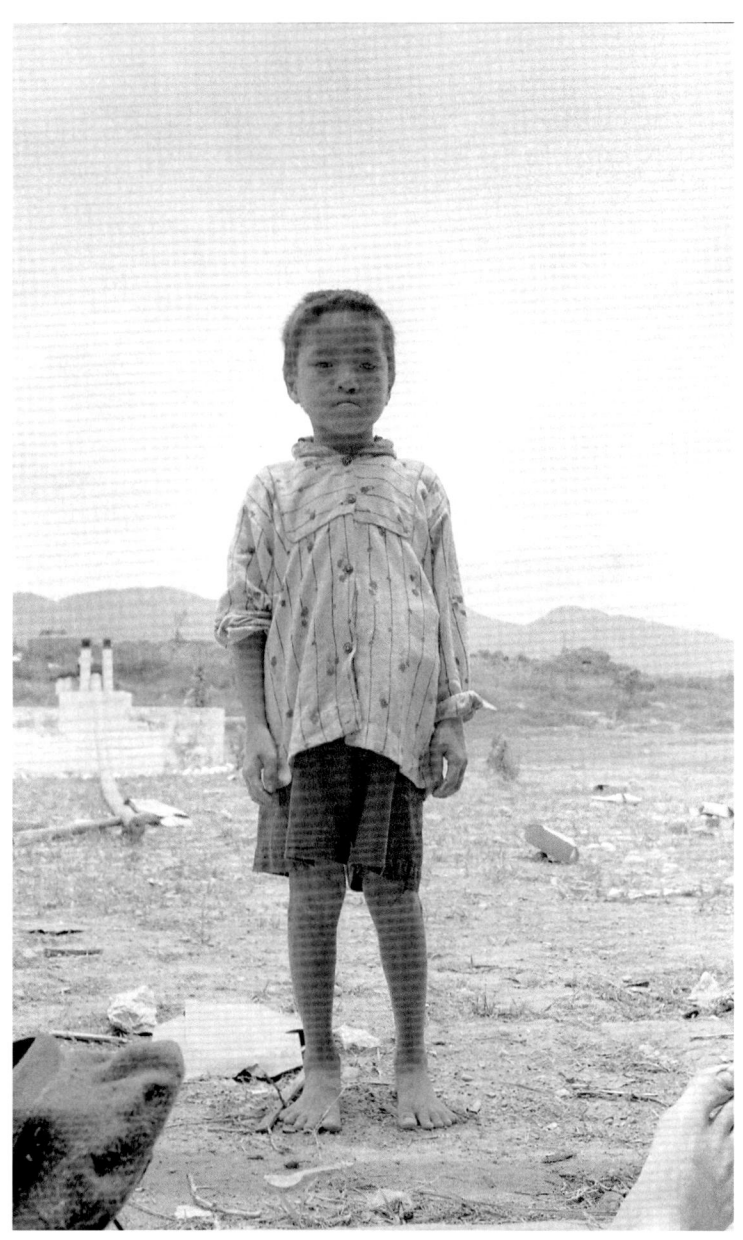

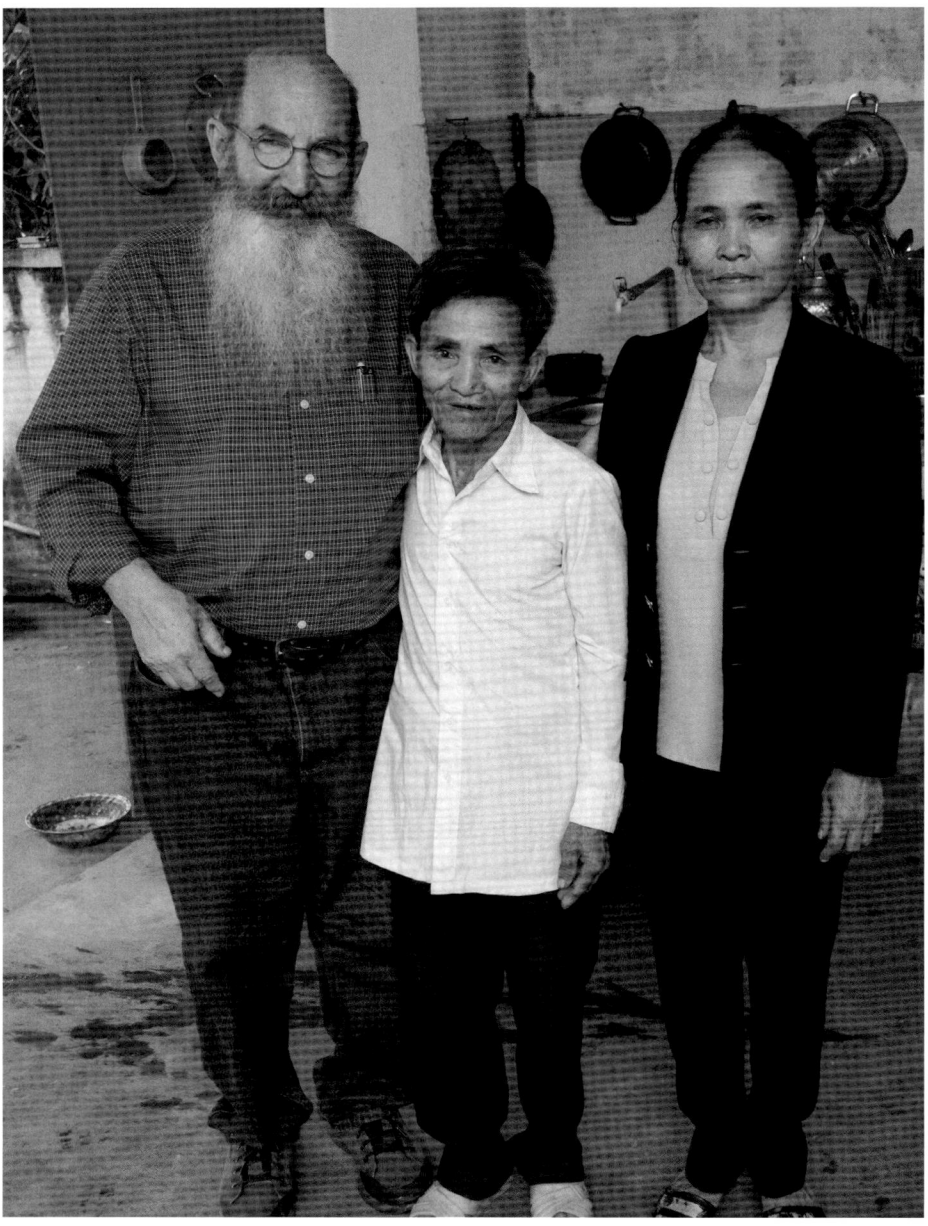

On 14 May 1970, Logue shot this photograph of Vo Sy, one of the youngsters in Hiêp Dúc who watched Ben Perry draw cars and their own portraits.

In Hiêp Dúc in 2016, James Logue meets again Vo Sy and his sister, Vo Thi Ba, with copies of the photograph of Vo Sy with Ben Perry in 1970.

profit. Now, in this truce with capitalism, the nation flourishes as Southeast Asia's economic success story.

Our guide to the battlefields, Nguyen Cong Thong, wears an olive drab t-shirt bearing the shoulder patch of 196th Light Infantry Brigade. He is cheerful, punctual, and well versed in the conflict. A 1975 high school graduate in his native Da Nang, he "lived" the war and its aftermath and is forthcoming about life in Vietnam, then and now.

From our hotel, Hôi An Essence Resort and Spa, Thong and our driver, Duc, take us south and west, alongside rice fields worked with both machinery and water buffalo and into Alpha's old AO in Que Son Valley.

"There's LZ West," Jim says quietly.

I gape at the mountain's nearly vertical green soar. Long gone from its crest and slopes are red gashes from the chemical scythe of Agent Orange.

Jim and I both yearn to stand atop the old fire base, but neither of us have legs or lungs to scale it, nor the stomach to encounter its namesake: *Nui Liét Kiém*, or "Mountain of Leeches." Instead, we go to church.

"It's still there!" Jim exclaims when Duc stops in nearby Viet An.

In late summer 1970, Jim accompanied Captain Donald Wilson, battalion chaplain, and Andrew Wommack, chaplain's assistant, to this Christian church and its adjacent school and orphanage. Logue's story in the battalion newspaper described how the chaplain's wife had coordinated efforts from Southern Baptists in Virginia to provide the locals with clothing, food, and school supplies. Captain John Wilson's mother headed similar efforts among Methodists in Alabama. Jim photographed Chaplain Wilson with youngsters, as well as the church, where a banner in the sanctuary was emblazoned, "John 3:16."

The church is new. Communists torched the old edifice but later allowed Catholics and Protestants to return and rebuild. Jim opens the sanctuary doors. There spread above pews is the old "John 3:16" banner someone saved from the conflagration.

Jim and I leave donations, along with copies of his 1970 photographs.

Hiêp Dúc today is unrecognizable from its condition fifty years ago, with its shops and thriving enterprises along clean, paved streets. For a mid-day break, Duc pulls into a truck repair shop, with a shady, open-air rest area. Mechanics on break thumb through photographs Jim took here on 14 May 1970. A passerby, wearing her conical *nón lá*, points to pictures of a barefoot boy in shirt and shorts. She knows him—Vo Sy, and his older sister, Vo Thi Ba—and will invite them here tomorrow morning to meet us.

The rest of the day we follow Alpha's faint trail, guided by Thong's geographical knowledge, Duc's driving skills, and Jim's cartographic "point men": his old AO map and area images from Google Earth. First, we wind along a road that narrows into a dirt path at "The Gap": the Song Thu Bon river, and across it, the green soar of the NVA's mountain haunts.

One battle site begins at the end of a neighborhood street. Beyond stretch a green field and distant woodlands, where on 5 May 1970, friendly fire fell on 2nd Platoon, wounding four and killing Duane Peterson of Isanti, Minnesota. Two months thereafter, Duane was to have married while on R&R in Hawaii.

As we peer at the distant tree line, laughter and music ring out from a nearby comfortable home.

"Wedding party," Thong explains.

Jim needs no map to find the dirt path, now a two-lane paved road leading north of Hiép Dúc. Beyond a bridge rises a small new hostelry, Phuong Dong Hotel, built above the site where Sergeant Donald Kuzilla died that rainy afternoon of 14 May.

That day seemingly dawned again the next morning in Hiép Dúc. We return to the automotive shop where a small, decrepit fan, looking as if it were new in 1970, stirs the air. Vo Thi Ba, wearing a stylish black jacket and pants, arrives with her husband, Dang Dinh Quyean, and her younger brother, Vo Sy, one of the children Jim photographed on 14 May 1970. All smile and shake our hands warmly.

They cluster over Jim's photographs, chatting with us via Thong's translation. In one photograph, Sy is one of the barefoot boys leaning on Ben's shoulder as the latter draws pictures on field-expedient canvases: cardboard from C-ration cartons.

With Thong interpreting, Jim describes how Alpha arrived on 14 May 1970, after four days without rations. Ba nods. She remembers fear and hunger, and how many subsisted on roots and hid in caves and jungles for safety from both armies. Still, civilians fell in the crossfire. Quyean pulls up his shirt to reveal scars from napalm.

"It was a horrible life because of the war," Ba says.

With G.I.s in this protected village, she came to welcome C-rations. One soldier, she recalled, wanted to adopt her and Sy and take them to America.

Yes, she recalls the NVA swarming into the village in April 1970, murdering many, confiscating foods, and damaging the American-built school and other buildings. Yes, she remembers that day in May when Alpha appeared and resupply choppers landed with C-rations, which soldiers shared with civilians.

After conversing with *these* veterans of the war, I will say this to the men of Alpha: "Yes, many civilians were your enemies. These things they remember fondly: sharing your rations, giving children candy, and one soldier drawing pictures for children. You shared food, built homes and schools. Medics and nurses bound wounds, and doctors brought life into the world. You despised every minute of every day, but you gave these people a chance for life, and left footprints in their memories."

It's time to go. We shake hands. Sy hugs Jim, who hands him three photographs he had taken of him and Ben on that long ago day. I snap a group photo of Jim, Sy, and Ba—three people from two worlds who met once in their youth, and now a full life later.

All the while, a slightly stooped elderly man with sparse, white chin whiskers stood aside listening. As we turn to go, he steps in front of Jim. For a moment, he studies Jim's face, and then smiles and with a slight bow speaks two letters in English:

"G.I."

And then he touches his heart.

Suggested Reading

Boot, Max. *The Road Not Taken: Edward Lansdale and the American Tragedy in Vietnam*. New York: Liveright Publishing Corporation, 2018.

Bowden, Mark. *Hué 1968: A Turning Point of the American War in Vietnam*. New York: Atlantic Monthly Press, 2017.

Burkett, B. G., and Glenna Whitley. *Stolen Valor: How the Vietnam Generation Was Robbed of its Heroes and its History*. Dallas: Verity Press, 1998.

Hastings, Max. *Vietnam: An Epic Tragedy, 1945–1975*. New York: HarperCollins, 2018.

Humphries, James F. *Through the Valley: Vietnam, 1967–1968*. Boulder: Lynne Rienner Publishers, 1999.

Kidder, Tracy. *My Detachment: A Memoir*. New York: Random House, 2005.

Logue, James Allen. *Vietnam Hiêp Dúc LZ West: Images of Alpha Company, 4/31st, 196th LIB, Americal Division*. blurb.com, 2011.

Marlantes, Karl. *What It Is Like to Go to War*. New York: Atlantic Monthly Press, 2011.

McMaster, H. R. *Dereliction of Duty: Lyndon Johnson, Robert McNamara, the Joint Chiefs of Staff, and the Lies That Led to Vietnam*. New York: HarperCollins, 1977.

Milam, Ron. *Not a Gentleman's War: An Inside View of Junior Officers in the Vietnam War*. Lubbock: Texas Tech University Press, 2009.

Moore, Lt. Gen. Harold G. (ret) and Joseph L. Galloway. *We Were Soldiers Once . . . And Young: Ia Drang—The Battle That Changed the War in Vietnam*. New York: Random House, 1992.

Nolan, Keith William. *Death Valley: The Summer Offensive I Corps, August 1969*. Novato, CA: Presidio Press, 1987.

———. *Sappers in the Wire: The Life and Death of Firebase Mary Ann*. College Station: Texas A&M University Press, 1995.

O'Brien, Tim. *The Things They Carried*. New York: Houghton Mifflin Harcourt, 1990.

Stanton, Doug. *The Odyssey of Echo Company: The 1968 Tet Offensive and the Epic Battle to Survive the Vietnam War*. New York: Scribner, 2017.

Wright, James. *Enduring Vietnam: An American Generation and Its War*. New York: Thomas Dunne Books, 2017.

Index